Navigation

THE TIME-LIFE LIBRARY OF BOATING
HUMAN BEHAVIOR
THE ART OF SEWING
THE OLD WEST
THE EMERGENCE OF MAN
THE AMERICAN WILDERNESS
THE TIME-LIFE ENCYCLOPEDIA OF GARDENING
LIFE LIBRARY OF PHOTOGRAPHY
THIS FABULOUS CENTURY
FOODS OF THE WORLD
TIME-LIFE LIBRARY OF AMERICA
TIME-LIFE LIBRARY OF ART
GREAT AGES OF MAN
LIFE SCIENCE LIBRARY
THE LIFE HISTORY OF THE UNITED STATES
TIME READING PROGRAM
LIFE NATURE LIBRARY
LIFE WORLD LIBRARY
FAMILY LIBRARY:
- HOW THINGS WORK IN YOUR HOME
- THE TIME-LIFE BOOK OF THE FAMILY CAR
- THE TIME-LIFE FAMILY LEGAL GUIDE
- THE TIME-LIFE BOOK OF FAMILY FINANCE

Navigation

By the Editors of
TIME-LIFE BOOKS

The
TIME-LIFE Library of Boating

TIME-LIFE BOOKS, NEW YORK

Published simultaneously in Canada.
Library of Congress catalogue card number 75-13778.

The navigational skills described in this book are essential in piloting a boat along inland and coastal waters. Celestial navigation—the art of establishing position in open water without the benefit of markers or soundings—is explained in another volume of this series.

The Cover: The 12-meter racing sloop *Columbia* shaves past red sea buoy #32 during a practice run on Long Island Sound. This buoy warns of a rock ledge off Stamford, Connecticut, and often doubles as a mark for racers. The light atop the buoy guides sailors at night, and a bell serves as a locator during fog.

The Consultants: Halsey Herreshoff, who was the navigator for *Courageous* in her successful defense of the America's Cup in 1974, has piloted sailing craft and powerboats for 25 years.

G. James Lippmann, a naval architect, is the executive director of the American Boat and Yacht Council.

Carleton Mitchell has logged more than 50 years as a racing skipper and cruising man, under sail and power, and is the author of seven books and scores of articles on nautical matters.

William Munro, a powerboatman with more than 30 years of experience, is a photographer and author of many articles for *Motorboat* magazine and other boating publications.

Valuable assistance was given by the following departments and individuals of Time Inc.: Editorial Production, Norman Airey; Library, Benjamin Lightman, Lester Annenberg; Picture Collection, Doris O'Neil; Photographic Laboratory, George Karas; TIME-LIFE News Service, Murray J. Gart; Correspondents Margot Hapgood (London), Maria Vincenza Aloisi (Paris), Jean Walker (Miami).

Contents

The Wayfinding Art

The Wayfinding Art

by Halsey Herreshoff

There are no highways at sea. When a boat sails out from the comforting familiarity of the harbor it moves into a wide-open, ever-changing world. Perspectives shift, distances become hard to gauge, and landmarks along the receding shoreline take on a new and often perplexing aspect. Ahead, all kinds of unseen dangers may lurk—sand bars, rocks, sunken wrecks and powerful tidal currents. To keep track of his exact location in this alien environment and to lay a safe course to his next destination, a boatman applies a basic and venerable skill: he navigates.

None of the techniques a navigator uses—especially when calculating his route along coastlines and through inland waters—are particularly mysterious or difficult to master. The navigator simply performs a kind of careful detective work. He reads the clues provided by his compass, his charts, his depth-finding equipment; he gathers evidence from the bearings of buoys and lighthouses; he pries out information from tide tables and coastal piloting guides; he picks up a hint or two from the look of the water or the feel of the wind on his cheek. Then, like a nautical Sherlock Holmes, he weighs all this information, deduces his position and plots his progress on a chart.

The particular kind of detective work a boatman uses to find his way when he is within a day's sail from shore—a process called coastal navigation, or piloting—will be set forth in the pages that follow. In mid-ocean, where there are no landmarks or buoys, another kind of pathfinding, called celestial navigation, comes into play. Here the navigator finds his own position from calculations on the positions of the sun and certain bright stars. This latter technique is described in another book in this series.

Coastal piloting can provide some of the most adventurous and satisfying moments in boating. I remember the sense of pride and pleasure I felt a few summers ago at making a tricky passage to my home port at Bristol, Rhode Island, through one of the thickest fogs I have ever been in. We had set sail right after breakfast from Block Island, about 10 miles south of the Rhode Island coast, aboard my 38-foot sloop, *Alerion*. The wind was blowing in from the southwest, strong and mist-laden, and as we nosed out past the harbor breakwater, the fog closed in. Visibility dropped to 100 feet, and *Alerion* sped onward in a puffy gray world all her own.

But even while wrapped in the dense fog blanket, we enjoyed a comforting sense of knowing exactly where we were. Before leaving the harbor, I had plotted a series of compass courses to various buoys and lighthouses along our route. Our first mark, a bell buoy some three miles to the northeast, marked a stretch of dangerous shoals and severe tide rips. A strong tidal current swept across our course, and unless I allowed for its effect, we could be set down onto the shoals. Now, as *Alerion* slid along through the fog, I checked her speed: 7.2 knots. Knowing the speed and the distance to the buoy, I could figure out the time of our arrival: just 25 minutes away.

At exactly 23 minutes from the Block Island breakwater, the muffled clank of the bell broke through the fog. A minute later the buoy itself hove into view. We were dead on course. With a flicker of pride at this initial victory, I altered course to our next compass heading, toward a lighthouse on the mainland. Again I checked the speed, worked in my estimate of the current's effect and calculated our passage time. Again we arrived at our mark, right on schedule. And so it went until, early in the afternoon, we picked up our mooring in Bristol Harbor at the end of a perfect passage.

Not all my pathfinding attempts—nor those of fellow navigators—have worked out so satisfactorily. Some years ago, as a fledgling 23-year-old lieutenant junior grade in the U.S. Navy, I served aboard a 750-ton minesweeper in the Pacific. One day I was piloting the vessel through a maze of islands and reefs in the Inland Sea of Japan. The visibility was good; nevertheless, we

Master navigator Halsey Herreshoff stands in the cockpit of the 12-meter sloop Courageous, whose courses he plotted during her successful defense of the America's Cup in 1974. Grandson of the illustrious yacht designer Nathanael Herreshoff, the author has spent some 25 years piloting sailing craft and powerboats of all sizes, and is, in addition, an accomplished naval architect.

moved ahead cautiously as the channel meandered among the natural hazards with only occasional buoys to mark the turns.

We had decided to follow the shoreline of a rocky island until it seemed safe to cut for an opening at the far end of the next big promontory. From time to time, I would glance at the chart, and compare its features with the look of the land on either side of us. Suddenly, an alarm went off in my mind. The chart and the landscape did not seem to agree. The depth finder showed the water shoaling rapidly to 27 feet, only twice the minesweeper's draft. Instead of following the channel, we were steaming headlong into a shallow bay. Through inattentiveness, I had lost my place on the chart and was heading in straight for the beach.

Frantically I signaled full power astern and counted some prickly moments until the ship lumbered to a halt. We managed to turn ourselves around and head back to the channel where we belonged, but I emerged from the episode a singularly red-faced junior lieutenant.

In all my later stints as navigator, however, I have been fortunate enough to stay out of serious trouble by being more attentive and consistent than I was that day. Basically, I try to apply a mixture of reasoned calculation and seat-of-the-pants judgments—a combination that has guided mariners for centuries. While today's boat pilot relies on some extraordinarily accurate and sophisticated tools to help him find his way, most of the fundamental concepts and practices of navigation have changed very little since the days of Columbus and Eric the Red.

The very first navigators simply used their eyes, along with a good bit of common sense. They picked out landmarks along the shore, watched where waves broke against rocks, looked for eddies and ripples that might indicate shallows, even hunted in the water's color for clues to the depth of the channel. Past sight of land, the early mariners steered by the stars or the track of the sun from east to west, or by the slant of the prevailing winds.

Some nautical pioneers used more esoteric natural aids. One of the great Viking explorers was a man named Floki Vilgjerdarsson, who discovered Iceland. On his voyages, Floki carried a cage of ravens. When he figured land was near, he opened the cage and released a bird. If it circled aimlessly, land was still far beyond the horizon. But if the raven flew off with a purpose, Floki followed it, knowing the bird would lead him to a landfall.

Lacking the inborn piloting instinct of ravens and other wild fowl—which no one has yet been able to analyze with certainty—human navigators through the centuries have come up with various man-made devices to help orient themselves. Bonfires on mountaintops lighted the seafarers of ancient Greece to harbors in the Aegean. The Egyptians, with a low silty coastline that offered few landmarks, erected a 400-foot-high lighthouse on the island of Pharos, just outside the harbor of Alexandria, in about 280 B.C. Topped by an open chamber where a log fire was kept burning, the lighthouse cast a light about 25 miles out to sea. The structure stood for more than a millennium as one of the wonders of the ancient world, beckoning sailors into port until it collapsed in the 1400s.

Besides referring to prominent markers ashore, early navigators developed a number of onboard navigating aids. The first and most basic was a tool for measuring water depth. In an Egyptian wall painting executed more than 3,500 years ago, a man stands in the prow of a river barge holding a long rod, called a sounding reed, for probing the bottom. Eventually navigators adopted the lead line—a weighted line equipped with graduated markings, and often with a bit of tallow on the end to bring up bottom samples.

By the late Middle Ages, mariners were relying on their lead lines to cross wide stretches of open water. "Ye shall go north until ye sound in 72 fathoms in fair grey sand," reads a set of 14th Century sailing directions on how to get from Spain to England. "Then go north until ye come into soundings of ooze, and then go your course east-north-east." Fourteenth Century lead lines must have been awesomely long; 72 fathoms is 432 feet.

A medieval sailor's most valuable tool, beside his lead line, was his magnetic compass. At first, mariners rigged compasses only in emergencies, when cloudy skies hid the sun or the North Star. The ship's pilot would rub an iron needle against a lodestone, a chunk of iron ore with the ability to magnetize other bits of the same metal. Then he skewered the magnetized needle through a wisp of straw and floated it in a bowl of water, where the needle would point in the general direction of north. Eventually compasses became permanent fixtures, much as they are today, with the needle swinging freely on a pivot. And by the time of Columbus, a calibrated card had been added to the compass for reading direction.

Columbus certainly used such a compass to find his way to America in 1492. He also carried a rough chart, drawn on sheepskin, on which he marked each day's passage across the ocean. His principal method for determining his position was a basic piloting technique called dead (short for deduced) reckoning. By referring to his compass to get his heading, and by measuring his speed and the time sailed, Columbus could calculate his position—at least theoretically—at any given moment.

But the Admiral badly misjudged his progress. His principal timing device was a sandglass, which the helmsman turned every half hour, and his sole method for judging speed was to watch bubbles or patches of seaweed flowing past his hull. Relying on this system, when Columbus reached the West Indies he figured he had sailed 3,466 miles; he thus overestimated the true distance by about 9 per cent.

Dead reckoning became a lot more precise a century later when English navigators came up with the first oceangoing speedometer. The device, called a chip log, consisted of a light towline with a pie-shaped sliver of wood on one end to act as a drag in the water. The line was knotted at regular intervals. Stationed in the stern, the navigator would toss the chip log overboard and let its line pay out astern. As the log hit the water he would set up a 30-second glass and count the knots that slipped through his fingers while the sands ran out. He could then convert his knot count into the ship's hourly speed. And though the chip log has long since disappeared from the navigator's arsenal, the term "knots" survives as the proper designation of a ship's pace measured in nautical miles per hour.

Even with a fairly workable speed gauge, however, the pilots of the old sailing ships often had trouble telling exactly where they were. Unseen currents could carry a ship hundreds of leagues off course, with no one the wiser. Compass needles, too, showed an uncomfortable habit of wandering. So navigators in the past, like sailors today, would try to confirm their dead-reckoned positions by other means. Near shore, they would take sights and make fixes on landmarks and buoys. On the high seas and in unmarked, uncharted areas, they used the techniques of celestial navigation.

As more and more ships sailed out to the far reaches of the earth, the tools and techniques of navigation were sharpened and refined. By the end of the 18th Century, a reliable ship's chronometer had replaced the sandglass. The deviations and variations in readings of compasses were carefully worked out and tabulated. Map makers drew up charts with ever greater precision, defining water depths, land features and compass directions. Each reef and promontory was given its known position on the earth's surface.

The most celebrated contributor to these advances in the art of navigation was an 18th Century British sea captain named James Cook, who mapped out vast stretches of the South Pacific, and also piloted the first ship to go south of the Antarctic Circle. Unlike most seafarers of his day, Cook was a scientist and an accomplished land surveyor. In 1768, the Royal Society sent him to Tahiti, with orders then to sail west in search of a huge continent that many geographers felt lay undiscovered in the Southern Ocean. Cook paused in Tahiti to take some astronomical observations. Then he sailed on to New Zealand and finally reached Australia—the missing continent.

Wherever he made a landfall, Cook surveyed and mapped the coastline.

His maps were not the imprecise and often wildly imaginative sketches set down by most explorers before him, but were charts of painstaking exactness with each detail clearly marked and meticulously positioned. In fact, his chart data was so reliable that some of it was still being used by the British Admiralty during World War II.

Since Cook's time, the only real change in the navigator's techniques has come from the use of electronic devices. Today, besides his charts and compass, a boatman can outfit his craft with electronic depth finders, radar sets to warn of any hazards unseen in storm and fog, and very elaborate radio equipment that can establish his position within a few yards on almost any well-traveled waterway on earth.

The ultimate in modern piloting gear—and certainly the fanciest equipment I have ever used—was lodged in the navigator's station aboard the 12-meter *Courageous,* winner of the 1974 America's Cup. Precise piloting is essential in a 12-meter race, for a skipper's tactical decisions depend on an absolute knowledge of his boat's position at every moment. As navigator on *Courageous,* it was my job to keep tabs on our position and compare it with that of the competing boat.

At the heart of *Courageous'* navigational setup was a digital computer, which analyzed every movement the boat made and predicted how the craft would behave on any heading in any wind condition. Readings from the various instruments aboard—wind gauge, speedometer, compass, heel-angle meter—were fed into the computer at the rate of four times a second. I would fix our starting position and our destination, and punch this information into the computer; the computer would do some quick calculations to disgorge our position. Also, it would help us decide, as we tacked upwind, the exact moment to change course and head for the mark. This last ability is what put us over the finish line first in the key race of the Cup trials against *Intrepid,* to determine which boat would defend the Cup against the Australian challenger. Each of us had won four races; this was the final one.

On the day of the race, a blustery wind blew in from the northeast, bringing with it a thin fog that cut visibility to about a mile. *Intrepid* nosed by us at the start and strode ahead toward the first mark on the course, 4.5 miles to windward. We were close on her tail, moving smartly, but we seemed unable to close the gap. Our main hope was that a piloting lapse would occur aboard *Intrepid.* And that is precisely what happened.

I was keeping a dead-reckoning plot on the chart, and knew that any moment we should come about if we were to arrive precisely on the mark with no distance or time wasted. Unsure in the poor visibility of exactly when to make our move, I punched the computer button for a readout. The computer's reply, couched in mathematical terms, was unmistakable: "Go now." We did—a critical 15 seconds before *Intrepid* made her move. We shaved past the mark in first place, and the race was ours.

Helping to guide *Courageous* to first place in those trials—and to ultimate victory in the America's Cup—provided the high point of my career so far as a navigator. But the satisfactions of everyday piloting can be just as rich: threading an intricate course along a winding channel, fetching a difficult mark in a pea-soup fog, or confirming a position from a set of quick, deft fixes. And on an ordinary cruise no elaborate computerized gear is needed.

Any competent navigator can plot his course with the use of only a few basic tools: compass, depth finder, speedometer or log, a good set of charts, a sharp pencil, a set of parallel rules, a pair of dividers to tick off distances, and a firm surface on which to work. Most important of all is to develop careful, common-sense procedures when putting the tools to work. A good navigator practices whenever he takes out his boat. He gets into the habit, even on easy trips when the weather is fair and the waters familiar, of plotting his course, timing his run, reading his depth finder and checking his position by taking the appropriate fixes. Then, when night falls or when the fog rolls in, he will have the skills and tools to find his way with purpose and conviction.

Soquel Cr.
Capitola
Aptos
Valencia Cr.
Aptos Cr.
Rio Del Mar
Seacliff Beach
SOQUEL COVE
S. P. R. R.
Granary Tr
Twin Lakes
R TRS
(KSCO) 1080 kHz
Black Pt
Soquel Pt
10 ft Rep (1971)
BW"SC"
WHISTLE
Mo (A)
NAVAL OPERATING AREA

The Underwater Terrain

The most vital service a chart performs is to describe the territory beneath the skipper's hull. Using a combination of numbers, color codes, underwater contour lines and a system of abbreviations and symbols, the chart tells a pilot all he needs to know about an area's undersea topography, including where he can safely venture and the sections he should avoid.

Most of the numbers on the chart represent measurements of the water's depth at mean low tide, taken at the spot by a hydrographic vessel. These soundings may be either in feet or in fathoms (a fathom equals six feet); the chart's legend will indicate which unit is used. Contour lines, which connect points of roughly equal depth, profile the bottom's shape; the lines are either numbered *(chart, opposite)* or coded *(chart, below)* according to depth. Color shadings also indicate depth, with the shallowest areas in the darkest tint. Rocks and reefs, and various other characteristics of the bottom, are marked by either standardized symbols or abbreviations, as described at right.

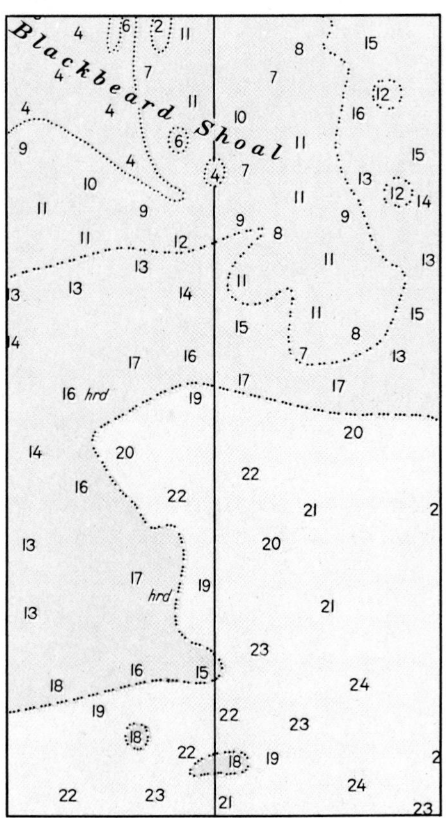

On some charts, as in this excerpt showing Blackbeard Shoal off the Georgia coast, the depth of each contour line is indicated by a system of dots. And even though the individual soundings are in feet, the dots refer to fathoms. Thus lines of single dots enclose areas of one fathom (six feet) or less, while lines of double and triple dots indicate depths of two and three fathoms respectively.

Wrecks, Rocks, Reefs

Cartographers choose from a selection of stylized notations, like the ones shown below, to indicate underwater hazards. A sunken wreck, for example, may be shown either by a symbol or by an abbreviation plus a number that gives the wreck's depth. A dotted line around any symbol calls special attention to its hazardous nature. Since slightly different symbols often indicate the same hazard, the boatman should consult the complete list in the pamphlet entitled *Chart No. 1,* published by the National Ocean Survey and available at both the NOS distribution office *(page 172)* and most marine-supply outlets.

Symbol text	Meaning
5½ Wk; 21 Wk	Sunken wrecks (abbreviation: Wk); a number indicates precise depth in feet at mean low water.
	A partly submerged wreck, showing part of its superstructure or hull at mean low water.
5 Rk	Sunken rocks (abbreviation: Rk); a number indicates the precise depth at mean low water.
Co 3; reef line; rky	Submerged reefs (abbreviations "Co" and "rky" indicate coral and rocky); a number gives the precise depth at mean low water.
Uncov 2 ft; (2); Uncov 2 ft; (2)	Rocks that are covered at high tide and uncovered at low; height is given in feet above mean low water. Parentheses enclose uncovered height.
	Rocks awash at low water.
	Rocks awash at low water.
(25)	A rock never covered by water, with height above mean high water.
Coral; Co; Co; Co	Coral reefs located offshore that are uncovered at mean low water.
Foul	An area fouled by wreckage, rocks or coral.

Bottom Quality

A system of cartographer's abbreviations, used alone or in combination, describes the composition of the bottom, allowing a skipper to pick the best holding ground for his anchor. He should look for hard sand (hrd S), for example, to hold him securely, trying to avoid a rocky (rky) or weed-choked (Wd) bottom that could snag his anchor or allow it to drag.

Abbreviation	Meaning	Abbreviation	Meaning
S	sand	*sft*	soft
M	mud	*hrd*	hard
G	gravel	*stk*	sticky
Sh	shells	*rky*	rocky
Wd	seaweed	*gy*	gray
Grs	grass	*br*	brown

Clear Warnings of Shoal Waters

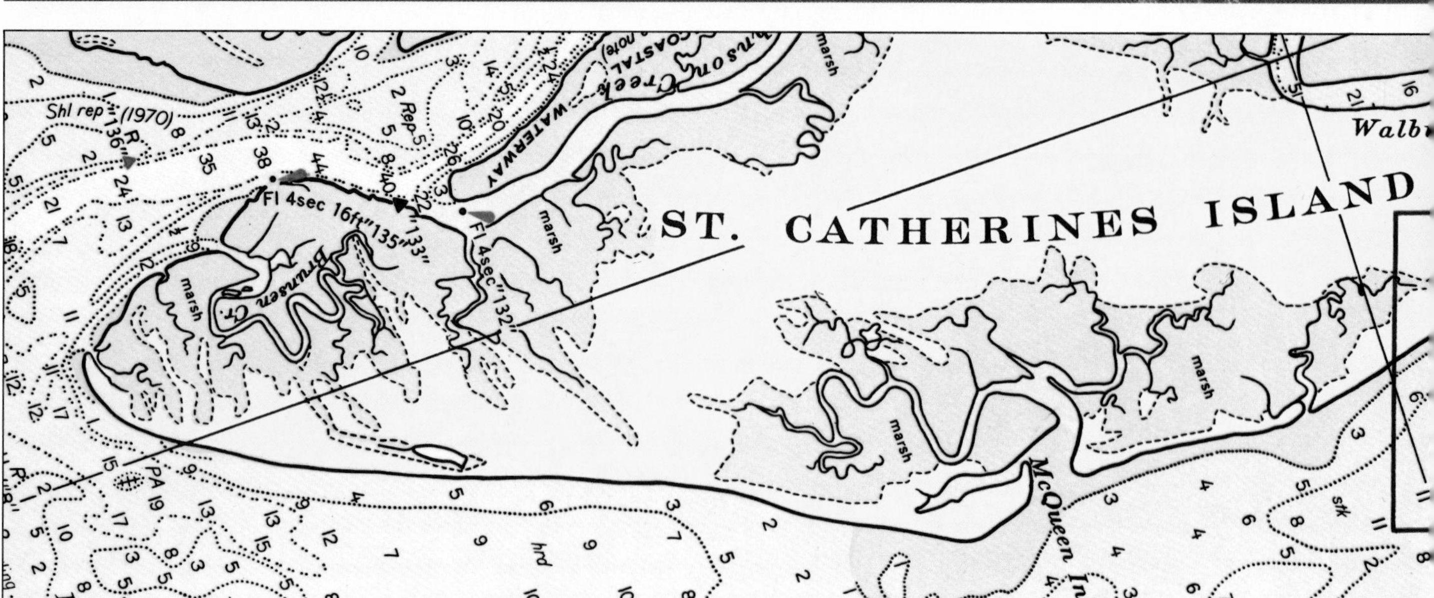

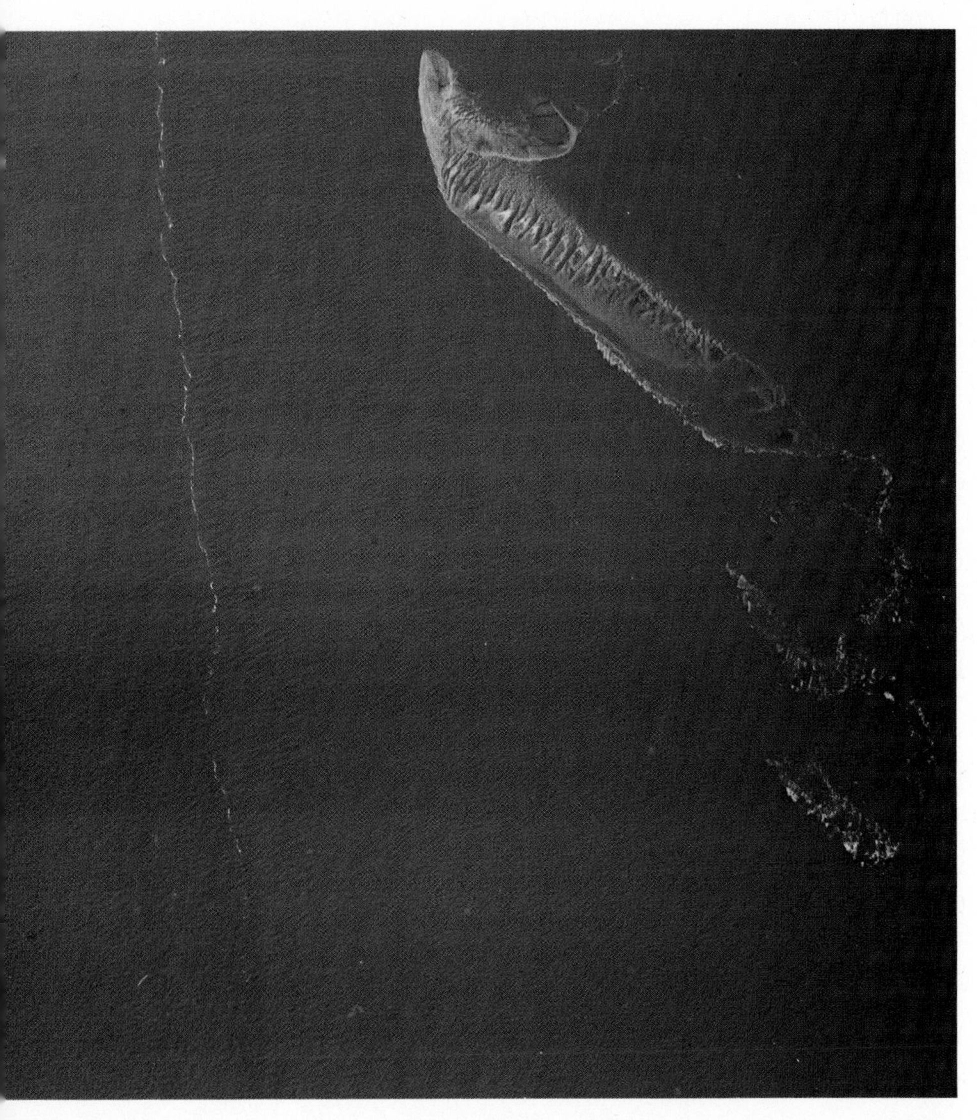

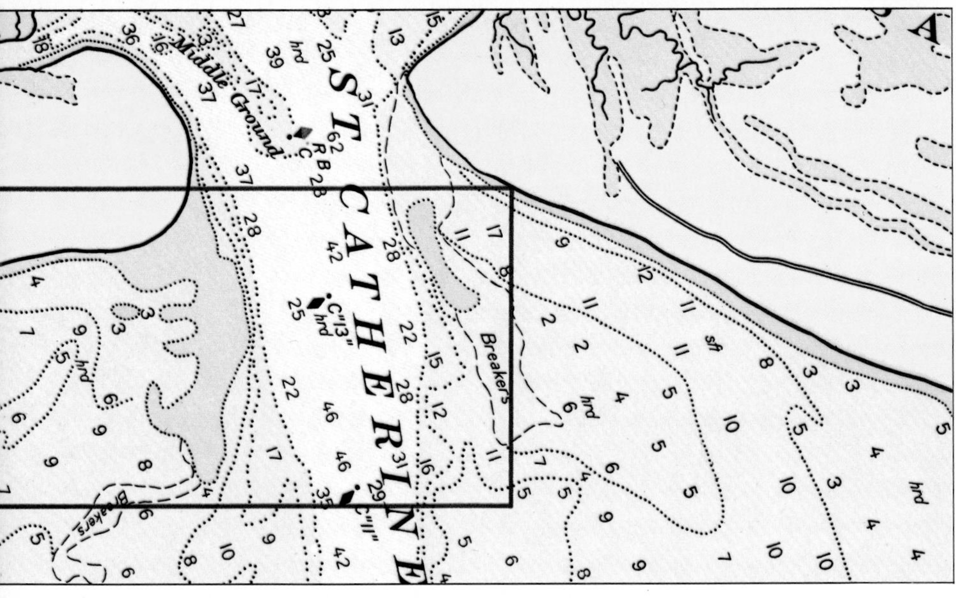

At the inlet to St. Catherines Sound, Georgia, shifting sand bars—which are seen in this aerial photograph as pale slashes—flank the channel and create a constant threat to navigation. But the color codes and symbols on the chart below (marked off with a blue rectangle corresponding to the area covered in the photo) give pilots clear warning of the hazards. The sand bars show up as green areas enclosed by dotted lines, indicating they are uncovered at low tide. Breakers are labeled; hard bottom is indicated by the abbreviation "hrd." "Middle Ground" is the name of a shoal just inside the inlet.

A Key to Prominent Checkpoints

To pinpoint the location of high, man-made landmarks such as water towers, smokestacks, flagpoles and radio beacons, cartographers use the standard symbol of a dot surrounded by a circle. A notation next to the symbol defines the landmark's precise nature—whether, for example, it is a large domed roof or small cupola—as explained in the table of selected landmarks below. If the dot is omitted, the notation will be given in lower-case type—indicating that the landmark's position is approximate.

⊙ CHY	The chimney of a building; the building is not charted, because the more visible chimney gives a navigator a better bearing.	⊙ GAB	A prominent gable on the roof of a building, providing a more precise bearing than would the building as a whole.	⊙ TR	A tower that is part of a larger building.
⊙ STACK	A tall industrial smokestack.	⊙ FP	A free-standing flagpole.	⊙ R TR	A radio tower—either a tall pole or a tall scaffolded structure for elevating radio antennas.
⊙ S'PIPE	A standpipe or a tall cylindrical structure, such as a water tower, whose height is greater than its diameter.	⊙ FS	A flagstaff attached to a building.	⊙ R MAST	A radio mast—a relatively short pole or scaffolded structure for elevating radio antennas.
⊙ TANK	A water tank that is elevated above the ground by means of a tall skeletal framework.	⊙ DOME	The dome of a building. If the building is well known, its name may appear in parentheses; e.g., DOME (STATE HOUSE).	⊙ LORAN TR	A loran tower—a tall, slender structure, braced with guy wires, for elevating loran antennas.
⊙ MON	A monument, such as an obelisk or statue.	⊙ CUP	A cupola—a small dome-shaped turret atop a building.	⊙ TELEM ANT	The large dish-shaped antenna—known as a telemetry antenna—of a missile tracking station.

Structures Drawn to Scale

For low-lying structures such as piers, ramps and bridges—and also for buildings and towns—cartographers have developed shorthand representations such as the ones shown here. Thus, various rectangular or triangular shapes may indicate streets with houses along them; old military forts are shown by an outline of their ramparts. Such symbols are drawn to scale, and depict the landmarks as viewed from overhead. Like all landmark symbols used on nautical charts, these are listed in Chart No. 1.

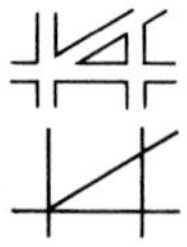

A grid of streets representing a city or town.

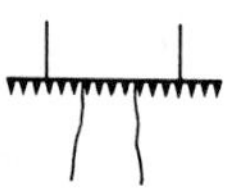

A dam. The tooth-edged line represents the dam structure; the lines below, the runoff.

A water-front ramp; broken lines indicate the portion submerged at mean low tide.

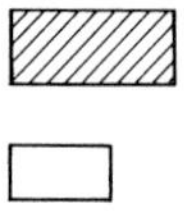

Groups of adjoining buildings; large rectangles are usually shaded, small ones blank.

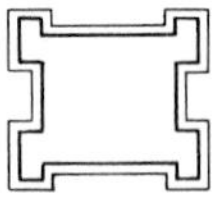

A military fort.

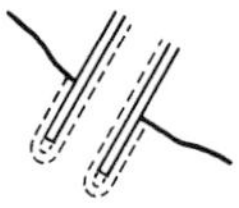

A pair of jetties; broken lines mark the extent of their underwater foundations.

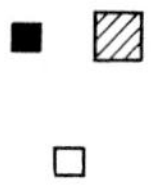

Individual buildings. Larger symbols are shaded, small ones filled in or left blank.

Short parallel docks projecting out into the water from a curved bulkhead.

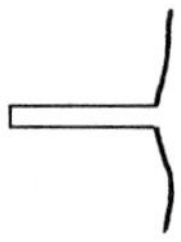

A long single pier projecting into the water.

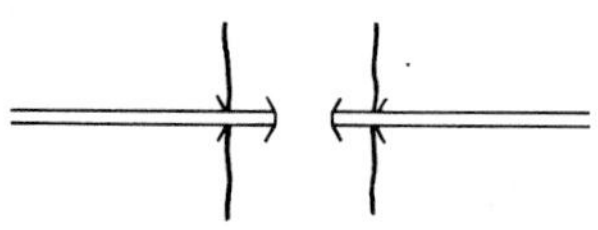

A bascule drawbridge, whose sections swing up like the gates at a railroad crossing.

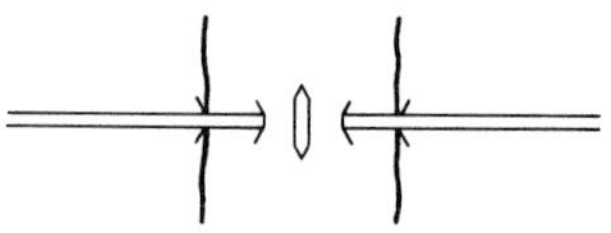

A swinging drawbridge. The center section turns upon a central pier.

Symbols for Landmarks

Besides a knowledge of the underwater terrain, the mariner needs a clear representation of the coastal landscape; the chart provides it. Coastlines are depicted at both high tide and low, inland topography is defined, and any landmark that might help a navigator fix his position is noted and labeled.

Some of the drafting techniques used to portray the shape and character of coastal areas are shown at right. Contour lines or hatch marks designate slopes and cliffs. Dots or speckles along the shoreline indicate a sandy or boulder-strewn beach. And green tints denote areas that are uncovered when the tide goes out.

A variety of dots, circles and other symbols *(opposite)* give the locations of prominent landmarks. And on some charts —most notably those for foreign waters —churches, temples and mosques merit their own symbols. Samples are shown below, along with stylized drawings of the buildings themselves.

Ecumenical Signposts

Spires make handy landmarks. On United States charts, they are shown merely by a circle. But for foreign waters, chart makers distinguish between religions with the special symbols at left below (the drawings at right are supplied here for convenient identification).

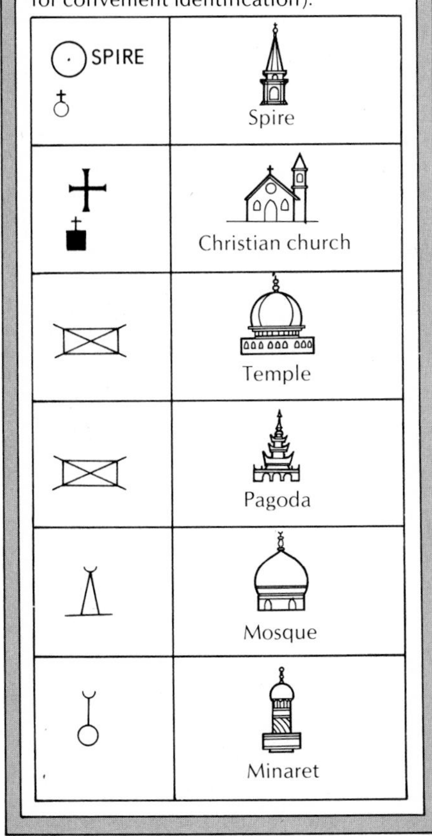

The Look of the Coast

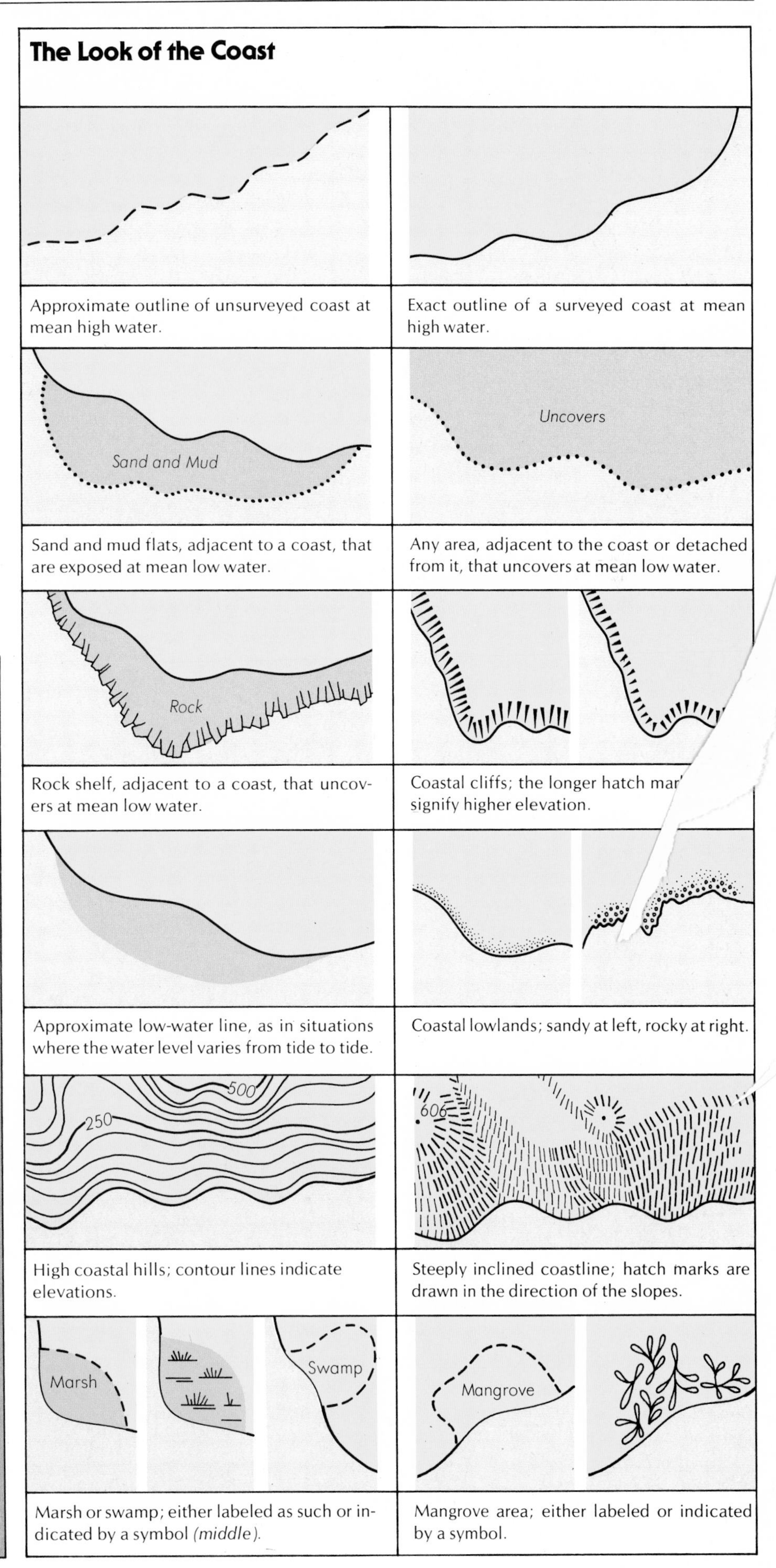

Approximate outline of unsurveyed coast at mean high water.

Exact outline of a surveyed coast at mean high water.

Sand and mud flats, adjacent to a coast, that are exposed at mean low water.

Any area, adjacent to the coast or detached from it, that uncovers at mean low water.

Rock shelf, adjacent to a coast, that uncovers at mean low water.

Coastal cliffs; the longer hatch mar[illegible] signify higher elevation.

Approximate low-water line, as in situations where the water level varies from tide to tide.

Coastal lowlands; sandy at left, rocky at right.

High coastal hills; contour lines indicate elevations.

Steeply inclined coastline; hatch marks are drawn in the direction of the slopes.

Marsh or swamp; either labeled as such or indicated by a symbol *(middle)*.

Mangrove area; either labeled or indicated by a symbol.

A Mariner's Match-up

Matching chart symbols to landmarks, a boatman traveling past Santa Cruz Harbor in Monterey Bay, California, can find his position by identifying prominent man-made features on shore. The large letters on the photograph above identify: (A) an 800-yard-long pier, (B) a conspicuous domed structure, (C) a stretch of buildings, and (D) the mouth of a small boat harbor. All four are reproduced (with duplicate letters for easy recognition) on the chart in stylized symbols: a long yellow ramp for the pier, a circle and dot for the dome, a grid for the buildings, and two broken lines for the harbor channel.

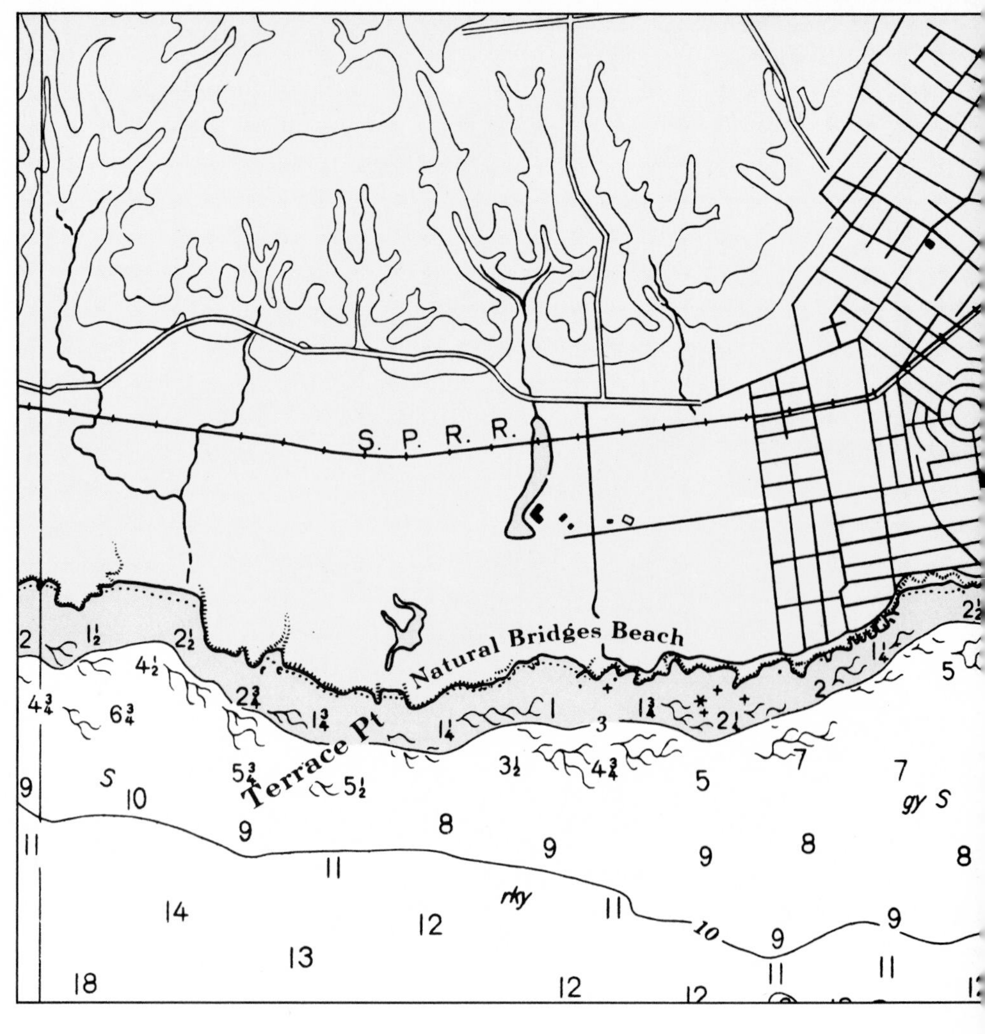

C
D

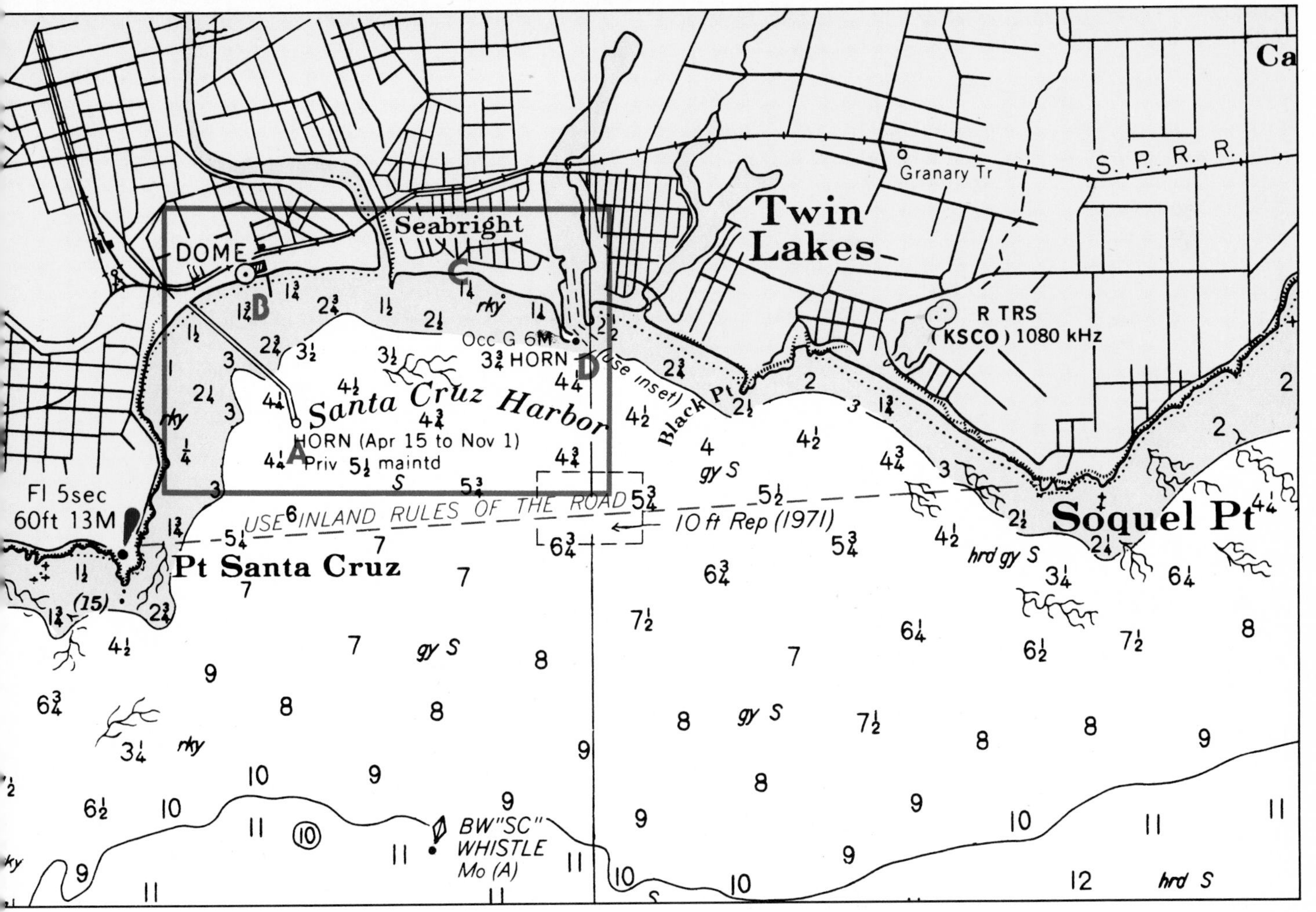
Ca
Granary Tr
S. P. R. R.
Seabright
Twin
Lakes
DOME
B
C
rky
Occ G 6M
3¾ HORN
D
(use inset)
R TRS
(KSCO) 1080 kHz
Black Pt
Santa Cruz Harbor
HORN (Apr 15 to Nov 1)
A
Priv 5½ maintd
Fl 5sec
60ft 13M
USE INLAND RULES OF THE ROAD
10 ft Rep (1971)
gy S
hrd gy S
Soquel Pt
Pt Santa Cruz
(15)
BW"SC"
WHISTLE
Mo (A)
hrd S

The Prime Locators

A typical nautical chart has built into it a brilliantly simple system for telling a boatman exactly where he is, and the direction and distance from any one place on the chart to any other. The principal element of this master key is a grid *(right)* superimposed over a chart's geographic forms. The grid's horizontal lines run in an east-west direction, and are parallels of latitude; the vertical lines, running north-south, are meridians of longitude. In this system, any location or position can be described or fixed in terms of the point where a parallel and a meridian intersect.

All major parallels and meridians are coded by degrees, counting upward from zero. The zero parallel, or base line of latitude, is the equator. From there, the parallels march north and south in progression until they reach 90° at the poles. The longitude base line, called the prime meridian, passes through Greenwich, England. This site was chosen in 1884 by an international conference of astronomers, largely owing to Britain's status as a maritime power—and because the Greenwich Observatory was the scene of extensive navigational research. From 0° along the prime meridian, longitude is reckoned east and west halfway around the world to a maximum of 180°, where the meridian runs through the Pacific Ocean.

As the chart excerpt on the opposite page shows, each degree is subdivisible into 60 units called minutes, with each minute representing one nautical mile, or about 2,000 yards. And each minute further subdivides into 60 seconds, or multiples thereof.

The basic reference point for calculating nautical directions is north; but a navigator has to contend with two "norths." One is true north, that is, the chart direction to the North Pole—where, on a globe, the meridians converge. The other is magnetic north, the place to which, basically, all compass needles point. These two locations are some distance apart *(globe, right)*; in making calculations, navigators must compensate for the variation.

The grid of latitude and longitude lines that overlays every chart enables a mariner to pinpoint any location on it. Longitude is reckoned by degrees east (E) or west (W) of the prime meridian, which runs through Greenwich, England, and latitude is indicated as north (N) or south (S) of the equator. Thus, the coordinates 20°W 20°N mark a spot just off Africa's west coast (blue dot).

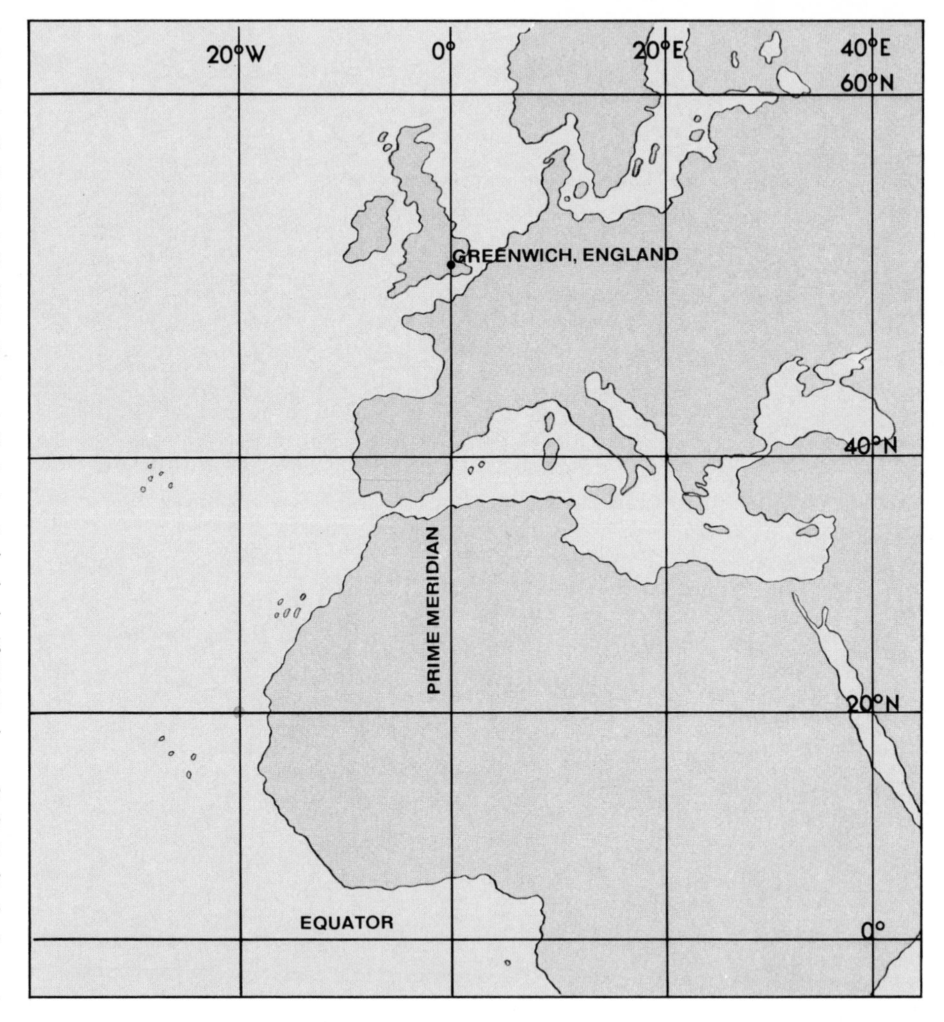

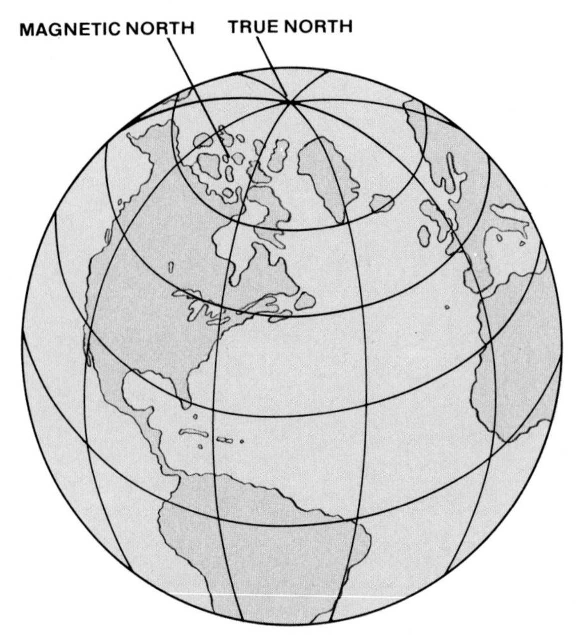

The northern terminus of the lines of longitude represents true north, but the North Magnetic Pole toward which compass needles generally point is 1,000 miles away at Bathurst Island, Canada. Navigators compensate for the variation between the two poles by using a device that is called a dual compass rose (opposite). The amount of variation differs with each locale.

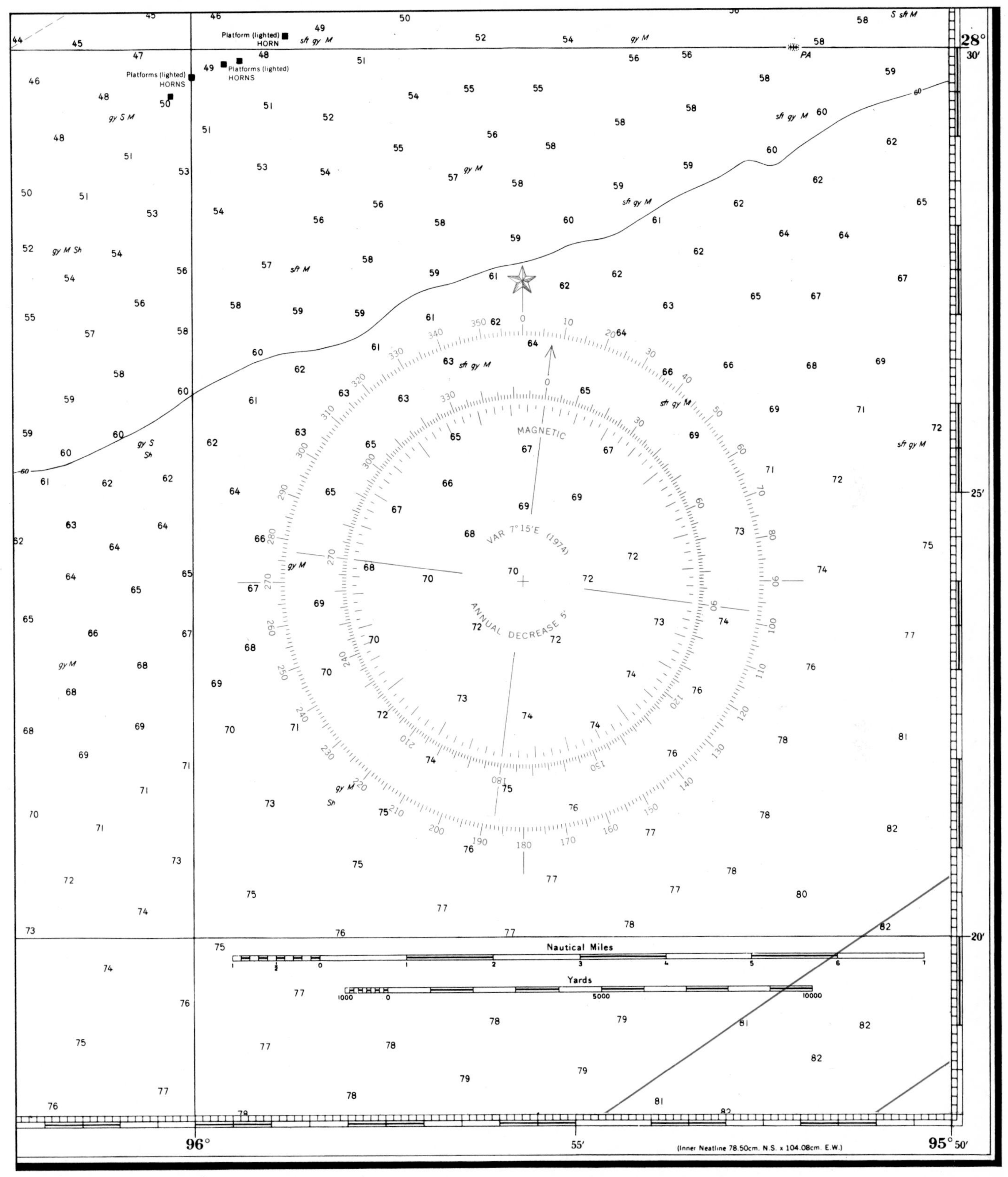

On this chart excerpt, a dual compass rose shows the variation between true north and magnetic north. The zero of the outer rose points to the geographic pole, while the inner circle's zero shows the compass direction to magnetic north. The difference between the two is the local variation, which increases (or decreases, as noted within this rose) each year because the magnetic field that is generated by the earth's moving molten core is in flux. In the margins of the chart are displayed the degrees of latitude (along the right-hand margin) and longitude (along the bottom margin). The margins further divide the area into minutes by means of the alternating lined and blank bands, and into six-second units, or tenths of minutes.

Mercator's Distortion

A chart is a flat representation of a section of the earth's curved surface. There are many ways to depict—or, as cartographers put it, to project—a round surface onto a flat one. The most popular projection for nautical charts is the Mercator, named after the Dutch map maker, Gerhard Mercator, who invented the technique in 1567.

The Mercator flattens out the earth so that lines of latitude and longitude can form a rectangular grid. To achieve this, the projection must stretch those parts of the globe not precisely on the equator. The amount of stretch increases in proportion to the distance from the equator. And wherever the stretch occurs, the distance between points on a chart will appear greater than it is on the earth's surface. The Mercator is devised so that the east-west stretch is balanced with a north-south stretch. Thus the mariner can use the latitude margin *(opposite)* as a scale for measuring all distances correctly.

In making a Mercator projection, a chart maker, in effect, uses one or more triangular earth peelings taken off from a pole to the equator. He then stretches each triangle so that its apex is as wide as its base, and it becomes a rectangle. At the same time, the rectangle is proportionately elongated to balance out the increasing amount of lateral stretch as the latitude approaches the poles.

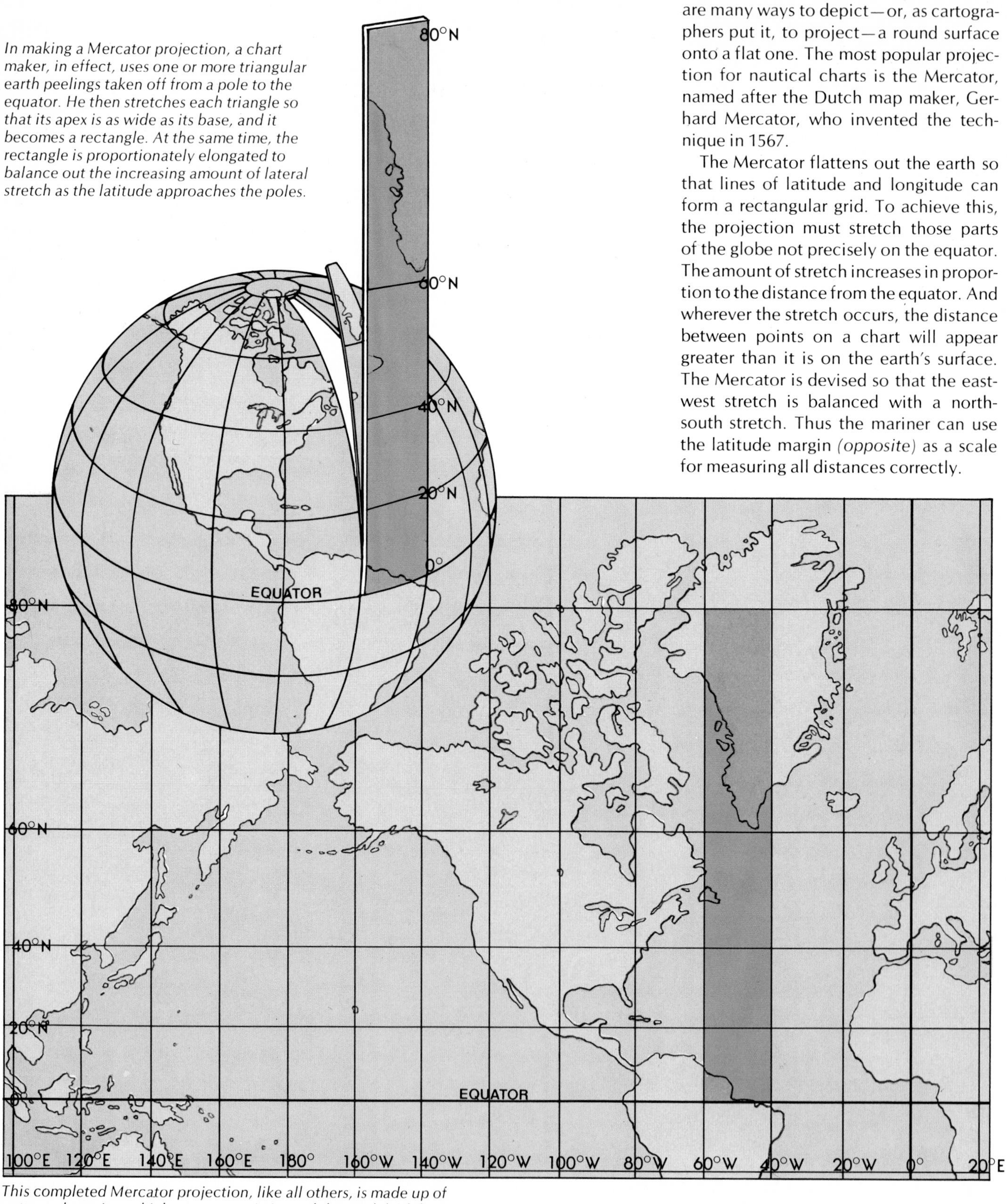

This completed Mercator projection, like all others, is made up of rectangular strips, which represent sections of the earth laid down adjacent to one another. The blue rectangle between 40°W and 60°W duplicates the strip peeled and stretched from the globe at top. In high latitudes the areas become enlarged and distorted. Thus, Greenland appears, proportionately, three times its true size.

Nova Scotian Coast

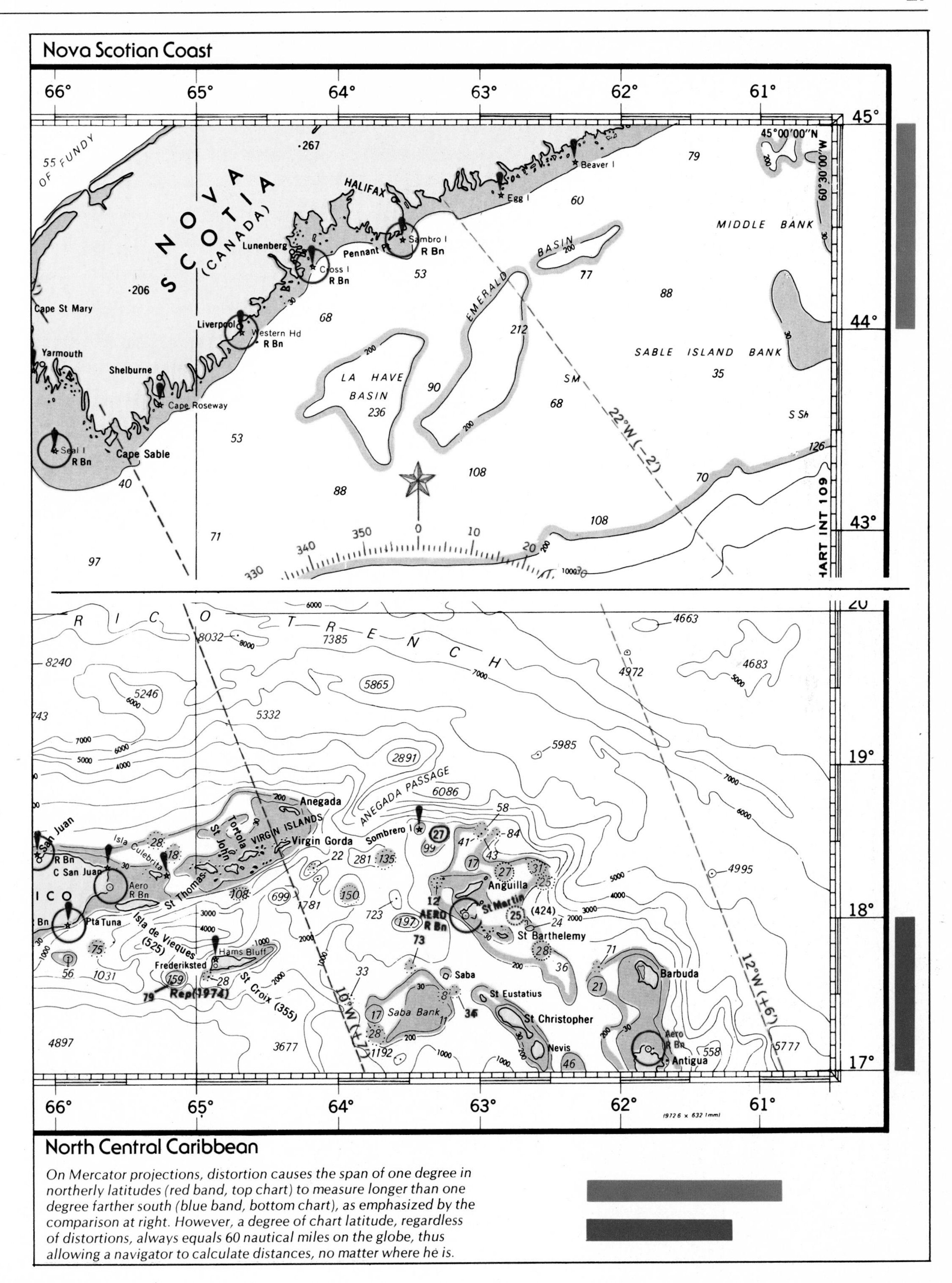

North Central Caribbean

On Mercator projections, distortion causes the span of one degree in northerly latitudes (red band, top chart) to measure longer than one degree farther south (blue band, bottom chart), as emphasized by the comparison at right. However, a degree of chart latitude, regardless of distortions, always equals 60 nautical miles on the globe, thus allowing a navigator to calculate distances, no matter where he is.

Bodega Bay
Bodega Head
Bodega
5533
165-SC
Napa
Napa R.
Petaluma
5603
TOMALES BAY
Petaluma R.
SAN PABLO BAY
5525
5402
POINT REYES
DRAKES BAY
San Rafael
Richmond
Tiburon
Berkeley
5599
Sausalito
5535
Oakland
Golden Gate
SAN FRANCISCO BAY
Farallon Islands
SAN FRANCISCO
Alameda
5532
Point San Pedro
San Mateo
5072
Half Moon Bay
Redwood City
5520
5531

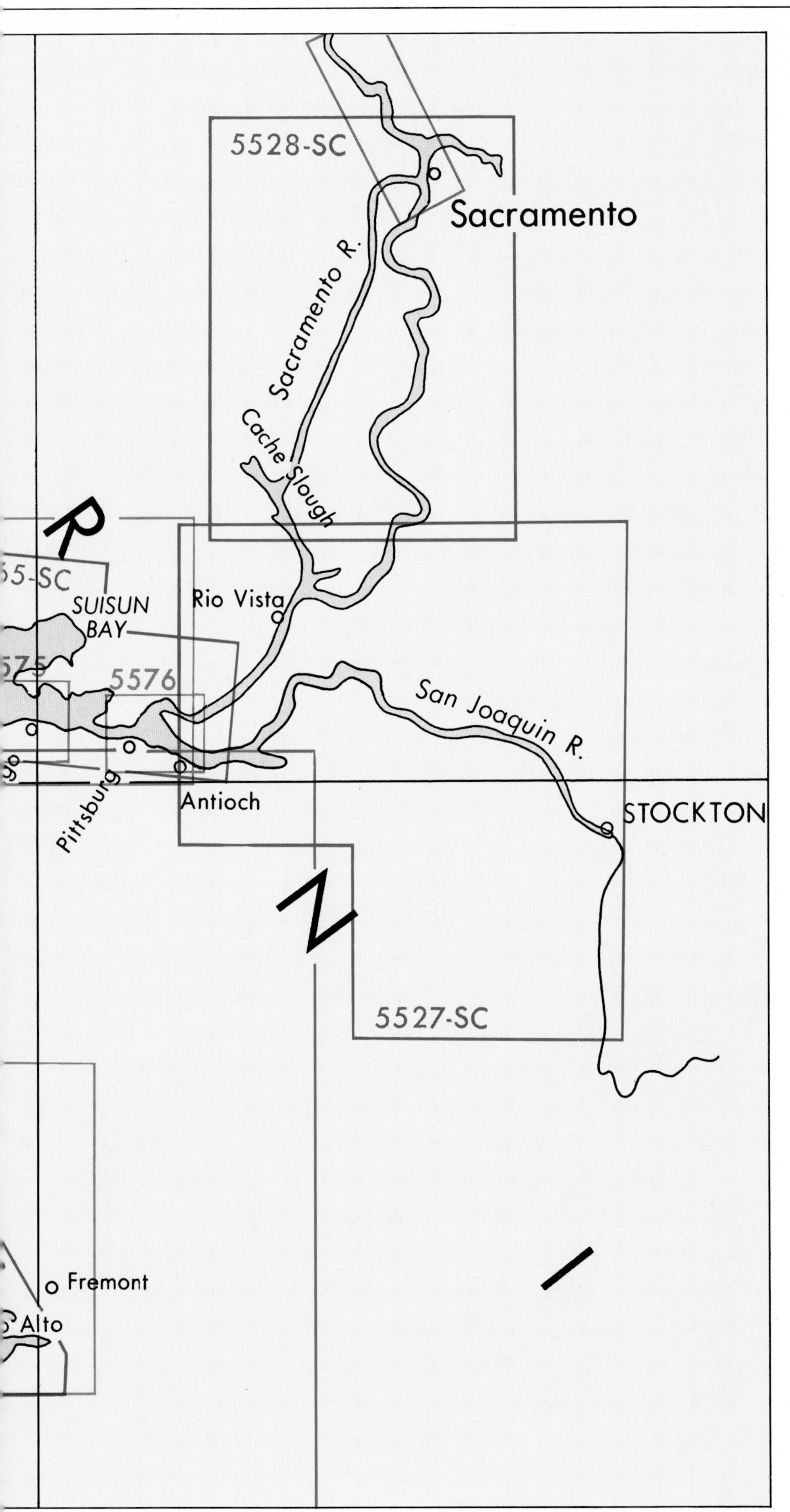

A Choice of Charts

Whenever a boatman heads out on a cruise, for a day or a month, he should carry a selection of charts that gives both an overall look at the general area he is traveling, and minute details on every harbor, channel, hazard and aid to navigation he may encounter. In choosing, he can use as a guide the chart catalogues of the National Ocean Survey *(pages 36-37)*, a federal agency that compiles most of the charts covering United States waters.

As the excerpt at left shows, these so-called catalogues are actually large annotated maps on which the areas covered by available charts are outlined in coded colors, each individual chart being designated by a serial number. Normally, the pleasure-boater uses four kinds of charts, which the catalogue outlines in three different colors. Two of these kinds, General Charts and Coast Charts, indicated by blue lines, embrace sizable stretches of water and coastline, and are essential for coastwise piloting. Harbor Charts, outlined in red, provide detailed close-up views of selected inshore areas.

In addition, many skippers carry a stock of Small-Craft Charts, outlined in green, which are designed especially for the recreational boatman. Essentially they are strips of Harbor Charts arranged along the axes of popular waterways, including tidal stretches of major rivers. They show all navigation aids and hazards in precise detail; they also contain tide tables, point out repair facilities and indicate the best cruising routes.

The National Ocean Survey catalogues also offer another category called Sailing Charts. These charts cover broad sweeps of ocean and are most often used for offshore navigation; they are too small in scale to be shown in the excerpt at left. A segment of one is shown overleaf, however, along with samples from other chart categories to illustrate the differences in scale and in detail.

This excerpt from a Pacific Coast chart catalogue shows the charts a boatman may select for navigation in the San Francisco Bay area. For his long-range coastal piloting and overall perspective he would use General Chart 5402 (blue outline). Coastal Chart 5072 gives more detail on the approaches to the Golden Gate. From there, if he were headed for, say, Vallejo, he would get Harbor Charts 5532, 5533 and, finally, 5525 for a look at his anchorage. Alternately he might select Small-Craft Chart 165SC (green outline), which covers all the bays in the area.

Closing In by Scale

Every chart represents a compromise between showing maximum area and maximum detail. The key to the compromise is scale. The effect of different scales is illustrated here by excerpts from four chart categories, as they zero in on an island *(red arrow on chart at right)* off Maine. As the chart scale increases, the focus narrows, but topographic features become larger and more detailed.

Cartographers describe a chart's scale by a numerical ratio, which defines the unit of chart space showing a corresponding unit of the earth's surface. On the segment at right, the scale is 1:1,200,000; i.e., one inch depicts 1,200,000 inches of actual distance, or about 20 miles.

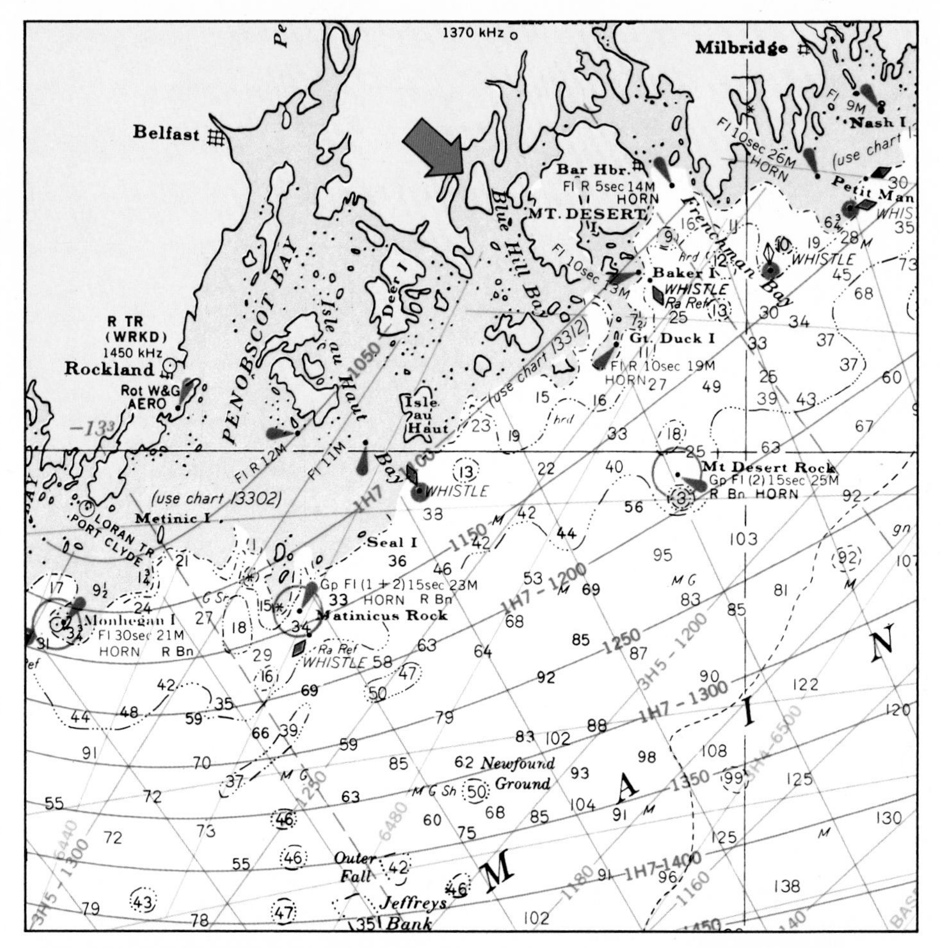

1:1,200,000 scale. *The Sailing Chart excerpted here encompasses an enormous stretch of water, but gives only scanty information on inshore areas: the island in Blue Hill Bay marked by the arrow appears in rough outline. Like other Sailing Charts, all of which have a scale of 1:600,000 or smaller, this one shows a few major lighthouses, includes offshore soundings in fathoms and is useful solely for making long-range approaches.*

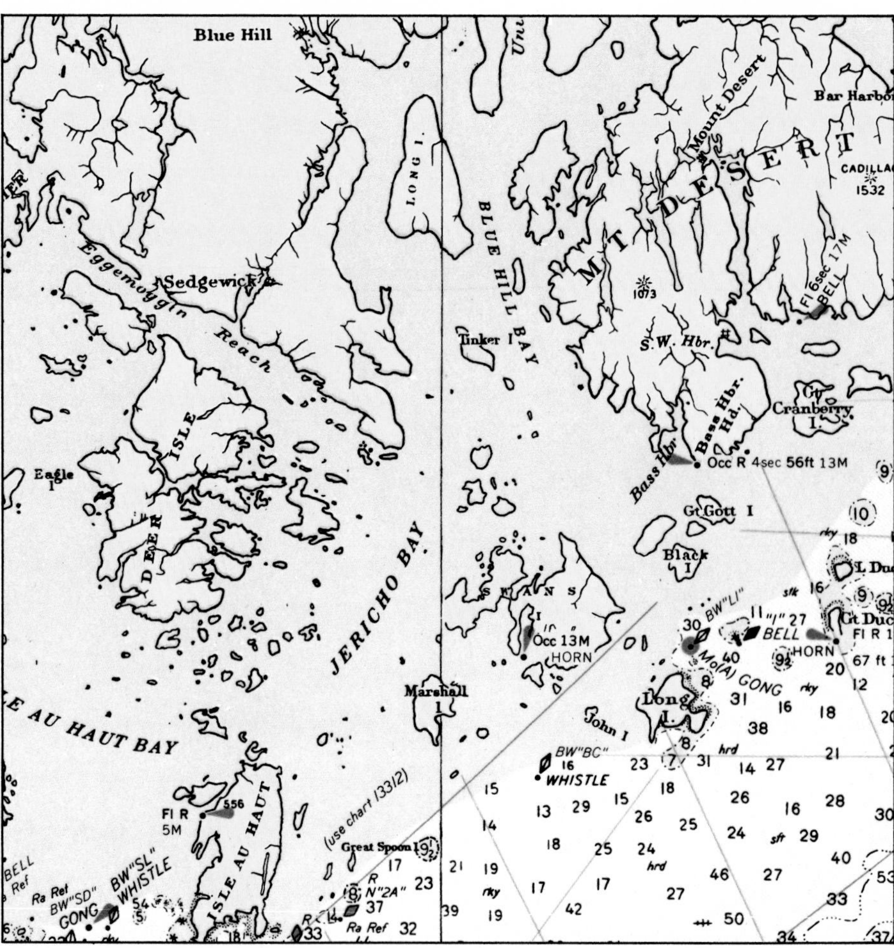

1:378,838 scale. *When scale increases, as with this General Chart, coastal areas are shown in somewhat greater detail. The island in Blue Hill Bay appears larger and has acquired a name: Long Island. But General Charts, ranging in scale from 1:600,000 to 1:150,000, still do not include the precise data that is required for close-in piloting. They are used for plotting courses along a coast—but outside of major rocks and reefs.*

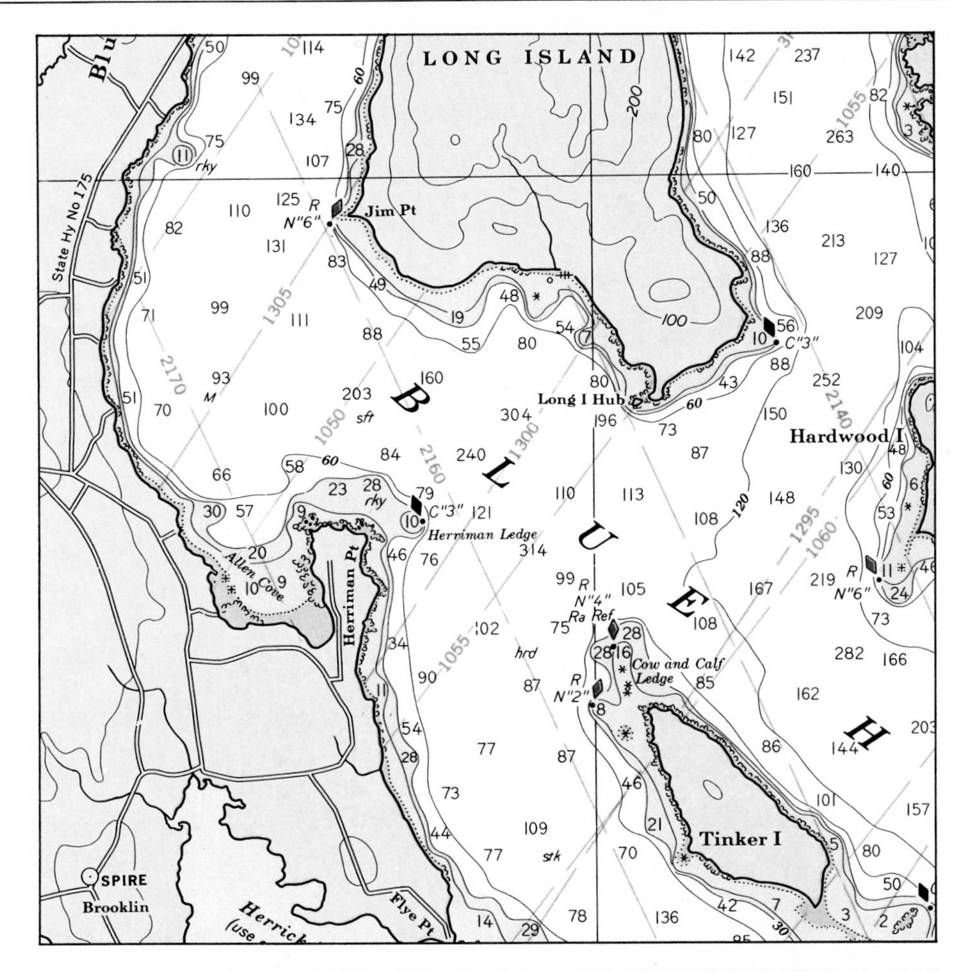

1:80,000 scale. *The amplified scale of a Coast Chart, like the example at left, allows the cartographer to incorporate the major navigational details necessary for inshore piloting. Here, a part of the intricate coastline of Long Island is carefully delineated; depth soundings in feet describe shoal areas and channels, and principal navigation hazards and aids are clearly shown. The perspective is still broad enough, however, to give the navigator an overview of his immediate area.*

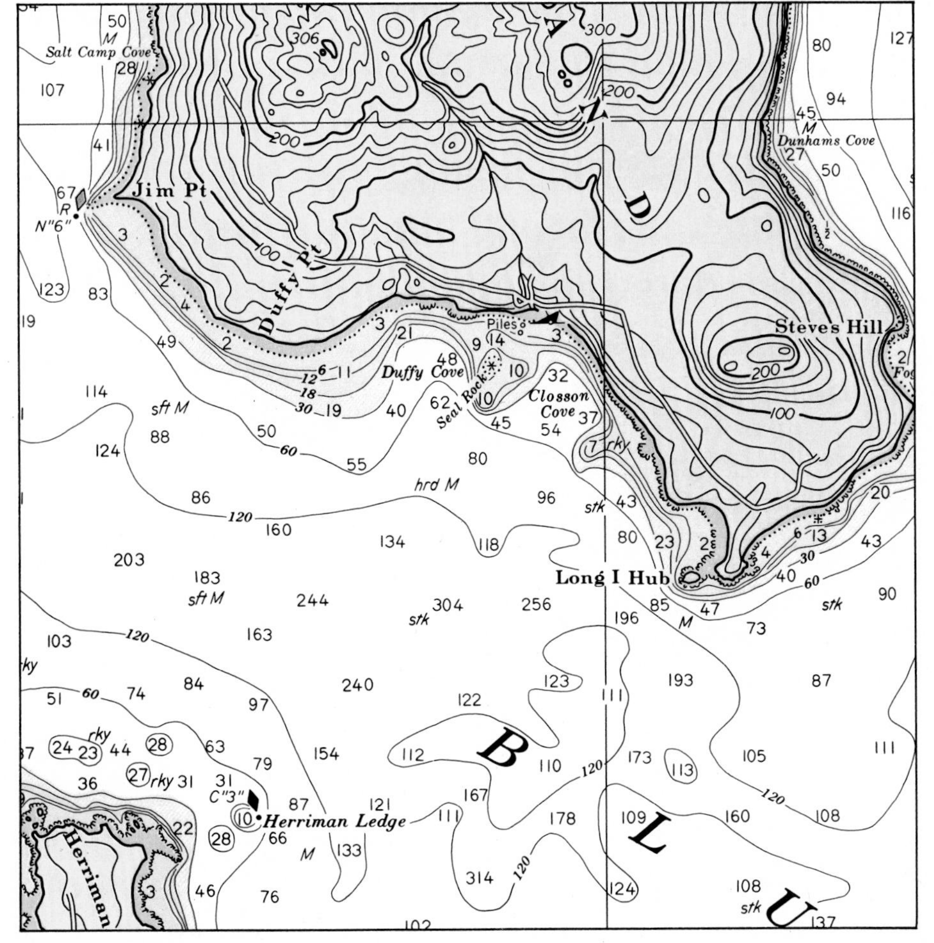

1:40,000 scale. *The closest view of all is provided by a Harbor Chart (Small-Craft Charts are similar in scale), which closely details the coastlines and bottom contours, and includes an elaborate schematic representation of inland topography. Here, Long Island has been scaled up so that even pilings between Duffy and Closson coves are clearly marked. Some Harbor Charts are drawn to an even larger scale than this one; they range from 1:50,000 to 1:5,000.*

Other Looks in Charts

While most cruising grounds in the United States are covered by the standard nautical charts issued by the National Ocean Survey (NOS), some areas require their own charts. Any skipper who travels on lakes, canals or rivers above the tidal zone can turn to specialized charts such as the ones shown here. They are compiled by the Defense Mapping Agency's Hydrographic Center, by the Army Corps of Engineers or by a regional NOS branch called the Lake Survey Center, and they can be purchased by writing to the agency that puts them out *(page 172)*. (For cruising in Canadian waters, you may obtain charts from the Canadian Hydrographic Service.) While these regional charts usually follow the general format of the NOS charts, they show some significant differences.

The Defense Mapping Agency's charts of foreign waters, for example, use data obtained from foreign-government surveys, and thus they sometimes resemble foreign-admiralty charts. Land areas are usually gray, as in the Bahamian chart below; depths may be in meters rather than fathoms or feet. Great Lakes charts *(top right)* and river charts *(opposite, below)* are sometimes marked with preplotted courses along channels or between major navigation marks; but course distances are given in statute rather than in nautical miles *(page 94)*. And while most charts use the standard NOS symbols for rocks, reefs, landmarks, buoys and lighthouses, the river and lake charts compiled by the Corps of Engineers often employ an entirely different set of symbols; they are described on the charts themselves.

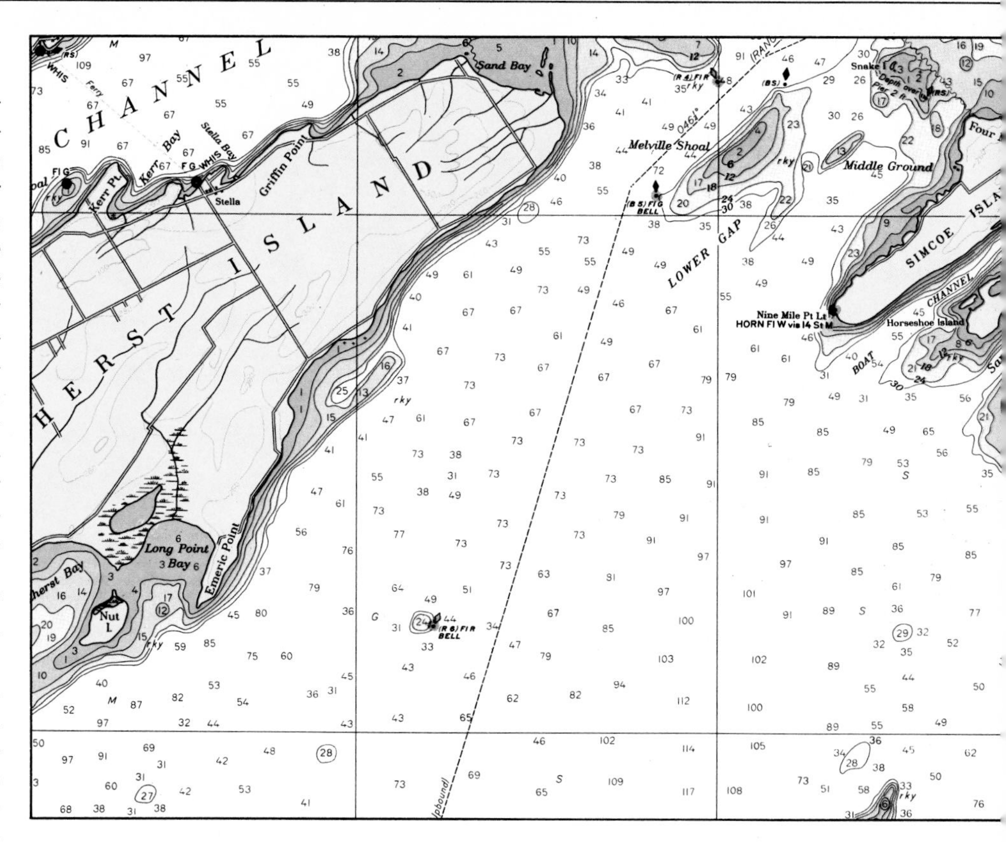

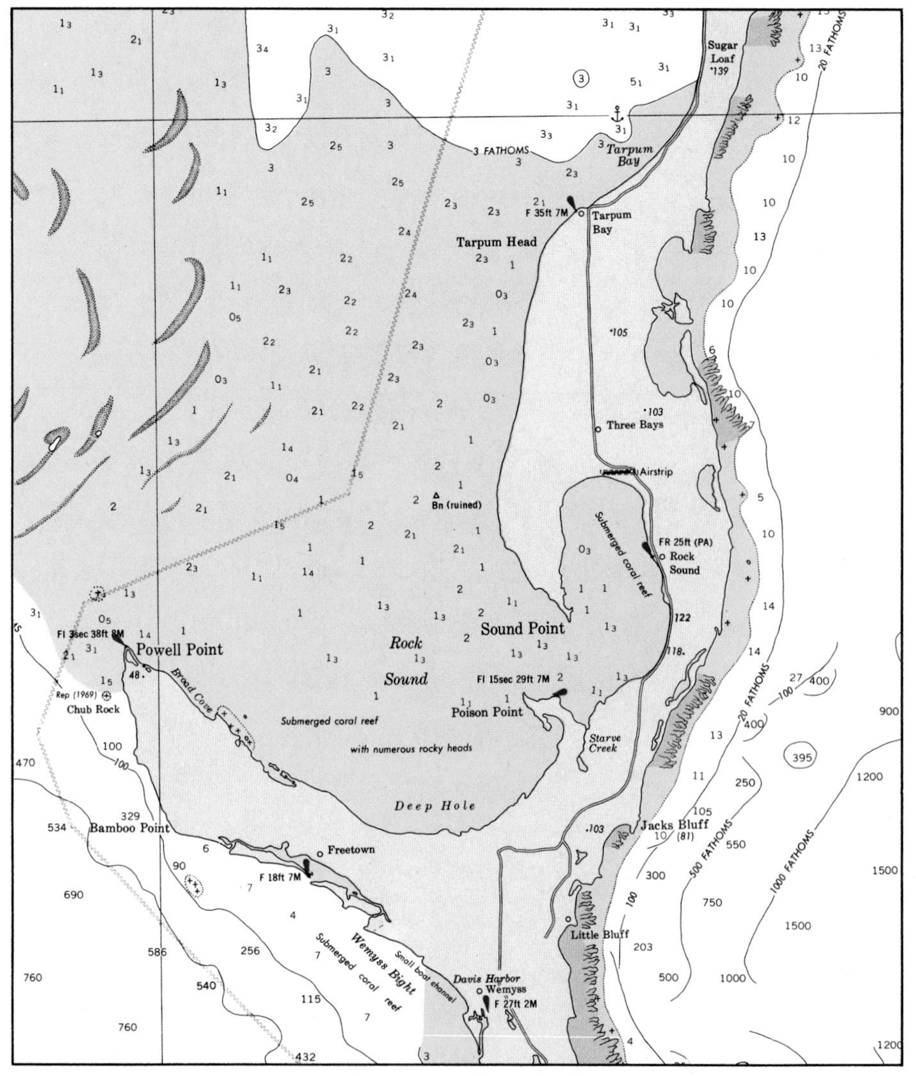

This chart excerpt of a part of Eleuthera Island in the Bahamas is typical of the international charts that are put out by the U.S. Defense Mapping Agency. The land areas are tinted gray, and shallow water is indicated by a distinctive aqua blue. Soundings are marked in fathoms; also, within areas of less than 11 fathoms, a small number next to the fathom mark defines depth to the nearest foot. But the navigator should not rely on such exact measurements, since revisions of these special charts are sporadic, and sand bars may have shifted and channels filled since the last survey.

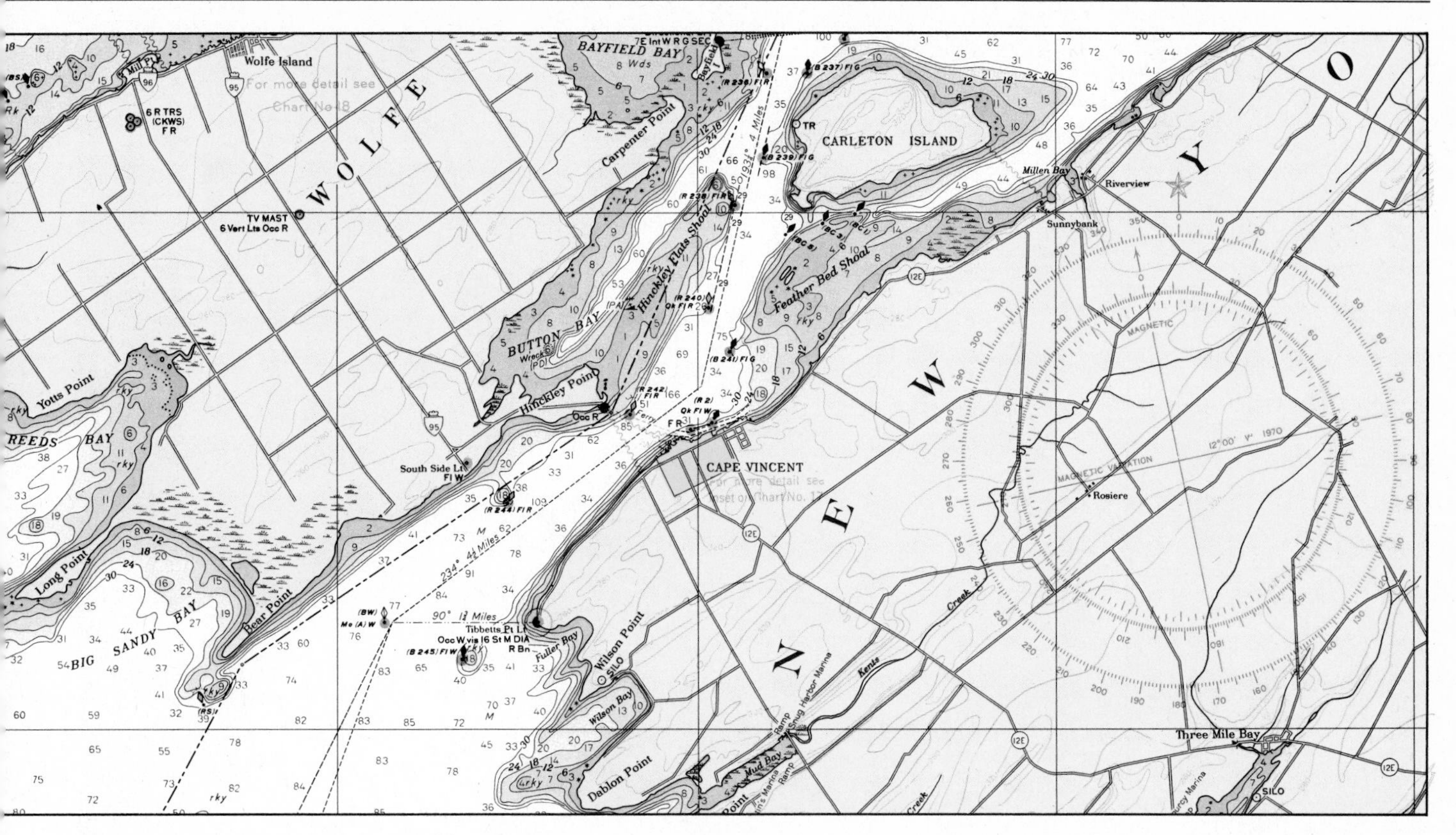

A tricky stretch of northeastern Lake Ontario is shown in this segment of a chart issued by the Lake Survey Center. As in all charts of the Great Lakes, where water level depends on seasonal variations in climate rather than the daily tide, depth soundings are based on an average of historical lows occurring during the winter months. Suggested course headings between major navigation marks and landfalls are shown by light dashed lines, which are accompanied by distances in statute miles and by compass bearings. The heavy broken line running by Wolfe Island is the United States-Canadian border.

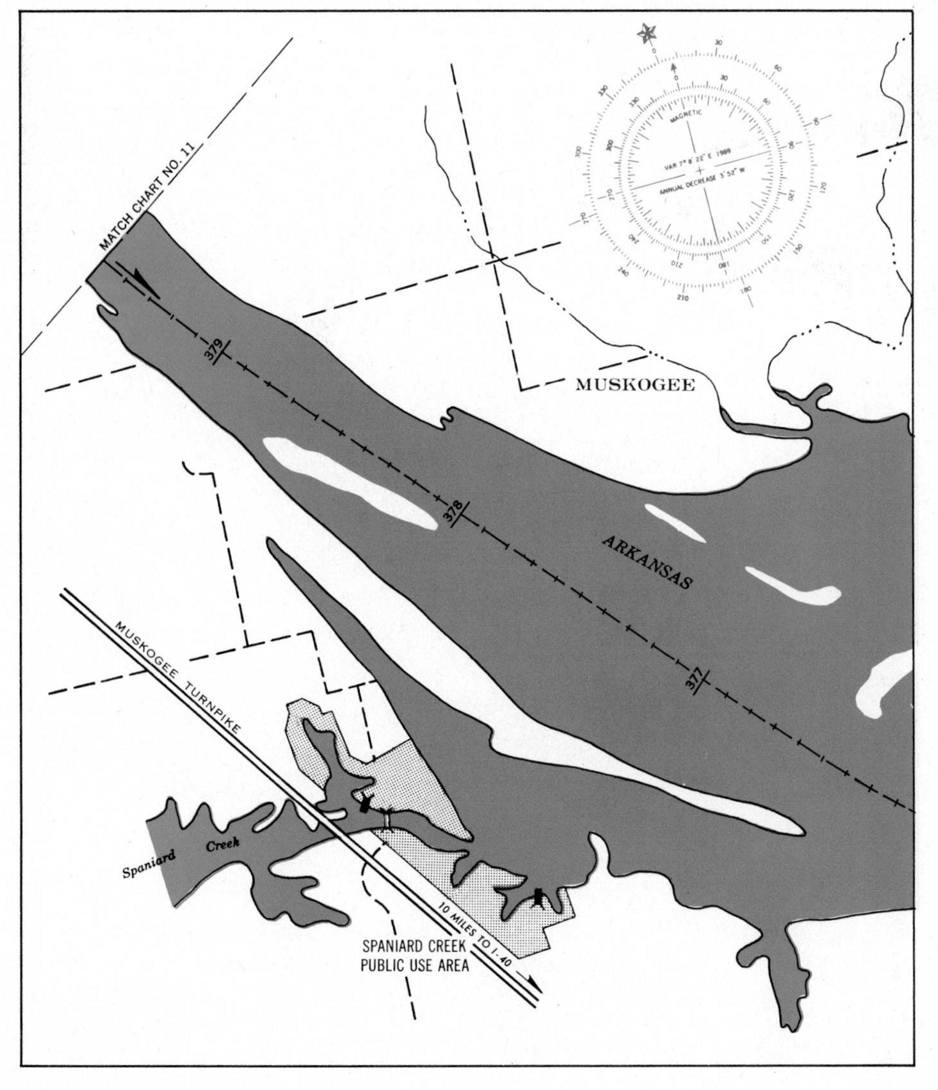

This three-mile strip of the Arkansas River near Muskogee, Oklahoma, is part of an extended river chart put out by the Army Corps of Engineers, which maps most major inland watercourses in the United States. Soundings are omitted because of the continuously shifting bottom contours, but a broken red line gives the safe channel. The line is marked for each statute mile; the numbers indicate the distance to the river's mouth, which is at the Mississippi. As in most river-chart formats, the Arkansas system is traced in separate chart sections, which are bound together sequentially in a booklet.

Steering a survey launch along a depth-sounding run, a helmsman stands before a panorama of dials and screens, which appears as complex as the control panel of a small airliner. Each course he runs is precisely predetermined, and the course data are fed into a computer. Underway, he steers by a sensor needle that remains centered in its dial when he is on course. To the helmsman's right, the tracer of a depth finder records a profile of the ocean floor on graph paper, in response to a series of depth soundings.

As the survey launch runs its depth-sounding course, the on-board computer records on magnetic tape the depth-finder readings and their locations, as determined by radio position-fixing equipment linked to the computer. Throughout the run an officer monitors the instruments by periodically checking the computer's tape print-out.

How Charts Are Made

To meet the unending need of mariners for up-to-date charts, specially equipped survey teams like the one on these pages keep a constant eye on the nation's waterways. These professional water watchers are members of the National Oceanic and Atmospheric Administration, which also maintains a staff of 100 map makers *(pages 36-37)* in a group called the National Ocean Survey in NOAA's headquarters in Rockville, Maryland. Together they revise the 971 different charts that are the cruising bibles for 18 million pleasure-boat owners and another 250,000 or so commercial mariners.

Some of the information is collected by planes armed with 400-pound aerial cameras; these aircraft fly more than 50,000 miles annually photographing changing shorelines and river courses. At the same time, a flotilla of powerboats, skillfully manned and lavishly equipped, develops data on water depths and bottom characteristics, as shown here. Cruising at 20 knots, this vessel uses highly sophisticated radio position-fixing equipment, electronic depth finders and computers that pick up information along the lines of meticulously plotted courses.

The results of these surveys—reams of computer print-outs, piles of handwritten notes, fat rolls of sequential nine-inch-square color transparencies—as well as reports from the Coast Guard, the Army Corps of Engineers and alert civilian boatmen, all find their way to the NOS's chart-making center, where cartographers transpose them onto charts.

To double-check the survey boat's position, seamen measure with sextants the angles from three onshore landmarks, and then, by triangulation, determine the launch's exact location at the start and finish of each day. These visual fixes serve to verify the position that the vessel's computer obtains out of its radio position-fixing equipment—which is vulnerable to atmospheric distortion.

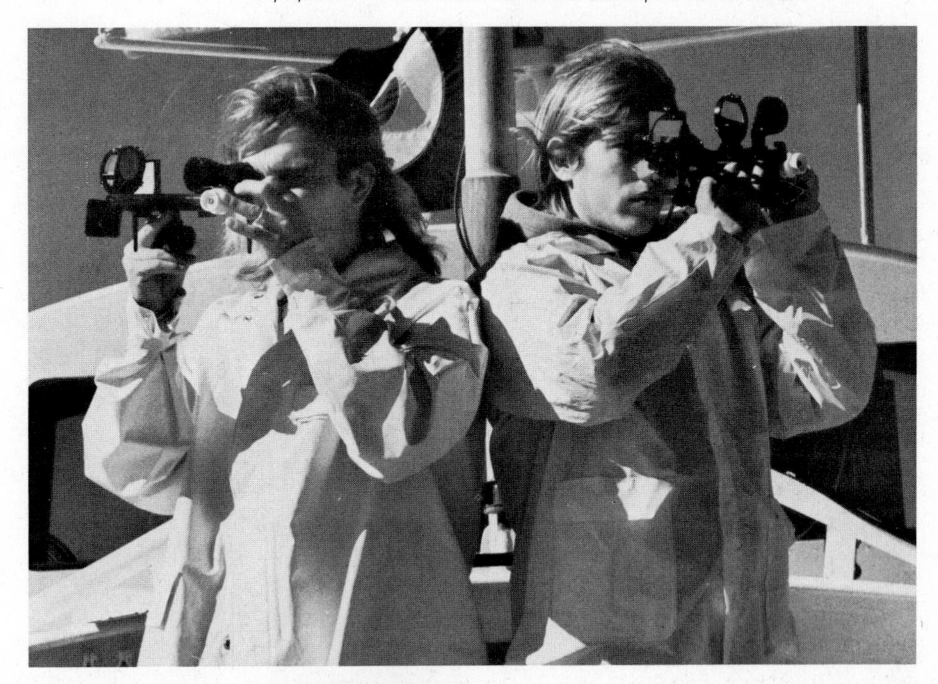

To obtain a specimen of the sea bottom, a crewman lowers a clamshell sampler over the side. When the device touches down, its two halves snap shut, collecting about two cups of material. The crewman then hauls the sampler aboard, examines the contents and marks his findings and their location in a record book. Later, this record of the bottom material (mud, sand or rock), its consistency (soft, sticky or hard) and any significant sea life on its surface (kelp or beds of seashells) will be used to update charts.

Cartographers at the National Ocean Survey office in Rockville, Maryland, work on revising charts—or creating new ones—for every patch of navigable U.S. waters. The map makers revise more than 550 charts annually, including some, like those covering the ever-changing offshore oil-drilling area between the Mississippi River delta and the Texas border, that have to be revised twice every year.

Correlating field data, a cartographer sifts out newly reported depth soundings, bottom information and menaces to navigation, such as submerged rocks and wrecks. Then he transfers them to the master drawing of a nautical chart that is under his right hand.

This cartographer corrects a section of coastline by tracing over the contours of an aerial photograph made to the scale of the chart. Placing the chart and transparent photograph atop a light-table, she records topographic information from the picture.

To transfer information from aerial photographs to a large-scale chart, the cartographer puts two transparencies into an aviograph, a stereo viewer with an attached scribing arm. As the cartographer moves a control handle, a pointer, visible through the viewer, traces the features he wants to transpose, while a pencil on the drawing arm (far right) re-creates the same details on the chart (foreground).

MASTERWORKS OF CHART MAKING

Not long ago, as measured by the main currents of history, most common sailors navigated by either pure guess or luck, or by their own crude sketches of coastlines. During much of the 15th Century the art of the nautical chart maker was not much more than a century old. Columbus had not yet exploded the boundaries of the known world, which still centered around the Mediterranean. But an era of great navigators was aborning. The few existing charts, laboriously created by a handful of talented cartographers, were coveted by kings and queens, and by a few powerful traders and sea captains. These works were treasured instruments of high ambitions; they could help guide fleets to commercial ports or the wealth of new lands.

The chart makers' creations were also remarkable for their artistic beauty. The exquisite example shown at right was drawn by two craftsmen in Barcelona in 1456—only 150 years after the creation of the earliest known nautical chart. The design is overlaid with an interlacing of straight-line navigation routes, called rhumb lines, that radiate from major ports and cities—and from compass roses. The artists added national flags, and miniature illustrations showed the principal buildings—some of them curiously capsized—at centers of trade and worship.

From this elegant base, the science of nautical cartography began to develop in earnest with the great voyages of exploration in the late 15th Century. In Portugal, Prince Henry the Navigator recruited Europe's finest map makers to chart his captains' discoveries along Africa. In Spain, King Ferdinand and Queen Isabella established one of the earliest government cartographic offices. In charge was a hydrographer who kept New World maps under lock and key. One hydrographic appointee was the Italian explorer Sebastian Cabot, who outraged the Spanish court when he tried to sell secret charts to his own country. Thereafter, no foreigner was allowed to hold the post.

The Spanish monarchs had hoped to set up a monopoly on charts, empowering their cartographic office with sole authority to draft and sell charts. But in Spain and Portugal, private map makers bribed seafarers returning from the New World for descriptions of lands, bays and harbors. And a black market in charts flourished in many Iberian seaports.

Though some of the early cartographers were explorers, such as Cabot and Amerigo Vespucci, who actually saw the areas they mapped, most map makers simply interpreted the reports of returning sailors—or plagiarized the work of fellow cartographers. Wherever the information originated, it was closely guarded. The Italian Battista Agnese, whose Pacific chart appears on pages 42-43, was elaborately secretive; neither his contemporaries nor historians ever learned his sources.

As exploratory voyages grew more numerous, cartographers scrambled to keep pace with the sailors—constantly adding new discoveries to their charts. And the science of cartography improved apace. Abetted by improved navigational instruments, Portuguese chart makers were the first to include lines of longitude. By the middle of the 16th Century, most maps had fully developed grids of latitude and longitude superimposed upon the spiderweb networks of rhumb lines.

Although many similarities exist in the products of the early chart makers, distinctive styles emerged in various locales. Catalan charts were noted for their decorative qualities, Portuguese works for their flamboyant colorings, and charts of the Italian school for their Spartan purity of execution. By the late 16th Century, the Dutch craftsmen had become preeminent in Europe; their bold, informative attention to coastal details dominated cartography for more than a century.

This 1456 chart of the Mediterranean was a climactic achievement of the Catalan school of cartography. The coastline and listing of towns and ports (in red) is meticulously accurate. But the artists stylized such features of unconcern to Mediterranean sailors as the Red Sea (lower right) and the Atlas Mountains (scalloped green frond).

This Portuguese chart of Brazil's northern coast was one of the earliest to indicate latitude. Drafted in 1519, the map illustrates explorers' impressions of the new land. The chart maker filled it with colorful birds, a plethora of place names and ferocious cannibals, who cut down trees yielding the purple dye called indigo. The most important parallels of latitude—dividing climatic zones—are drawn across the face of the map; others are indicated by the beaded north-south line along the right margin.

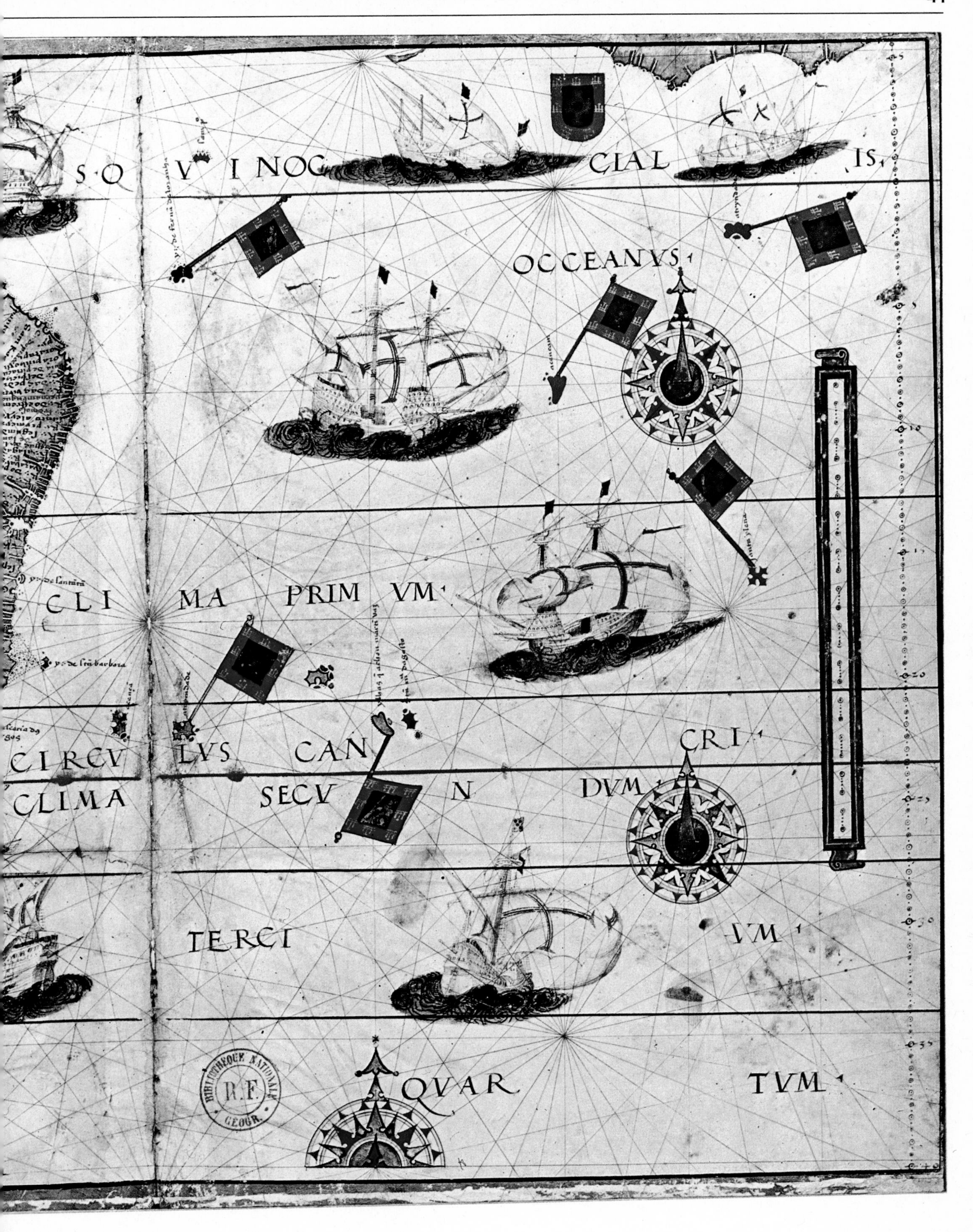
S·Q V I NOC CIAL IS
OCCEANVS
CLI MA PRIM VM
CIRCV LVS CAN CRI
CLIMA SECV N DVM
TERCI VM
QVAR TVM
BIBLIOTHEQUE NATIONALE R.F. GEOGR.

This chart of the Pacific, created in 1555 by a Genoese, Battista Agnese, reveals the state of exploration at the time. China, Ceylon and the Philippines are shown, but Australia and New Zealand had yet to be discovered. The chart includes one of the earliest indications of tides: at the head of the Gulf of California, flecked with a reddish tint, an inscription notes that high-water depth is 11 brazas (a braza is the span of a man's outstretched arms) and low-water depth is eight brazas. Also, Agnese overlaid the map with a grid showing both latitude and longitude —one of the first chart makers to do so.

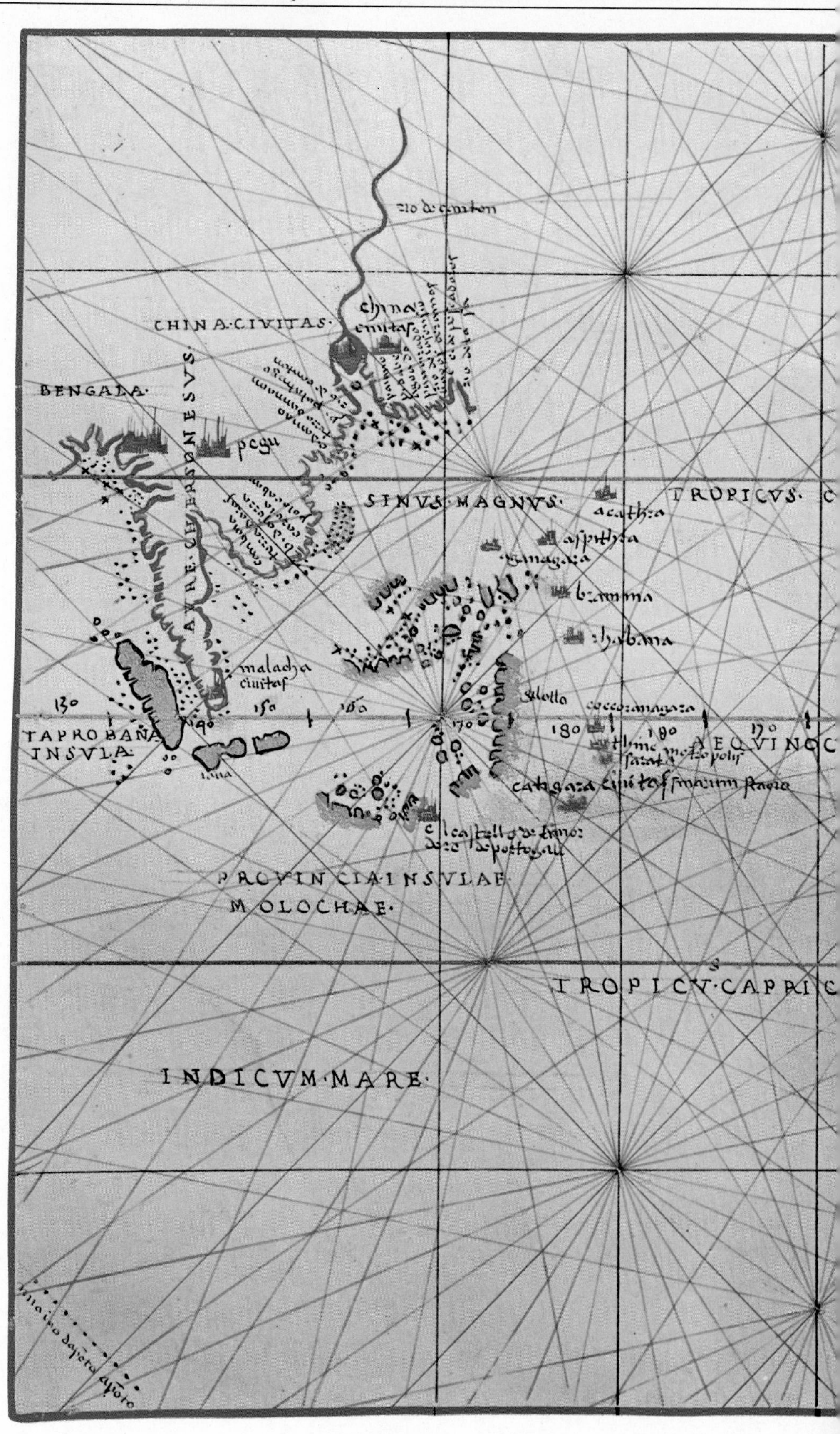

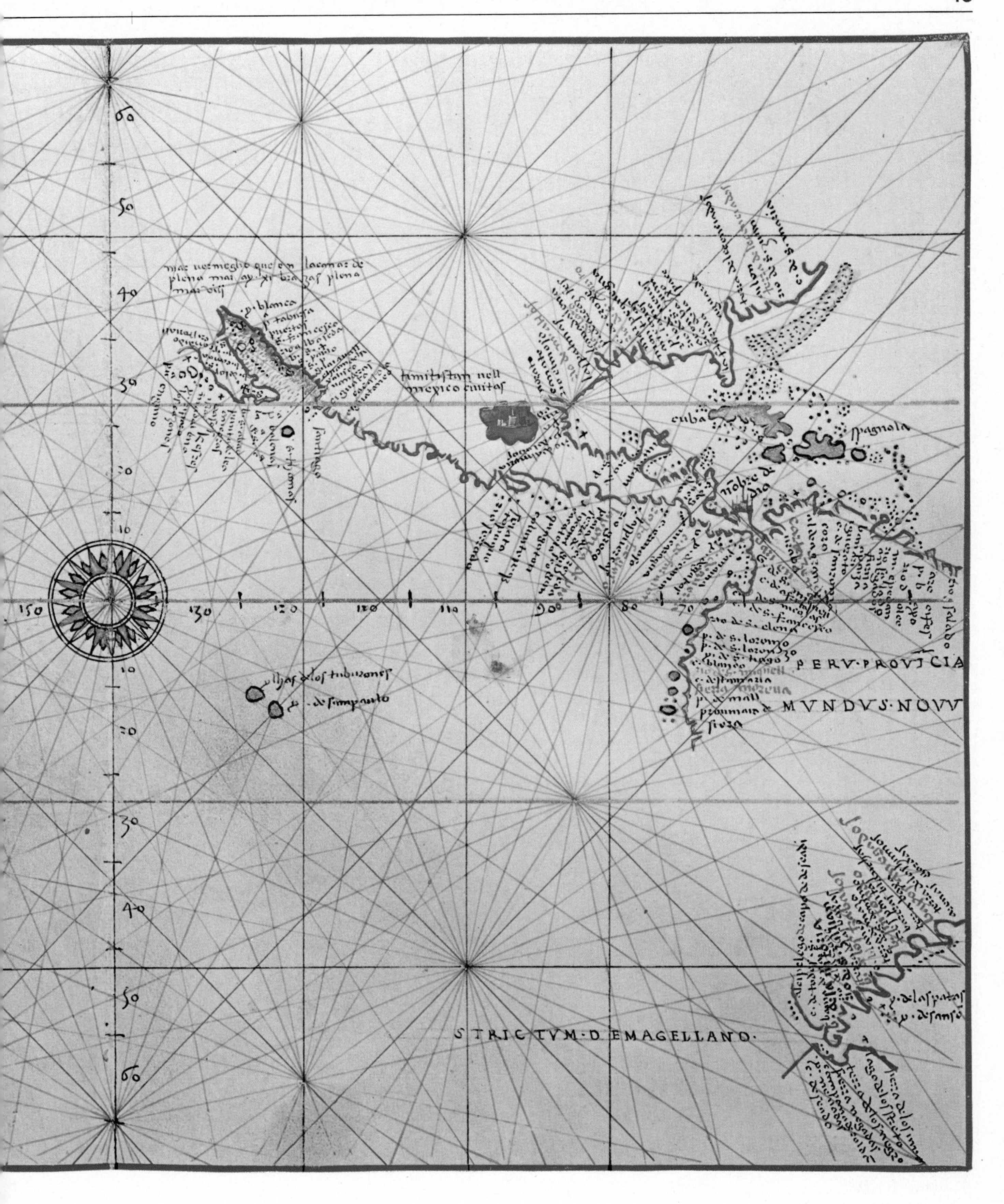

timitistan nell
mexico civitas
cuba
spagnola
nobre de dio
PERV·PROVJCIA
MVNDVS·NOVV
STRICTVM·D EMAGELLANO·

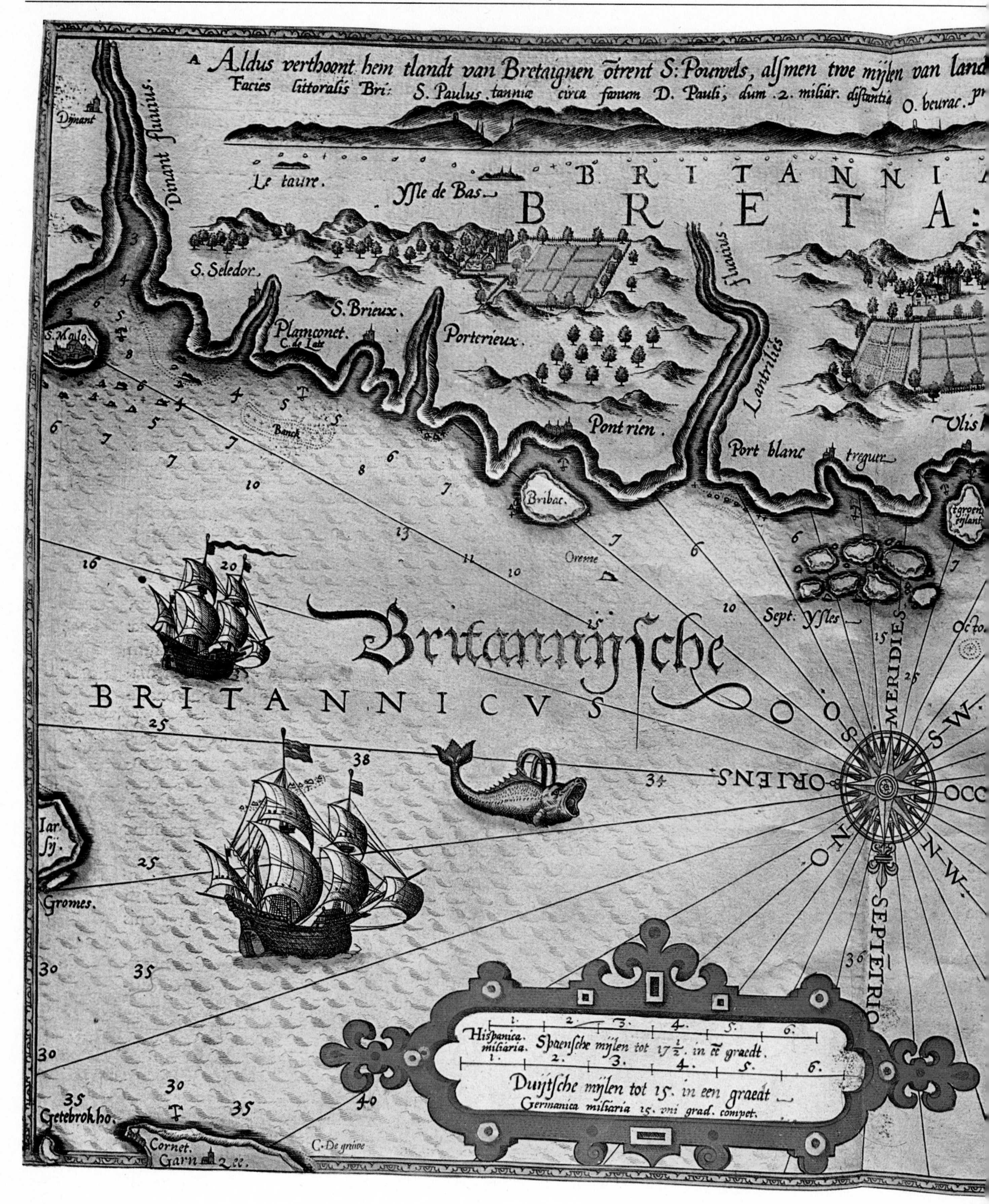
Aldus verthoont hem tlandt van Bretaignen otrent S: Pouwels, alsmen twe mijlen van land
Facies littoralis Bri: S. Paulus tanniæ circa fanum D. Pauli, dum 2. miliar. distantia
O. beurac.
Dinant fluuius
Le taure.
Ysle de Bas
BRITANNI
BRETA
S. Seledor.
S. Brieux.
Plamconet.
Porterieux.
Lantriliis
fluuius
Pont rien.
Port blanc
treguer
Bribac.
Oreme
Sept. Ysles
Britannische
BRITANNICVS
ORIENS
MERIDIES
SEPTETRIO
Gromes.
Hispanica miliaria. Spaensche mijlen tot 17½. in eē graedt.
Duijtsche mijlen tot 15. in een graeat
Germanica miliaria 15. vni grad. compet.
Getebrokho.
Cornet.
Garn
C. De gruve

In this 1583 chart of the coast of Brittany, the Dutchman Lucas Janszoon Waghenaer introduced systematic depth indications, pointed out hazardous rocks and shoals, and sketched the coast's profile (top). English sailors admired Waghenaer's work, and for centuries called any collection of piloting charts a waggoner.

2

Dotting the coastal and inland waters of the United States are tens of thousands of objects designed to tell a boatman where he is and where he should or should not go. These aids to navigation, as they are called, communicate their message by almost every imaginable means. Some ring bells or gongs, or sound horns or whistles; others signal their information mainly by shape, color or distinctive markings; some of them are designed to reflect radar or searchlight beams efficiently; and still others reach 10 or more miles across the sea by the use of high-intensity lights or radio waves.

The largest aids to navigation are lighthouses and beacons—descendants

SIGNPOSTS FOR SAILORS

of ancient Mediterranean towers that displayed wood or coal fires to warn ships off dangerous shores. Buoys are smaller but much more numerous; they make up about 60 per cent of the total of all nautical signposts. Sturdy tank-mounted structures such as the wasp-waisted model at left are anchored in depths of up to 450 feet. Designed for use in exposed locations, these buoys possess steel skeletons nearly 20 feet tall and are capable of withstanding extreme forces of wind and water that would have hopelessly overmatched their predecessors, the wooden-keg buoys or crude logs used to mark navigable waterways in centuries past. Farther inshore and in channels, simpler cylindrical or conical buoys suffice. In shallow water, the role of buoys is often assumed by signs that are called daymarks; they are displayed on pilings or spars driven into the bottom.

All of these various communicators speak to boatmen by means of a relatively simple language that can be easily deciphered and put to use with the help of charts, light lists *(page 73)* and other publications of the federal and state governments. The various sorts of navigable waters in the United States are subject to four major buoyage systems, which are described in detail on the following pages. The four systems differ from one another in minor respects, but each system operates on the same underlying principle: in concise and compelling language they all try to keep the boatman out of trouble, sometimes by indicating the proximity of specific dangers or, more basically, by offering the navigator a means of determining his location—the fundamental information that spells the difference between simply reacting to danger and anticipating it.

These aids to navigation are carefully maintained—in most cases by the United States Coast Guard—and are steadily replaced with more advanced designs. But they are not infallible. Lights or other electronic equipment can fail. Buoys sometimes drag from their appointed positions, particularly during heavy weather when the navigator is most in need of them. And communication can break down even when the device is functioning properly. Buoys that have been emplaced to warn of a shoal may become a liability if the shoal shifts in a storm. In fog, atmospheric conditions can play all sorts of tricks with sound, altering the apparent direction from which a boatman believes he hears a gong or whistle, for instance, or even changing a whistle's special identifying tones.

A skipper should never rely upon a single navigation mark to give him warning of possible danger. Instead, he should make use of all of the information conveyed to him by all of the aids that he can see or hear, or that he detects with his electronic equipment *(pages 130-133, 136-139)*. When used in this manner and with understanding, the aids to navigation are the seaman's best friends. After the safe negotiation of a long passage in dirty weather, the flashing light on the far horizon that signals "this is the way home" can be the most welcome sign a sailor ever sees.

As fog rolls in toward Santa Barbara, California, a sentinel buoy at the entrance to the harbor employs both light and bell to guide the mariner to a safe return.

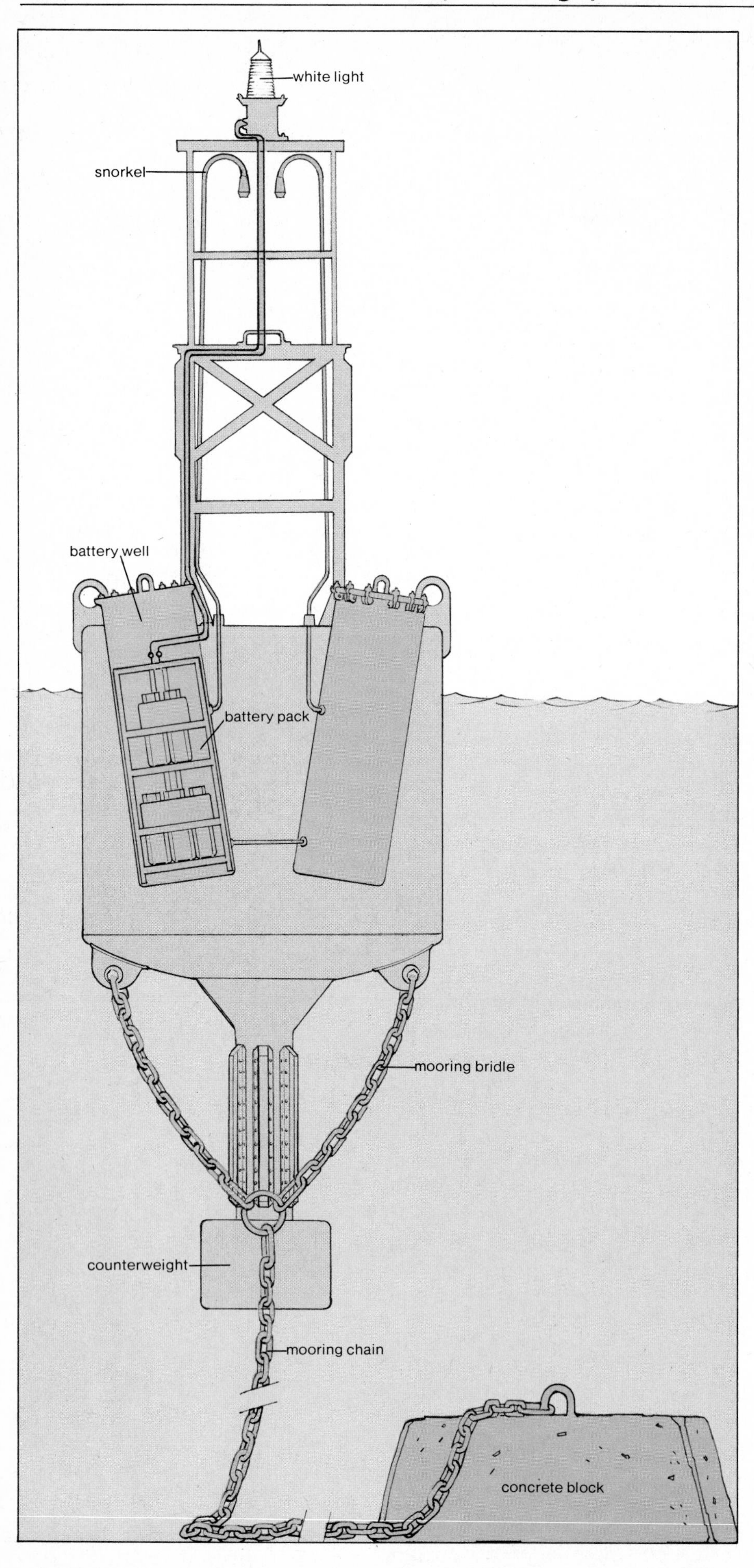

Flashers and Sounders

Buoys are the aids to navigation most commonly encountered. Some are simple metal cylinders moored to the bottom. But many, particularly those located offshore, are complex mechanisms that carry special devices for calling attention to their locations at night or in bad weather. Buoys like the one at left, a new design that is gradually replacing the traditional wasp-waisted buoy seen on page 46, light up. Lighted buoys commonly carry a blinking white light, as here; or they may emit coded signals of various colors and patterns, which are described on the following pages and on page 72. Others, like the four shown opposite, also use bells, gongs, horns or whistles to send out distinctive sound signals. Like the light signals, these noisemakers are identified both on charts and in United States government publications called light lists *(page 73)*, which help the mariner to locate buoy positions—and his own—in times of poor visibility.

Most of these aids to navigation are totally automated, and require only periodic servicing, which is done by the Coast Guard. Lights, for example, are powered by batteries housed in waterproof pockets and are capable of lasting up to three years. Light-sensitive crystals that operate in a manner similar to photoelectric cells switch on the lights automatically whenever the sunlight starts to fade below a certain intensity.

Sound buoys are operated in the main by wave action; the motion of the sea causes their bells and gongs to ring, or air to flow through carefully designed chambers to blow whistles. And though the noisemakers are of immense value to the navigator, especially along a fogbound coast, they have a limited range: the loudest of them usually can be heard no farther off than half a mile. By contrast, a lighted buoy like that at left can be seen for distances of up to seven miles.

Attached firmly to a sunken concrete block by a bridle and a slack chain, this lighted buoy is held upright by a counterweight so that its light can be seen at maximum distances. Two battery packs, mounted in waterproof wells, supply a steady 12-volt current; a snorkel from each pocket carries air to the batteries and lets gases escape.

A bell buoy produces an erratic pattern of sounds of a single tone as wave action causes its four tappers, hinged atop the buoy's frame, to strike the lip of the bell. The tappers are equipped with governing devices that limit their swing in order to prevent them from doing any damage to the buoy.

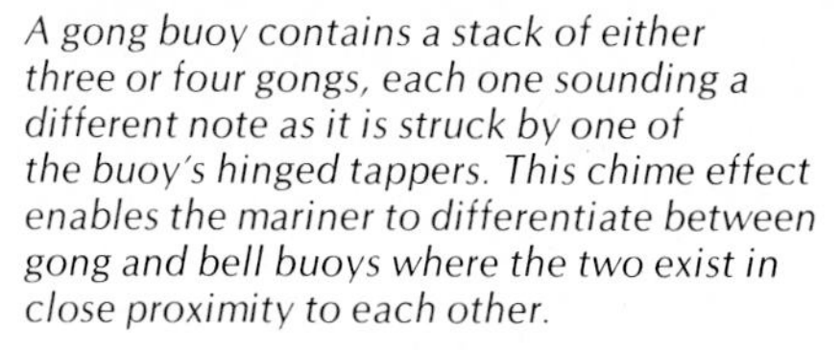

A gong buoy contains a stack of either three or four gongs, each one sounding a different note as it is struck by one of the buoy's hinged tappers. This chime effect enables the mariner to differentiate between gong and bell buoys where the two exist in close proximity to each other.

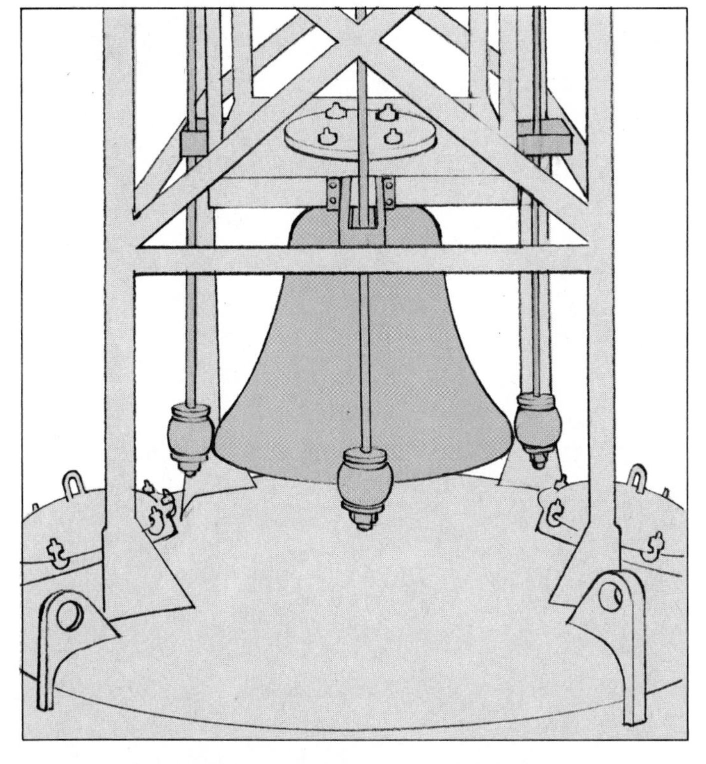

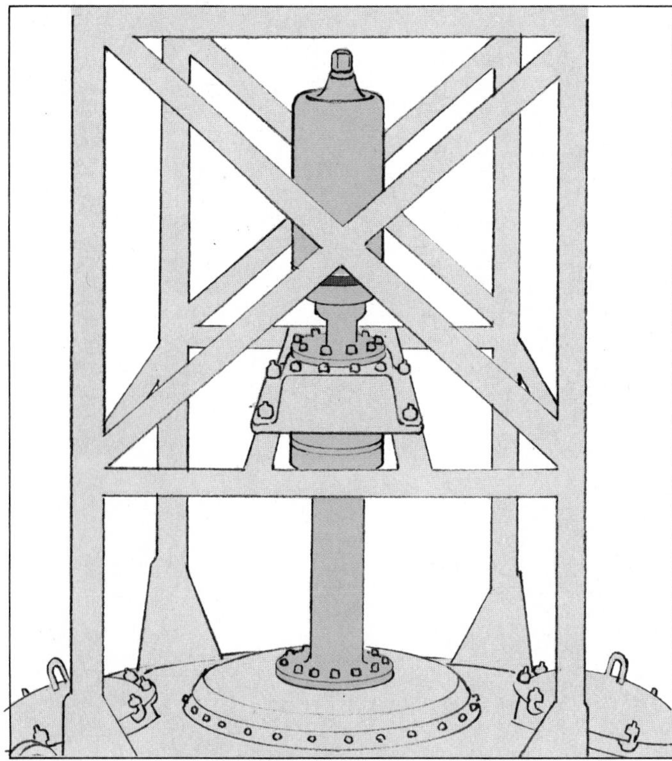

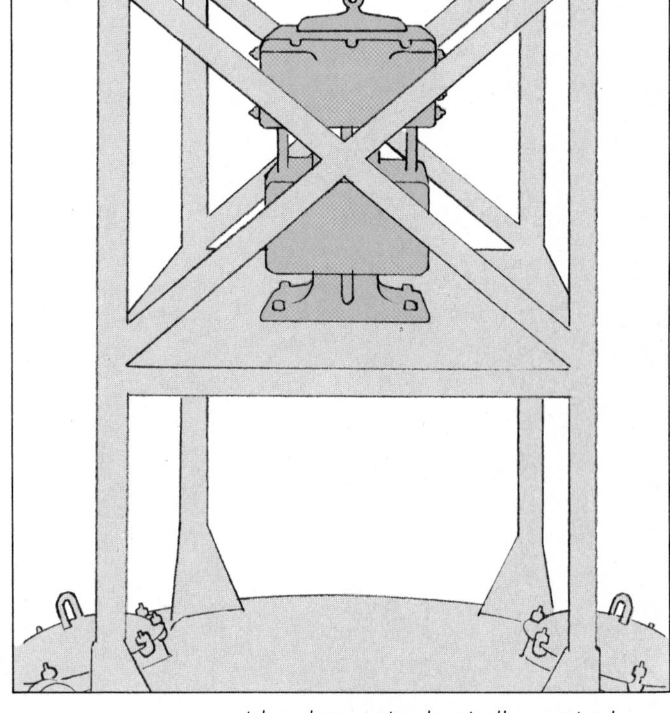

As a whistle buoy rises and falls with the action of waves, water is forced in and out of a tube in the center of the buoy. When the water enters, it pushes the air within the tube, forcing it under pressure through an aperture in the top, producing a loud whistle.

A horn buoy emits electrically energized blasts of predetermined lengths and intervals toward all points of the compass. The power comes from the same type of battery system that works the light shown opposite.

"Red, Right, Returning"

Of the four buoyage systems employed in the United States, the most important one is that used in the waters outlined at right, which are officially termed Navigable Waters by the Coast Guard. And this system of aids to navigation serves as the basis for the other three.

Essentially, the system depends upon observance of one basic rule. When returning to the land from seaward, a boat must leave all red marks to starboard and black to port, following a traditional mariner's dictum: "red, right, returning."

Such marks are coded not only by color but by number and sometimes shape —and this code is matched to a system of chart symbols *(Appendix)*. Floating red marks with a conical outline—commonly known as nuns—carry even numbers. Floating black marks, or cans, are cylindrical in shape and bear odd numbers. Daymarks are affixed to stakes or pilings driven into the bottom, and convey similar messages.

Other marks in the system convey other messages: which of two channels is preferable, or where to anchor. The most common of these marks are shown here, and their typical uses are illustrated in the composite harbor scene on pages 52-53.

In the Navigable Waters buoyage system (blue outline), a boat bound inland leaves red marks to starboard. This system's arbitrary subsystem designates "inland" as southerly (or westerly) along the Atlantic Coast; on the Gulf Coast, inland is westerly and northerly; and on the Pacific, northerly.

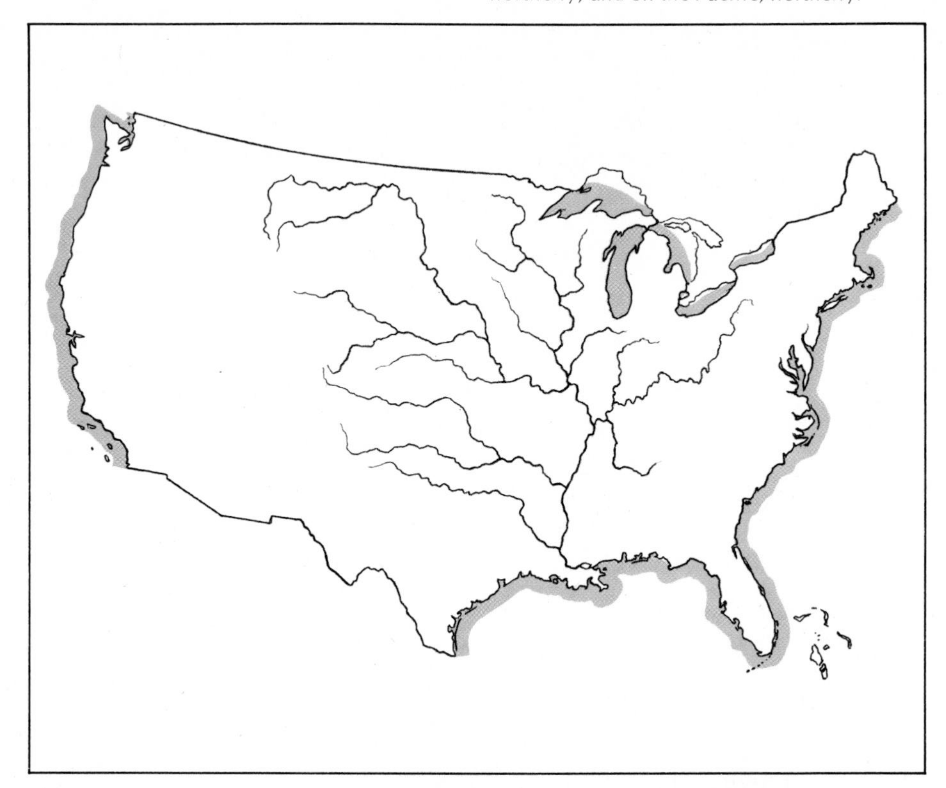

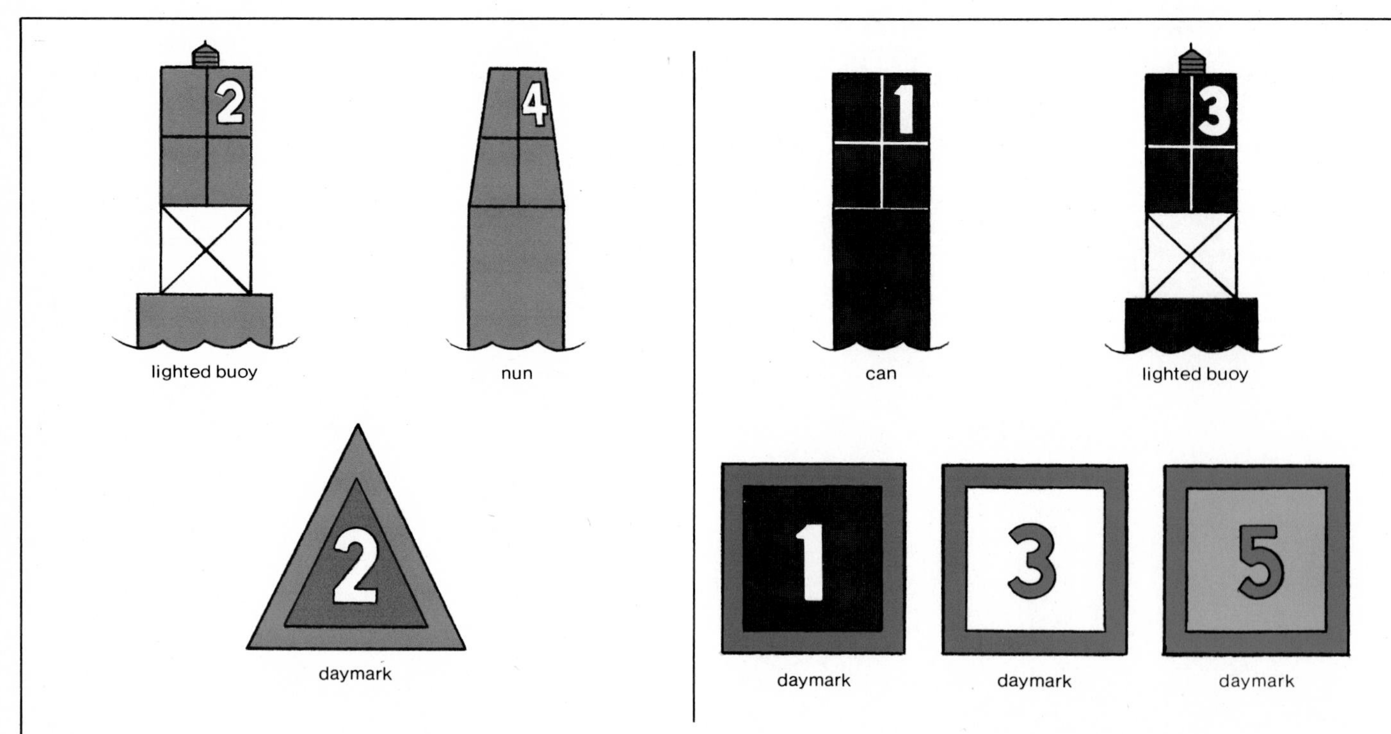

When bound inland from the sea, red even-numbered marks like the lighted buoy above and nun at upper right are kept to starboard. So are triangular red daymarks, which rest on pilings in shallower water. A lighted red buoy may flash red—or, to avoid confusion, white if there are other red lights nearby.

Heading in, black cans or lighted black buoys, which are odd-numbered, must be left to port. The buoy's light may be either green, which is the alternate color code for portside marks, or white. Square portside daymarks have green borders, although the interiors may be black, white or green.

Special-purpose buoys like those shown below can be found in all United States waters. They indicate conditions such as the presence of fish nets that might foul propellers, or quarantine areas where incoming vessels must moor until cleared. Exclusion buoys indicate extreme hazards.

Diamond-shaped daymarks like these have no special meanings. With or without notations, they are used to mark such points of navigation—or dangers—as the end of a jetty, or to call attention to a hazard around the bend of a channel. In their case, color is used only to attract a skipper's attention.

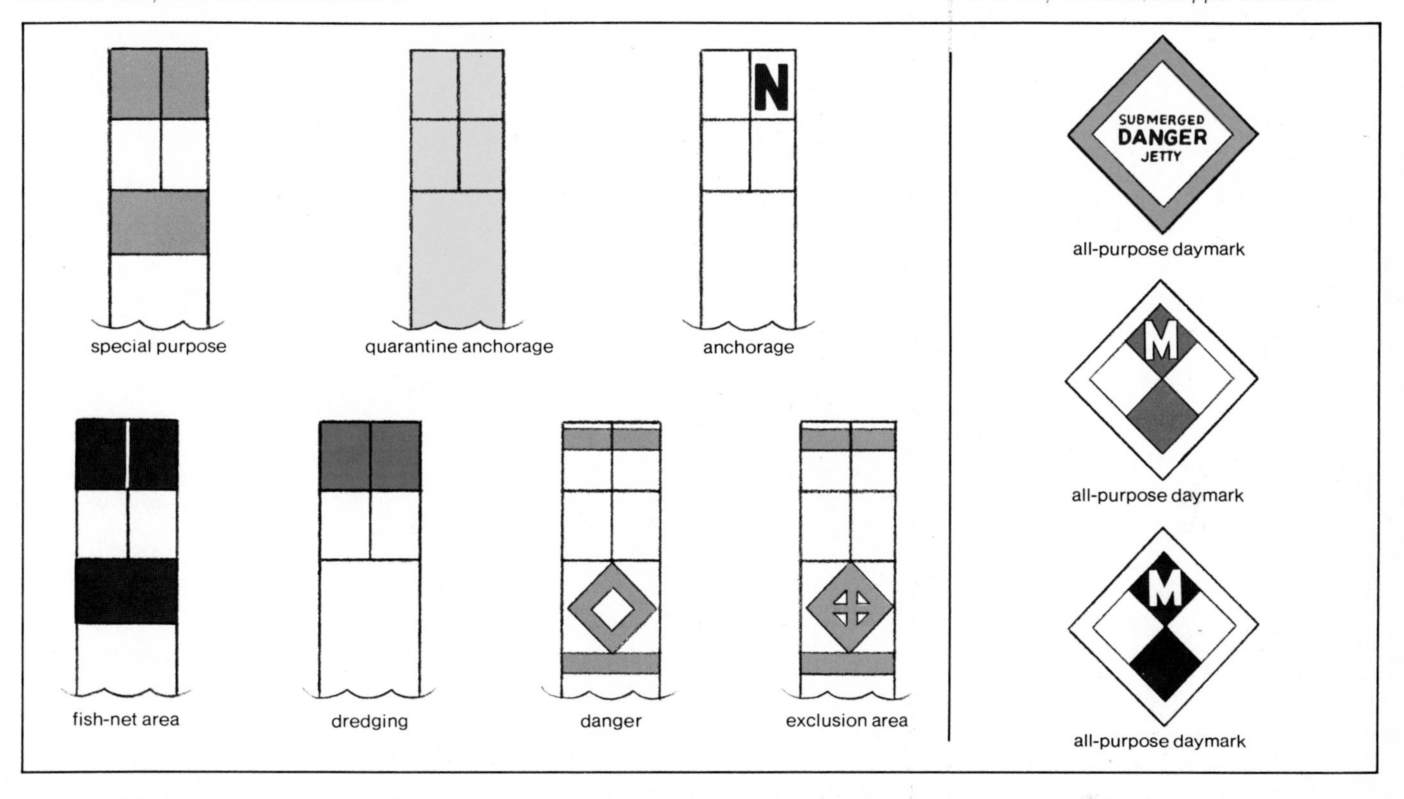

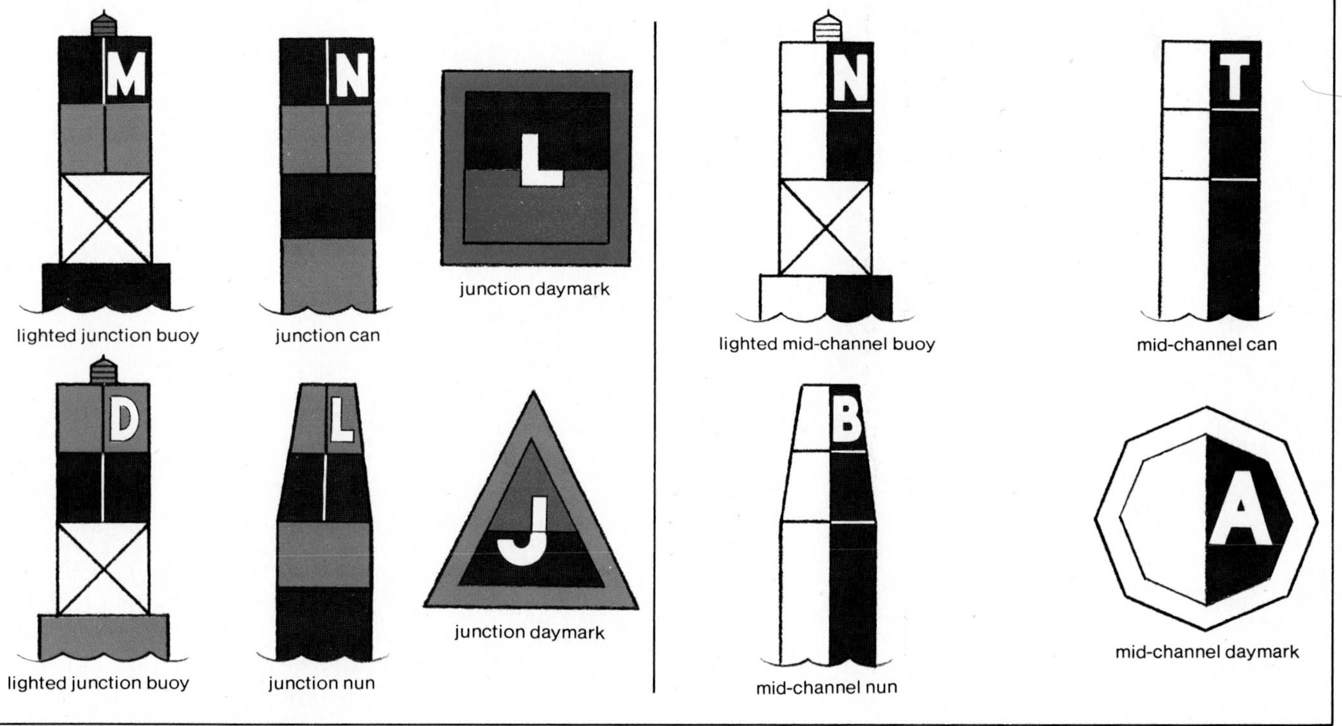

Markers like these indicate the junction of two channels and can be passed to either side. But when a black band is on top, the preferred channel is to starboard; lights may be green or white. A red band on top means the better channel is to port; lights may be red or white. The letters are for identification.

These aids indicate the middle of a channel and, like junction marks, can be passed to either side. The octagonal daymark is used only for mid-channel marks. Such aids may be equipped with white lights that signal with sequential short and long flashes. Sometimes they include identifying letters.

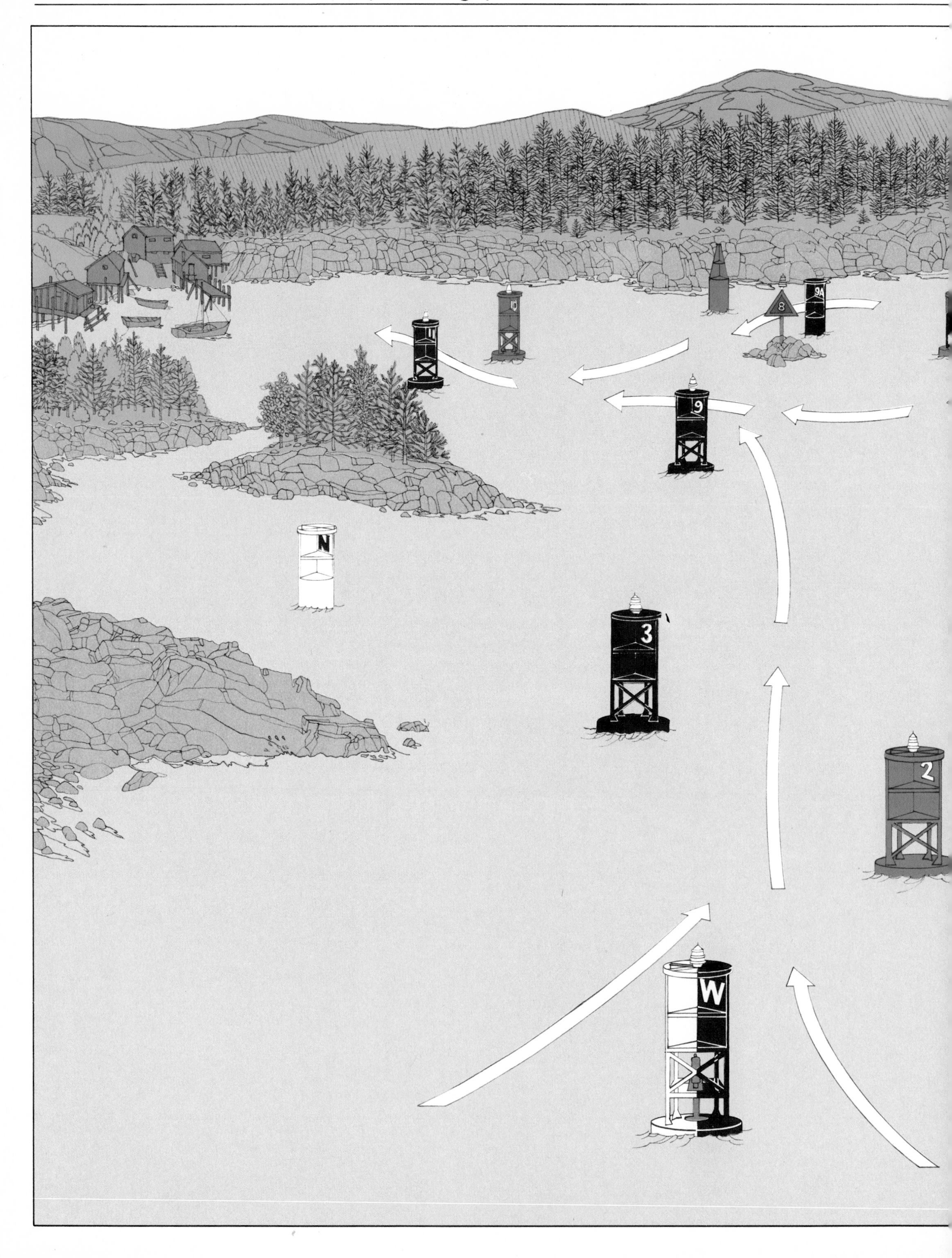

10
11
8
9A
9
N
3
2
W

The scene at left represents a mythical section of the Maine coast, whose buoys are part of the Navigable Waters system. Although buoys and markers in reality would not be as large as seen here, this view reflects a situation boatmen might encounter. Two channels and a shallow bypass lead to the same harbor. Skippers must read the buoys as detailed below. The accompanying drawings are for quick identification.

The black-and-white whistle buoy marks a channel entrance. It is passed to either side.

Red lighted buoy #2 is passed to the right by any boat returning from the sea—that is, in the direction indicated by the arrows.

Off to starboard, black-and-white buoys warn the mariner of underwater fish nets.

An orange-rimmed diamond daymark signals an underwater hazard: a collapsed jetty.

Past lighted buoy #3, anchorage buoy "N" denotes that there is a berth for vessels.

The skipper turns left around lighted black buoy #9 to head for the inner harbor.

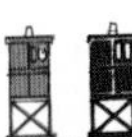

Dead ahead, two lighted buoys—one red, one black—form the "gate" to the harbor.

At top right, red bell buoy #2 and black #3 designate the gate to the second channel.

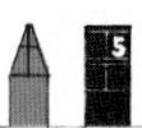

A nun to the right and a black can to the left (upper right) delineate the second channel.

A junction buoy dead ahead marks the intersection of the deepwater channel with the shallower one that lies to starboard.

A beacon, which is to starboard of a boat following the deeper channel, marks a rock. Ahead lie the buoys of the harbor gate.

Threading the Intracoastal

On the East and Gulf coasts of the United States, the Navigable Waters system described on pages 50 and 51 overlaps for long distances with another buoyage system—the Intracoastal Waterway, or ICW. The ICW consists of a series of connected natural channels that afford small boats a protected passage of 2,700 miles from Manasquan Inlet, New Jersey, to the Rio Grande in Texas. Its aids to navigation are basically identical to those of the Navigable Waters system; in fact, along most of the ICW its marks differ only in that they carry broad yellow bands.

But, wherever the Intracoastal Waterway intersects or coincides with the Navigable Waters system, the mariner must exercise special care as he proceeds. In such areas, the only navigational aids seen are those of the Navigable Waters system; they do, however, carry small yellow triangles or squares *(opposite)* that give directional signals to guide boats bound through the Intracoastal Waterway. To follow the ICW under these circumstances, a navigator must therefore ignore the meaning of the marks of the Navigable Waters system, and follow the course given to him by those small yellow triangles and squares.

The Intracoastal Waterway, outlined in blue on the chart below, intertwines along its course with the Navigable Waters system. Throughout the ICW, boats moving away from Manasquan Inlet and toward the Rio Grande are considered to be heading inland, and they must follow the special yellow ICW code.

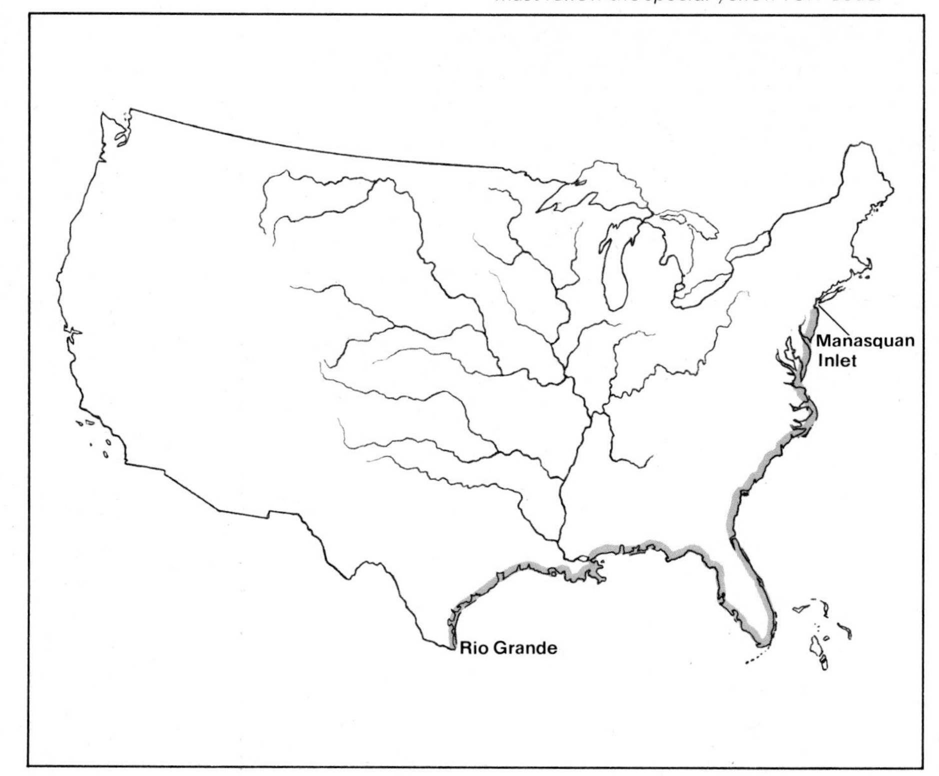

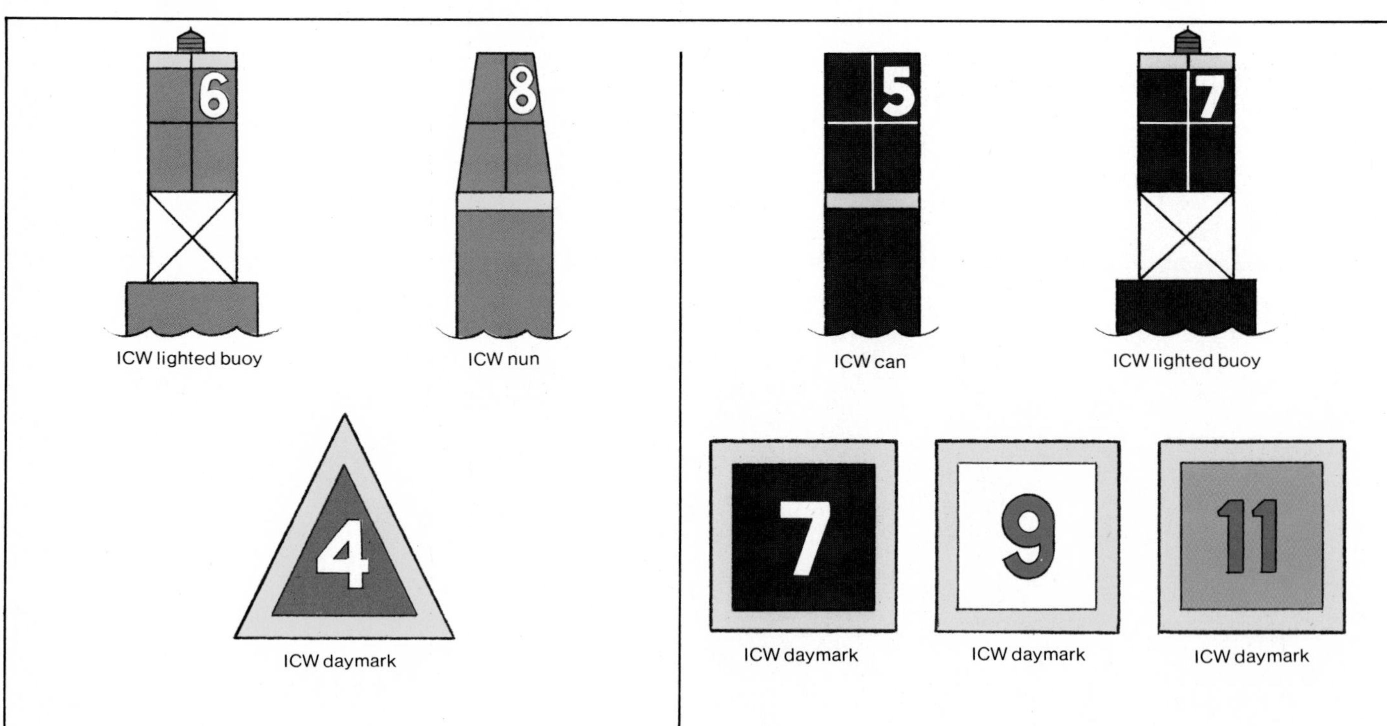

Even-numbered red buoys and triangular daymarks, which also carry the ICW's yellow bands, are kept to starboard when bound inland—as defined in the chart above. Lights are red, as here, or white. Starting at Manasquan Inlet, mark numbers usually run only up to 99, then begin again at 1.

A boat moving down the ICW from New Jersey toward Texas leaves these odd-numbered yellow-banded black buoys (with green or white lights) and square daymarks to port. The green, black or white colors of the daymarks serve as additional reminders that they are to be left to port.

So-called dual-purpose marks like those shown below are primarily part of the Navigable Waters system, and their shapes and colors give directions for its channels. Secondarily, they indicate the course of the ICW. A yellow square means that a boat following the ICW should leave the mark to port.

dual-purpose daymark

dual-purpose daymark

dual-purpose daymark

dual-purpose daymark

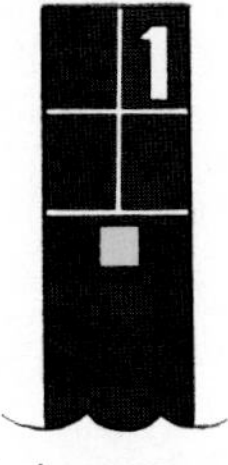

dual-purpose can

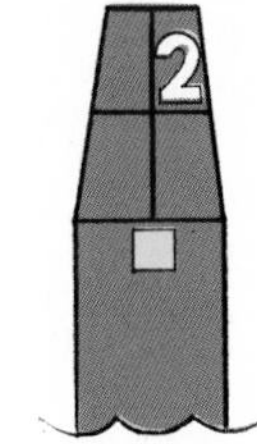

dual-purpose nun

The yellow triangles on these dual-purpose marks say that they should be kept to starboard by a boat running in the Intracoastal Waterway. The numbers on such marks are a part of the odd-left, even-right coding of the Navigable Waters system, and have no relation to the Intracoastal.

dual-purpose daymark

dual-purpose daymark

dual-purpose daymark

dual-purpose daymark

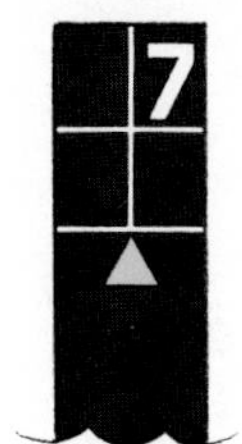

dual-purpose can

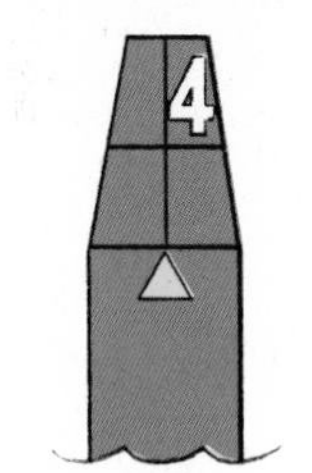

dual-purpose nun

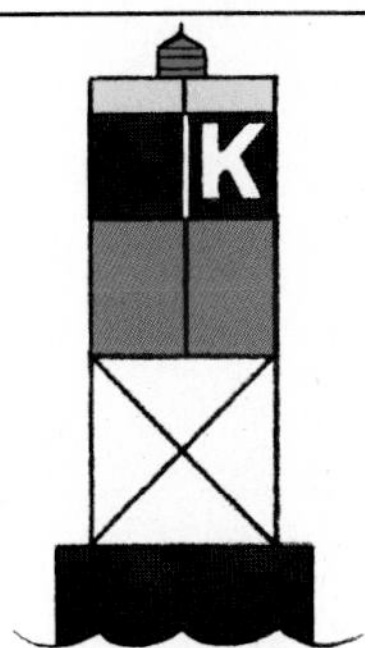

ICW lighted junction buoy

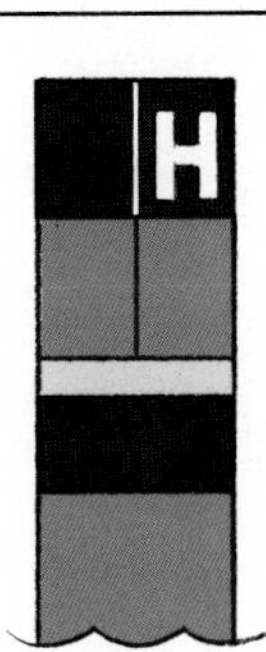

ICW junction can

ICW junction daymark

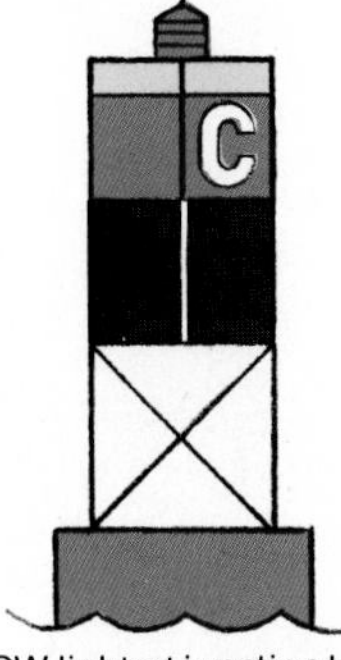

ICW lighted junction buoy

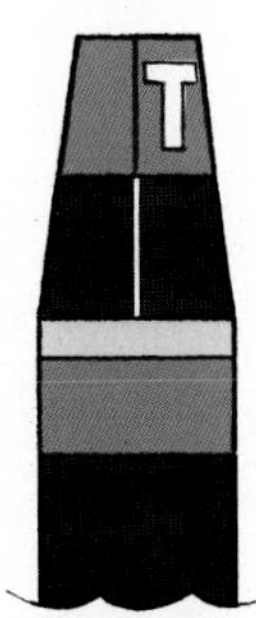

ICW junction nun

ICW junction daymark

Yellow-banded ICW junction marks indicate intersecting channels. A black band on top means the preferred channel is to starboard (the light can be green or white), red on top that it lies to port (the light is red or white). The better channel is to starboard of the square daymark, to port of the triangle.

ICW mid-channel daymark

The octagonal shape, black and white interior and yellow border of this daymark signal the center of the ICW channel. It can be passed to either side. Such mid-channel daymarks often bear white lights. The letter "E" identifies the mark when compared to its identically lettered chart symbol.

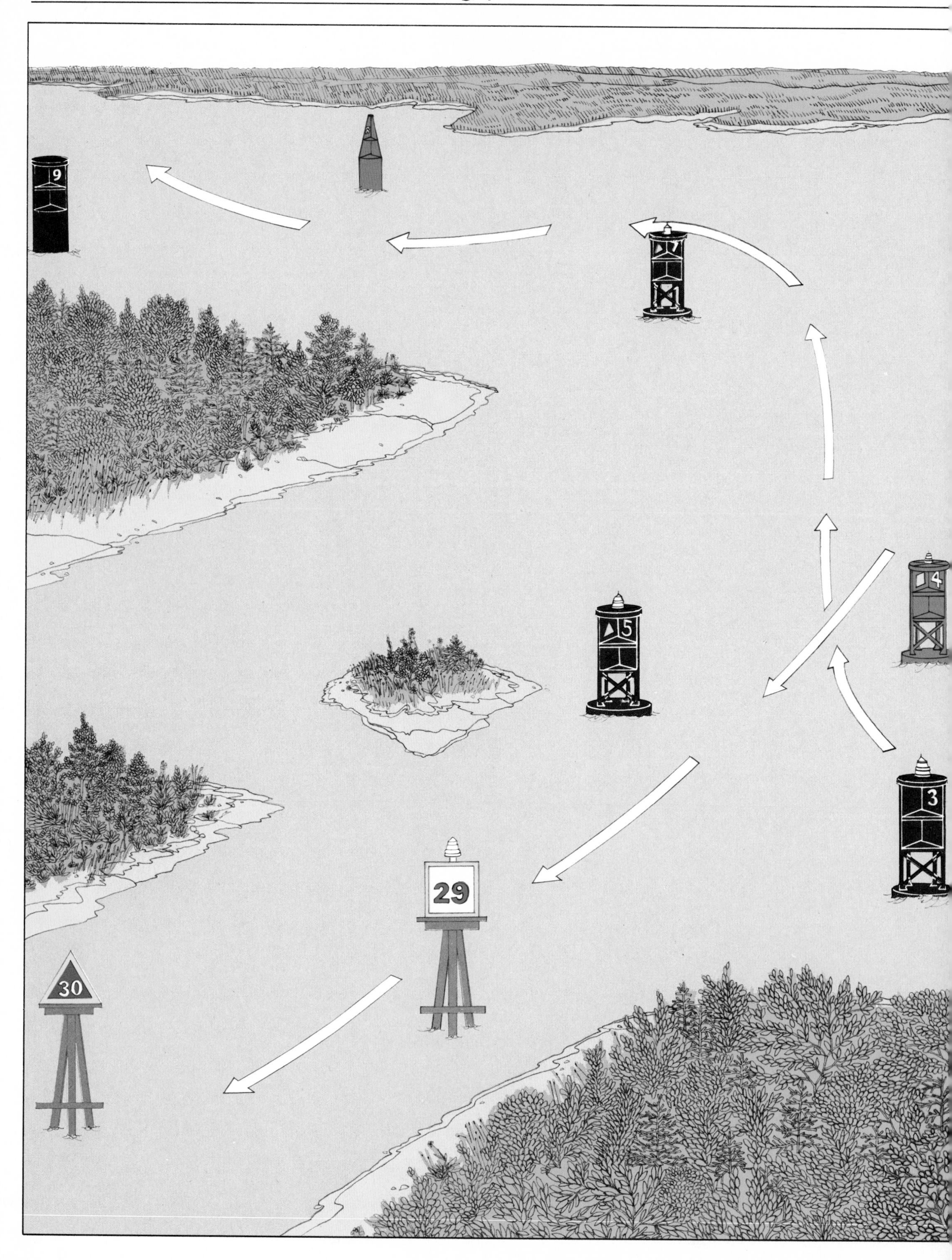
9
7
5
4
3
29
30

A typical intersection of two buoyage systems—the Intracoastal Waterway and Navigable Waters—is diagramed here. The ICW channel begins at top right; to travel in it, a skipper must be aware of the principle of dual-purpose marks (page 55). The Navigable channel, entered from seaward at bottom right and crossing the Intracoastal channel, is relatively simple to follow.

Cruising down the ICW, the skipper leaves square daymark #25 (top right) to port.

Red nun #24, carrying the ICW's distinctive yellow band, is kept to starboard.

The yellow triangle on dual-purpose buoy #6 tells the ICW skipper to leave it to starboard.

Although buoy #7 is black, the yellow triangle indicates that Intracoastal Waterway traffic must leave it to starboard.

Despite the red color of buoy #4, the yellow square tells the skipper to leave it to port.

Navigable Waters traffic entering from seaward leaves red lighted buoy #2 to starboard, and black buoy #1 to port.

Crossing the ICW channel, Navigable Waters traffic ignores yellow markers on red #4 and #6, and on black #5 and #7, leaving them to starboard and port respectively. Red #8 and black can #9 mark the channel continuation.

Running the Rivers

The Western Rivers buoyage system employs certain specialized aids to deal with the peculiarities of river navigation. Notable among these are "passing" and "crossing" daymarks *(below)*. The passing daymarks are set down where the river channel runs close along one of its banks. As with other aids used in all the systems, their colors, shapes and lights indicate on which side they are to be passed. Crossing daymarks are positioned in places where the river channel crosses to the opposite bank.

In addition, the system frequently employs aids called ranges. These are two marks used together. A skipper positions his boat to line up the range nearer to him with another range farther away, and follows an imaginary line drawn through them to keep on course. Such ranges are also used in other systems, but they are seen most often on Western Rivers.

Western Rivers has a few additional distinctions. Since the changing velocity of river currents causes buoys to vary position more than elsewhere, most Western Rivers marks are not charted. Aids are not numbered or lettered. Occasionally, a mark will, however, show the distance *(opposite)* from one point to another.

Outlined in blue below, the Western Rivers buoyage system is employed on the Mississippi and its tributaries (most other major rivers in the United States are governed by the Navigable Waters system). Here, as elsewhere, leave red marks to starboard when proceeding inland—that is, moving upstream.

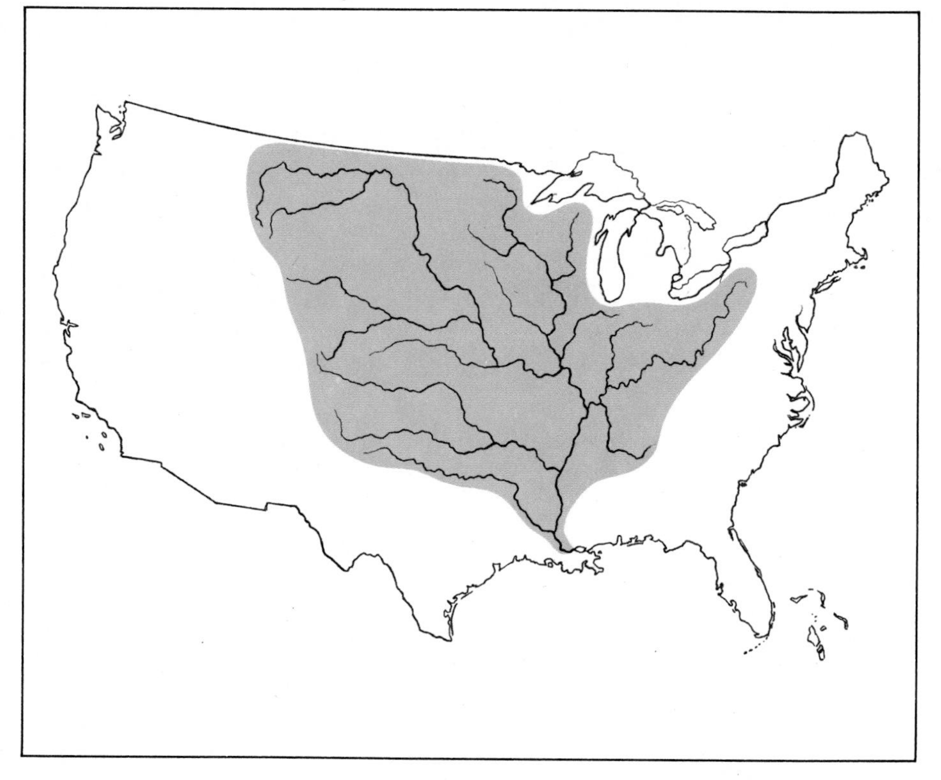

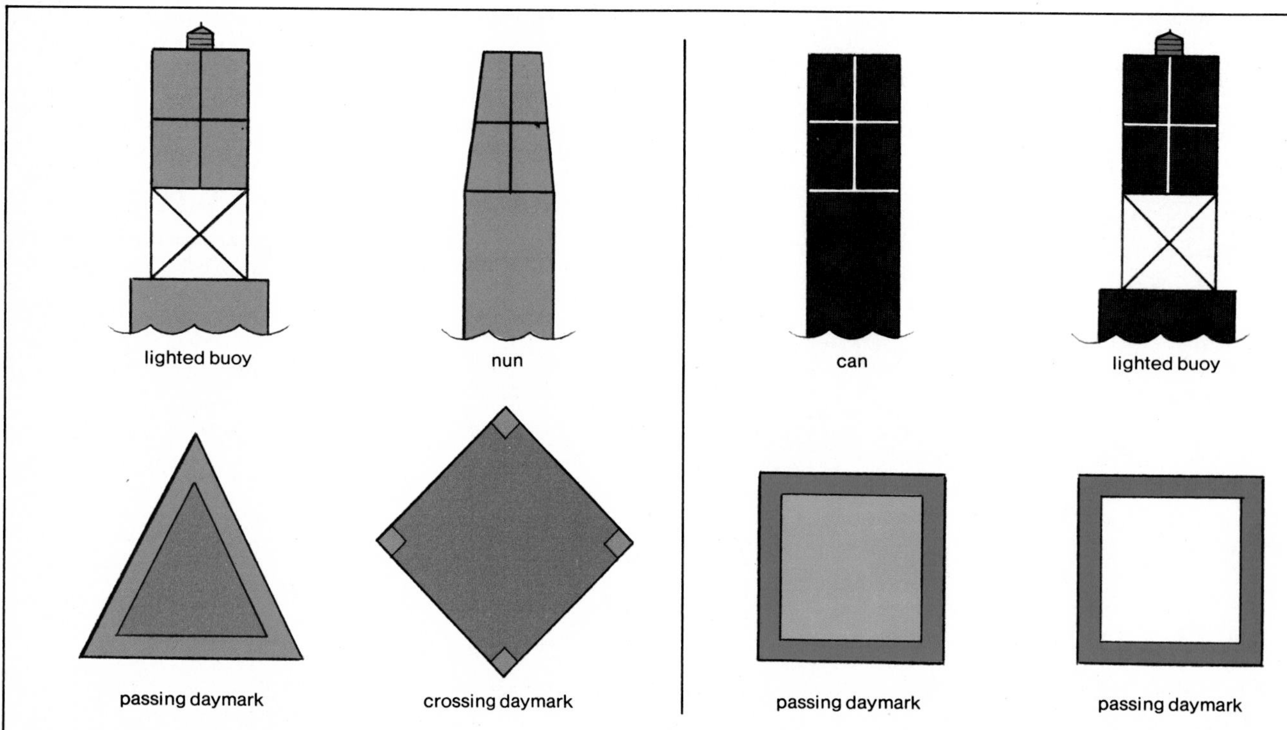

Moving upriver, a boat leaves the red nun and red-lighted (or white-lighted) buoy at top to starboard. The triangular red passing daymark, marking a channel near a riverbank, is also left to starboard—as is the red crossing diamond, which indicates that the channel is shifting to the other bank.

Black cans and lighted buoys are left to port en route upriver, as are green or white, green-bordered passing daymarks. As elsewhere, buoy lights are green or white, predominantly green. The green or white diamond-shaped crossing daymarks (near right) are also passed to port. There are no black daymarks.

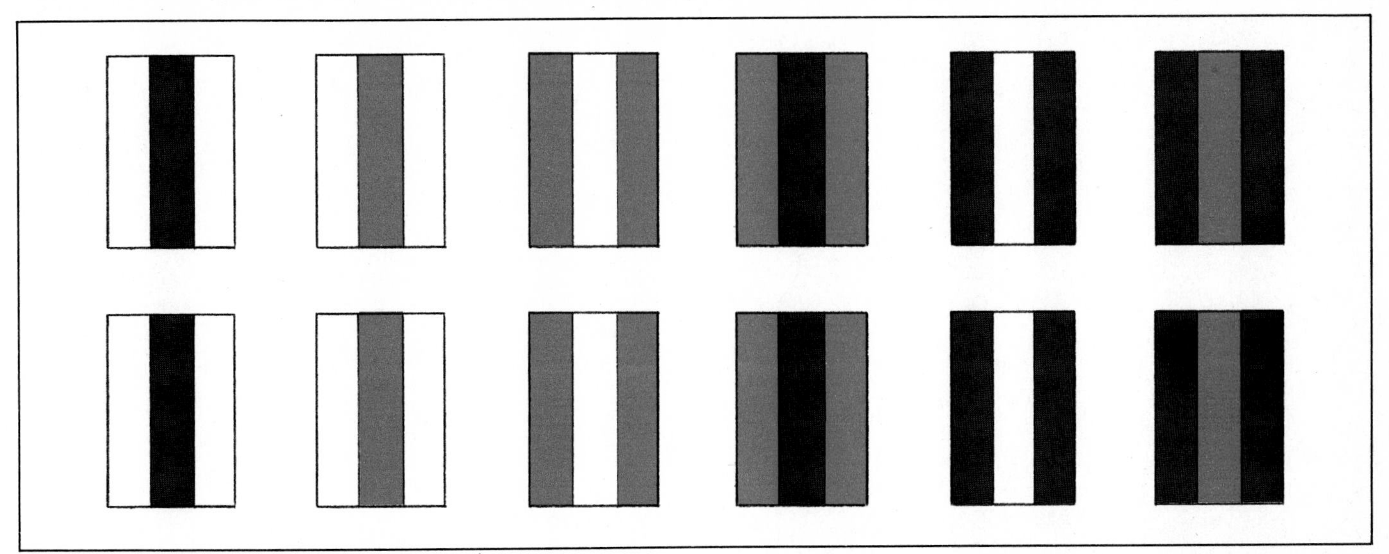

Range marks used on Western Rivers—and in the Navigable Waters—are shown above. The Intracoastal Waterway uses similar range marks, which also carry that system's distinctive yellow bands. In all systems, the basic colors serve to make the marks stand out against their backgrounds. Red, for example, might be used when green farmlands line the shore. Many ranges carry lights; again, the colors do not indicate direction but are selected for maximum visibility against the night landscape.

131.4

mile board

Mile boards on the Western Rivers mark the distance upstream from a given spot—either the river's mouth or the point of its confluence with another river. This one might be telling the mariner that he is 131.4 miles upstream from the Mississippi's Gulf outlet.

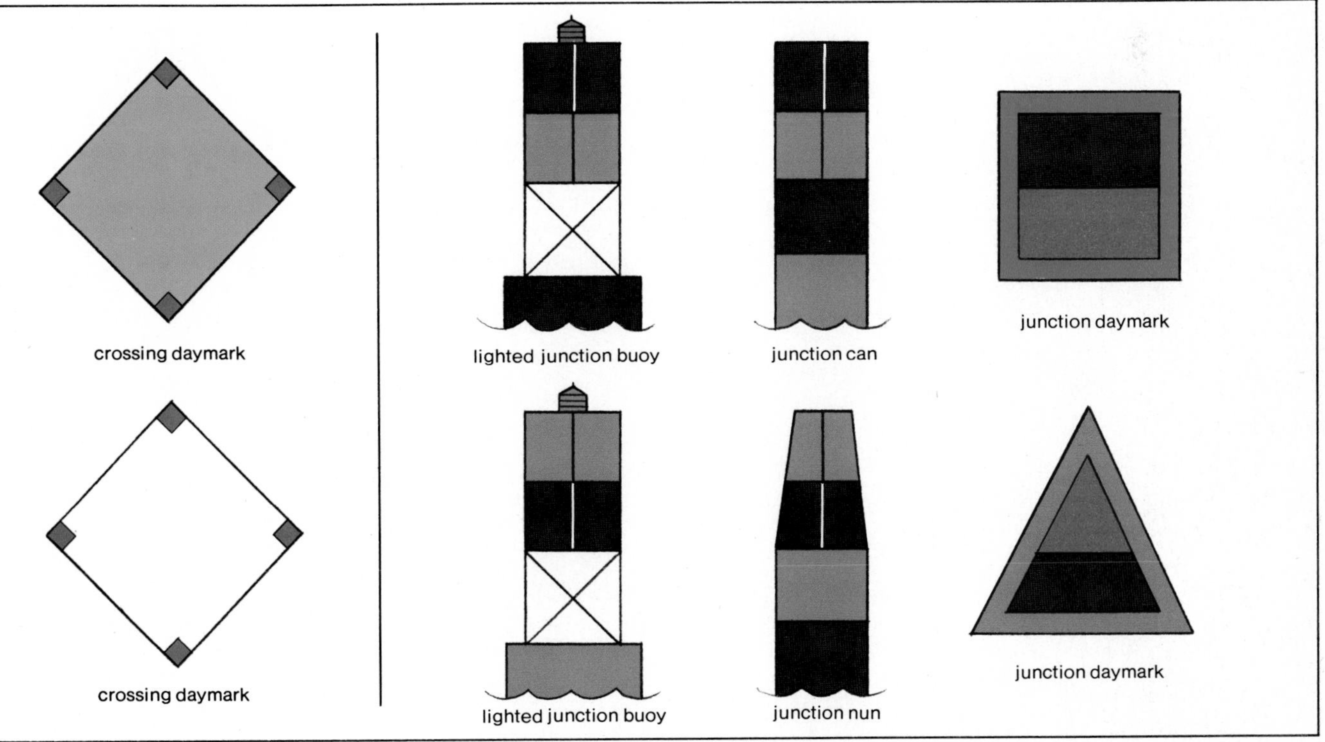

These buoys and daymarks, like those on pages 51 and 55, signal the convergence of two channels. And their color coding is the same: a black band on top says the preferred channel is to starboard (its light, if any, is green or white); a red band (or a red or white light) says that the channel is to port.

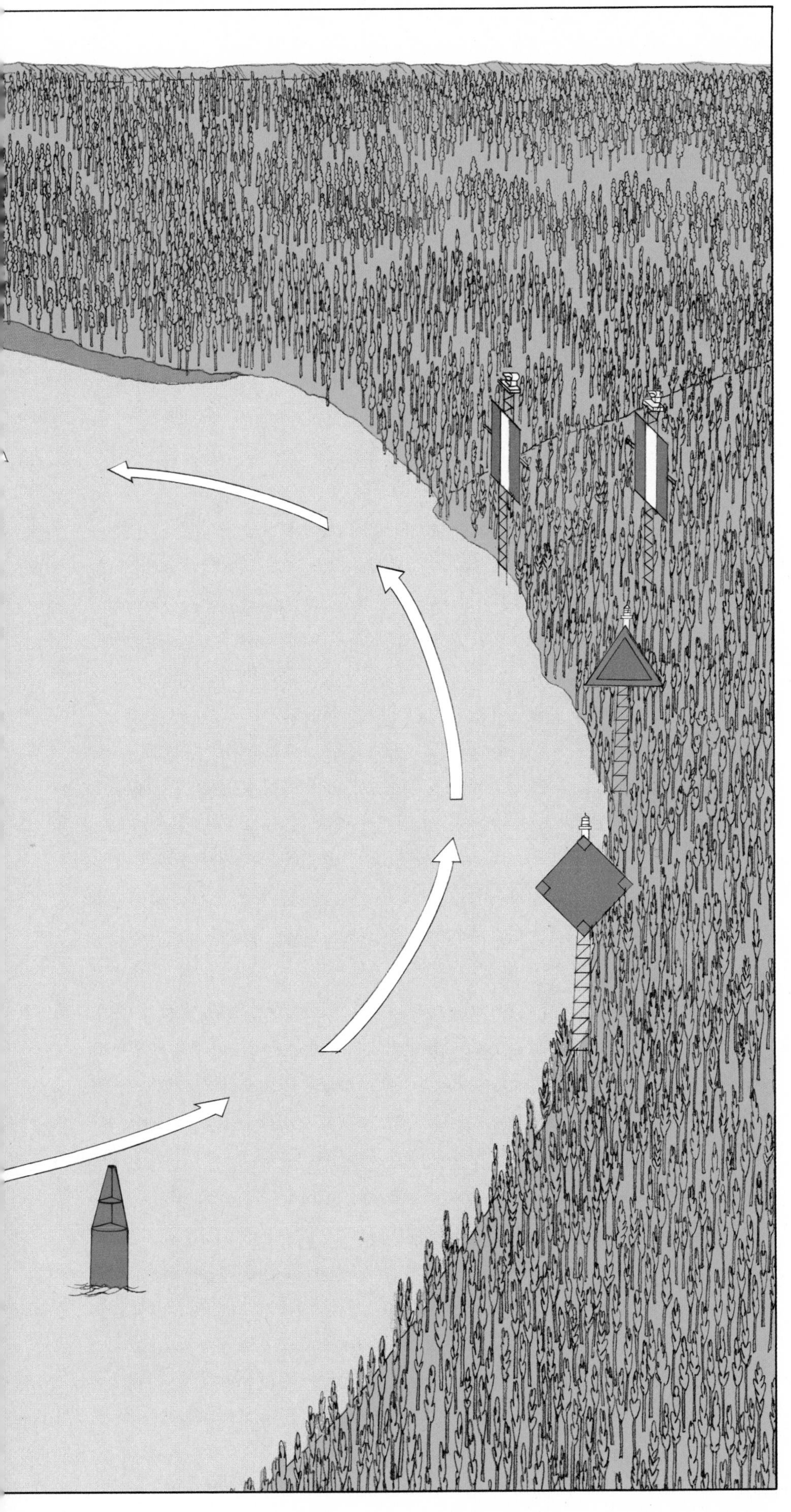

The scene at left represents an imaginary section of the Mississippi, whose traffic is governed by the Western Rivers buoyage system (pages 58-59). Traveling upriver, a skipper would follow the buoys and other marks in the manner described below.

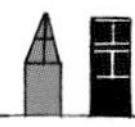

Red nuns and black cans—which are laid down in abundance because flood currents often move them or sweep them away altogether—mark mudbanks to the right and left sides, respectively, of the river channel.

A red diamond-shaped crossing daymark signals deep-draft upstream traffic to cross the river and head toward it in order to stay in the deepest water of the mainstream. Shallow-draft vessels might cut the corner to avoid the mainstream's strong current.

A triangular red passing daymark indicates that the mainstream channel continues to run closely along the right-hand bank.

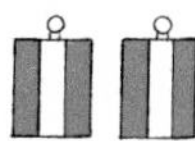 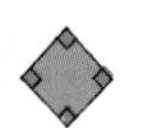

A pair of ranges, when aligned astern, directs traffic toward a green crossing daymark, farther upriver and on the opposite bank.

At a fork in the river, a red-and-black junction daymark signals by the red upper sector that the preferred channel is to port.

Square passing daymarks on the mainstream arm of the fork indicate that the deepwater channel is close by the left-hand bank.

In the secondary channel, square and triangular passing daymarks show that either bank is suitable for navigation.

A System for the States

In virtually all United States waters not under federal jurisdiction, a fourth buoyage system takes over. This is the Uniform State Waterway Marking System (USWMS) used on large bodies of water that lie wholly within the borders of a state—e.g., Lake George in New York.

The system uses two special types of marks: "regulatory" and "cardinal." Regulatory marks are painted with orange crossed diamonds, diamonds, circles or rectangles *(right)* that convey specific messages; they may carry white lights.

Cardinal marks *(bottom right)* are used in areas where there is no well-defined channel—or where the mark might be approached from any one of several points. Their color coding indicates the direction of safe water and the course the boat should take to reach it. For example, the black-topped buoy tells the boatman to stay to the north or east of it, the red-topped to the south or west. The red-and-white-striped buoy signals an obstruction between it and the nearest shore. Cardinal marks, too, carry white lights, or none.

The USWMS uses black and red odd- and even-numbered channel buoys that employ the "red, right, returning" code—and one other distinctive mark, a mooring buoy *(below)*, is colored blue.

The shapes and patterns of these orange-and-white regulatory emblems give commands, warnings or information. A diamond with a cross means "keep out," a diamond alone means "beware," a circle says "obey regulations," and rectangles give directions.

SWIM AREA
boats excluded

ROCK
danger

5 MPH
caution

MURPHY SLOUGH
FRESNO CANAL
directions

mooring buoy

Mooring buoys like the one above carry a distinctive marking throughout the system: a broad blue band runs around an otherwise white float. In busy channels, these mooring buoys carry white flashing lights.

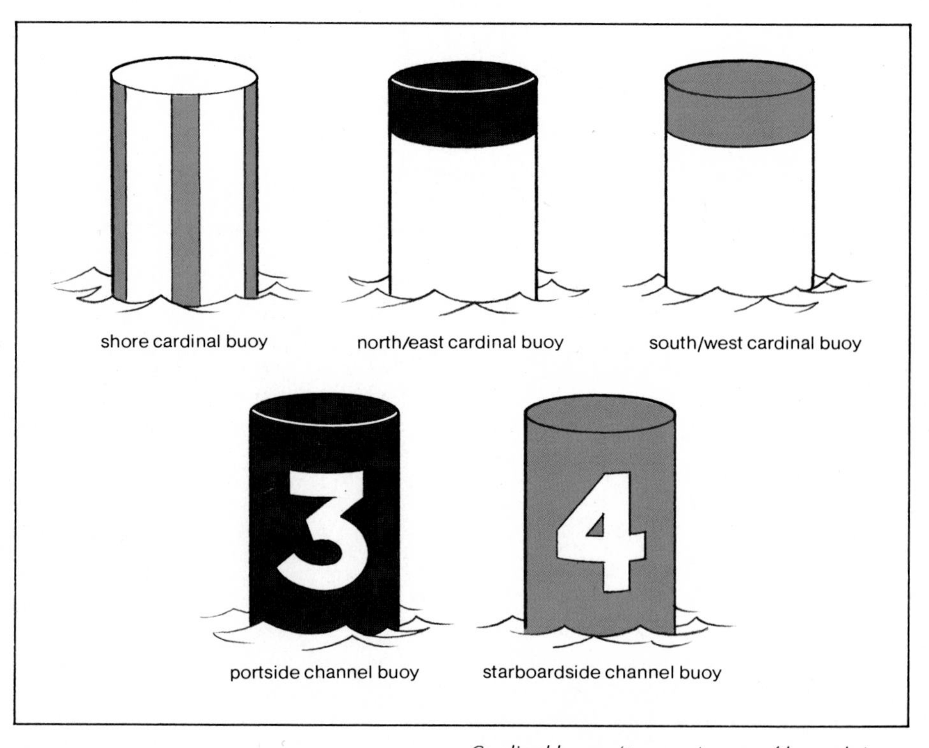

shore cardinal buoy | north/east cardinal buoy | south/west cardinal buoy

portside channel buoy | starboardside channel buoy

Cardinal buoys (top row) warn of hazards in different directions. A boat must not pass between shore and a red-and-white-striped buoy. It should proceed north or east of a white buoy with a black top, and south or west of one with a red top. Black channel buoys are left to port, red to starboard.

The hypothetical lake at left lies wholly within the borders of a single state and thus employs the Uniform State Waterway Marking System described opposite. In the deployment of navigation aids shown here, north is to the top of the page—as is the direction of the lake's source.

Traffic heading up the lake avoids the rocks in the foreground by passing to the north or east of the black-topped cardinal buoy.

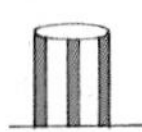

A vertically striped shore buoy warns vessels to steer clear of the rocky hazard that lies between it and the nearest land.

Off to port, a cross-and-diamond exclusion insignia on the square daymark directs boats to keep away from a swimming beach.

To starboard, a plain diamond—indicating danger—on the daymark underscores the presence of the rocky hazard.

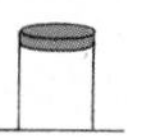

The red-topped cardinal buoy beyond the rock should be passed to the west by boats heading up the main channel, or to the south by a boat proceeding into the cove.

A blue-striped buoy such as the one in the cove is to be used for mooring.

A line of red buoys should be left to starboard when moving toward the lake's source.

Black buoys should be left to port when proceeding through these narrows.

Its light gleaming beneath the crown of a 166-foot tower, the Bodie (pronounced "body") lighthouse marks dangerous shoals near Cape Hatteras, North Carolina. The island is named for the numerous bodies washed ashore after repeated shipwrecks.

Guiding Lights

By far the most visible and dramatic of all navigation aids are the large, complex structures known as light stations, whose powerful beams, frequently augmented by other warning signals, guide mariners over broad stretches of open water. The most familiar of these structures are lighthouses, such as the Bodie Island station looming above the shrubs of a North Carolina sandspit at left. The Bodie light, like scores of others perched on coastal headlands or offshore islands, casts its beam almost 20 miles over the ocean—as it has steadily for more than a century.

While a fair number of the nation's lighthouses have done similarly long service—and retain such old-fashioned features as living quarters for a resident keeper—the majority are fully automated. Besides having a complex and sophisticated lens *(overleaf)*, most of the stations now send out radio beams *(top right)* for electronic navigation by RDF *(pages 130-133)*, and are equipped with foghorns *(right, below)* that can be switched on by remote control from the nearest Coast Guard station.

On every light station, the radio beacon, the foghorn and the light itself emit their signals in characteristic, coded sequences that allow the mariner to quickly identify the source. Bodie Island Light, for example, gives two brief white flashes every 30 seconds. This identifying signal, or light phase, is noted next to the station's position on the nautical chart for the area, and is also included in a multivolume Coast Guard publication called the light lists *(page 73)*. The light lists also give the pertinent characteristics of all the foghorns and radio beacons.

Another important piece of information included in the light lists is the visible range of each station. This depends on two main factors: the height of the light above the water and the luminosity of its lamps. The listings give the distance at which the light is visible on a clear night—called the nominal range; this figure provides the navigator with a valuable clue for judging his position when the light first comes into view.

Like many light stations, the one below sends out a continuous, distinctive radio signal that can be picked up by any boat equipped with a radio direction finder (RDF). Here, the signal consists of three alternating short and long tones—symbolized by the varying widths of the stylized radio waves. While beacons on some older stations may be separate structures as here, on modern stations they are in the form of a thin antenna attached to the lighthouse.

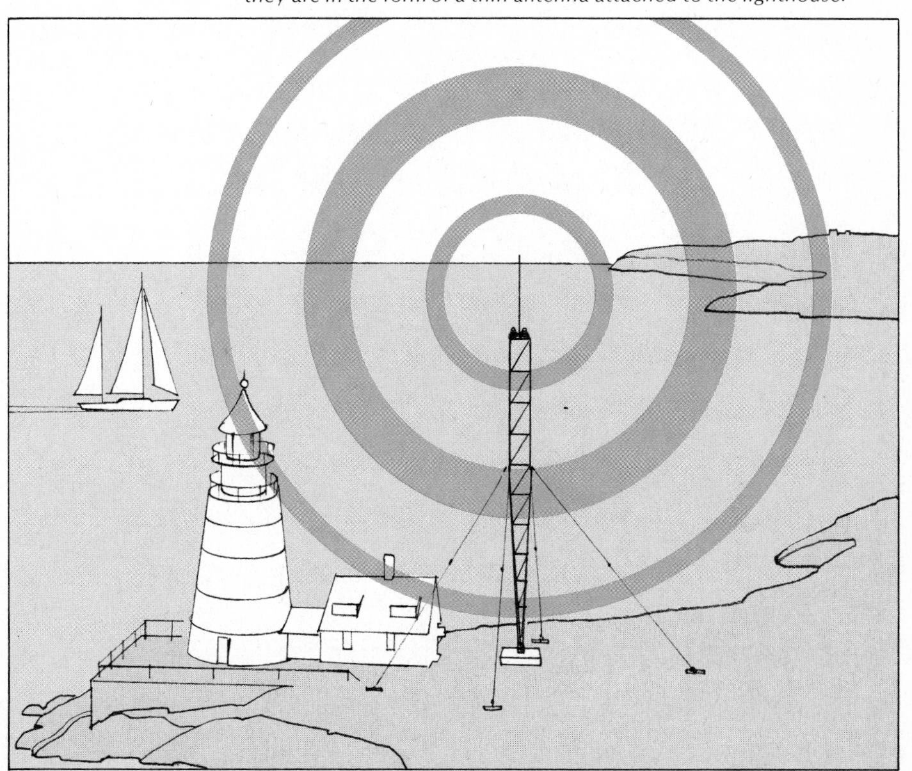

A Fog Warning that Sometimes Goes Askew

While no warning devices announce themselves with more authority than electric foghorns, now housed in many light stations, the message they deliver is sometimes ambiguous—as shown by this schematic aerial view of a powerboat passing a light station. The reason is that the sound waves from the horn often encounter different air temperatures, which cause the waves to speed up, or slow down, and bend out of shape. The foghorn at left is surrounded by an area of cool air (tinted light blue), which transmits the sound waves in a slow, regular pulse. But when a segment of the waves meets a patch of warm air (tinted blue-gray), the warm air causes these segments to push slightly ahead. To a listener on the boat, the source of the signal then seems to be off the starboard quarter *(arrow)*, even though the foghorn's true position is directly abeam.

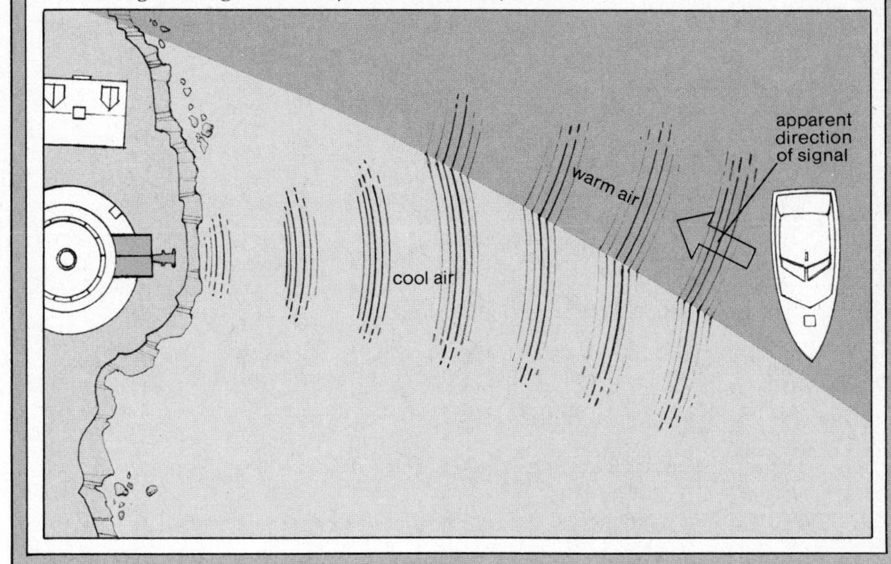

The Fresnel lens in the light station at Point Loma, California, consists of 12 vertical glass panels tapering on top into rows of prisms that form a crown. In each panel, concentric segments of prismatic rings encircle a central bull's-eye. This lens is eight feet high and weighs nearly a ton, yet because it is mounted on a friction-reducing mercury float, a relatively small electric motor can revolve it around the 1,000-watt bulb that is located inside the structure.

Mariner's Magic Lantern

The powerful beams that emanate from a typical light station owe their brilliance to a massive lens invented in 1820 by the French physicist Augustin Fresnel. A complex structure of cut-glass prisms, the Fresnel lens surrounds a light, collecting and intensifying rays so dramatically that on a clear night a 250-watt incandescent bulb may be seen 15 miles away.

This amazing optical achievement was the masterwork of an unassuming technician who lacked both a laboratory and basic scientific instruments. An engineer in Napoleon's army, Fresnel was relegated to overseeing road construction. When off duty, he pondered the nature of light, using a sheet of paper with a small hole covered by a drop of honey to serve as a makeshift lens. Despite the lack of proper equipment, Fresnel learned enough to begin authoring papers that helped establish the wave theory of light, now a basic law of physics. Eventually, Fresnel was assigned to the French Lighthouse Commission where, putting his theories into practice, he developed his lens.

Besides intensifying the strength of the light, a lighthouse lens is now so constructed that, when rotated, it sends out a characteristic coded signal *(below)*.

Crowning a steel tower that rises above the Southern California palms, the Fresnel lens at Point Loma directs its light into a predawn mist. Even though its effective range is reduced by the morning haze, the light still manages a beam strong enough to be picked up several miles out in the Pacific Ocean.

This simplified top-view drawing of a Fresnel lens shows how its panels produce a series of flashes—thereby giving a lighthouse its identifying signal. Each panel transmits light beams as a separate column. Thus, as the lens turns, light columns flash, then appear to go dark, in a recognizable pattern.

The key to the effectiveness of the Fresnel lens, illustrated here in cross section, is an ingeniously arranged set of prisms at the top and bottom of each panel; these prisms bend the light's rays so precisely and effectively that virtually all of the rays go out in orderly, intensely focused beams.

The navigational torch passes as the lightship Ambrose makes a farewell circle around its successor, an offshore light tower, in 1967. With the crew lined up on deck and signal flags flying to indicate that it is underway, the vessel leaves its post in New York harbor, where lightships had served since 1823.

Deepwater Stations

In open water where the depth is too great to construct conventional lighthouses, offshore shoals and heavily traveled seaways are marked by the three types of light stations shown here—the lightship, light tower and so-called large navigational buoy (LNB). Each of these deep-water stations has its own coded light, radio beacon and fog signal. The lightships, painted a fire-engine red, are the oldest and most colorful. But during the 10 years from 1965 to 1975 most of them were replaced either by the more modern light towers *(left)* or by LNBs. Indeed, in 1975 only two major lightships were still operating in United States waters: one off Nantucket Island in Massachusetts and the other at the mouth of the Columbia River in Washington.

Both the light towers and the LNBs represent substantial advances in efficiency and in ease of operation. The towers *(right)*, often called Texas Towers because they are adaptations of offshore oil rigs, sit firmly on bedrock: unlike the lightships, they cannot be driven out of position by storms. Some towers carry a skeleton crew of four or five men, and others need no crew at all—while the lightships demand an operating force of a dozen men or more. All the LNBs *(below)* are totally self-operating, and are cheaper to install than the towers, though the range of their lights is not as great.

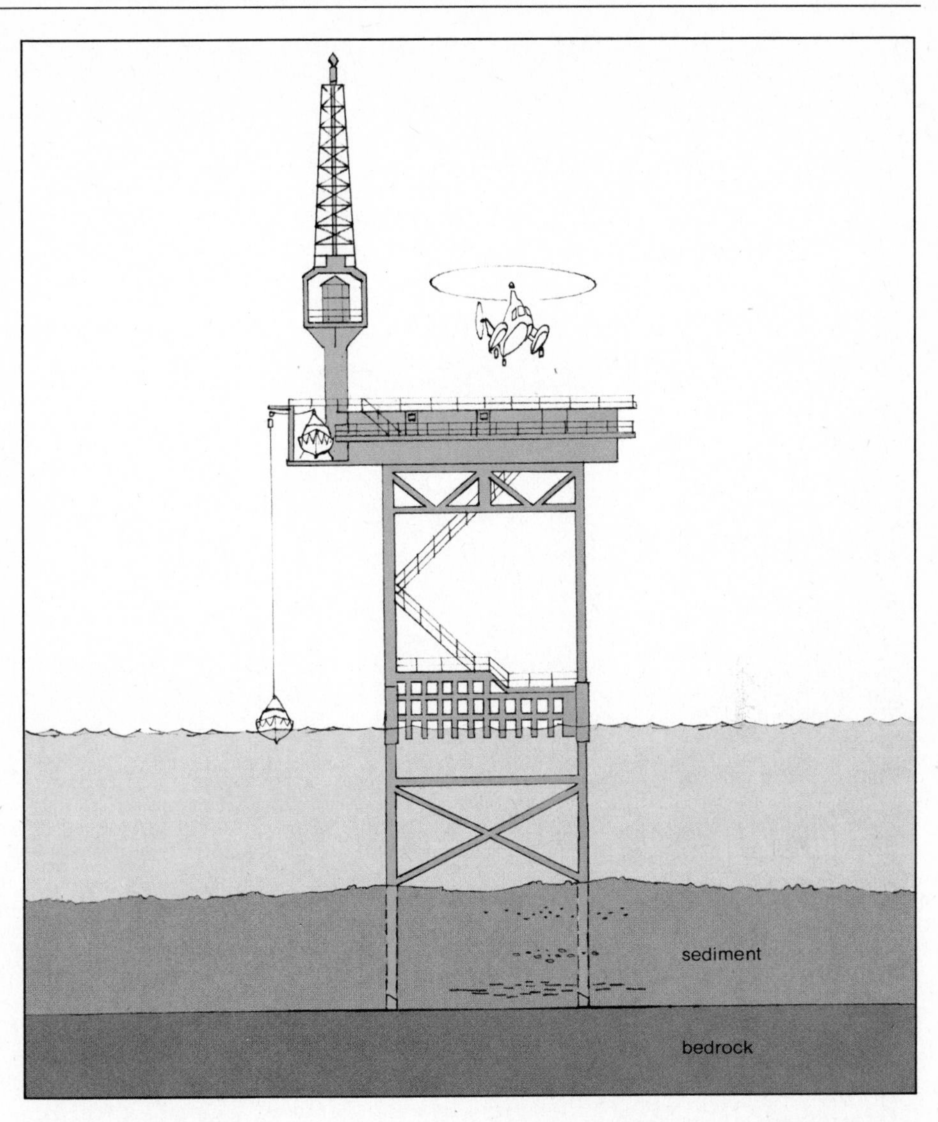

This simplified drawing of a light tower shows the station's basic structure. Pilings driven to the bedrock of the continental shelf support the tower. Its light, visible for 23 miles, is housed under the radio beacon, which transmits a coded signal 75 miles. Quarters for the five-man crew, plus storage area for supplies, are tucked into the platform on top of the girders; the roof serves as a launching pad for a supply helicopter.

Totally automated, this large navigational buoy (LNB) stands ready to be towed to its site, where it will be secured by a 10-ton concrete sinker and a 7,000-pound anchor, and then inspected quarterly by maintenance crews. Forty feet in diameter with a 42-foot tower, the LNB has a light visible 10 miles away, a radio beacon that carries 25 miles and fog signals audible at 2.5 miles. Screens around the tower act as radar reflectors.

Winking a welcome—and a warning—in the dusk, a 70-foot-high beacon signals to seamen from a jetty at Little Creek Harbor, Virginia. Somewhat like a small-scale lighthouse, this beacon is equipped with its own foghorn and coded light beam, which is visible up to 12 miles at sea in perfect weather.

Beacons and Ranges

Many lighted aids to navigation are less imposing and have a shorter range than full-scale light stations—but they still rise more dramatically above the water and their signals show farther than ordinary lighted buoys. These middle-distance lights principally include beacons, such as the structure at left marking the entrance to a small harbor, and range lights, which are pairs of lighted structures (also equipped with the range daymarks shown on page 59) that indicate a main channel.

Both beacons and range lights are permanently fixed installations. Even though they are intended for fairly close-in piloting, they share important features with the larger light stations. They flash on and off with an identifying code, which is described in the light list *(overleaf)*. Both ranges and beacons carry special lenses to concentrate their beams. On beacons, the lens is generally a cylindrical, nonrotating type of Fresnel called a drum lens, while range lights, which are designed to shine in only one direction *(bottom right)*, have flat lenses similar to the kind found in theatrical spotlights. All beacons and range lights are fully automated, down to the capability of changing burned-out light bulbs *(top right)*. In addition, the larger beacons, like most light stations, may be equipped with foghorns.

A cutaway of a beacon's so-called drum lens shows the automatic bulb changer found in most small- to middle-sized navigation lights. Here, six incandescent bulbs are screwed into a hexagonal holder. When a bulb burns out, an electric current is diverted to a small motor that rotates the holder. As the spent bulb (gray) moves out of the way (arrow), a fresh one (yellow) is brought upright. At the same time, a third bulb (blue) slips into position as the next replacement.

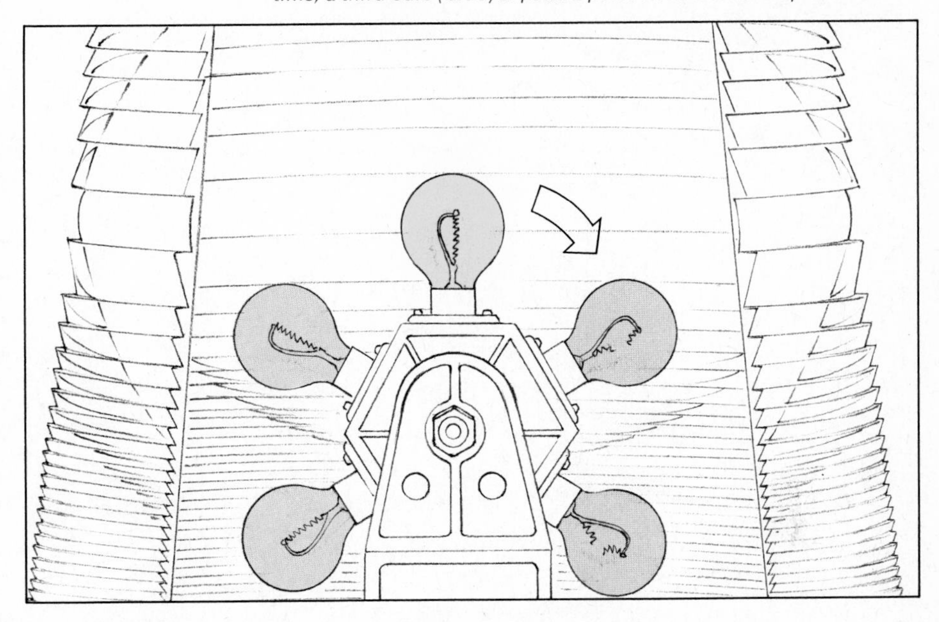

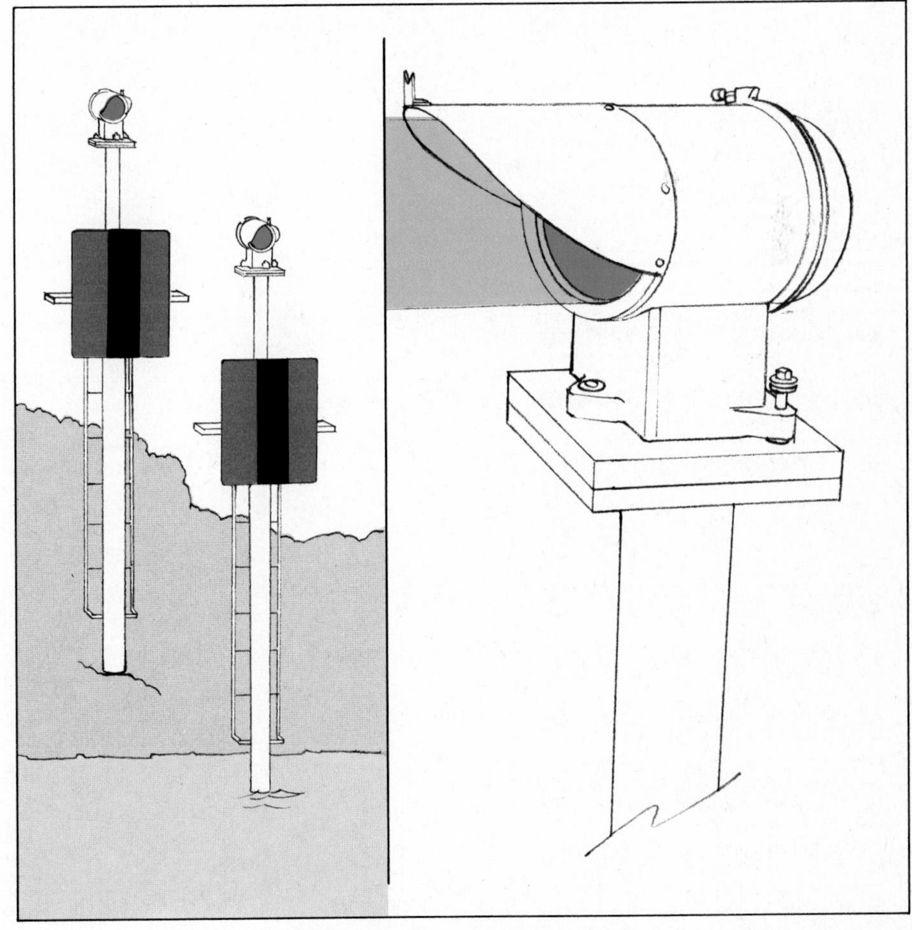

Like all range lights, the pair of lights here (above, left) are set one in front of the other—thus giving a boatman who lines them up a sure course along a channel. To assure that the nearer of the two ranges does not block the more distant one, the second range is mounted slightly higher up. For daytime identification, lighted ranges have distinctive daymarks. Each light is set in a hooded fixture (right) to create a one-directional beam that is brightest when viewed head on.

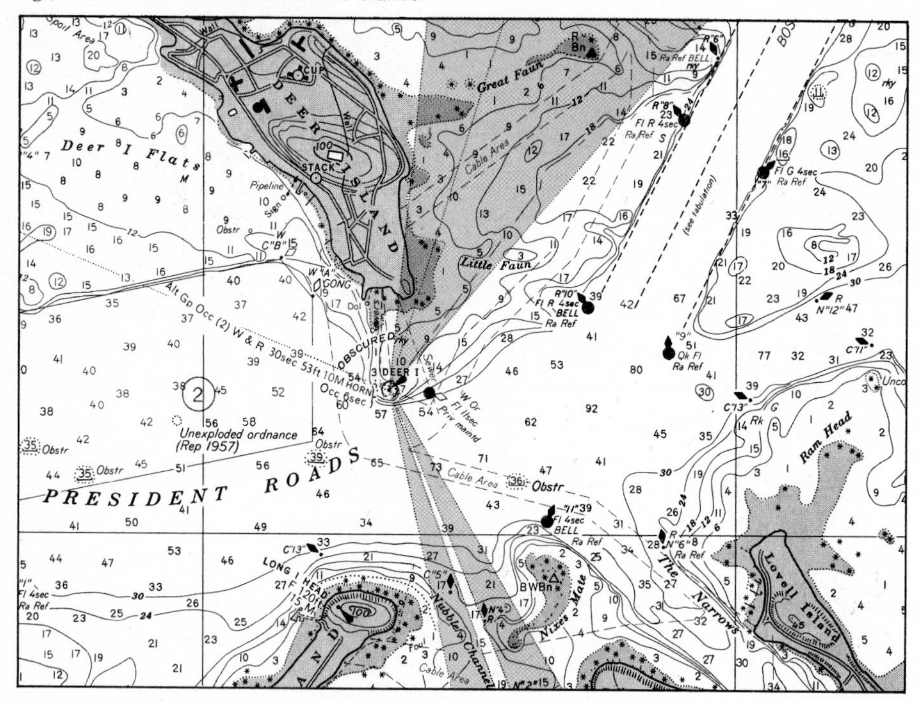

Color sectors beamed from Deer Island Light mark approaches to Boston Harbor. Shown on the chart by dotted lines, the sectors are tinted here for easy recognition. The red sector to the north warns of shoals. Below, a white sector between red and green ones signals a clear channel between two islands.

The Language of Lights

Not only is every light coded with one of 13 basic identifying characteristics *(below)*, but many also have color sectors that serve as warnings and guides *(left)*. Created by tinted filters placed in front of the light, color sectors cast hues over sweeps of water to declare danger zones and delineate navigable channels.

A navigator can decode a light's signature by watching it steadily for one minute, preferably with a watch in hand. After timing the periods of brightness and dark, and noting the color variations, if any, he then consults a book no boat should be without: a light list. Published by the Coast Guard in five volumes, the light lists index geographically every navigation aid in specified areas. The lists present information about each light *(opposite)*, including the color sectors, foghorn signals, radio-beacon data, and, of course, its coded signature using the abbreviations explained in the chart below. An additional abbreviation, Alt., for alternating, indicates that the identifying flashes in the signature alternate among two or more colors.

The Thirteen Basic Signals

In this graphic representation of basic light signatures, with their abbreviations, white triangles indicate brief flashes, white rectangles longer periods of light.

Light Pattern	Abbreviation	Description of Light
	F. = Fixed	A continuous, unblinking light.
	F. Fl. = Fixed and flashing	A continuous light, varied at regular intervals by flashes of greater brilliance.
	F. Gp. Fl. = Fixed and group flashing	A continuous light, varied by groups of two or more flashes.
	Fl. = Flashing	A light that flashes at regular intervals of not less than two seconds and whose period of darkness exceeds the period of light.
	Gp. Fl. = Group flashing	A light that sends out groups of two or more flashes at regular intervals.
	Gp. Fl. (1+2) = Composite group flashing	A flashing light in which the flashes are combined in alternating groups of different numbers.
	Mo. (A) = Morse code	A flashing light whose blinks signal letters in Morse code—in this case, dit-dah for A.
	Qk. Fl. = Quick flashing	A light that flashes 60 times or more a minute, used only on buoys and beacons.
	I. Qk. Fl. = Interrupted quick flashing	A light in which five seconds of quick flashes is followed by five seconds of darkness.
	E. Int. = Equal interval (Isophase)	A light with equal periods of light and darkness; sometimes described as an isophase light.
	Occ. = Occulting	A light that is eclipsed at regular timed intervals, but whose period of light is always greater than the duration of darkness.
	Gp. Occ. = Group occulting	A light with regularly spaced groups of two or more occultations.
	Gp. Occ. (2+3) = Composite group occulting	A light whose occultations combine in alternate groups of different numbers.

The identifying features of various lights around Lake Huron appear on this page reprinted from the Great Lakes light list. By consulting the entries in each column for Thunder Bay Island Light, for example, a navigator would discover that the light is located in a white conical tower; that it emits a white flash every 15 seconds, visible for a radius of 28 miles; that the station includes a radio beacon; and that its two-toned foghorn gives two blasts every 30 seconds.

(1) No.	(2) Name / Characteristic	(3) Location (Lat. N. / Long. W.)	(4) Nominal Range	(5) Ht. above water	(6) Structure (Ht. above ground / Daymark)	(7) Remarks / Year
	LAKE HURON, MICHIGAN					
	WEST SIDE					
	EAST ALPENA CHANNEL					
	— Buoy 5	In 17 feet	....	....	Black can	White reflector. Private aid.
	— Buoy 6	In 16 feet	....	....	Red nun	Red reflector. Private aid.
	— Buoy 7	In 15 feet	....	....	Black can	White reflector. Private aid.
	— Buoy 8	In 14 feet	....	....	Red nun	Red reflector. Private aid.
	— Buoy 9	In 20 feet	....	....	Black can	White reflector. Private aid.
	— Buoy 10	In 14 feet	....	....	Red nun	Red reflector. Private aid.
	— Buoy 11	In 14 feet	....	....	Black can	White reflector. Private aid.
	Thunder Bay Wreck Buoy WR 2	In 18 feet. 45 03.7 83 23.6	....	....	Red nun	Red reflector.
	WEST SIDE (Chart 537) (NO 14646)					
	Middle Island Buoy 14	In 24 feet, northeast end of shoal.	....	....	Red nun	Red reflector.
1313	**Thunder Bay Island Light** **Fl. W., 15^s**	On east shore of island. 45 02.2 83 11.7	28	63	White conical tower, dwelling attached. 67	RADIOBEACON: Antenna 640 feet 181° from light tower. See p. XVIII for method of operation. DIAPHONE, two-tone; 2 blasts ev 30^s (2^sbl-2^ssi-2^sbl-24^ssi). 1832
1313.51	STONEYCROFT POINT LIGHT **Fl. W.**	.... 45 06.4 83 18.5	....	....	TR on red skeleton tower	Private aid. Maintained from Mar. 15 to Nov. 15 1971
1314	*Nordmeer Wreck Lighted Bell Buoy WR1.* **Qk. Fl. W.**	In 35 feet 45 08.1 83 09.3	7	....	Black	Ra ref. 1,150 feet, 102.5° from last reported position of wreck.
1315	**Middle Island Light** **Fl. W., 10^s**	On east side of island, 45 11.6 83 19.3	18	78	White conical tower with orange bands in middle, dwelling detached. 71	1905
1316	STONEPOINT LIGHT **Alt. Fl. W. & R., 60^s** 3^s Wfl., 27^sec. 3^s R fl., 27^sec.	On end of the loading dock. 45 17.8 83 25.1	25W 21R	55	White cylindrical structure	Private aid. 1955
	Stoneport Approach Buoy 1	In 25 feet	....	....	Black can	White reflector.
	Stoneport Buoy 3	In 23 feet	....	....	Black can	Private aid.
	Stoneport Buoy 5	In 23 feet	....	....	Black can	Private aid.
	Stoneport Buoy 7	In 23 feet	....	....	Black can	Private aid.
	Presque Isle Harbor Entrance Shoal Buoy 2.	In 20 feet	....	....	Red nun	Red reflector.
1317	PRESQUE ISLE HARBOR RANGE FRONT LIGHT. **F. G.**	On west shore of harbor. 45 20.3 83 29.4	....	23	KRW on white pole 18	Higher intensity beam on bearing 274° diminishing around remainder of horizon. 1870
1318	PRESQUE ISLE HARBOR RANGE REAR LIGHT. **F. G.**	790 feet 274° from front light.	....	36	Rectangular international orange daymark with white vertical stripe. 33	1870–1967
1319	HARBOR LODGE RANGE FRONT LIGHT. **F. R.**	In 10 feet 45 20.5 83 29.2	....	16	International orange daymark on white pile.	Private aid maintained from May 15 to Oct. 31. 1957
1320	HARBOR LODGE RANGE REAR LIGHT. **F. R.**	In 6 feet, 500 feet 338.5° from front light.	....	21	International orange daymark on T. V. antenna.	Private aid maintained from May 15 to Oct. 31 1957
1321	**Presque Isle Light** **Fl. W., 15^s (5^sfl)**	On north end of Presque Isle. 45 21.5 83 29.5	21	123	White conical tower, dwelling attached. 109	1840–1871
1322	*Adams Point Lighted Buoy 1* **Fl. W., 6^s**	In 42 feet, north of point.	7	....	Black	Ra ref.

A NOBLE LINE OF NAUTICAL SENTINELS

While automated lighting devices and electronic signals gradually assume the task of guiding mariners through darkened waters, old-fashioned lighthouses like the one at right and those on the following pages linger in the mariner's memory—and many still stand—as traditional symbols of hope and safety. These towering edifices of stone, brick, iron and wood, built in the 19th Century on lonely reefs and promontories, represent an age when men and women routinely risked their lives so that lights would beam their warning to seafarers.

Virtually every light erected in those days was an engineering triumph, a hard-won victory by daring and resourceful people. The saga of establishing a tower on Minot's Ledge *(right)* exemplifies the struggle. During lowest ebb tide, Minot's Ledge pokes only three feet above the chop of Boston Bay. In 1847 workmen began to drill holes for the pilings of a manned iron beacon. Twice waves swept all traces of their work from the ledge, both times washing men into the sea but miraculously drowning no one. Then after three years of such daredevil labor, the beacon was finished and two keepers scrambled aboard. In the spring of 1851 a raging storm crumpled the tower and the two men inside were killed.

In 1855 military engineers started construction of a new tower, this time of stone. Again tides and weather hampered work; men continually grabbed for life lines as breakers swept the rocks. Nevertheless, the workers managed to sink iron rods into holes drilled in the rock to reinforce foundation rows of granite blocks. Then the men formed sandbag dams around each block to keep the sea from washing away their mortar before it set. After five years of agonizing labor, a three-man crew rowed out to take charge of the tower—which stands to this day.

Like the builders of these lights, the men and women who lived in them were a hardy, independent breed who voluntarily consigned themselves to desolate towers and lonely lightships. They often had to row miles for food and use collected rain water to drink and bathe in.

Danger was a constant companion, and not just in the form of weather. One lightship in New York harbor was rammed by passing ships twice in one day—and survived. In Florida, light towers and lightships were attacked by Seminoles during the 1836-1837 uprisings. But the greatest threats were from storms and waves. A 35-foot wooden lighthouse on a pier at Michigan City on Lake Michigan crumpled during a storm in 1886, and the keeper, an 80-year-old woman, just managed to totter away before it fell.

Even on calm days, the keeper's lot was hard. He had to haul fuel to the lamp, and constantly clean its chimney and trim its wick. All glass surfaces of the lanterns had to be polished. And to keep down dirt that could foul the lenses, floors and walls were scrubbed weekly. To make sure the keeper never lagged in his duties, inspectors arrived unannounced.

While many keepers undertook this demanding existence alone or with buddies, others took along their wives and children. Sometimes family members found themselves joined for life not only to the keeper but to the light. Kate Walker tended a lamp in New York harbor for 35 years after her dying husband told her, "Don't forget to keep the lamp burning, Kate."

Abbie Burgess, the eldest daughter of the keeper of Matinicus Light off Maine, personified the dedication of a keeper's child. Twice, while still a teenager, Abbie found herself in charge of the light when storms stranded her father on the mainland and waves roared over the rock. Both times she kept the lamp burning nightly for almost a month. After the father retired, Abbie married his successor's son and remained for 14 more years. In 1875 she was appointed assistant keeper at White Head Light, Maine. Musing on her years in the tower, she wrote: "If I ever have a gravestone, I'd like it to be in the form of a lighthouse or beacon."

Rising 97 feet above Boston Bay, Minot's Ledge Lighthouse endures the crash of surf. The picture was made more than 50 years ago.

Built on a rock six miles off the coast of northern California, this granite tower above St. George's Reef took eight years to complete in 1892, and cost over $700,000—the most expensive lighthouse of its day. Workmen had to live on a schooner moored nearby and go to work in a cage on a wire strung from the boat's mast to the rock.

The Bluff Shoals Lighthouse in Pamlico Sound near Cape Hatteras, North Carolina, rests on pilings 12 feet above the water. At this height in relatively sheltered waters, it has seldom been hit by waves. The clapboard, houselike design of the light was typical of those first put up in Middle Atlantic bays and inlets during Victorian times.

A 19th Century wooden lightship marking the Vineyard Sound channel off Massachusetts displays oval daymarks atop its masts; at night kerosene lamps were raised below them. Keepers on lightships had arduous duty. They served 30 days without relief, were tossed about by storms and kept an anxious eye on shipping that might ram them.

The Carysfort Reef Lighthouse along Florida's Atlantic coast was designed to stand against the wind and waves of the area's frequent hurricanes by presenting only skeletal iron surfaces to the elements. The lighthouse replaced a lightship withdrawn from duty after its captain and a crewman were killed by Indians in 1837.

Served by an enclosed walkway, the Isle of Shoals Lighthouse five miles off New Hampshire looms like a fortress with a tower of granite blocks two feet thick. Originally conceived as a modest stone structure, the lighthouse was massively reinforced to protect it from anticipated attack by Confederate gunboats during the Civil War.

The ornate Racine Reef Lighthouse in Lake Michigan, embellished by a rococo frosting of ice, rises tier upon tier from an octagonal concrete foundation to spindly stovepipe and flagpole—a classic example of Victorian wedding-cake architecture, and an ultimate symbol of the austere pride of the old-time light builders and keepers.

N
30
60
E
330
300
W
DANFORTH
CONSTELLATION

3

On a clear day a boatman traveling short distances in familiar waters can usually make intuitive judgments on all the crucial components of navigation—direction, distance, speed and time. But on any longer, more difficult journey, he must consciously apply the navigational tools—and the skills in using them—that have guided mariners for centuries. The most critical of these tools is the compass. It issues a constant report on the boat's heading, and can also be used as a sighting instrument to determine the directional relationship of the boat to some mark ashore or on the water. The boat's speedometer—or its tachometer—delivers an instant-by-instant mea-

THE BASIC PILOTING TOOLS

sure of through-the-water speed. These data can be used to plot a course on a chart with the help of other tools. Parallel rules, for instance, enable a navigator to draw a line in a direction precisely defined by his chart's compass rose. Dividers help translate speed into distance on the chart. And by manipulating all these ingredients of direction, speed, time and distance, a navigator can make a plan not only for reaching a distant destination at a predetermined hour, but also for checking his position en route. Each step of the trip is recorded on the chart, creating a basis for computing the next step. Thus, a navigator gains an overview of his situation.

In theory, all these plans and devices should enable a boatman in coastal waters to determine his position with scientific precision. In practice, however, some uncertainties inevitably creep into his calculations. Taking compass sightings from a pitching deck, for instance, can be an exercise in guesswork and near frustration. Magnetic headings can be deceptive, since any piece of ferrous metal or small electric current aboard a boat may lead a compass astray—and the navigator, too, unless he has corrected or allowed for the deviation. Speedometers and tachometers faithfully record speed through the water but cannot take into account the effects that winds and currents have on a vessel's speed over the bottom.

Navigation is, thus, as much an art as a science. Nevertheless, a boatman can do a good deal to minimize uncertainty. He should install his compass with exquisite care, adjust it with precision, treat it with consideration and periodically check its accuracy. Happily, methods of verifying this vital instrument's performance have improved since the days of the "pilot's blessing" used by Columbus' navigators—raising a hand to point to the North Star and then lowering it in a steady arc onto the compass.

Today's boatman also has the aid of such conveniences as red-filtered night lights that allow him to read instruments or a chart without reducing the sensitivity of his night vision, as would happen if he were using a conventional white light. Binoculars help him to pick out the visible objects on which most of his calculations depend; a pair of 7x50 binoculars, which are hefty enough for steadiness in handling, should supply about as much magnification as the average boatman will need.

As additional help, today's naval architects usually include, in plans for boats even as small as 24 feet, a special space for the navigator to stow and use his equipment. Ideally, on a power cruiser the space will be next to the wheel; on a sailboat, belowdecks near the companionway. It should be sheltered and offer the best possible visibility all around, room to spread out charts, and secure stowage for tools. Few boats meet all these requirements. But even if a navigator has to keep his equipment in a duffel bag and unfurl his charts on the lid of the ice chest, he will quickly find that using his tools becomes second nature—and navigation an engrossing challenge that is as exciting and rewarding as any other game of skill.

In this helmsman's view of a compass, the fluid-filled dome, lighted for night steering, acts as a lens to magnify the part of the compass card that indicates the ship's heading.

As a boat turns from one heading to another, everything aboard turns with it —except the compass card. As shown at right, the card's N marking keeps pointing north no matter what the boat's heading. When a boat falls off to the right of the correct course, the lubber line does too, and both must then be steered to the left until the lubber line swings back to the proper course. Neophyte helmsmen, plagued by the illusion of a moving compass card, sometimes try to steer the card instead of the boat, thus increasing the steering error and the difficulty of getting back on course.

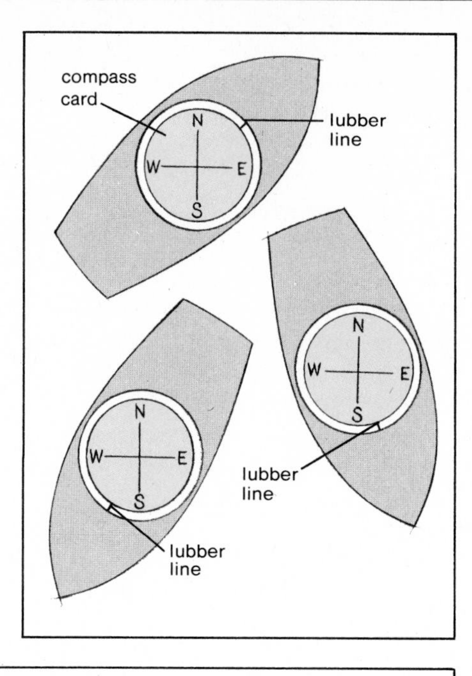

How a Compass Works

A mariner's compass, like the one at left, below, is designed to give a navigator, at a glance, his boat's correct heading relative to the direction of magnetic north. The compass' prominently displayed dial, called the compass card, is plainly marked with directions expressed in degrees, and is usually illuminated for night steering by a light with a red filter that preserves the helmsman's night vision.

On most compasses, a vertical pin called a lubber line is fixed to the compass housing—and thus, in effect, to the boat itself—to indicate the precise direction in which the boat is heading. Some compasses have similar pins—called 90° lubber lines—mounted at 90° intervals around the card for use in determining when a landmark is directly abeam or astern.

Another pin, centered on the compass card and taller than the others, is called the shadow pin. It is so named because expert navigators use the angle of its shadow to determine—by complicated calculations involving the known position of the sun—a ship's true, rather than magnetic, heading. For most boatmen, however, the shadow pin is used to determine position by taking bearings on fixed visible objects such as buoys, smokestacks and lighthouses. But sometimes, in seeking to take a bearing with the boat's steering compass, a navigator finds his view impeded by a mast or other shipboard object. In such circumstances, a hand-held bearing compass like the one on the opposite page is a great convenience.

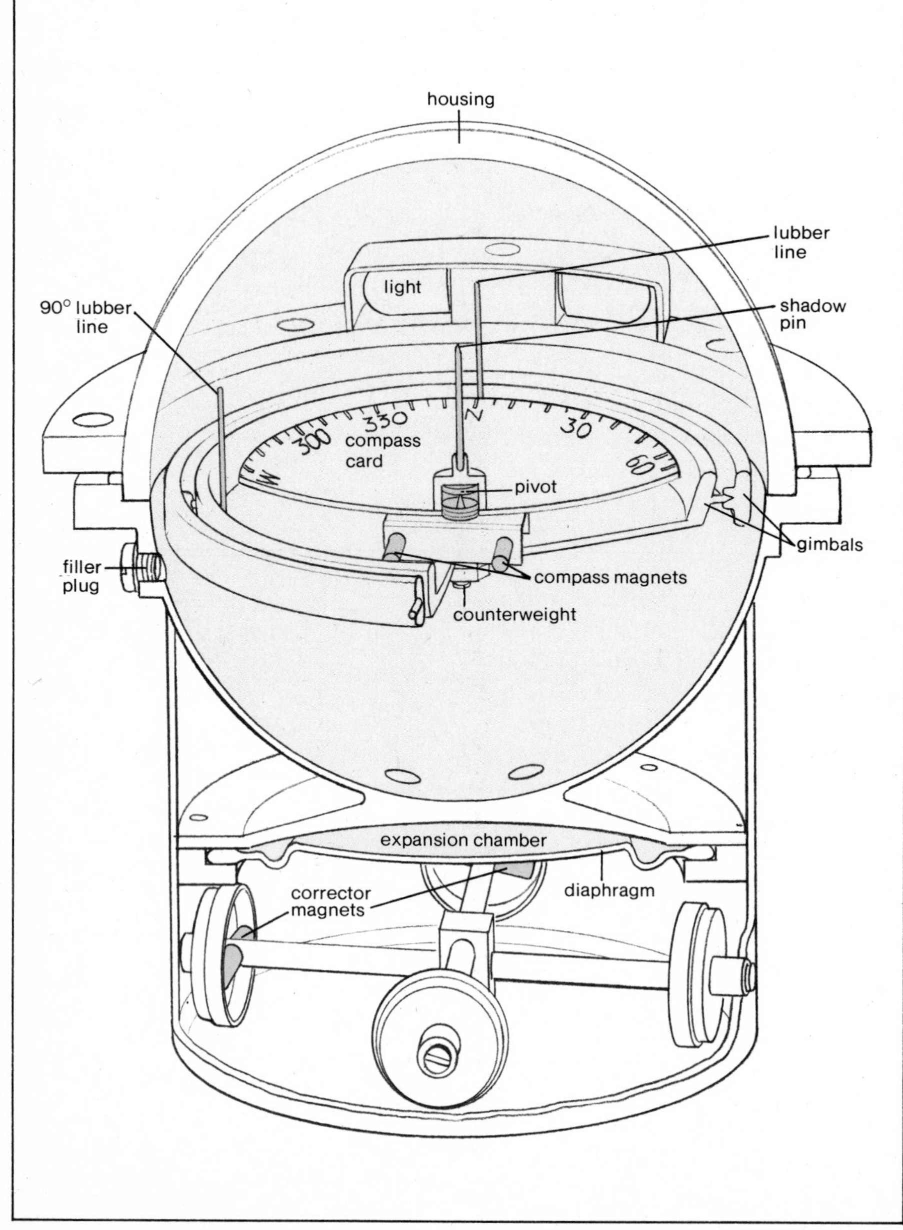

Inside a compass, as shown in the cutaway drawing, are gimbals and a counterweight to keep the card level when the boat tilts. The card—and the attached magnets aligning it with the earth's magnetic field—balance on a pivot. The housing is filled, through an opening sealed by a plug, with clear, highly refined kerosene. The fluid buoys up the card, reducing pivot friction, and damps the oscillations caused by vibration. A flexible diaphragm beneath lets the fluid expand and contract with changes in temperature. Corrector magnets in the base aid in adjusting the compass after its installation.

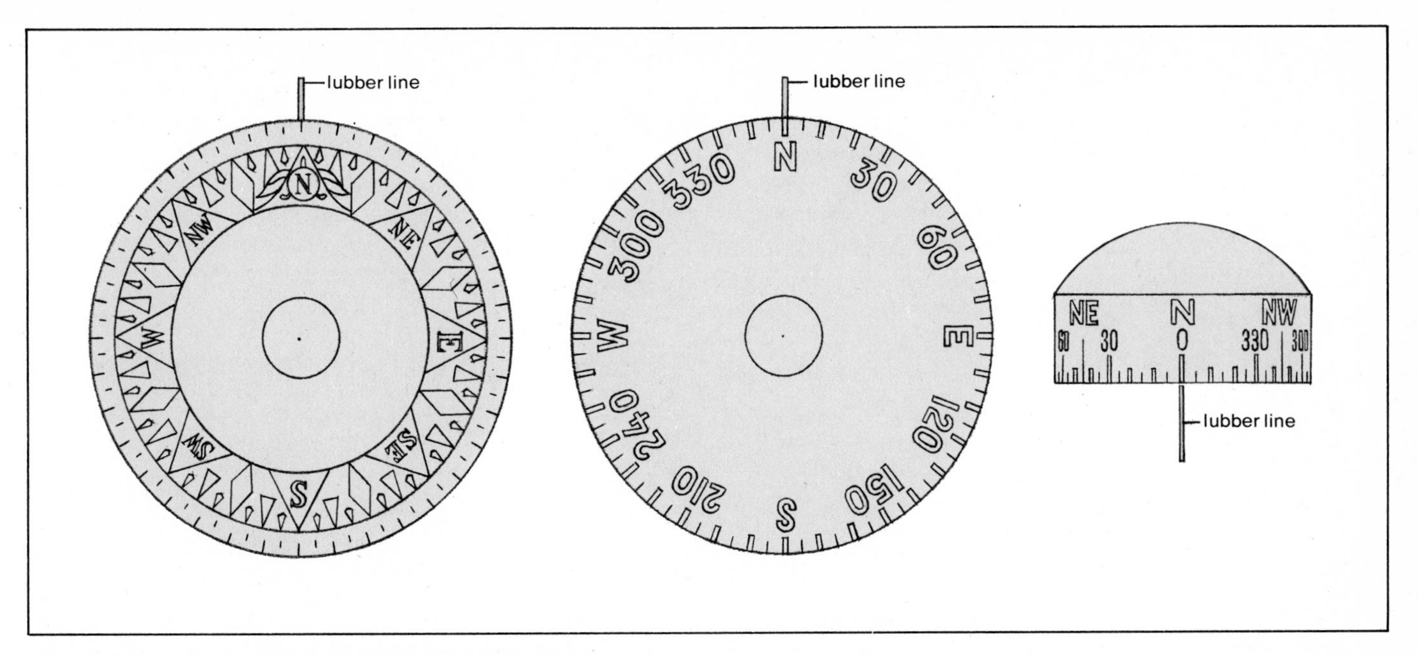

Until about 1900, compass cards were marked with the 64 directional points and half points shown at left, above. Most cards are now measured off by degrees (center), a system that offers greater precision and simplifies navigational calculations. Small boats are frequently equipped with an aviation-type compass (right); it features a card shaped like an inverted cup, with the degrees marked on the side and the lubber line set aft. When a boat using one of these aviation compasses strays to the left of the course, the lubber line moves to the right of the correct reading —the reverse of the usual response.

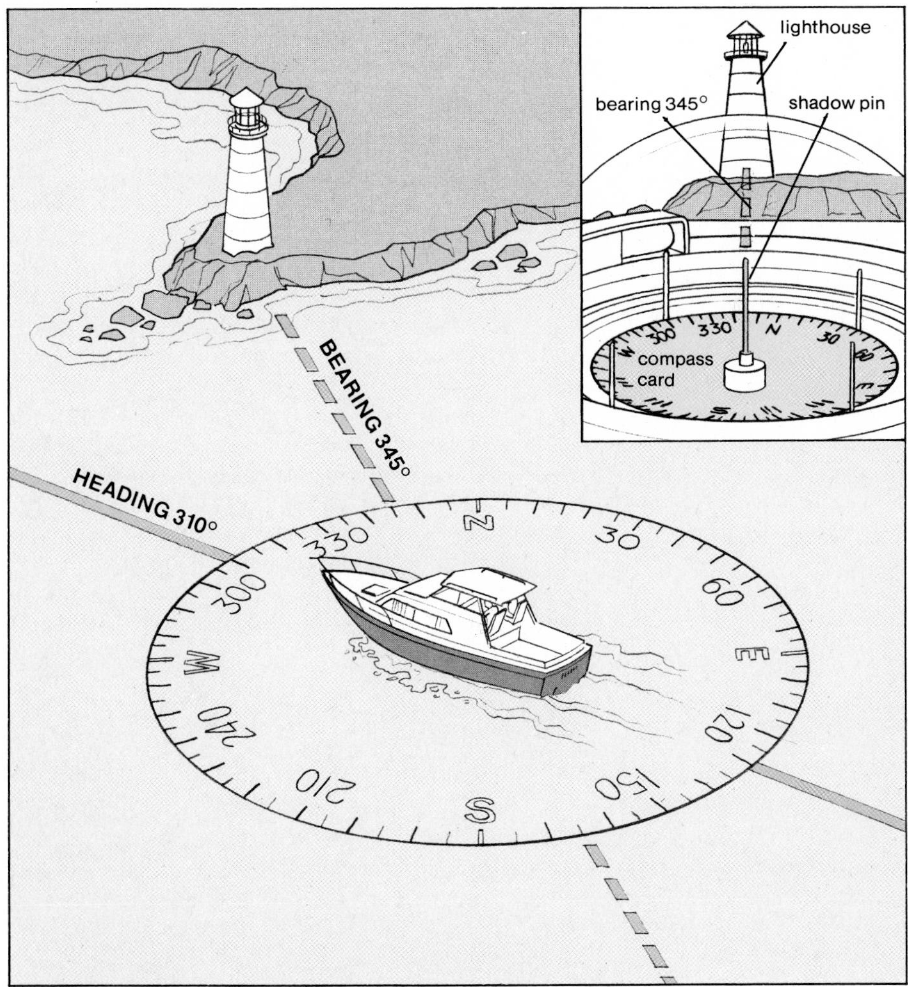

A compass not only defines the mariner's course but can also serve as an invaluable instrument for taking sightings and fixing a boat's approximate position. On the boat above, the compass shows the helmsman that he is on a course of 310° magnetic. Off to his right is a lighthouse whose position is marked on his chart. Sighting across the compass' shadow pin (inset), he determines that the bearing from the boat to the lighthouse is 345° (broken line). On his chart he draws a line from the lighthouse bearing 345°. He knows that he must be somewhere along that line, and he can reasonably assume that he is near its intersection with his 310° course line.

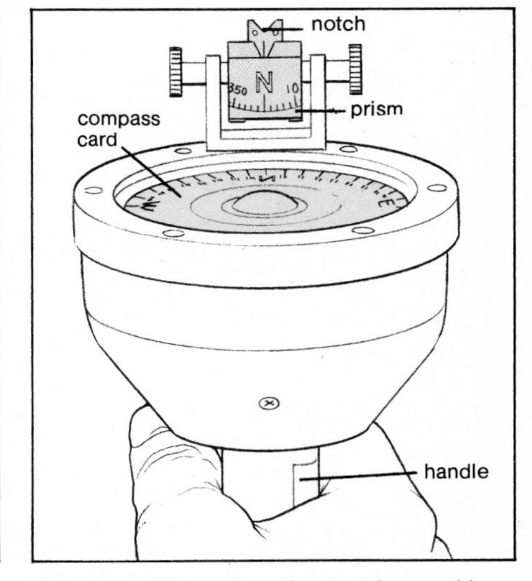

The hand-held compass above is designed for taking bearings. Holding the device at eye level, the navigator centers an object in the sighting notch and reads the bearing from the compass card through a reflecting prism. Such a compass usually contains a battery-powered light that is for night use.

To align a compass, the boatman begins by stretching a string from the center of the bow to the center of the stern, thus establishing the vessel's center line. The compass is then installed with the lubber line and shadow pin directly beneath the string. If it is necessary to offset the compass from the center line, a second line should be constructed by measuring out carefully from two points on the boat's center line, creating a parallel on which to place the compass.

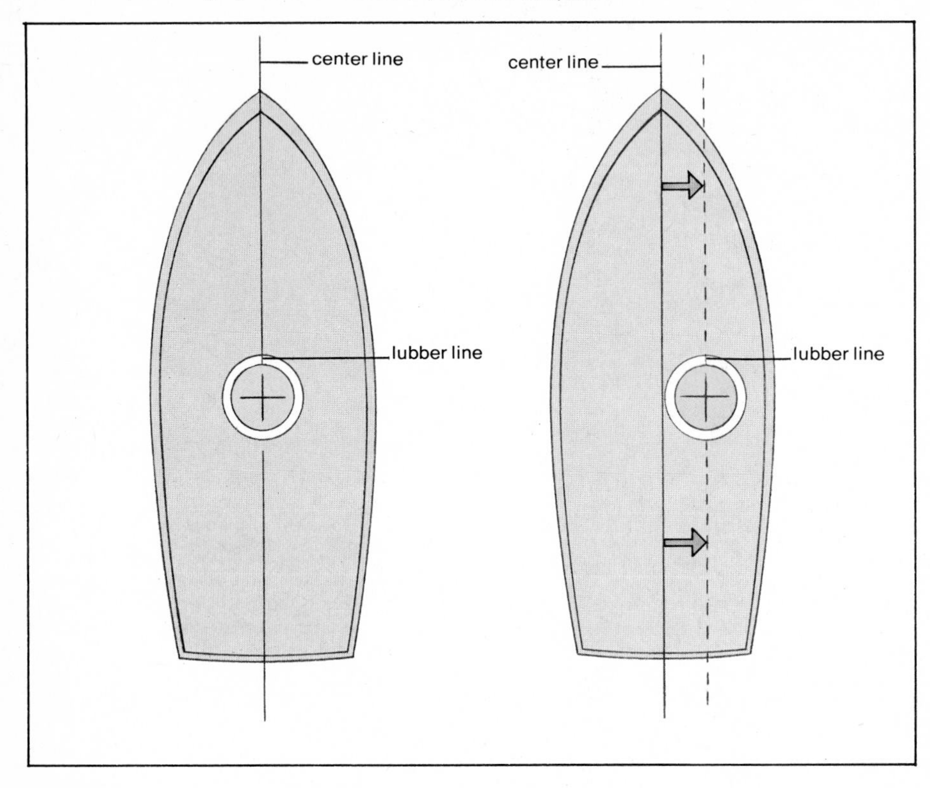

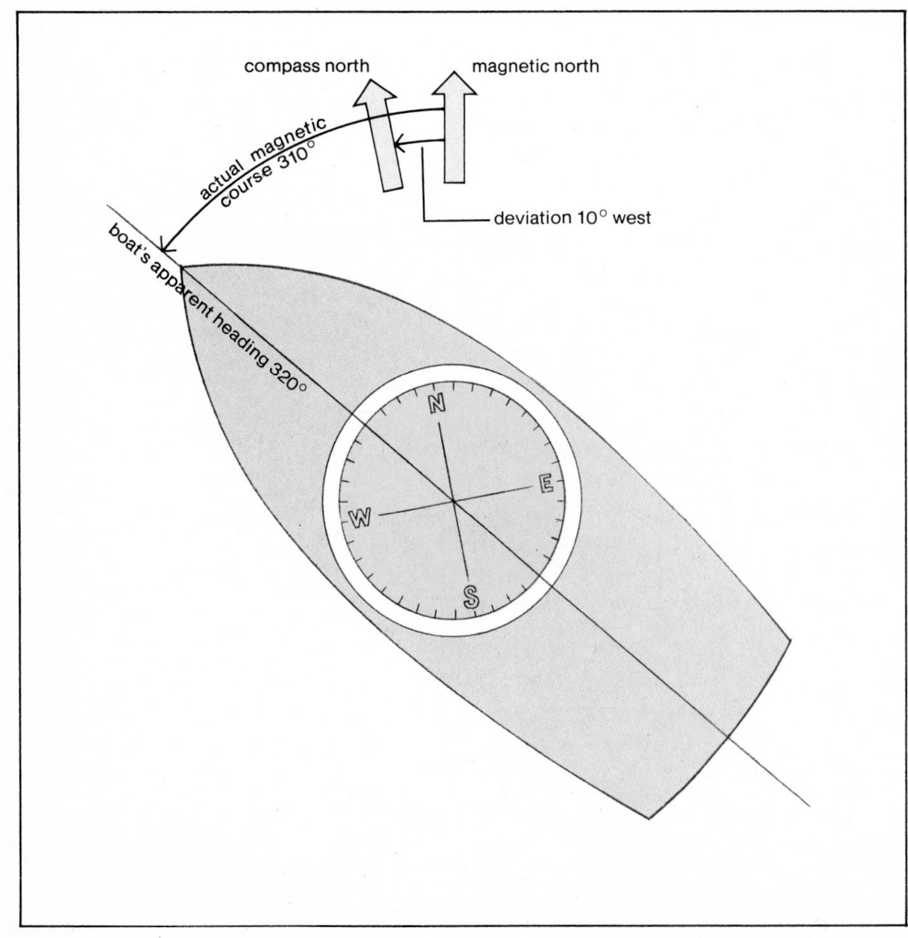

Installing and Adjusting

Two critical factors can prevent a boat's compass from helping to guide the mariner on his intended course. One is misalignment, and the other is deviation. To eliminate the former, a boatman need only be sure that the compass' lubber line and shadow pin align precisely with the boat's fore-and-aft axis, as shown at left. But to correct the latter, he must first understand the effect on the compass reading of various equipment aboard the boat, and then undertake a fairly complex set of procedures to compensate.

Ideally, the compass should be located well away from electronic equipment or any sizable piece of ferrous metal, such as the engine or a metal steering wheel. But since the prime consideration in the placement of a compass is visibility to the helmsman, some deviation may be inevitable. The extent of deviation on a boat may be so extreme that the skipper will have to call in a professional compass adjuster. Usually, however, the boatman himself, by following the procedures explained on pages 88-89, can adjust the compass so that deviation can be reduced to a minimum.

In so doing, he should run his boat along a sequence of known headings to be sure that his needle gives him an accurate reading of his boat's course. He should always begin by checking the four so-called cardinal points of the compass—north, south, east and west (beginning with north, since that is the base point of all compass calculations)—until he is certain he has established his instrument's degree of error at all points.

The compass on the boat at left has a deviation of 10° west; i.e., when the boat is headed directly toward magnetic north, or 000°, the compass points to 010°. Therefore, a helmsman steering by the faulty compass on a course of 320°, as here, will actually be on a magnetic heading of 310°. If his landfall is 20 miles away, this built-in error could cause him to miss it by nearly four miles.

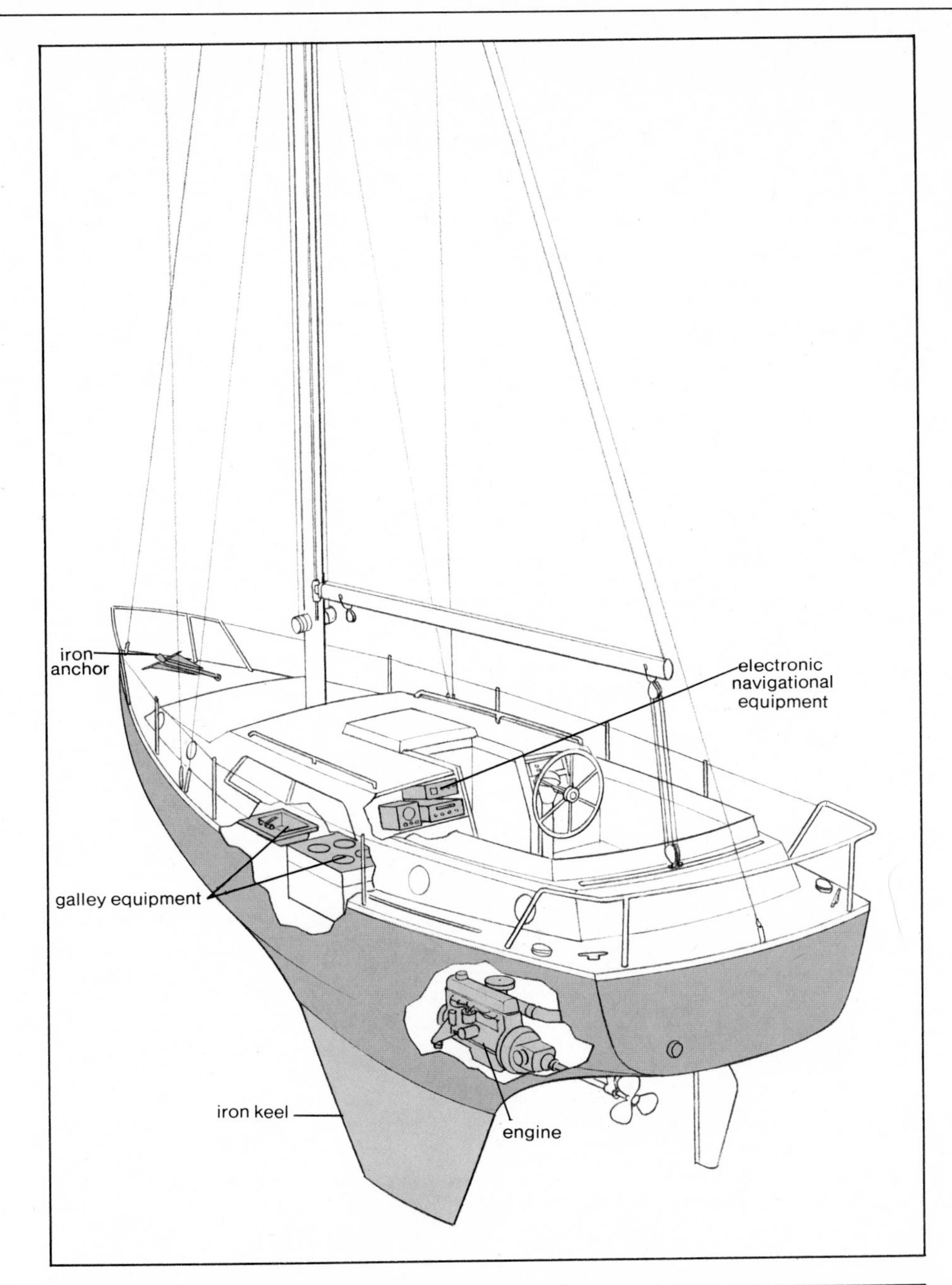

Any boat may be loaded with metal gear and electrical equipment likely to cause compass deviation. The effect can be minimized by using nonmagnetic metal such as bronze or the special steels that often serve for railings, standing rigging or steering wheels—and by keeping pairs of current-carrying wires close together to neutralize the effect of their electromagnetic fields. The boatman should also check his compass for changes in deviation when he turns on his engine or any electric motor, or when he brings aboard additional equipment such as a toolbox.

An Inclination for Beer

Small and apparently harmless items of equipment often cause compass deviations. Tiny motors and switches usually located near the compass, such as those that operate the windshield wipers, horn, lights, pump and ignition, can distract a compass. So can a beer can—or even the steel grommet on the yachting cap of a helmsman bending over the binnacle. A professional compass adjuster once struggled with an erratic compass on a boat used for fishing excursions. He finally found the trouble: an ice chest that was installed near the compass was full of canned beer at the outset of every trip and was usually empty on the return trip. His solution was to adjust the compass so that it registered due north when the chest was half full.

To reduce deviation in a typical mariner's compass to a practical minimum, a skipper uses the two pairs of corrector magnets, mounted in the compass base on brass shafts; he changes their setting with adjusting screws. On a north-south heading, the north-south corrector magnets are used to correct the compass, on an east-west heading, the other corrector magnets are employed.

east-west corrector magnet
north-south corrector magnet
directional magnets
adjusting screw
brass rod
north-south corrector magnet
adjusting screw
east-west corrector magnet

Compass corrector magnets move in pairs as their axes are turned by a key, made of brass or other nonmagnetic material. In the cutaway drawings below, the unadjusted compass at left is seen to have a deviation of 10° east. When the key is inserted in one end of the north-south corrector (right) and given a slight clockwise turn, it moves the corrector magnets, causing north on the compass card to swing onto the lubber line.

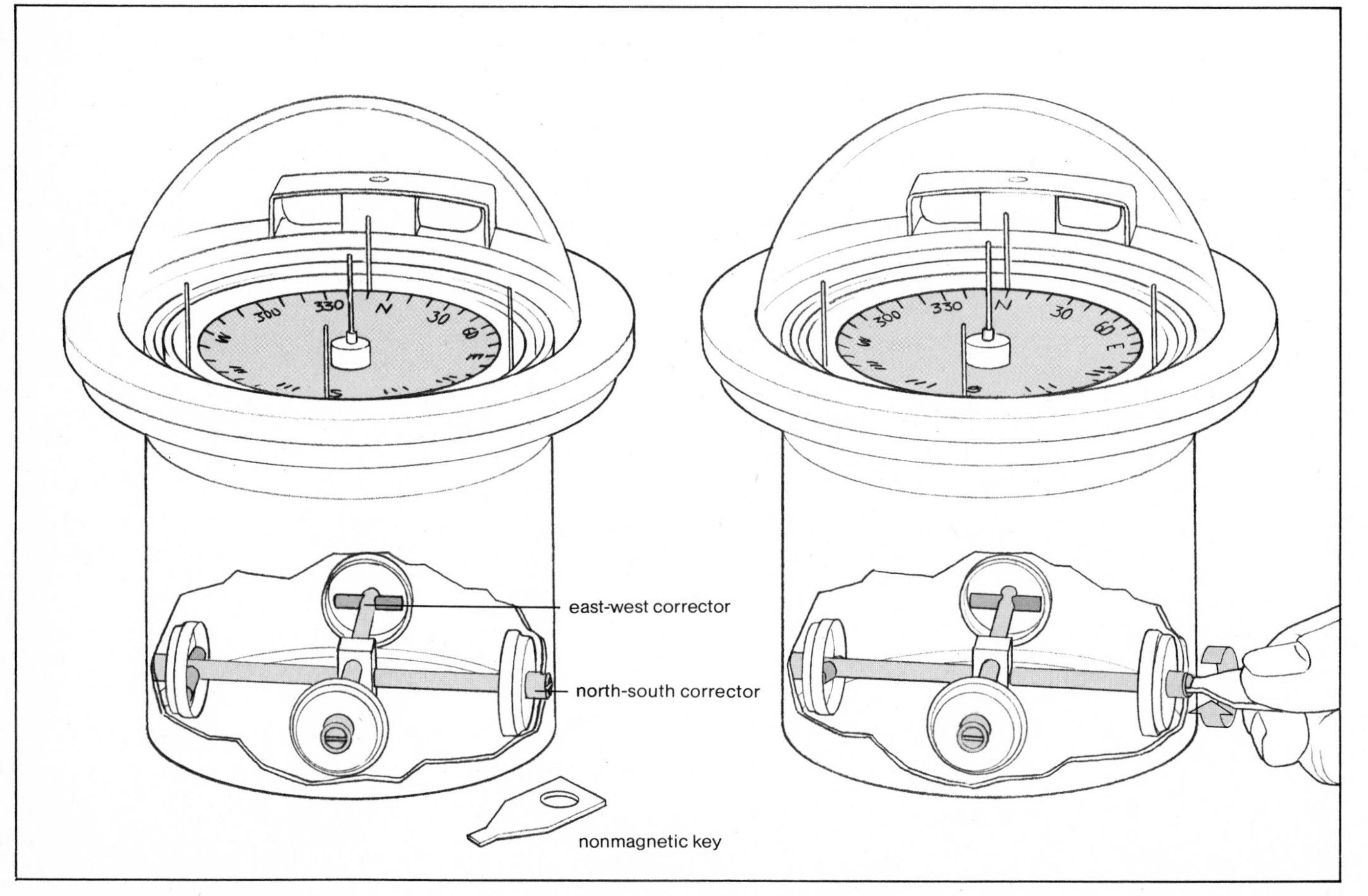

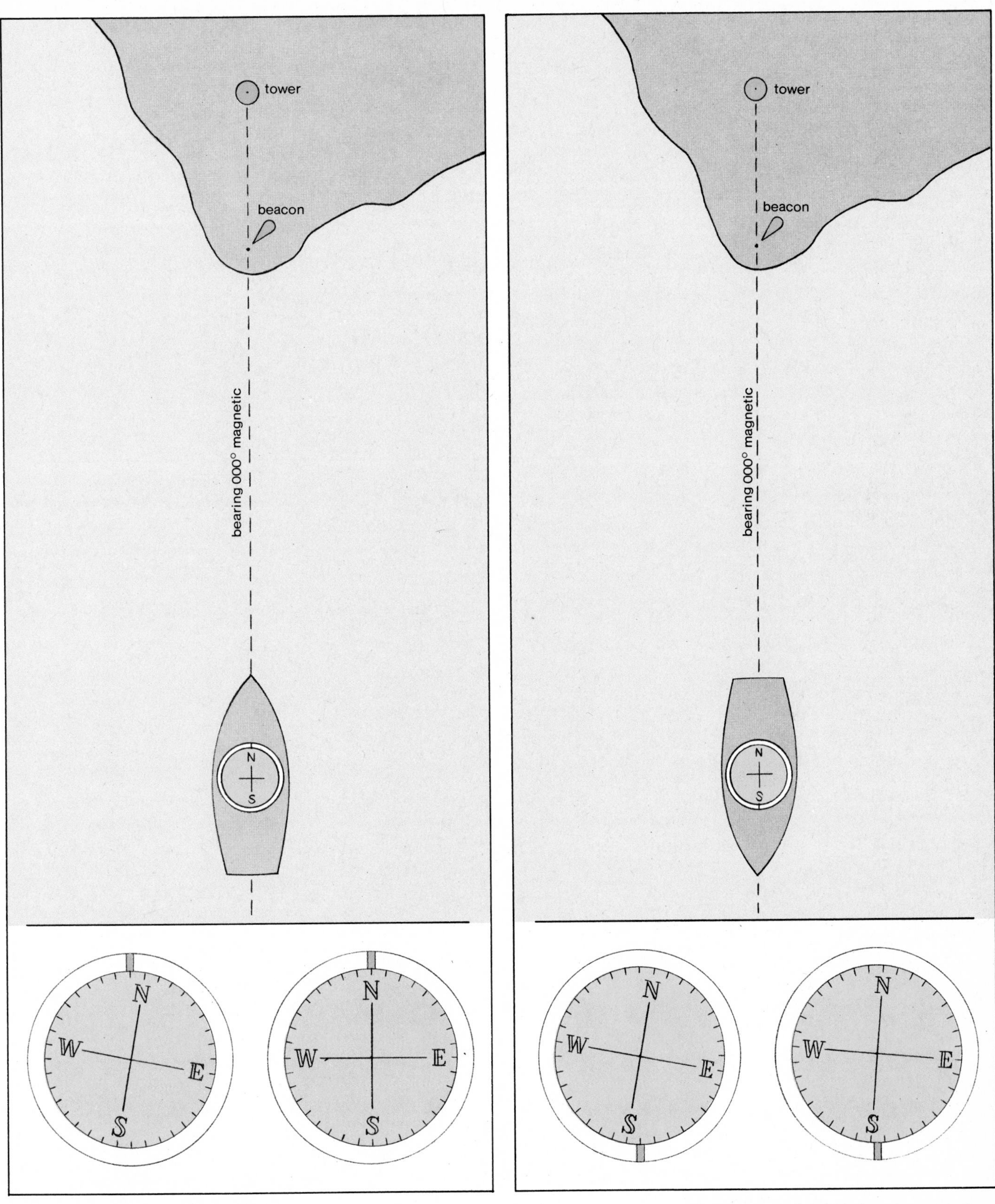

To correct deviation on a compass' first cardinal point, north, a skipper locates two fixed, charted objects that set a magnetic north-south line. When he puts his boat on that line, the compass' lubber line will be at magnetic north. If the compass is off—as it is above, by 10°—the deviation can be corrected by resetting the corrector magnets.

After correcting for deviation at a magnetic heading of north, the skipper aligns the boat's stern with the north-south range to correct deviation at south, or 180°. This will affect his north correction, so he corrects for only half the deviation at 180°. He repeats both operations, reducing deviation as much as possible. Then he can make similar adjustments on an east-west line of range.

After correcting deviation on the cardinal points (in blue, below), a skipper should check deviation at 15° intervals and keep track of the errors. He cannot make further corrections—to do so would affect his cardinal-point adjustments—but he needs to know for reference the amount of deviation. The skipper of the boat at right has begun checking by crossing the line of a range bearing 230° while steering a compass course of 015°. When the two range markers align, the range bears 229° by his compass and he knows that on a ship's heading of 015° his compass has a 1° easterly deviation.

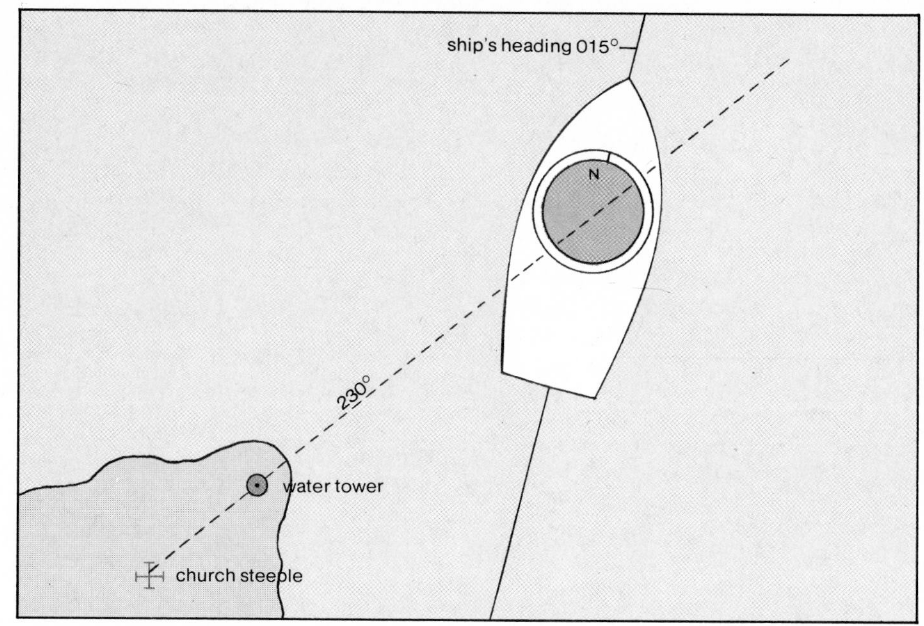

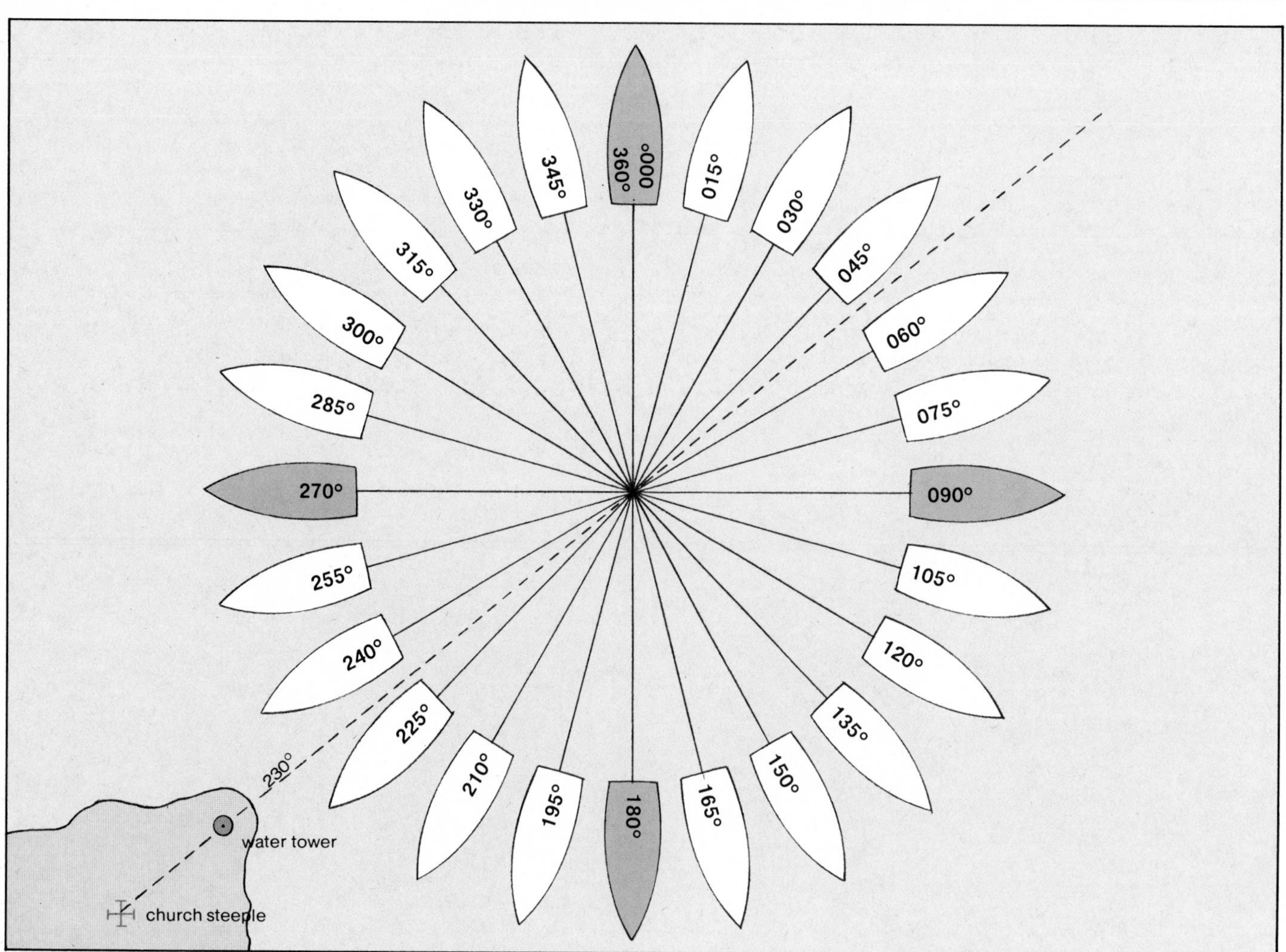

In determining deviation on headings all around the compass, a mariner must perform the maneuver illustrated at top on no less than 24 headings, including cardinals, and as a final check he must complete the circle by running a last heading on north. He can carry out this operation, called swinging ship, in various ways. He can sail his boat across the line of the range on each of the headings, as shown above. Or he can anchor his boat and warp it around from one heading to the next. If it is inconvenient to make all the deviation notations at one time or on a single range, the skipper can check deviation at some headings on one range and do the rest later on another range.

Data on compass deviation at each of the cardinal (blue) and intercardinal headings should be compiled on a table like the one below, listing the bearing of the range used, the ship's heading, the compass bearing of the range at that heading, and the amount and direction of deviation noted.

MAGNETIC COURSE	MAGNETIC BEARING OF RANGE	COMPASS BEARING OF RANGE	DEVIATION
000°	230°	230°	0
015°	230°	229°	1°E
030°	230°	228°	2°E
045°	230°	227°	3°E
060°	230°	226°	4°E
075°	230°	225°	5°E
090°	230°	225°	5°E
105°	230°	225°	5°E
120°	230°	226°	4°E
135°	230°	227°	3°E
150°	230°	228°	2°E
165°	230°	229°	1°E
180°	230°	230°	0
195°	230°	231°	1°W
210°	230°	232°	2°W
225°	230°	233°	3°W
240°	230°	234°	4°W
255°	230°	236°	6°W
270°	230°	235°	5°W
285°	230°	235°	5°W
300°	230°	234°	4°W
315°	230°	233°	3°W
330°	230°	232°	2°W
345°	230°	231°	1°W
360°	230°	230°	0

Plotting the deviation data on a graph should result in a smooth curve connecting the established points. One dot falling outside the curves—as at 255° below—can be disregarded as an error in observation. But an erratic pattern would indicate that either the data or the compass is awry.

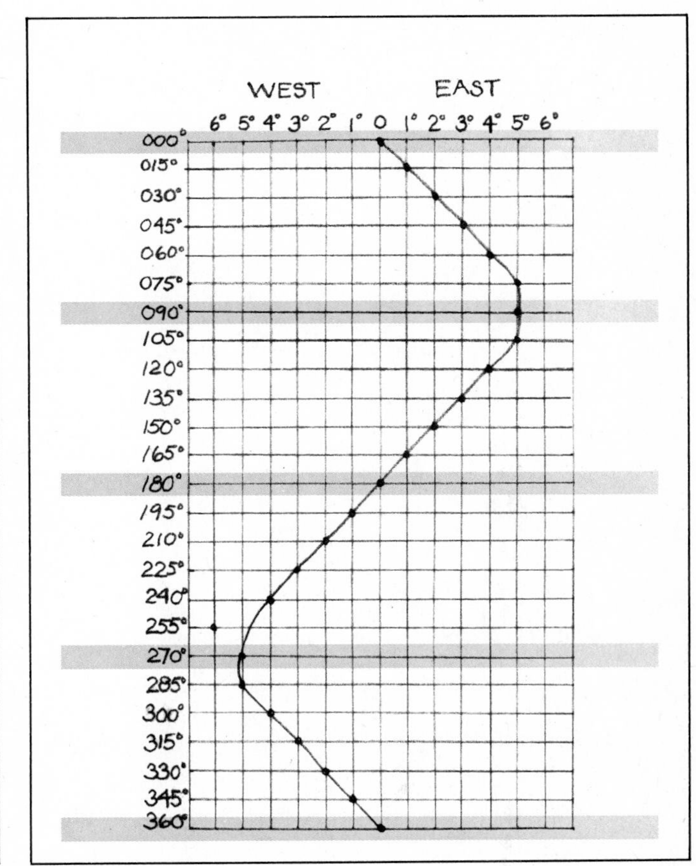

	MAGNETIC COURSE	COMPASS COURSE
NORTH	000°	000°
	015°	014°
	030°	028°
NORTH EAST	045°	042°
	060°	056°
	075°	070°
EAST	090°	085°
	105°	100°
	120°	116°
SOUTH EAST	135°	132°
	150°	148°
	165°	164°
SOUTH	180°	180°
	195°	196°
	210°	212°
SOUTH WEST	225°	228°
	240°	244°
	255°	260°
WEST	270°	275°
	285°	290°
	300°	304°
NORTH WEST	315°	318°
	330°	332°
	345°	346°
NORTH	360°	360°

Deviation data refined and corrected by being plotted on a graph, as shown above, can be converted into two columns of figures like those at left, and then posted near the compass for the helmsman's guidance. The first column lists the magnetic headings at which deviation has been observed. The figures in the second column, arrived at by adding the amount of observed deviation to, or subtracting it from, the magnetic heading, show the compass courses to be steered to achieve the correct headings. Thus, to steer a course of 015° magnetic, the helmsman puts the boat on a compass heading of 014°.

A measured mile, like the one bracketed in blue on the portion of a Boston Harbor chart shown above, can be used to check a boat's speed. It has a range at each end and is labeled with a true, rather than a magnetic, bearing since in most places magnetic north shifts slightly year by year. A skipper brings his boat up to a predetermined tachometer or speedometer reading before entering the course, starts timing at the first range and steers at a constant speed along the course's magnetic heading. At the mile's end his stopwatch reads—in this example—6 minutes 20 seconds, or 380 seconds. He divides 380 into the 3,600 seconds in an hour and gets a speed of 9.5 knots.

Time, Speed, Distance

In addition to direction, a navigator plotting a course must deal with the key elements of speed, time and distance. Time and distance are fixed and precisely measurable quantities, but a boat's speed —like its compass heading—is variable. Most modern powerboats and many sailboats have fairly accurate speedometers, but their delicate mechanisms can be affected by current, by their placement on a boat's hull, and by wear and tear. A boatman should therefore check his speedometer's accuracy periodically.

The best way to run a speed check is by measuring with a stopwatch *(left)* the time a boat takes to traverse a known distance at a steady pace, and then divide the time into the distance to get the speed. The most convenient distance is a precisely measured mile—some 90 of which have been established at various convenient locations in United States waters.

Timing a run over a measured mile is easier and more precise under power than under sail; but it is possible to sail a measured mile under reasonably constant conditions and get a good idea of a speedometer's accuracy. The skipper should run the measured mile at least once in each direction in order to balance out the accelerative or deterrent effects of wind or current, and for best results, he should do it several times at various speeds in each direction.

Most powerboats and auxiliary sailboats, whether they have speedometers or not, usually carry tachometers. By entering the results of his runs over the measured mile in a table like that at right, center, and plotting his entries on a graph, a boatman can use his tachometer as a reliable index to speed.

Thus, by one means or another, the mariner can find a way to measure his boat's speed through the water. But he must remember that, because of the effects of wind or current, this speed may be different from the boat's speed over the bottom. When making navigational calculations, he must include as a factor the speed of any current he encounters *(page 158)*, in order to establish his true speed over a given portion of the chart.

Once he knows his boat's speed, as explained in detail overleaf, he can then divide that speed into the distance indicated on his course line to compute the amount of time that will be required to reach his destination. Or, alternatively, he can multiply the speed and time to ascertain the distance the boat has traveled over some portion of a course leg.

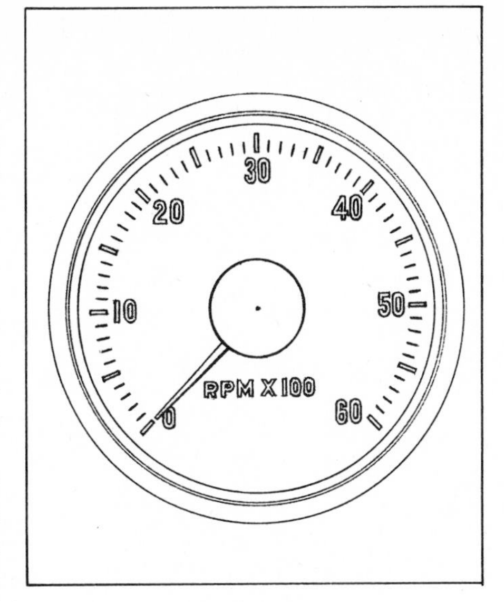

The tachometer (left), a standard device on most inboard and larger outboard craft, monitors engine revolutions per minute—in this case, zero to 6,000 in increments of 100. As set forth below, a boatman who has timed his craft over a measured mile at various tachometer readings can then use the results to gauge his speed at each setting.

The columns of figures below list the data for speed computations, obtained by running a powerboat back and forth over a measured mile at eight tachometer readings from 600 to 4,000 rpm's. Since this boat has a planing hull, which meets less water resistance above a certain speed, its velocity does not increase in a steady proportion to increased rpm's as is the case with some hull types.

RPM	NORTH - SOUTH TIME	NORTH - SOUTH SPEED	SOUTH - NORTH TIME	SOUTH - NORTH SPEED	AVERAGE SPEED
600	14 MIN. 36 SEC.	4.1	9 MIN. 40 SEC.	6.2	5.1
1500	6 MIN. 32 SEC.	9.2	5 MIN. 28 SEC.	11.0	10.1
2000	4 MIN. 14 SEC.	14.2	3 MIN. 47 SEC.	15.9	15.0
2300	3 MIN. 6 SEC.	19.4	2 MIN. 54 SEC.	20.7	20.0
2600	2 MIN. 28 SEC.	24.3	2 MIN. 20 SEC.	25.7	25.0
3000	2 MIN. 11 SEC.	27.5	2 MIN. 6 SEC.	28.6	28.0
3500	1 MIN. 58 SEC.	30.5	2 MIN. 1 SEC.	29.8	30.1
4000	1 MIN. 41 SEC.	35.6	1 MIN. 43 SEC.	35.0	35.3

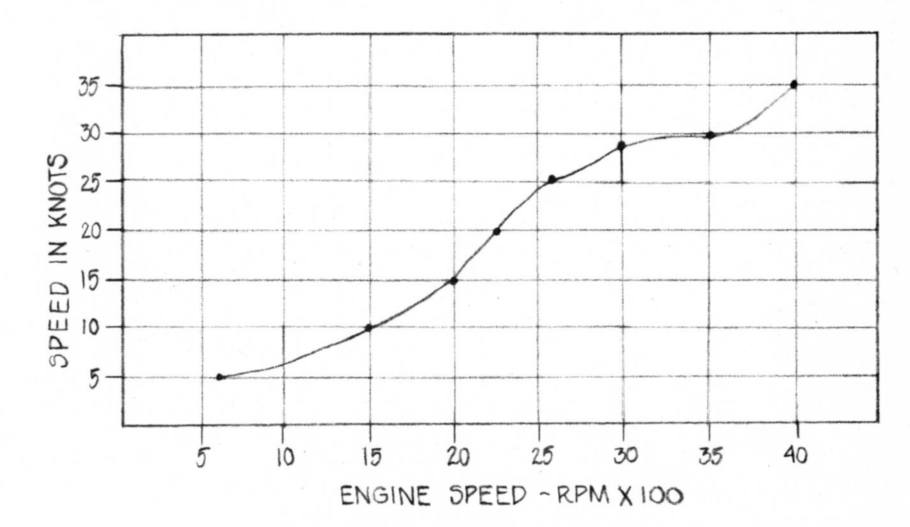

The graph above shows the last step in translating tachometer readings into speeds through the water. The skipper plots the graph from the data in the table above. Like the pilot checking his compass for deviation, he hopes to achieve a smooth curve that indicates his instrument is well calibrated, and his own observations and computations are accurate. This graph shows a jump in speed at about 2,000 rpm's—normal for a powerboat with the type of hull that begins to plane above a certain speed. Since this step-up and the other curves are relatively smooth and consistent, the pilot now has an accurate speed gauge for tachometer readings from zero to 4,000.

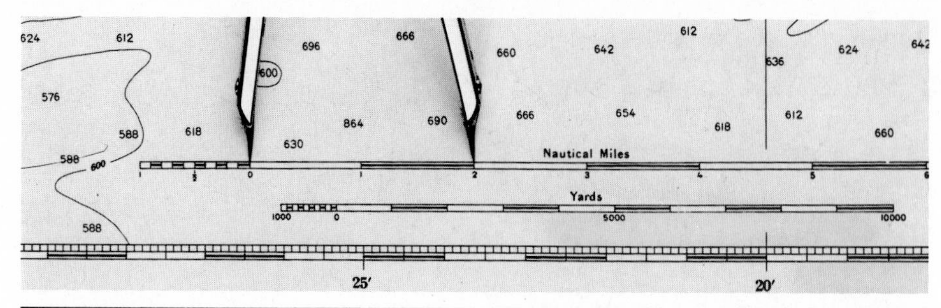

To measure short distances on a chart, a navigator uses a pair of dividers, opening them to span a given distance, then comparing the span to one of the scales (right) included on most charts. As an auxiliary scale he can use the latitude marks that appear along a chart's vertical edge: a minute of latitude equals one nautical mile.

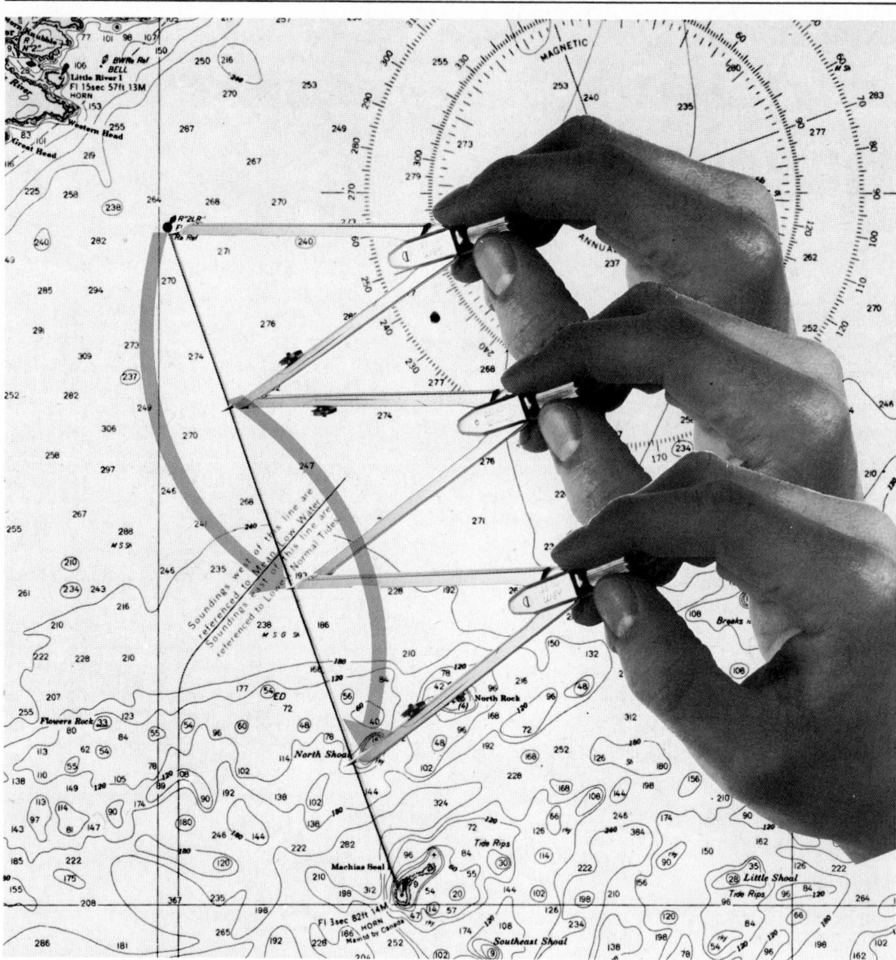

To measure course lines that are too long to be covered by the span of the dividers even when fully extended, the navigator should open them to a convenient distance—perhaps two or three miles, depending on the chart's scale—and then "walk" them as shown over the course leg for its full length. Often the dividers will not reach the end of the line on the last regular step, leaving a gap in the measurement. When this happens, pivot the dividers once more, then close them to fit the gap. Measure this shortfall on the scale and add it to the sum of the other steps.

The Basic Measure

The nautical mile is based on the earth's circumference. The ancient Greeks laid the groundwork for the nautical mile when, hypothesizing that the earth was round, they divided its circumference into 360°. Sailors subsequently found that one sixtieth of a degree, called a minute of arc, was a convenient measure of shorter distances. They renamed it the nautical mile and used it as the basis for their navigating calculations—with uneven results, since the nautical mile varied depending on the prevailing estimate of the earth's size. In 1929, an international agreement permanently established the nautical mile at 1,852 meters, or about 2,000 yards.

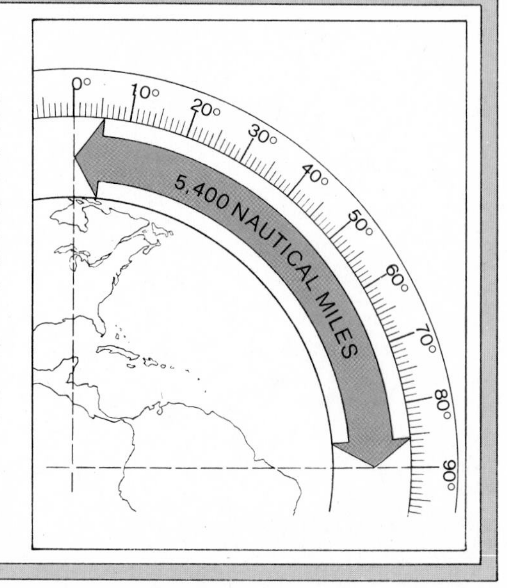

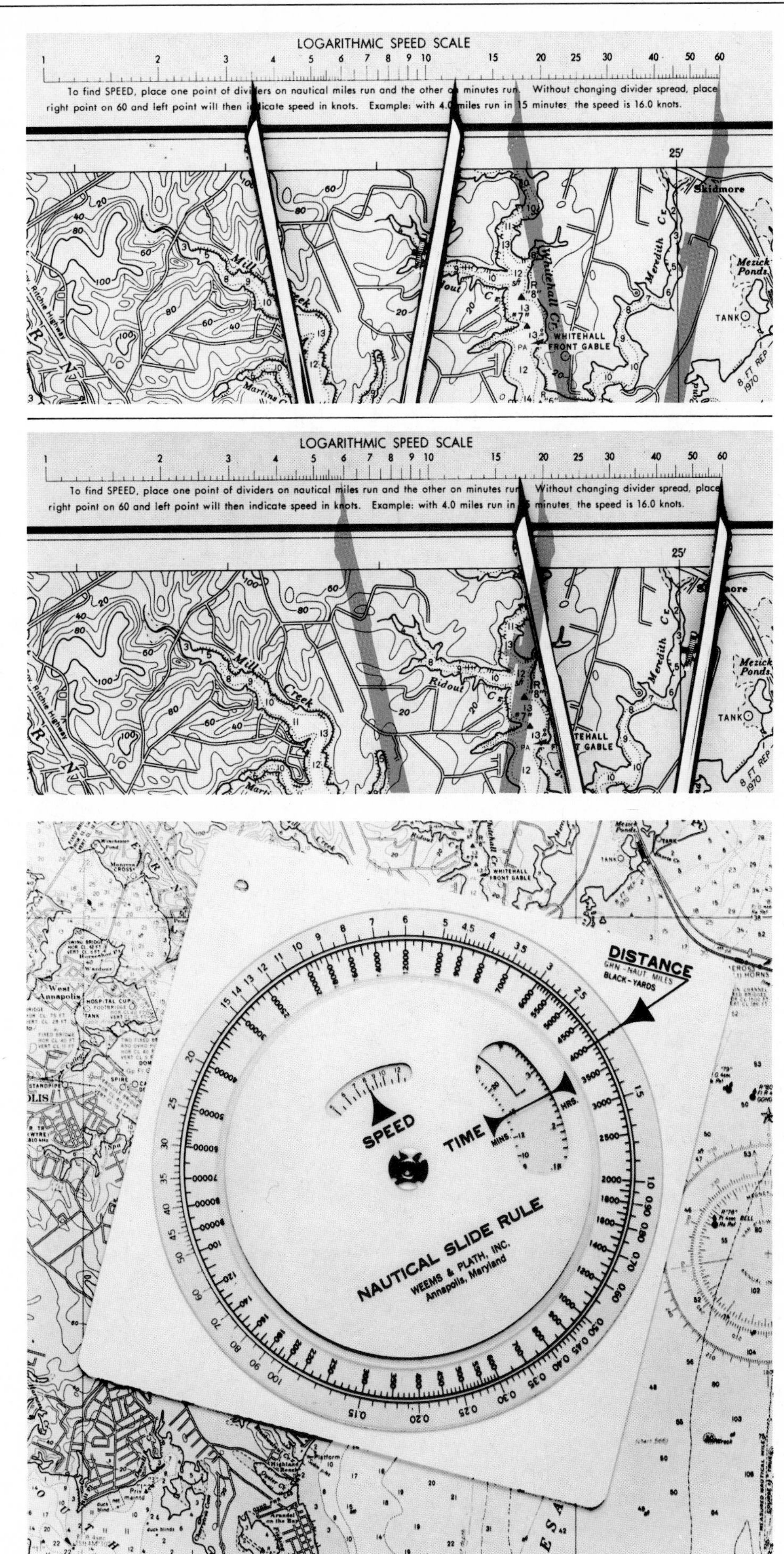

A convenient aid for determining speed, time or distance when two of the three factors are known is the logarithmic scale printed on many charts. To find the speed of a boat that has covered 3.5 nautical miles in 12 minutes, for instance, place one point of a pair of dividers at 3.5 on the scale. Open the dividers so the right point rests on 12, the elapsed time in minutes. Shift the dividers so that one point (blue dividers) precisely touches the scale at 60 minutes; the other point now lies on the speed of the boat—17.5 knots.

By reversing the steps above, the navigator can find out how much time it will take to cover a given distance—say, six miles—at his established speed of 17.5 knots. To do so, he places the dividers' right point at 60 on the scale and the left point on 17.5. Once again keeping the dividers set to this distance, he moves the left point to 6 (blue dividers) and reads the time, a little more than 20 minutes, from the right point. Alternatively, a pilot can estimate how far he will travel at his known speed in a specified time by setting the right point on the number of minutes, then reading the distance at the left point.

Another way to compute time, distance or speed is to use a circular slide rule, especially adapted for use by the seaman from the landsman's conventional slide rule. On the circular rule at left, distances in nautical miles and in yards appear on the rim of a large dial. A concentric smaller dial has two windows, one for reading speed in knots and one for reading time in minutes or hours. By dialing two known factors, the third can be found automatically. Here the slide rule shows that a boat traveling two nautical miles (4,000 yards) in 15 minutes (quarter of an hour) has a speed of eight knots.

Drawing a Parallel

Every pilot needs to know the exact magnetic direction of any course to be drawn on his chart. To get that information he uses the compass rose included on all charts. But since a course line drawn across a chart segment will rarely, if ever, intersect the center of a compass rose, a navigator requires some means of moving the line to the rose in order to determine its compass heading. The reverse is also true: if the navigator wishes to draw a line along a particular magnetic heading, he needs a reading from the inner—or magnetic—circle of the compass rose in order to guide his rule.

Navigators can use any one of a number of mechanical devices for making this transfer of information, and each navigator will decide for himself which tool he likes best. Shown on these pages are the two commonest, handiest and most accurate of these contrivances. The first, demonstrated at right, is a set of parallel rules, a hinged device dating from the late 16th Century. The second *(opposite)* is a more recent invention, the course protractor.

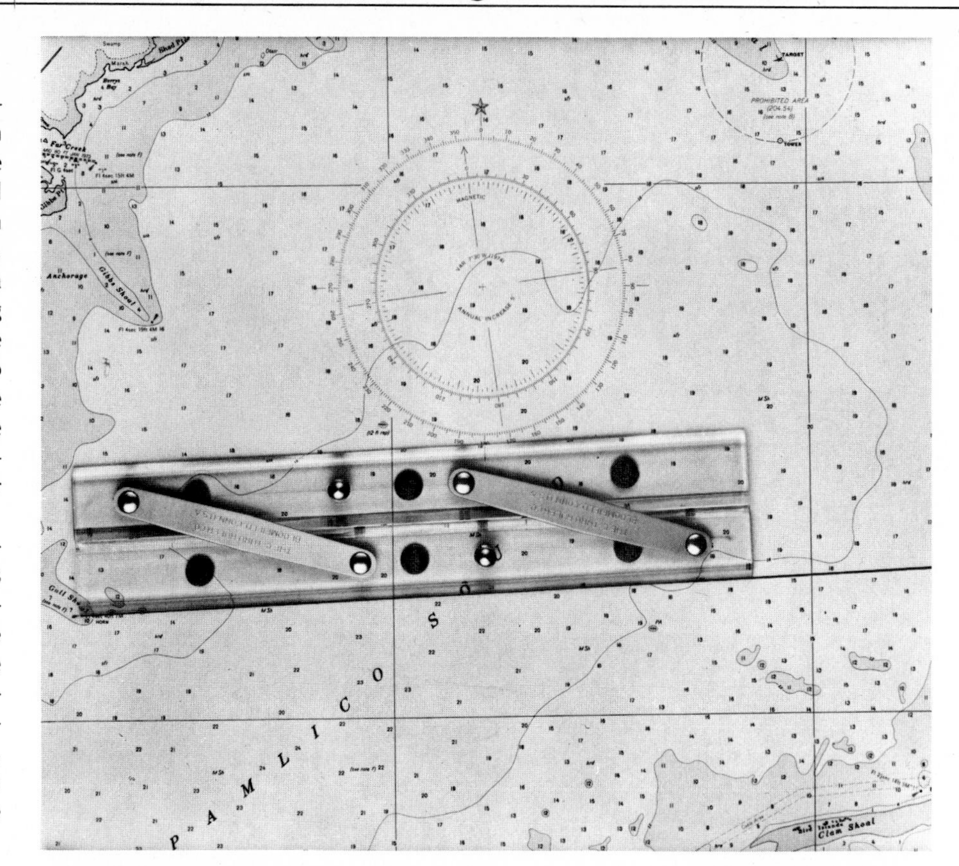

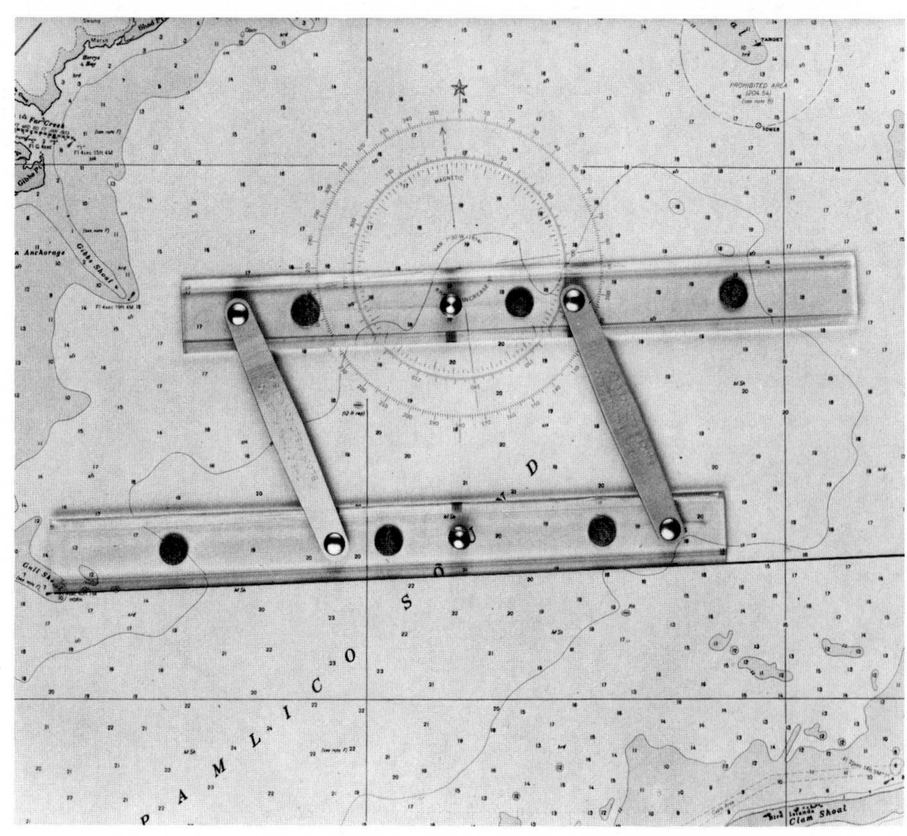

Using parallel rules to find the direction of an easterly trending course line on his chart, a navigator sets one edge—here the bottom—of the rules on the line (top picture). Then he opens the rules until the top edge intersects the rose's center. The easterly point of intersection with the inner magnetic circle—in this case 95°—is the course line's bearing. If the rose is too far from the course line to reach in one step, he "walks" the rules to the rose by opening them partway, holding the rule he has just moved firmly in place and swinging the other up to it, taking small steps to avoid slippage.

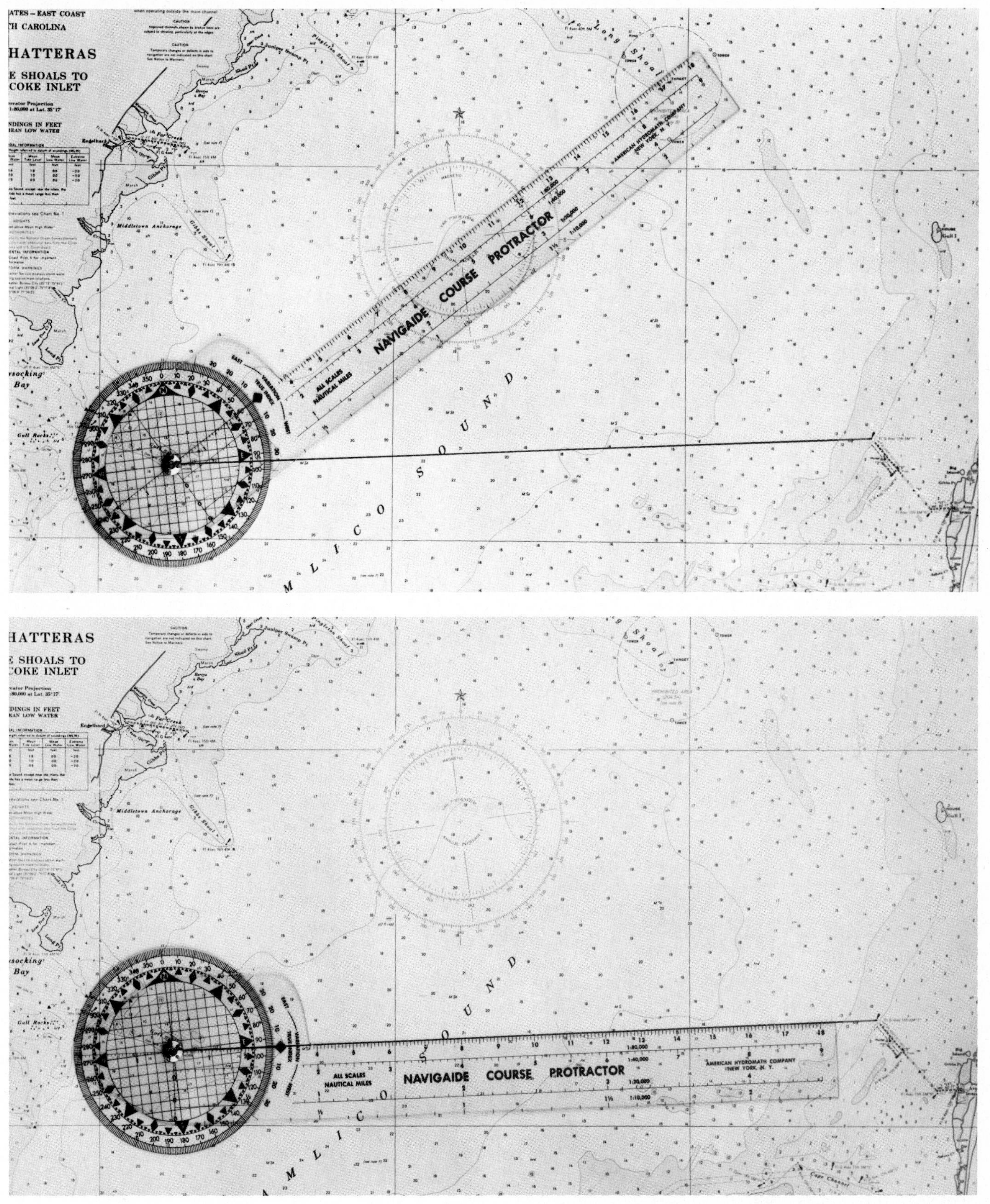

Using a course protractor to find the direction of a line of his chart, a navigator places the center hole of the disc at one end of the line with the upper edge of the arm intersecting the center of the chart's compass rose. The inner circle of the rose yields a reading of 60° magnetic. He revolves the disc until its figure 60 lines up (top picture) with the true index pointer. Holding the disc, which is oriented now with the rose, in this position, he rotates the arm until its top edge lies along the course line (lower picture). The figure on the disc opposite the true index pointer is the direction of the line—95°.

Laying Out a Course

A navigator equipped with a chart, a compass and the various devices for ascertaining speed, time and distance has all the tools needed for coastal navigation—except one. He still lacks a means of recording his course and position as he moves along, and of setting down on his chart the observations he uses in determining this critical information.

This process of marking a chart with information about a ship's movements is the culmination of the navigator's art. In practice it becomes a concise diary of a voyage, a clear record *(opposite)* of the navigator's intentions, predictions, observations, corrections and verifications.

For reasons of speed and clarity, the diary is written in a kind of navigator's shorthand *(right)*, easy to learn and easy to read. It is usually inscribed on a chart with an ordinary pencil, and an experienced navigator always has a supply of pencils, as well as a pencil sharpener, conveniently stowed by the chart table. An eraser, preferably one that works when wet, is handy, too, not only to correct mistakes but to clean old journeys from the chart so it can be used for future voyages.

The Navigator's Shorthand

Every navigator works out his own chart-notation system. The chief attributes of a good system are clarity and consistency so the navigator is never confused by his own code. The six symbols below are used almost universally by yachtsmen. They make it possible for anybody aboard a boat to figure out the chain of events on a trip like the one charted on pages 100-101, and to pilot the vessel in an emergency. A navigator may not use every symbol each time he leaves port, but he ought to be familiar with them all and know how to use them when he needs to.

C 072 MAG
D 26 S 15

A solid line represents a boat's course. Its direction is indicated by a letter C above the line, followed by three digits. MAG, for magnetic, is often omitted if all headings are magnetic. Below the line are the length of the course leg and the intended speed. This example shows a 26-nautical-mile course of 072° covered at 15 knots.

1745
195 MAG

A dashed line, easily distinguishable from a solid course line, stands for a bearing on a charted object. The direction from the boat to the object, in this case 195°, is written below the line in three digits. The time the bearing is taken—written in the four-digit form of a 24-hour nautical clock—appears above the dashed line.

1325 DR

A dot on a course line indicates a boat's position. By adding a semicircle, the time and the letters DR, the pilot specifies a dead-reckoning position. The least reliable type of position, it is entirely deduced from course, speed and time. This notation indicates where a pilot thinks he is or will be in the future.

0815 EP

A square around a dot on a course line, the letters EP and the time denote an estimated position. This symbol is used when the pilot has a bearing on a fixed object or a depth sounding *(page 129)* to combine with his projected course line. An EP is more reliable than a DR position, but is still about half guess.

1040 FIX
R FIX

An encircled dot marks a fix, a location confirmed by passing near a charted mark such as a buoy, or by taking nearly simultaneous bearings on two or more fixed objects *(below)*. The location is marked with FIX and the time. R FIX means running fix, a position derived from two bearings taken at different times.

0945 RDF FIX
RAD FIX

The navigator employs a triangle around a dot to indicate a fix based on information from electronic navigational aids *(pages 124-141)*. Each triangle is labeled to indicate both the time of the fix and the instrument used. For example, RDF FIX stands for a fix from a radio direction finder. RAD FIX means radar fix.

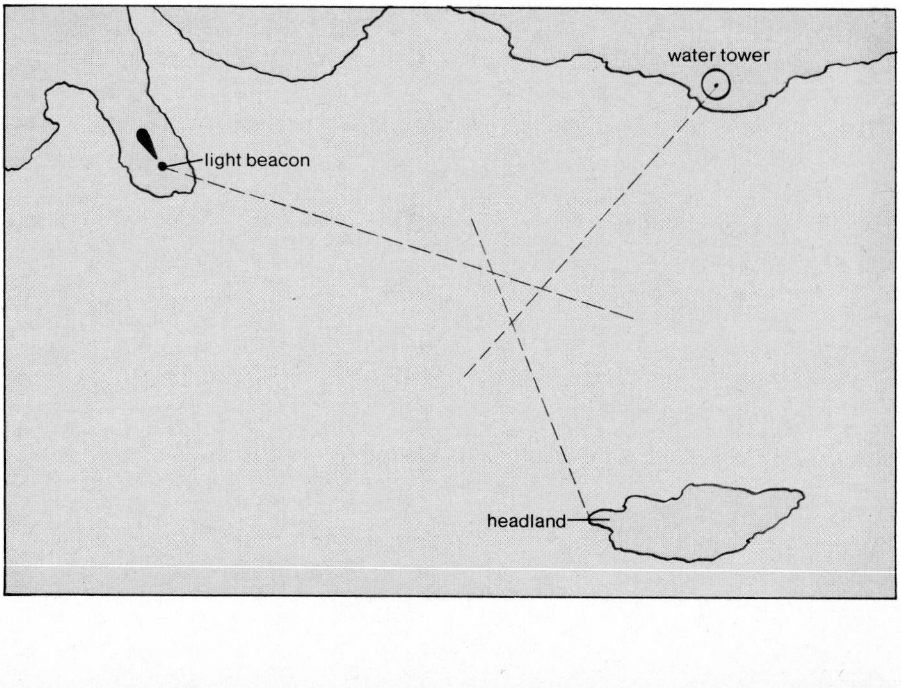

The most reliable way to determine a boat's location is by making a three-way fix (right). To make one, the boatman takes bearings on three charted objects; they should be widely separated so as to keep their bearing lines from crossing at an angle of less than 60°—but not more than 120°. Theoretically these three lines should all meet at a single point. In practice, slight errors in observation cause the lines to form a triangle, known to navigators as a cocked hat. But the boatman knows he is somewhere within the triangle, and as long as the triangle is small, the fix is usually close enough for his purposes.

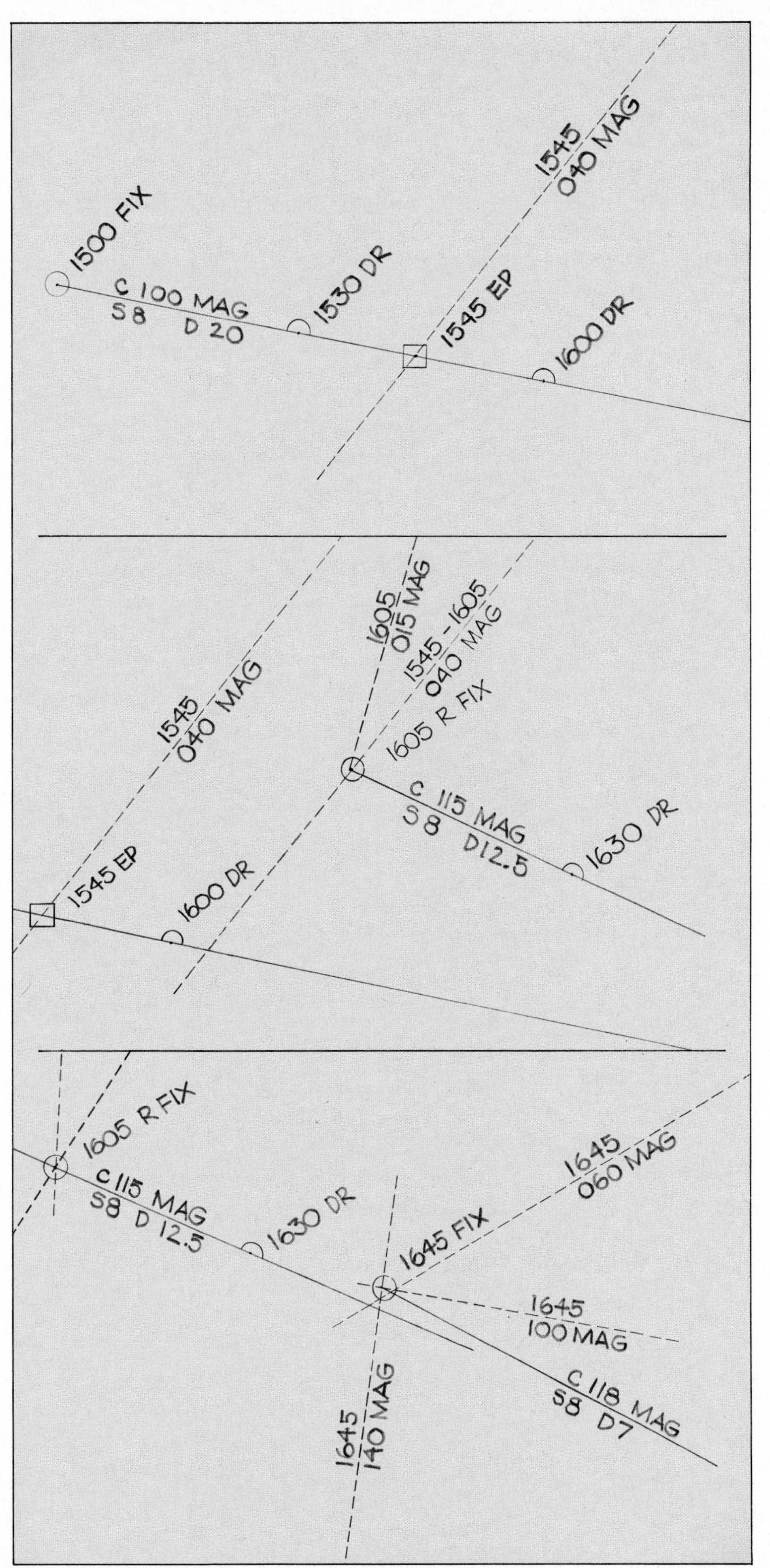

In compiling his shorthand record of a voyage, the navigator always begins with a fix. Fix data are usually written roughly perpendicular to the course line, while course data are written parallel to it. This skipper starts off at 1500 (3 p.m.), planning to go 20 miles at eight knots on a 100° course. He marks as DR positions his predicted locations for one half hour and one hour later. At 1545, he takes a bearing on a fixed, charted object, draws a dashed bearing line and labels it with time and direction. Knowing his boat is on this line, he marks its intersection with his course line as an estimated position.

At 1605, the skipper "advances" the 1545 bearing by marking off on the course line his reckoning of the distance covered in 20 minutes, then drawing a dashed line parallel to the 1545 bearing and labeling it with two time entries (1545-1605). At the same time, he takes a second bearing on the object that gave him the EP above. The intersection of this dashed line and the one representing his advanced bearing is labeled as a running fix. From this fix (which shows he is well off course), he draws a new course line to his destination—115° at eight knots for 12.5 miles—and predicts his position at 1630.

At 1645, 40 minutes after his running fix, the boatman sights three charted landmarks. He takes a bearing on each of them and draws on his chart the corresponding dashed bearing lines. He enters the resulting cocked hat as a fix; like the running fix above, it falls to one side of his plotted course line. Again, the navigator revises his course line. Beginning at his new fix, he plots a course of 118° for the seven miles remaining to his destination. He will continue to plot his position and make course adjustments that will bring him closer to his journey's safe end.

A Masterly Plot

A master navigator who can plot a proper course through multiple hazards can be as valuable to a boat as its helmsman. Shown on the chart at right is a portion of such a plot, which was compiled by navigation consultant Halsey Herreshoff one foggy summer morning as he cruised along the Maine coast.

Navigator Herreshoff first plotted a dead-reckoning course toward Flint Island, south of his anchorage in Pleasant Bay, then weighed anchor at 0945 and set out at a steady six knots.

A glimpse of the red beacon south of Norton Island through a rift in the fog at 0959 gave him a reassuring estimated position, and when at 1004 Flint Island loomed through the mist, bearings on its northern and eastern tips gave him a fix. The fog was lifting now, but in these waters morning fogs are notoriously unpredictable. Anxious, among all the rocks, to keep a constant check on his position, the skipper continued to plot every change of heading. He sprinkled his course lines with dead-reckoning positions and tested these assumptions as often as he could.

A fix at 1041 showed that he had been set, or swept off course, by a tidal current out of Western Bay. Beset again by fog and lacking a fixed visible object on which to take a bearing, he relied on a depth sounding at 1052 for an estimated position. For half an hour or so he motored east, holding closely to his plotted course, then turned 22° north. During the next hour, a string of islands off to port, glimpsed through breaks in the fog, gave him a running check on his position.

By noon the sun had burned off the fog and a fix at 1232 showed that he had been set by another tidal current. His next objective as he headed north was a clearly visible gong buoy, but midway to it, as a routine precaution, he took a bearing and noted an estimated position. From the buoy, the skipper proceeded by line of sight on up the coast (and off the chart). On the following pages are step-by-step illustrations and explanations of how an experienced pilot creates a course plot like this one, as he moves along.

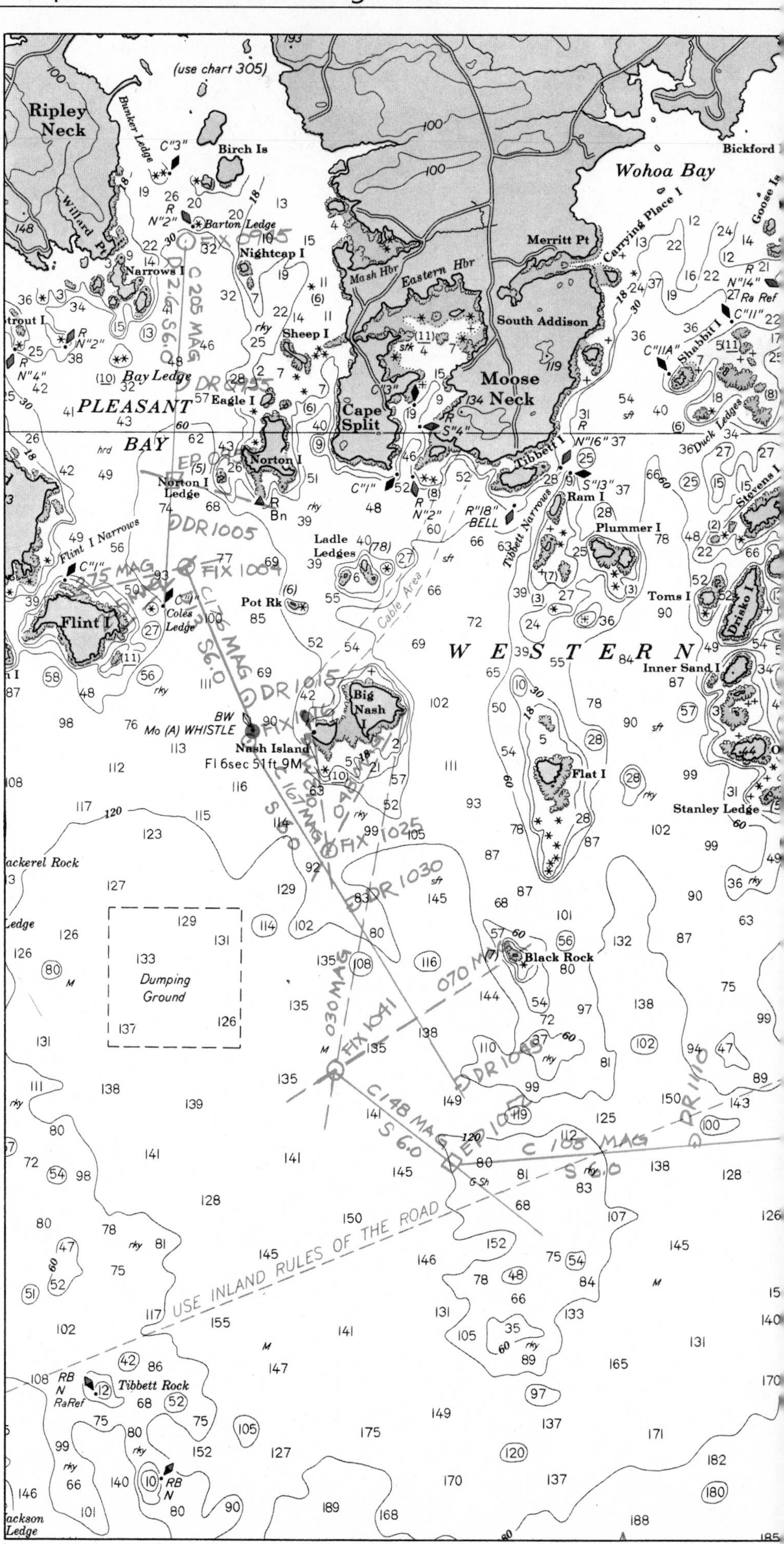

On the chart at right, the course through the myriad rocky islands off the Maine coast has been marked with a blue tint for greater legibility, though in practice the navigator would have made all of his notations with a black pencil that was easily erasable.

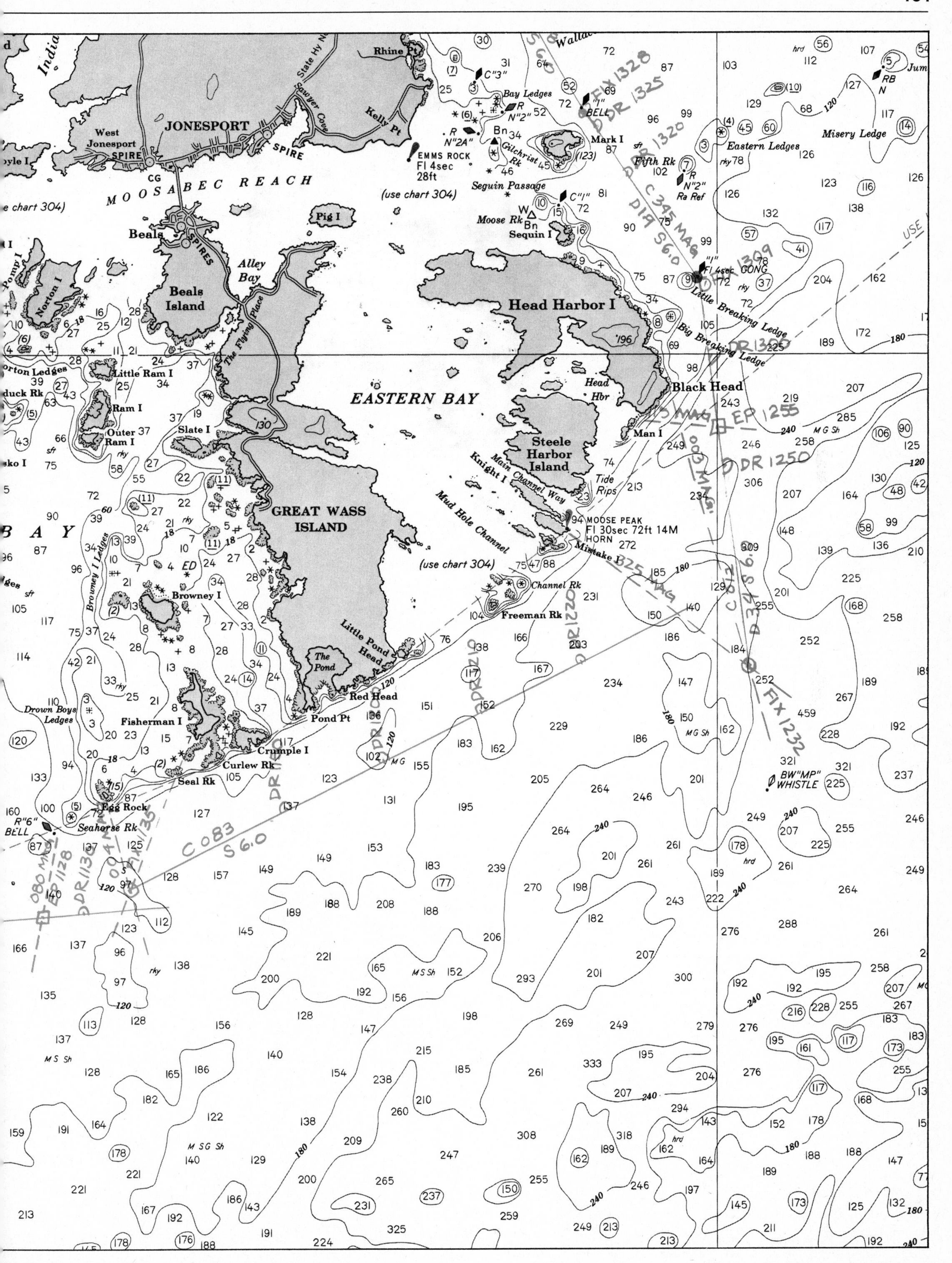
JONESPORT
West Jonesport
SPIRE
CG
MOOSABEC REACH
(use chart 304)
Beals
SPIRES
Beals Island
Alley Bay
The Flying Place
Pig I
Norton I
Little Ram I
Ram I
Outer Ram I
Slate I
EASTERN BAY
GREAT WASS ISLAND
Browney I
Browney I Ledges
Drown Boys Ledges
Fisherman I
Crumple I
Curlew Rk
Seal Rk
Egg Rock
Seahorse Rk
R"6" BELL
The Pond
Little Pond Head
Red Head
Pond Pt
Rhine Pt
Sawyer Cove
Kelly Pt
State Hy No
Bay Ledges
EMMS ROCK
Fl 4sec 28ft
Gilchrist Rk
Seguin Passage
Moose Rk
Sequin I
Mark I
Fifth Rk
Eastern Ledges
Misery Ledge
Head Harbor I
Head Hbr
Steele Harbor Island
Black Head
Man I
Little Breaking Ledge
Big Breaking Ledge
Knight I
Main Channel Way
Mud Hole Channel
Tide Rips
MOOSE PEAK
Fl 30sec 72ft 14M
HORN
Mistake I
Channel Rk
Freeman Rk
BW"MP" WHISTLE
"1" Fl 4sec GONG
"1" BELL
FIX 1328
DR 1325
DR 1320
C 345 MAG
DIA S6.0
DR 1309
DR 1300
EP 1255
DR 1250
FIX 1232
C 083
S6.0
EP 1128
FIX 1135

4

Before taking his boat out on a trip, especially in unfamiliar waters, a thoughtful skipper should always set aside time to ponder his course. Like the pilot of the sport fisherman at left, he may be planning no more than a 30-mile afternoon spin around Key Biscayne. Or he may be contemplating a week's cruise on the Great Lakes or along the Pacific Coast. In any case, he should consider the nature of the waters he will pass through and estimate his probable travel time; also, he should determine what navigation aids will help him on his way and how he will deal with tidal conditions or other special cruising problems he may encounter. Navigating foresight is as important

PILOTING POINT-TO-POINT

to sound boating as is checking out an engine or bringing proper safety gear.

A pilot who does his homework, and makes careful use of his findings, usually collects as dividends a safe, relatively easy trip—and the fun of exercising his piloting skills. But by failing to anticipate possible hazards, or by failing to apply the information on his chart or within his field of vision, he can easily curtail not only the pleasure of the cruise but the cruise itself. Recently, a $150,000 brand-new 48-foot cruiser fitted out with everything available for pinpoint, all-weather navigation—compass, chronometer, depth finder (or echo sounder), radar and loran—came to grinding grief in Long Island Sound because the skipper failed to read his chart and to keep an eye out ahead. Steering around the wrong side of a buoy, he hit a reef that sheared off both rudders, both struts, both shafts and both propellers.

The pilot of the sport fisherman shown on these pages, however, has made his preparations before leaving the pier: he has studied a chart of the area, chosen a route, and made mental notes of navigation aids and possible hazards. As shown on the map on the next two pages and in the photographs and chart sections that follow, his course takes him across Biscayne Bay, through a narrow channel between coral reefs, around a lighthouse, along the edge of a huge sand bar and back through a busy shipping lane to Miami.

He notes from the chart that for most of the way his path will be marked by buoys and beacons. A number of landmarks on shore may also help to keep him oriented. He makes a preliminary decision on how he will use these resources. For most of the trip he will be piloting from one point to another by line-of-sight navigation and by taking soundings. In stretches of more open water, where reference points are not always immediately visible, he will engage in a couple of dead-reckoning exercises, calculating the direction—and probable travel time—from his last accurately determined position to a further point marked on the chart but beyond his line of sight. Here and there he will use his depth finder to keep from straying into shallows, or even as a means of fixing his position.

Throughout the trip he will supplement the chart's general guidance by keeping a sharp lookout. His chart, though meticulously prepared and conscientiously updated by the National Oceanic and Atmospheric Administration, will not tell him the exact water depth in an area where dredged material is being dumped or the extent to which last week's storm shifted a sand bar.

Such close attention to the water and to his charts is not mere fussbudgeting. During his circumnavigation of Key Biscayne, the pilot of the sport fisherman will be operating on a sparkling afternoon under near-perfect conditions. If he makes a mistake, he will have time to stop and correct it. Still, he executes every maneuver with utmost precision, not only from a sense of seamanly pride, but also to prepare himself for rougher days. In fog or stormy weather, a pilot's calculations must be quick and unfailing, and may spell the difference between making port safely or not at all.

The sport fisherman rounds the first mark on the cruise: a black can marked "1," which the skipper properly leaves to starboard (page 50) as he heads out from the Miami River.

Blueprint for a Short Cruise

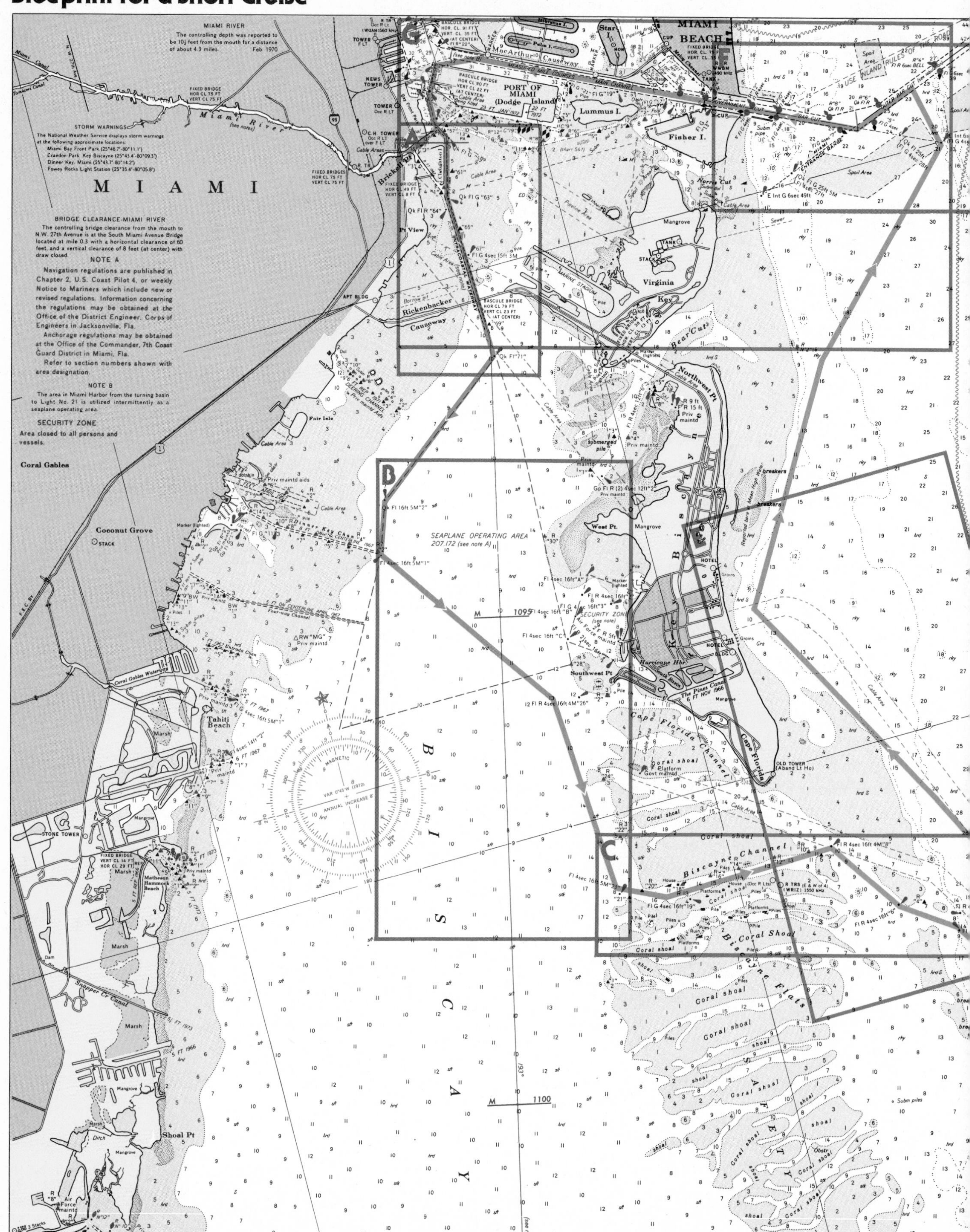

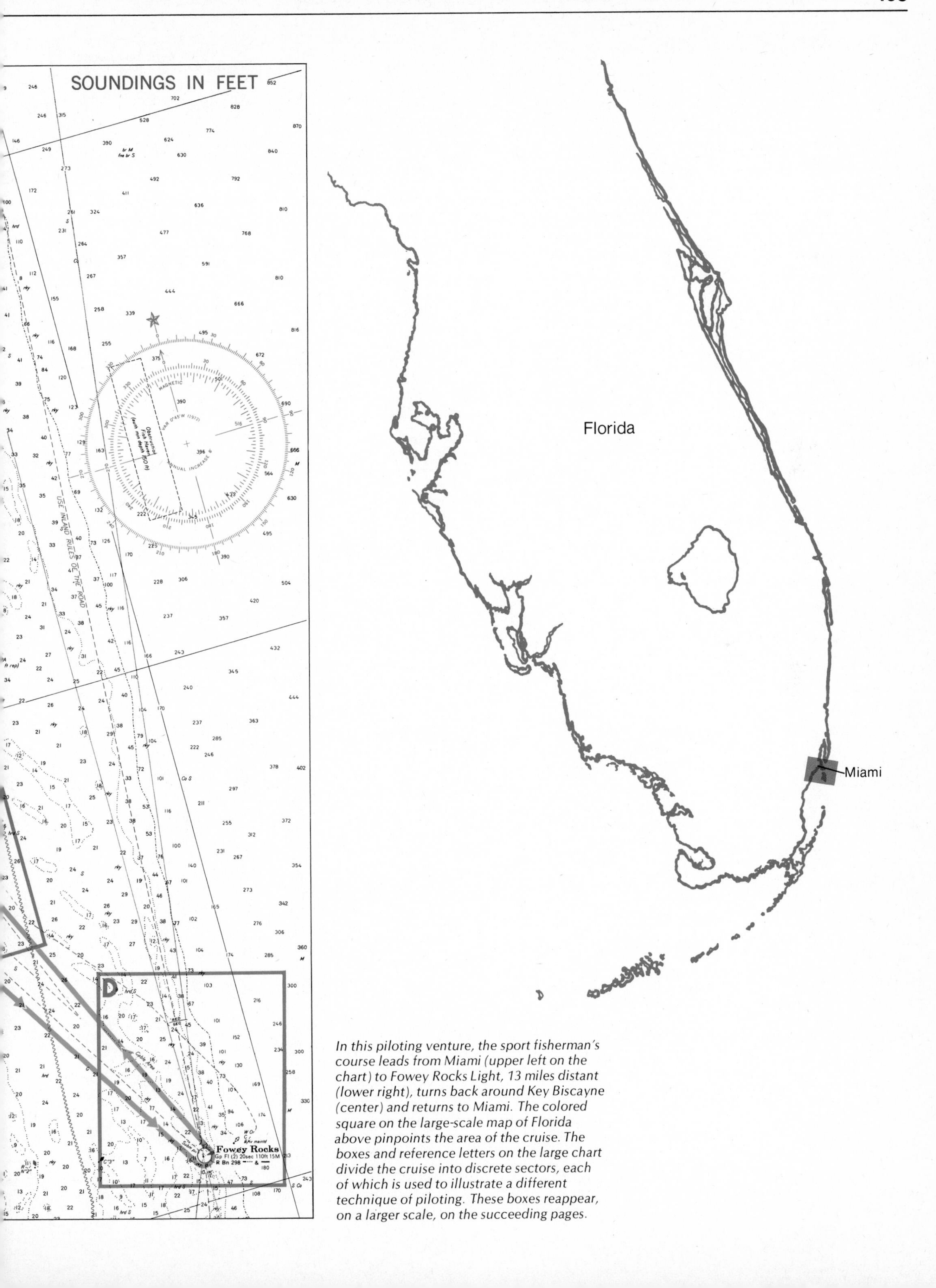

In this piloting venture, the sport fisherman's course leads from Miami (upper left on the chart) to Fowey Rocks Light, 13 miles distant (lower right), turns back around Key Biscayne (center) and returns to Miami. The colored square on the large-scale map of Florida above pinpoints the area of the cruise. The boxes and reference letters on the large chart divide the cruise into discrete sectors, each of which is used to illustrate a different technique of piloting. These boxes reappear, on a larger scale, on the succeeding pages.

First Leg of the Journey

After leaving its pier at the mouth of the Miami River, the sport fisherman making the short Florida cruise shown on these pages rounds triangular Claughton Island and enters the channel of the Intracoastal Waterway, or ICW.

In the top photograph on the opposite page, the boat is passing the spot indicated by the large figure 1 on Sector A of the chart *(right)*. Throughout this part of the journey, and until he enters the more open waters of Biscayne Bay, the pilot is guided by a series of aids to navigation lining the sides of this straight and narrow channel. As everywhere else along the ICW, the red-colored and even-numbered aids should be left to the starboard side of a boat traveling south, as here, or west. Odd-numbered and black are left to port. A part of each aid is painted yellow to show that the channel is a part of the ICW.

The channel here is kept dredged to a minimum depth—known as a controlling depth—of seven feet, and the pilot must take care to keep within the boundaries delineated by the beacons. He knows that his boat draws nearly three feet, and the numbers on the chart indicating depth in feet tell him that there are many shallower spots outside the channel.

Continuing on its southward course, the sport fisherman arrives at the point designated by the large figure 2 on the chart. Here a causeway crosses the ICW by way of the bascule bridge (a drawbridge with two counterweighted spans) shown in the lower photograph on the opposite page. The chart tells the pilot that when the bridge is closed it has a high-water vertical clearance of 23 feet. A large yellow sign on the bridge informs him that clearance is 25 feet at low tide.

If his boat carried a mast too tall to clear the bridge, he would stop short of the bridge and signal by three blasts of a horn or whistle for the bridge to be raised. However, it is illegal to request the raising of a drawbridge for a boat whose profile can be lowered enough to clear. And since this boat can clear simply by lowering its outriggers, the skipper dips them and powers through.

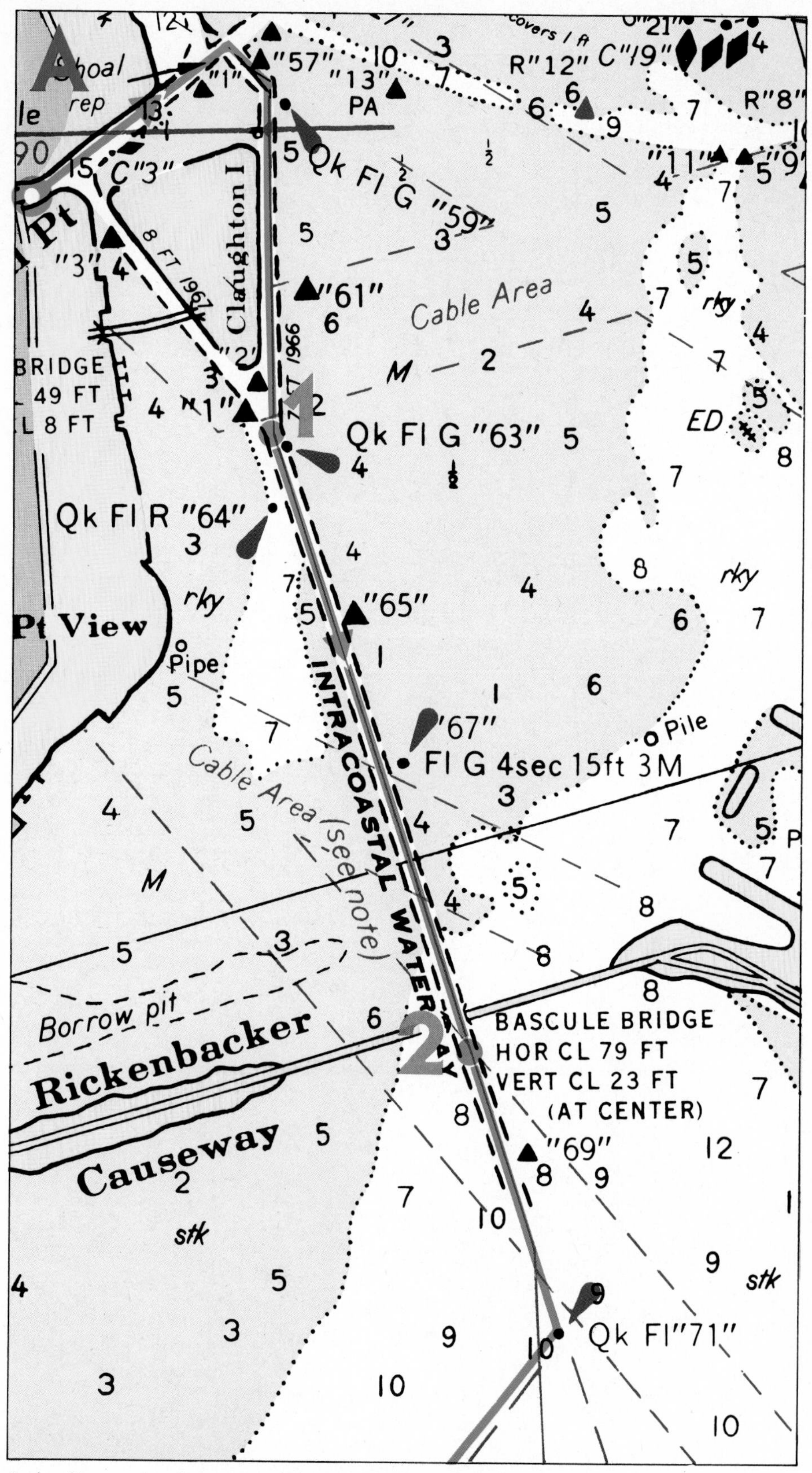

Broken lines on the chart segment above show the portion of the ICW traversed by the sport fisherman on the first leg of its voyage. The heavy green line traces the boat's course. Other information shown on the chart—and important to the pilot—includes the navigation aids marking the channel, landmarks such as bridges and prominent buildings, the depth of the ICW channel, and the horizontal and vertical clearances of the bascule bridge at figure 2. Motoring straight along this well-marked channel, the pilot can navigate visually, with no need to plot a prior course line.

1 As the powerboat churns south along the ICW channel, the skipper leaves to port the square-shaped beacon—called a daymark—that is black and odd-numbered. To his right is a small red buoy, temporarily replacing a beacon that is under repair. The yellow paint on the navigation aids identifies them as part of the Intracoastal system.

2 With outriggers lowered, the boat skims beneath the bascule bridge marked on the chart segment at left. The skipper of any sizable boat should consider before starting a trip whether he will encounter drawbridges that must be raised for his vessel. If so, he should consult the Coast Pilot as to whether there are hours during which the bridge cannot be raised for water traffic.

Plotting a dead-reckoning course, the pilot uses his parallel rules as a straight edge to draw a line on his chart from his departure position to his intended destination. Being careful to keep the rules aligned with this course, he then walks them over to the compass rose on the chart and reads that the compass heading of this course is 232° magnetic. He writes this figure, for future reference, alongside the course line, then steers his boat as close to 232° as possible.

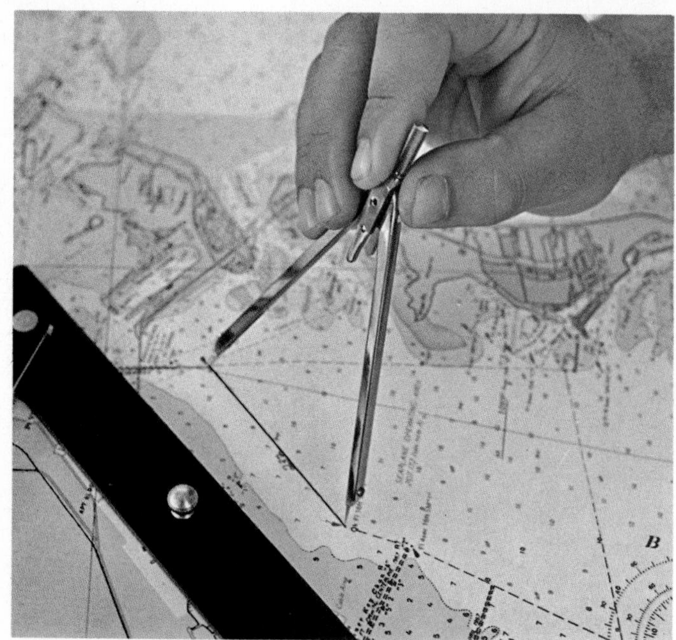

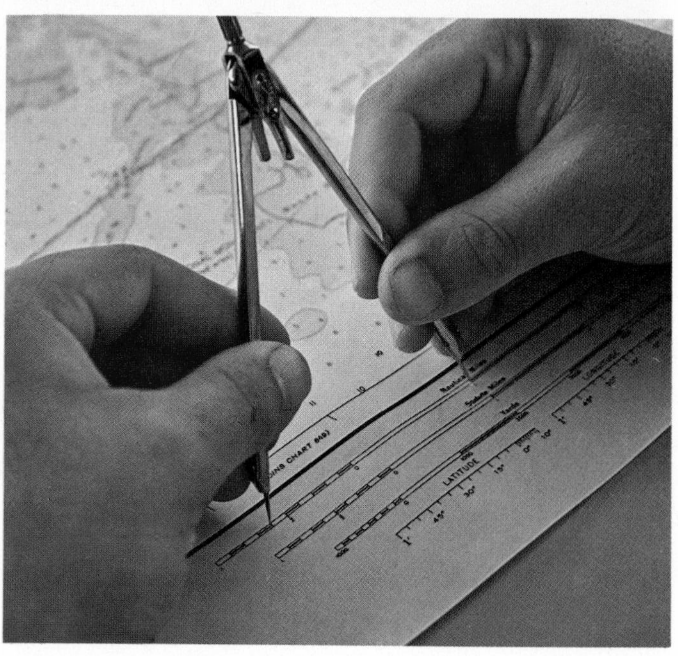

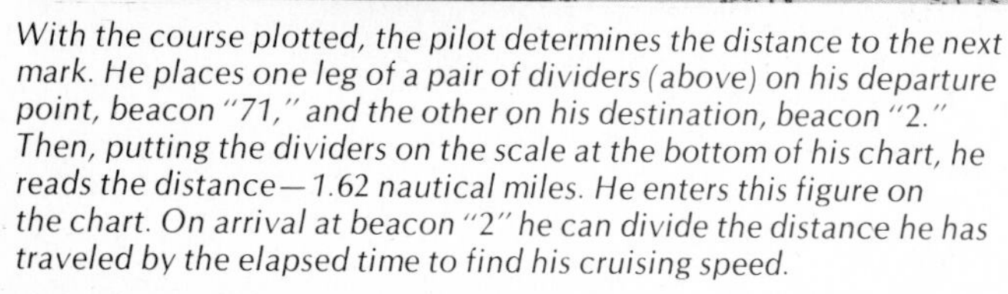

With the course plotted, the pilot determines the distance to the next mark. He places one leg of a pair of dividers (above) on his departure point, beacon "71," and the other on his destination, beacon "2." Then, putting the dividers on the scale at the bottom of his chart, he reads the distance—1.62 nautical miles. He enters this figure on the chart. On arrival at beacon "2" he can divide the distance he has traveled by the elapsed time to find his cruising speed.

Dead Reckoning

Leaving the Intracoastal Waterway sector shown on the chart on page 106 the sport fisherman's skipper is preparing to make a short run across Biscayne Bay, then around Fowey Rocks *(pages 114-115)* and home again. Before moving out where navigation aids may be spaced too widely for line-of-sight piloting, he plots a course, using the centuries-old technique called dead reckoning, or DR for short.

The objective of this leg of the trip is to get from beacon "71," shown at right, near the southern end of the ICW channel to beacon "2" *(chart, page 111)*, farther to the southwest. With a soft pencil—for easy erasure later—he draws a straight line on his chart from "71" to "2." Then using his parallel rules *(top left)*, he determines his compass heading for this course. Next he takes a measurement on the chart *(bottom left)* to find the distance between beacons. He enters both figures along the course line on his chart.

With the DR course set, the pilot notes that his departure time from beacon "71" is 12:45 p.m., or 1245 hours on the 24-hour clock used in navigation. He adds this figure to the distance and direction data he has written on the chart, and revs up the boat to a comfortable cruising speed. At this point, his tachometer—which shows the number of revolutions his engine makes per minute—reads 3,100 rpm's. Though his boat lacks a speedometer, like any careful skipper he has established from previous calibration tests *(pages 92-93)* that at those rpm's, under average conditions of wind and weather, he will be moving at about 25 knots. By keeping a close eye on his tachometer, he can try to hold a steady pace and arrive at the destination at a calculated time.

In common practice, however, winds, currents, imperfect steering and compass deviation will inevitably deflect a boat from the exact course line penciled on the chart; and the longer the run, the greater the deflection. But on the brief trip from "71" to "2," theory and practice coincide. There is almost no current here; the wind is negligible; and the distance is so short that minor steering errors have no significant effect. Within a few moments of leaving beacon "71," the pilot can see and identify beacon "2." He steers straight to it and arrives at nearly 1249 hours, having covered the 1.62 nautical miles in 3 minutes 50 seconds. By dividing the distance by the time, he can confirm that his boat is holding its speed of about 25 knots. With these data, he confidently begins the next leg of his voyage.

As he leaves "71" on his new heading of 232°, the skipper notes that the time of departure is 12:45 p.m. and enters it on his chart. He will also note on the chart the time of his arrival at beacon "2."

The tachometer on the dashboard counts the engine's rpm's, in this case 3,100. By regularly checking his tachometer, the pilot can keep his engine running steadily.

1 By lining up two fixed objects, such as the two beacons above—both are identified on the chart—a pilot gets what is called a range; that is, he knows he must be along a line running through the two objects. To find out where, he notes the intersection of this line with his boat's course line; his position is at the point of intersection.

2 A reading of 10 feet on the depth finder at right confirms the sport fisherman is at large figure 2 on the chart opposite. Many boatmen use depth finders in this manner, as navigation aids to check depths en route against the chart's notation of bottom depths along their course line. Depth finders also warn of potentially dangerous shoals, such as the one shown opposite on the chart of Sector B of the Biscayne Bay voyage.

Two Checks on Position

Passing beacon "2" *(upper left corner of chart),* the sport fisherman turns toward "1," clearly visible half a mile or so to the south. While a shipmate steers toward this next point, the navigator plots a new and slightly more complicated DR course for the third leg of his short trip off Miami.

He intends to go from beacon "1" to beacon "23" at lower right in the chart, but as an exercise in piloting he decides to verify his position en route. To do so he divides the leg into two roughly equidistant parts, each with a different course heading. For the first part, he picks a heading that will bring him to a spot—large figure 1 on the chart at right—just offshore, from which he can visually line up two aids to navigation, as shown in the corresponding photograph at left.

Before arriving at this spot, the pilot draws a line to it on his chart from beacon "1." By using parallel rules, compass rose and dividers *(page 108),* he determines that his chosen spot is about two nautical miles from beacon "1" on a course of 145° magnetic, and notes these facts on the chart. As the boat rounds beacon "1" and sets off on the new course, the pilot records the time of departure as 1300. He then draws a line *(heavy broken line on chart)* that passes through the two beacons near his checkpoint and intersects his course line at large figure 1. From the point of intersection, he draws another line to beacon "23." He calculates this line as bearing 175° magnetic and the distance as 1.8 nautical miles.

Traveling at its predetermined cruising speed of about 25 knots, the boat arrives at figure 1 in just under five minutes. The pilot notes the time, looks to his left, and sees that the two beacons he has selected for his checkpoint line up like the sights on a rifle. Sailors refer to such an alignment of two charted objects as a range; and when a vessel establishes itself along a range, the craft is said to be on a line of position, or LOP. On this chart the LOP is the broken line that intersects with the boat's course, giving the pilot a so-called fix that pinpoints his position.

Noting on the chart the time of the fix, the pilot puts the boat on its new course of 175° and heads for beacon "23." Since the chart's sounding marks show that this new route skirts a shoal, the pilot switches on his depth finder *(left)* as a double check on the precision of the course he is steering. If the finder indicates depths of less than 10 feet, the skipper knows he is wandering from his proper course and must sheer off into safer water.

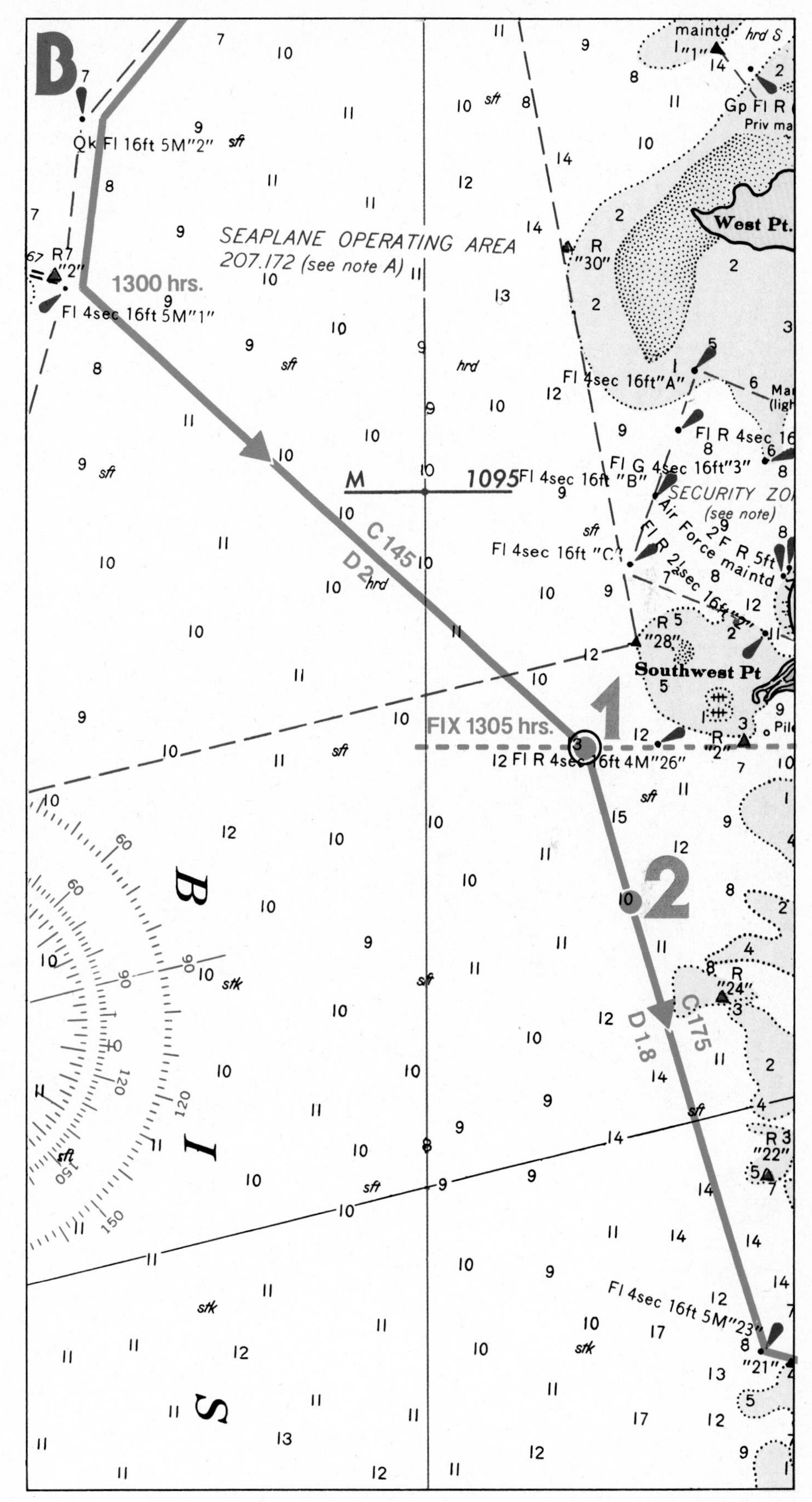

The dead-reckoning plot above is set down in boatman's shorthand (pages 98-99). Departure time from mark "1" is noted in the 24-hour system used by navigators. The course (C) is labeled according to its magnetic bearing. Distance (D) is in nautical miles; and a broken line indicates the line of position used in making a fix, with the time noted. A dot within a circle at large figure 1 marks the fix.

1 *Having passed beacon "23" at the end of his course (preceding page), the pilot enters Biscayne Channel (large figure 1 on the chart below). There he follows a trail of daymarks—here fixed on unlighted beacons—that outline the channel's northern edge. Since the boat is now heading seaward, the red daymarks are to port.*

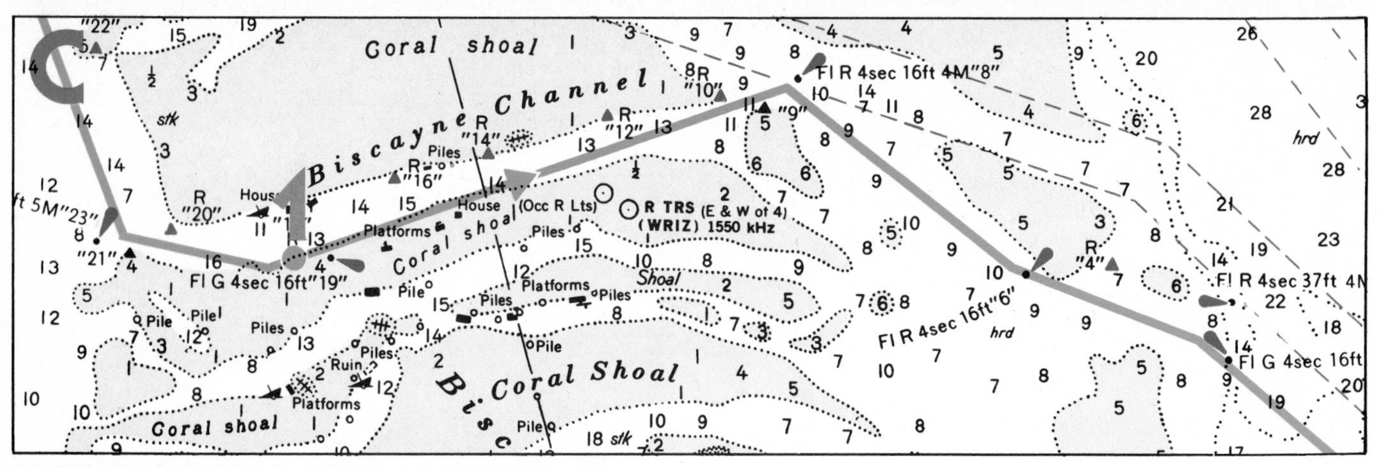

Consulting Sector C of the chart, the pilot recognizes the triangles he sees along his course (photograph at top) as the daymarks on the chart. Wrecks, pilings and houses on stilts are also indicated. But pilots should be alert for unexpected hazards; bottom contours change and new obstructions crop up oftener than do new charts.

Negotiating a Narrow Channel

As the pilot enters Biscayne Channel just past large figure 1, he notes lighter-colored waters off to port, indicating shoal water not far outside the string of red daymarks. By keeping a sharp eye out for such signs of danger, a boatman can run safely through channels that are less clearly marked than the one off Biscayne—though he should move at a cautious pace and keep his depth finder turned on.

Rounding the Far Turn

1 *Trailing a welter of spray, the sport fisherman rounds Fowey Rocks Light (large figure 1 on chart), the outermost limit of the trip. The light's tower, erected in 1876, is a favorite homing point for local boatmen; by night, its beam can be seen for 15 nautical miles in all directions. Also at Fowey Rocks is a radio beacon whose signal can be used by a boat's radio direction finder (page 130).*

2 *The sport fisherman leaves Fowey Rocks rapidly astern as the pilot and crew head back toward Miami. In order to double-check his course at this point (large figure 2 on the chart), the pilot can take a compass bearing directly astern; the light should bear 154°—exactly 180° from the course that is being steered.*

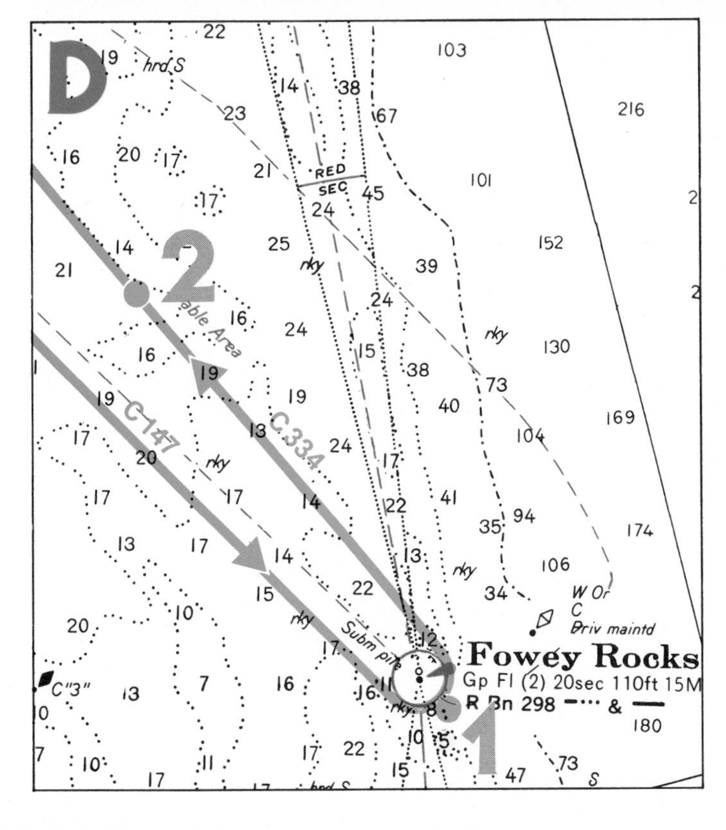

The pilot charts the course to Fowey Rocks (147° magnetic) and the homeward course (334°). Printed beneath the light's name is the key information on Fowey's characteristics. Translated, the abbreviations read: light flashes in groups of two every 20 seconds; the light, 110 feet over high water, is visible for 15 nautical miles; the frequency of the radio beacon is 298 kilohertz, broadcasting in Morse Code the letter B (dash-dot-dot-dot), plus an extended dash.

Doubling on Safety

Heading in from Fowey Rocks, the skipper sees that the dead-reckoning course he has plotted skirts a reef. To make sure he is far enough away from the reef, he computes his distance from a fixed object ashore— in this case, an abandoned lighthouse— by a technique called doubling the angle on the bow.

At large figure 1 on the chart, he takes a bearing on the lighthouse, using a hand bearing compass, a portable instrument whose face is bracketed by a sighting arrangement *(top, opposite)*. The lighthouse bears 20° west of his course of 334°. He marks this bearing *(broken line)* and the time, 1540, on his chart.

Continuing along his course, the pilot keeps checking the bearing of the lighthouse. When, at about 1544, the angle between his course and the lighthouse has doubled to 40°, he draws a second bearing on his chart. Where this second line intersects his course, he establishes a fix.

He knows from his first bearing that the interior angle at the south end of the triangle's base is 20°; the second bearing tells him the interior angle at the apex must be 140° (40° subtracted from the 180° of his straight-line course). Since the three interior angles of a triangle always add up to 180°, the other base angle must be 20°. If the base angles of a triangle are equal, its two sides are of equal length. Knowing his speed and the time elapsed, the pilot also knows that the distance from figure 1 to the fix is 1.5 nautical miles. He is, therefore, 1.5 miles off the light— enough to miss the reef.

Wishing to run close alongshore, the pilot now picks out a highly visible object on the shore ahead that will give him a bearing just skirting the shallow water. The most visible object is a large white hotel *(opposite, bottom)*, marked at the upper left corner of the chart segment. He draws a line from this fix to the hotel, and finds that its bearing is 330°. This line becomes his so-called danger bearing— so long as he stays outside it, he is safe. However, in these clear waters and in his shallow-draft boat, the pilot rightly decides (at large figure 2) that he can run along the danger bearing.

Just south of the first hotel is another hotel. By drawing a line through the second hotel, perpendicular to his course line, the pilot discovers that when the first hotel is dead ahead and the second exactly abeam he will have a fix at the point where he wants to change course again. When the moment arrives, he makes the fix and sets off on the new course.

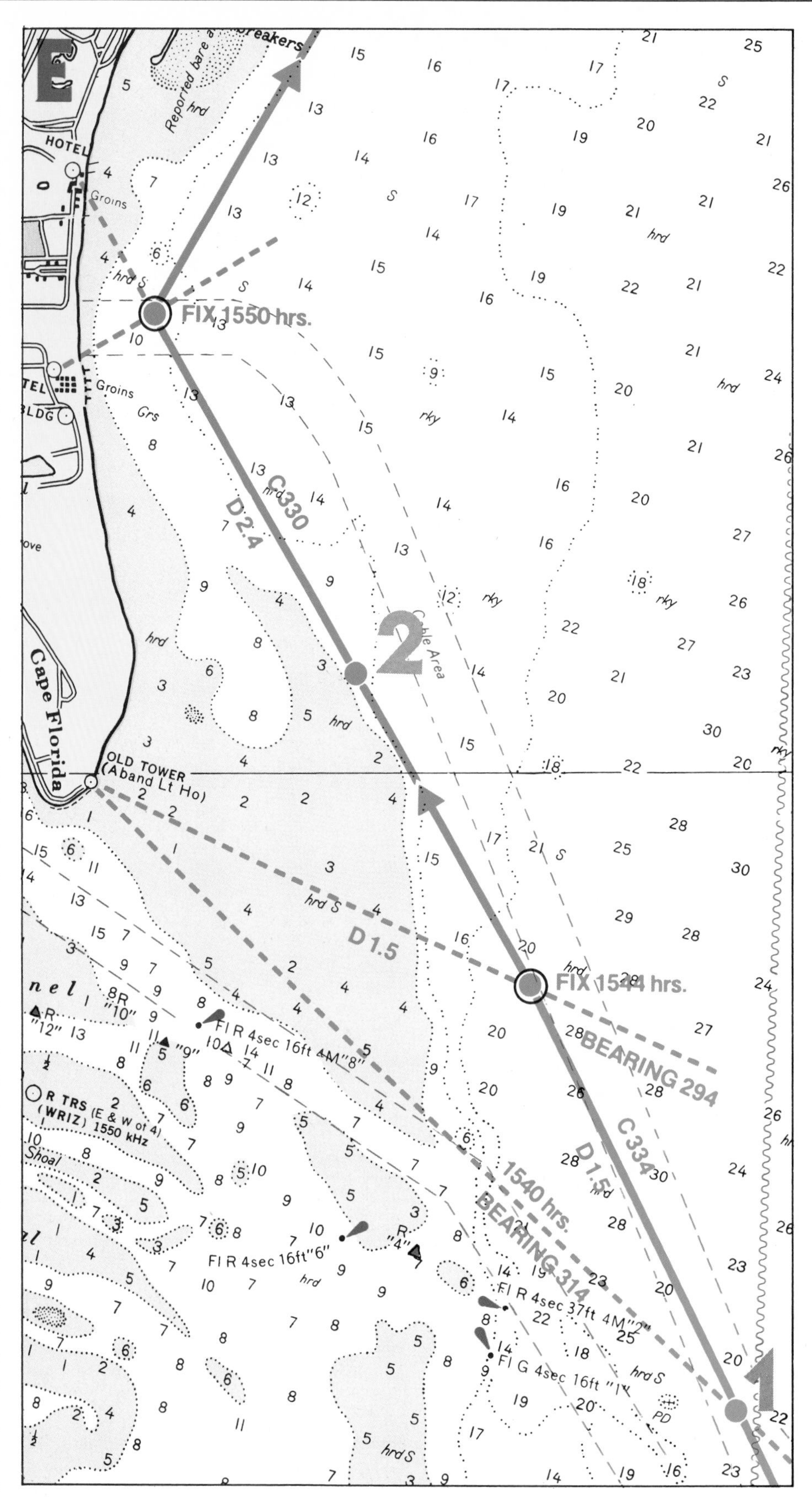

En route to Miami the skipper skirts a sand bar off Cape Florida, taking fixes to keep a safe distance away. He then heads for a hotel at top left on the chart, makes another fix and turns right to start his run up the coast.

1 Using a hand bearing compass, the pilot notes that from figure 1 on the chart the abandoned lighthouse bears 314° and that the time (right) is 1540. A hand bearing compass should be checked with the ship's compass to make sure the readings coincide, and should not be used on a steel boat because the deviation is variable.

2 The hotel shown here, seen from large figure 2 on the chart opposite, provides an excellent landmark on which to take a danger bearing and, later, to take another bearing for the fix at top left on the chart. Any large stationary object that is marked on a chart may be used for these purposes. Buoys should be shunned, if possible, as they have a tendency to shift position.

Having powered away from his last fix (preceding page), the pilot nears a passage between two spoil areas (where dredged material is dumped). In these spoil areas, bottom depth is kept at a minimum of 16 feet—but this information is not on his chart, nor is it available in other commonly published navigational guides. Since dumping often makes water too shallow for passage, the pilot avoids these sectors as he heads for the channel that leads to the Miami harbor.

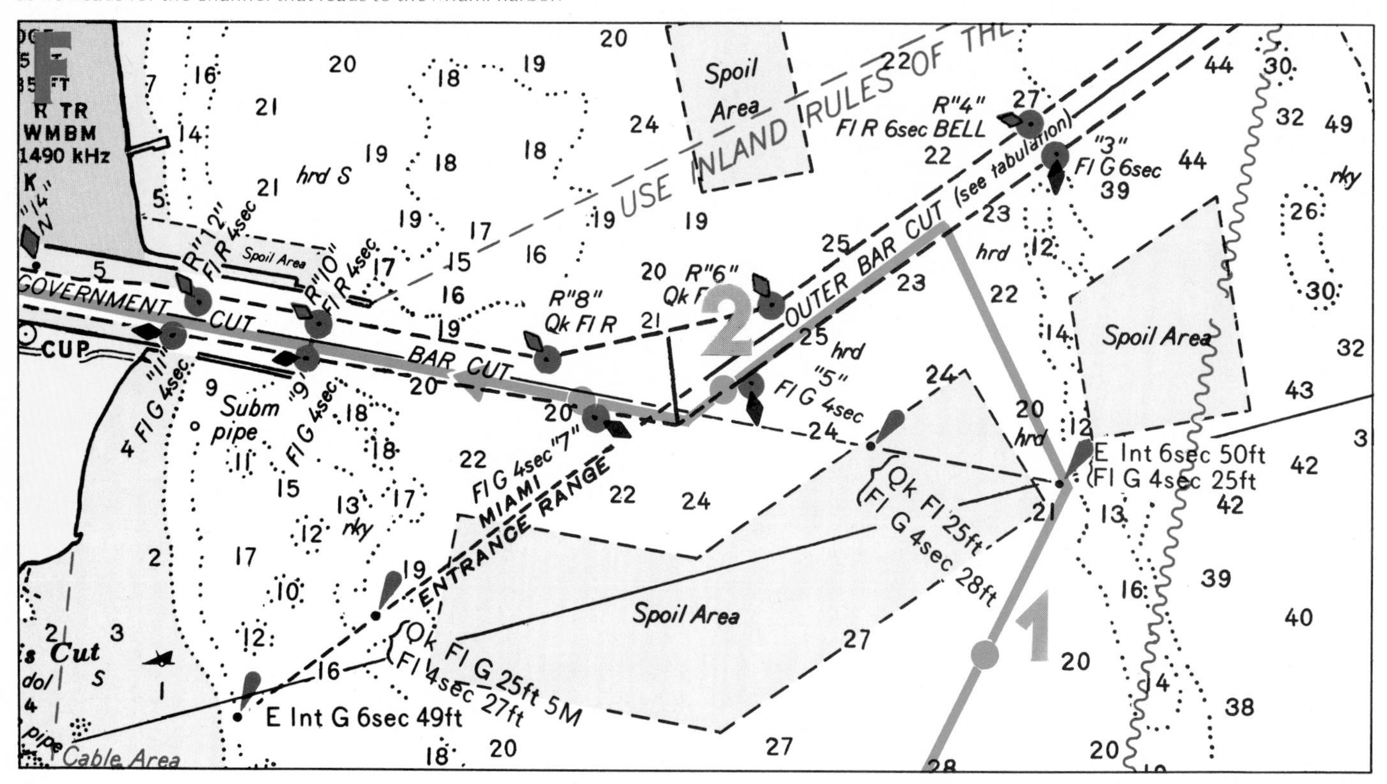

1 As he reaches large figure 1 on the chart, the pilot sees, just to his left, stakes rising from the water to mark one of the spoil areas, which he will avoid. The letters fixed onto the stakes are some of those in the words "Great Lakes," the name of the firm commissioned to dredge the channel.

2 *At this point the pilot has entered the Outer Bar Cut segment of the main channel by turning to port after crossing the sight line between buoy "5," shown here on his port hand, and buoy "3" to starboard. The sport fisherman is now at large figure 2 on the chart at left, properly leaving the black, odd-numbered buoy to port. The square shape at the top of the buoy is a radar reflector, which helps vessels to locate the mark during times when visibility is poor.*

On the final leg of the trip, the pilot, having skirted the spoil areas and entered the dredged channel of Outer Bar Cut, now prepares for the long, straight run through Bar Cut and Government Cut. To align himself properly in the channel, he will use the range located east of the bend where Bar Cut joins Outer Bar Cut.

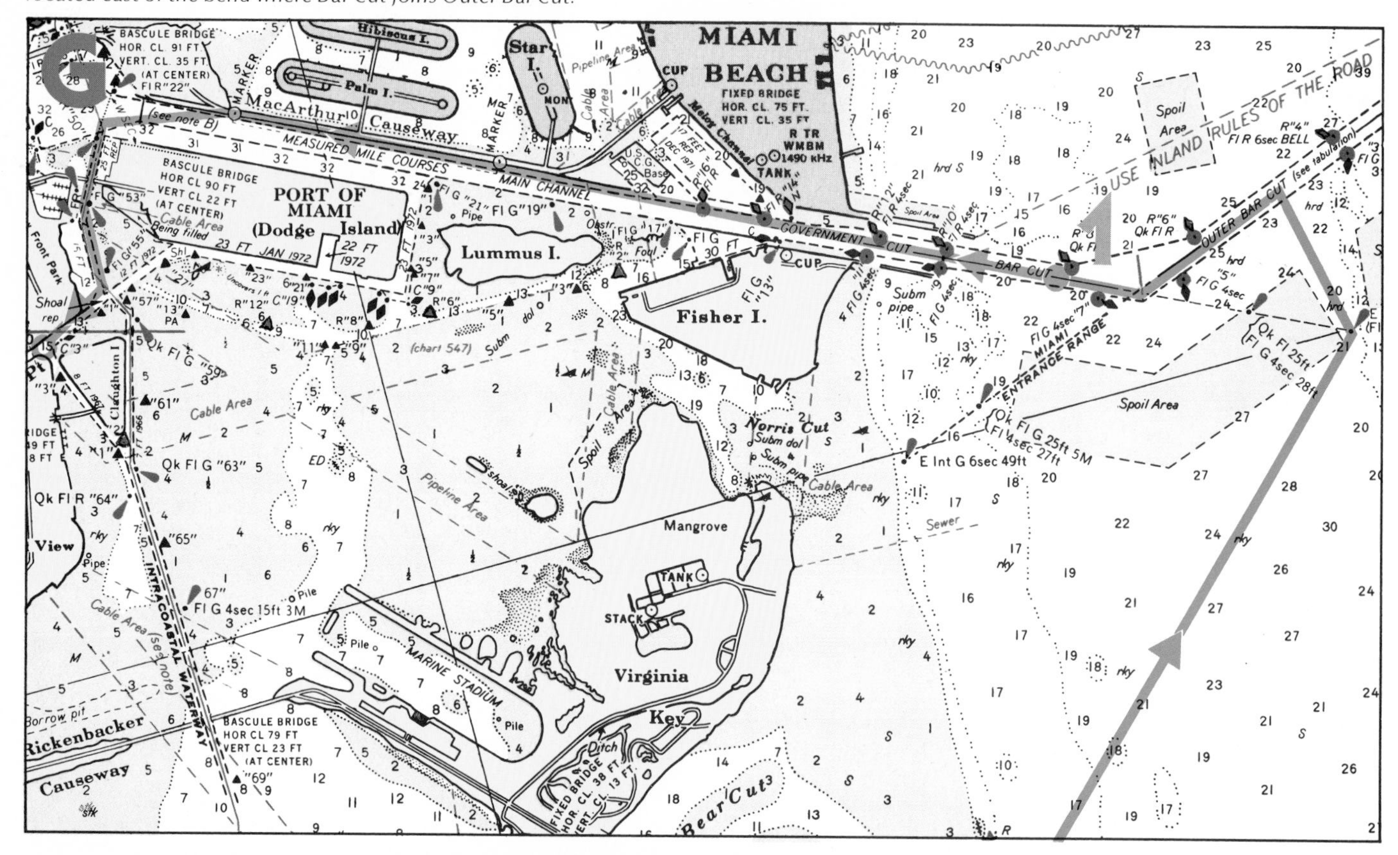

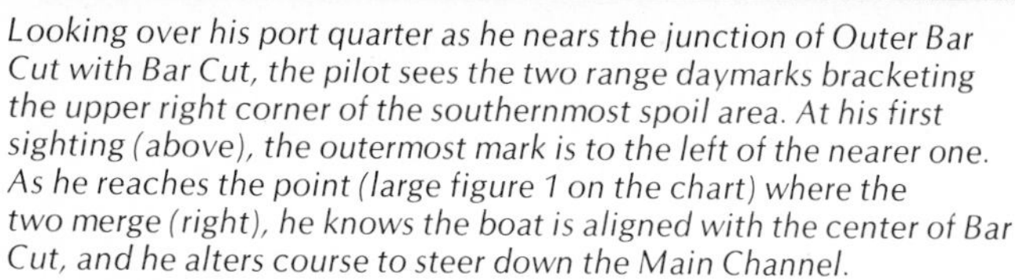

Looking over his port quarter as he nears the junction of Outer Bar Cut with Bar Cut, the pilot sees the two range daymarks bracketing the upper right corner of the southernmost spoil area. At his first sighting (above), the outermost mark is to the left of the nearer one. As he reaches the point (large figure 1 on the chart) where the two merge (right), he knows the boat is aligned with the center of Bar Cut, and he alters course to steer down the Main Channel.

Homing On the Range

1 *As the sport fisherman speeds toward Government Cut, the red-and-white-striped daymarks of the range are in line with his course, and dead astern. Later on, when darkness falls, the range will be distinguishable as flashing green lights projected down the line of the channel; the characteristics of these lights are marked on the chart. At the end of Government Cut, the skipper will turn around mark "50" (overleaf) and head back to the mouth of the Miami River.*

Last Lap

The skyline of Miami lies behind the cruise's last navigational checkpoint as the pilot heads for home. The mark is Intracoastal Waterway beacon "50," and its flashing red light and flanking triangular shapes signal the skipper that he should leave it to starboard.

FEET
FATHOMS
OFF
SENSITIVITY
0
10
20
30
40
50
RAY-DF 80
BFO
GAIN
TUNING
VOLUME
LONG ISLAND

5

THE BOATMAN'S MAGIC BOXES

Americans love gadgets. In their daily lives they are perhaps more attracted—and better served—by gadgetry than are any other people on earth. And United States boatmen are totally in tune with this national trait. When navigating lakes and rivers and ocean waters, especially at night and in bad weather, they call on an array of electrically powered boxes to see far beyond the limits of eyesight, to hear sounds past the range of the human ear and to pinpoint a boat's position on open water.

Of these seemingly magical boxes, the most commonly used is the depth finder, or echo sounder, which bounces sound waves off the bottom and translates the return signals into water depth—and in some cases even locates fish. Equally useful is the radio direction finder (or RDF). From distances of over 50 miles these simple receiving sets can indicate bearings on a network of Coast Guard-operated radio antennas whose locations are fixed on nautical charts. Omni (short for visual omnirange radio) is a more elaborate version of RDF equipment, transplanted to boats from aircraft cockpits. More accurate—and far more expensive—than ordinary RDF apparatus, omni picks up signals from radio beacons established for the use of aviators. On larger pleasure boats, radar listens for echoes of its own transmissions to pinpoint obstacles and to make accurate position fixes. Perhaps the most sophisticated of all the boxes is a special radio called loran (an acronym for long-range navigation) that can locate a vessel's position within a labyrinth of navigational hazards—or in the most open stretch of water.

All these devices except omni were developed to a level of practical application for military purposes during World War II. The principles of sonar, used by subchasers, are now at work in depth finders. Shipboard radar evolved from British ground radars used to intercept German aircraft.

After the war, electronic navigational aids were bulky and expensive, and thus limited to commercial vessels. In recent years, design advances—especially miniaturization—have put these electronic marvels well within the reach of many pleasure craft and their owners.

The effective use of these instruments, like the use of a compass and parallel ruler, must be keyed to nautical charts. Comparing echo-sounder readings with charted depth soundings, for example, can help identify a boat's position. The numbers appearing on the face of a loran set correspond to the numbered grid lines used for position fixes on loran charts. And RDF bearings on charted radio beacons provide lines of position.

Like all tools, even these sophisticated instruments have their limitations. During thunderstorms, for example, loran readings are difficult to make. RDF is unreliable at dawn and dusk when the sun interferes with radio waves, making accurate fixes almost impossible. Heavy rain, which bounces back radar impulses, appears on a radarscope as an opaque wall; and even on the clearest days, radar blips can be ambiguous. One man, thinking his boat was about to be crushed by what the radar showed to be a huge ship approaching from astern, rushed on deck with a life preserver to find that the threatening ship was actually a Navy blimp.

As a guide to the proper use of these sometimes puzzling gadgets, the following pages explain the functions and limitations of all the boatman's most familiar electronic boxes, from a simple depth finder costing about as much as a good camera to a sophisticated radar set whose price rivals that of a small automobile. By understanding them, and their occasional idiosyncrasies, a skipper can guide his boat safely through the most complex hazards over fog-shrouded or night-darkened waters.

The basic tools for electronic navigation include a radio direction finder, shown here on a chart table; a two-way radio on the bulkhead at right; and a depth finder affixed to a shelf.

The commonest depth-indicator box (below) is the flasher type, named for the quick-blinking neon lights that record depth on a clocklike face. The flashes show at two places on the face: at "0" for the outgoing pulse, and at the number corresponding to the water depth when the echo returns. The knob at lower left turns on the depth finder and adjusts its sensitivity to tune out any extraneous echoes. A switch at lower right sets it to read in feet or in fathoms.

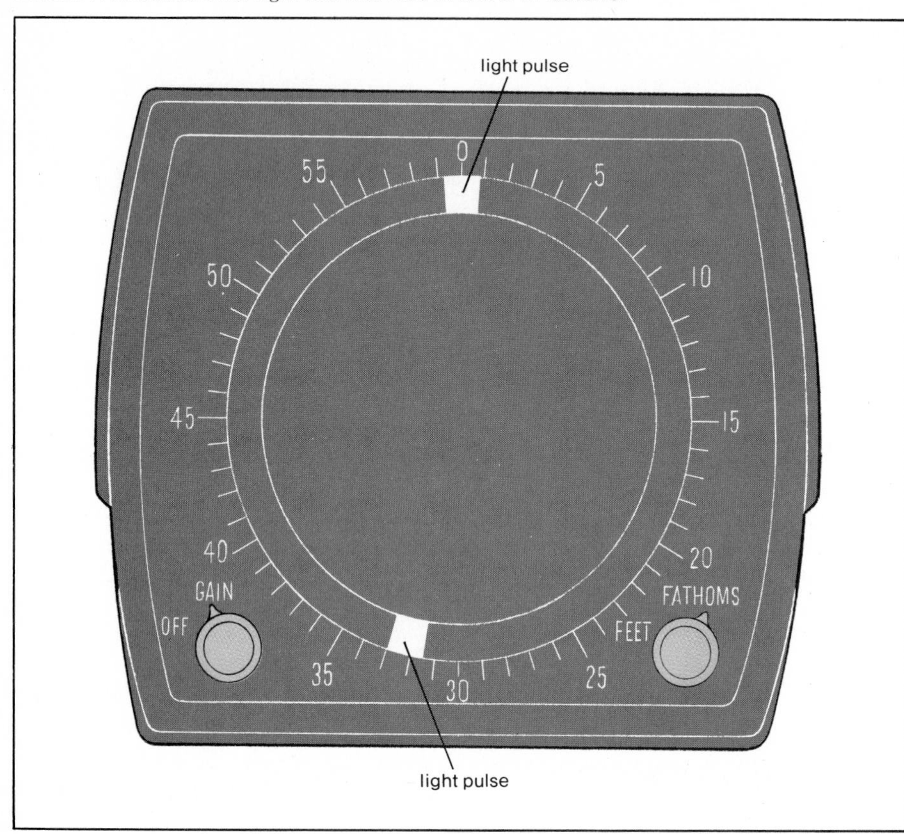

Sounding by Echo

Every skipper who cruises lakes, rivers or coastal waterways is nagged by the thought of running aground. For centuries the only defenses against this ignominy were a sharp eye and a lead line constantly wielded to take sounding on the water's depth. Nowadays, the lead line's job has been taken over by electronic sentinels called depth finders. As shown on this page, they come in different styles with different faces. But all depth finders function basically the same way: they measure the time a sound pulse takes to reach the bottom and return, and then convert the delay into a depth reading.

For sending and receiving the pulses, the echo sounder relies on a transducer *(below, left)*, which acts alternately as a loudspeaker and a microphone. It transmits as many as 20 ultrasonic pulses each second and picks up their echoes. Then a depth-indicator box *(left and below)* translates the time between transmission and echo reception into numerical readings of either feet or fathoms.

A skillful boatman can use an echo sounder in two additional ways: he can double-check his boat's position and navigate a course *(pages 128-129)* by following the bottom terrain; and if equipped with an ultrasensitive depth finder, he can even search out fish for his dinner.

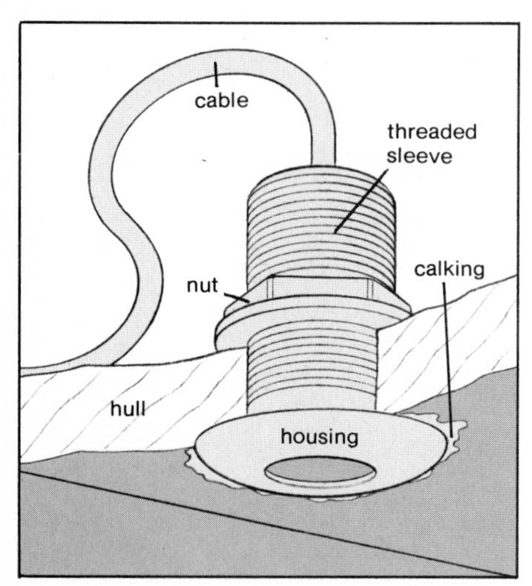

A conventional depth-finder transducer is contained in a threaded sleeve that is passed vertically through a boat's hull, calked and held tightly in place by a nut. The smoothly rounded exterior housing eliminates water turbulence—a source of false readings. The cable carries electrical impulses to this sender-receiver and back to the indicator box.

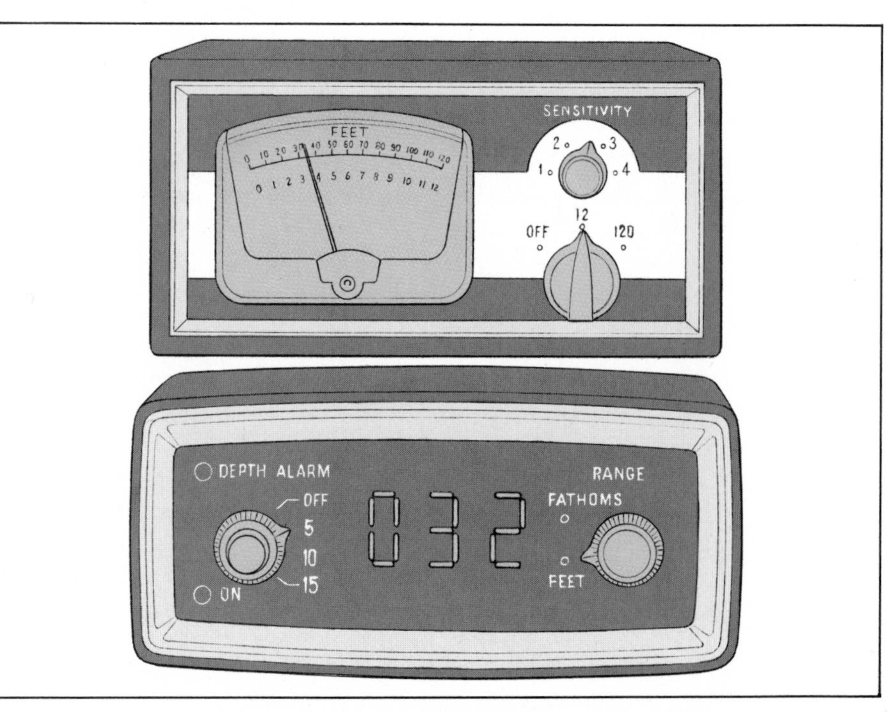

Echo sounders show depth either on a meter (top) or with lighted numbers (bottom). The meter gives accurate readings down to 12 feet —i.e., with the switch at 12; set at 120, it gives general readings to 120 feet. A sensitivity knob reduces irrelevant echoes. The digital model has a feet-fathom selector at right. At left is a base knob for an alarm that sounds when the depth reads less than a preset level; the inner knob is an on-off switch, and also adjusts brightness.

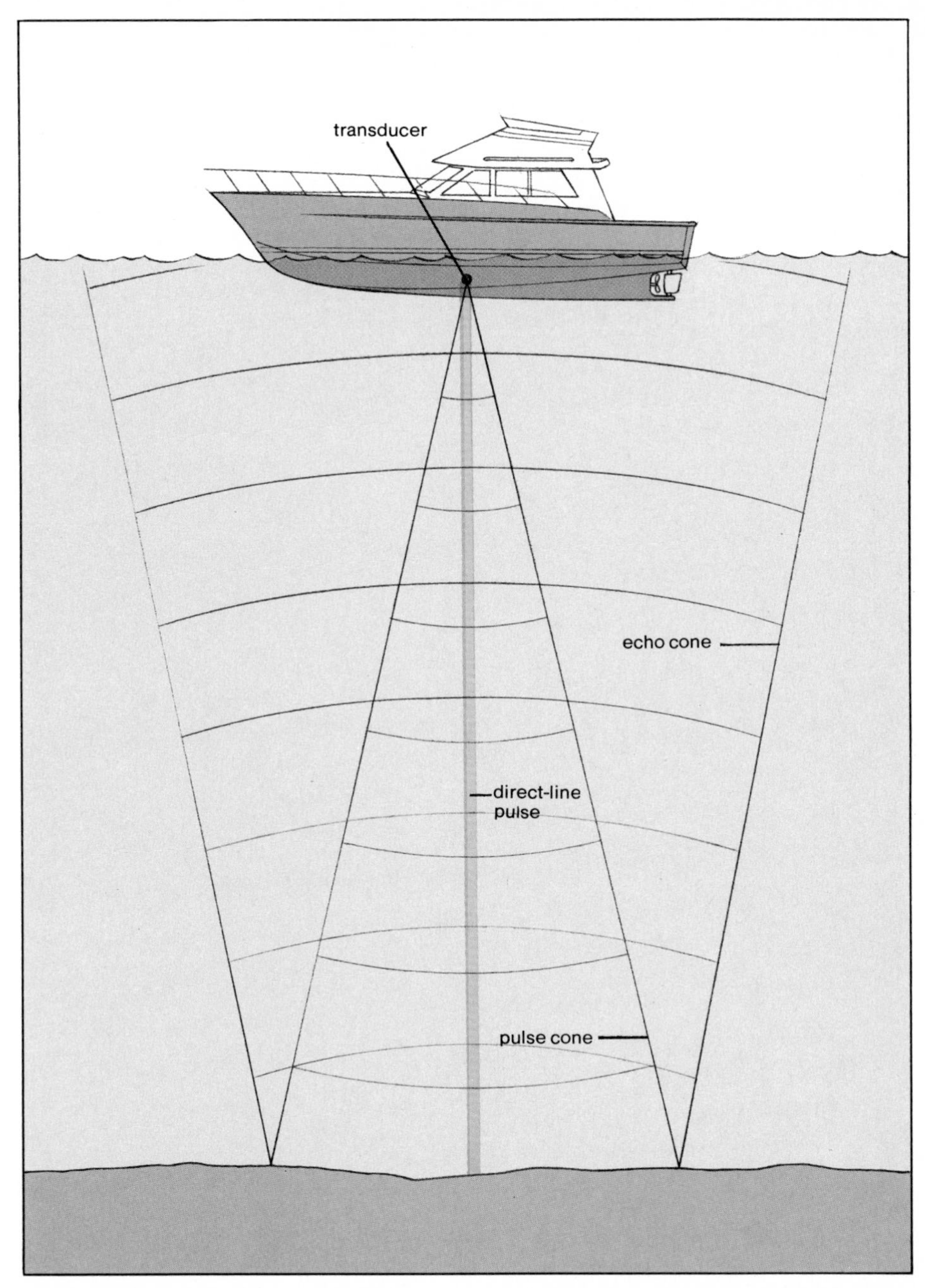

The arc-shaped sound pulses sent from a depth finder's transducer go down in a cone pattern until one portion of a pulse arc hits something. That pulse instantly rebounds, giving the depth finder a readout on the distance between the closest underwater object and the transducer. In the case of a flat bottom, as at left, all pulses except a direct-line-rebound pulse are reflected away from the transducer in an ever-widening echo cone. On a very uneven bottom, however, the transducer may pick up a rebound from a shallow ledge astern—rather than a direct-line rebound from far below.

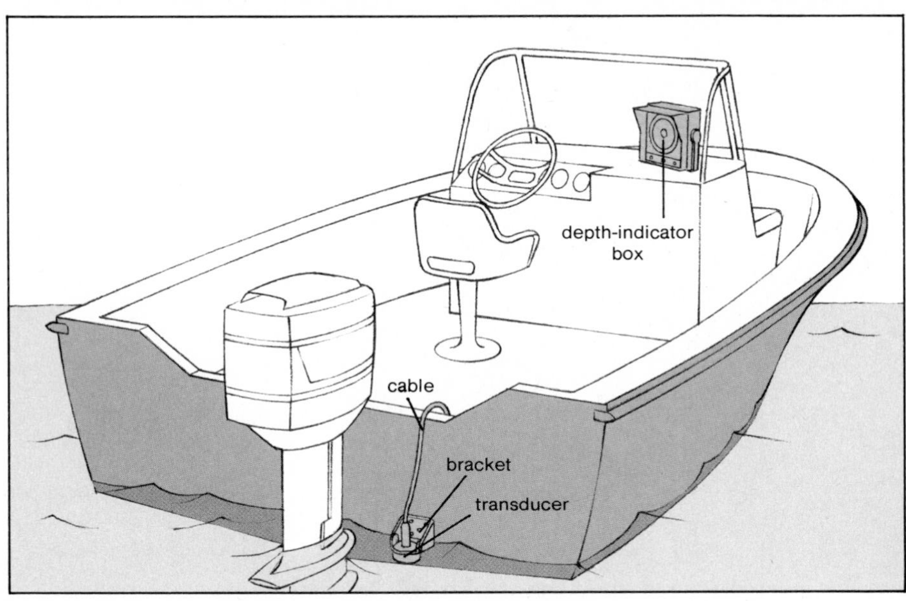

An easily demountable transducer for an outboard runabout can be attached to the transom either by a bracket, as here, or by a suction cup. The depth-finder cable should be routed as far as possible from the engine to preclude electrical interference by the spark plugs, which could distort the electronic signal. From the transom, the cable runs forward to the depth-indicator box.

When cruising a coastline with an evenly sloping sea bed, a skipper can navigate even in poor visibility by using a depth finder to match his course to charted bottom contours. Here, a pilot bound for Provincetown, Massachusetts, heads in toward Cape Cod until the depth finder tells him he has reached a 60-foot contour. Steering a course (broken line) that keeps the depth-finder reading at 60 feet, he is able to follow the contour safely around the tip of the Cape.

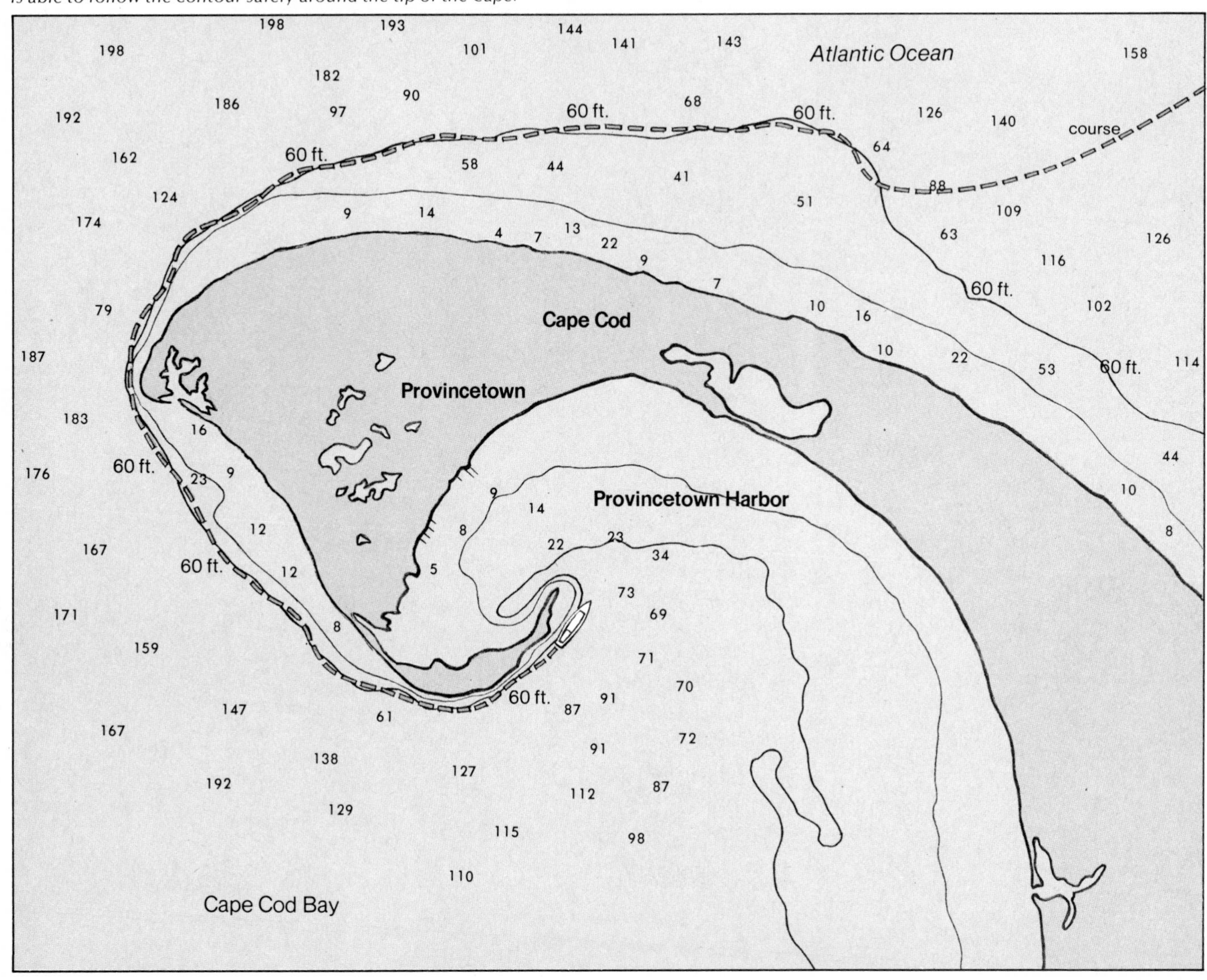

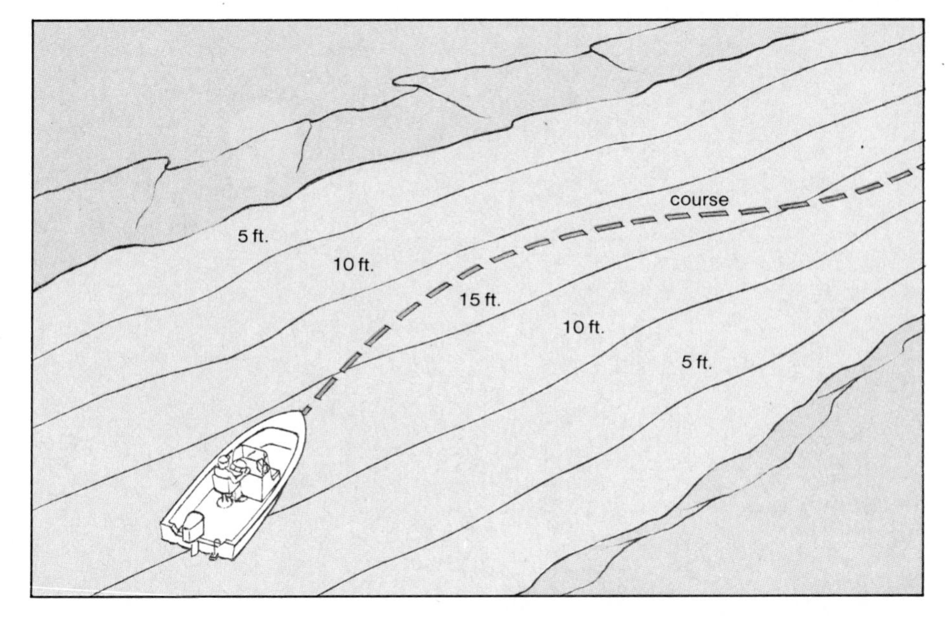

This vessel is using its depth finder, combined with a gently zigzagging course, to stay in the navigable water of a narrow estuary. The pilot first angles his craft toward one bank, keeping on that heading until his depth finder shows the water depth beginning to decrease. Then he bears away toward the opposite bank, continuing to change direction whenever the depth finder shows the water becoming uncomfortably shallow.

Where the bottom slopes irregularly offshore, such as occurs west of Moss Landing, California (below), the pilot making a blind landfall must remain alert to his depth finder's readings. Heading in, he will see his depth-finder reading increase suddenly from 25 to 88 fathoms as he passes over Monterey Canyon. Matching this increase to contour lines on his chart, he can fix his position at about three and a half miles from the harbor entrance, on a bearing of 62° magnetic.

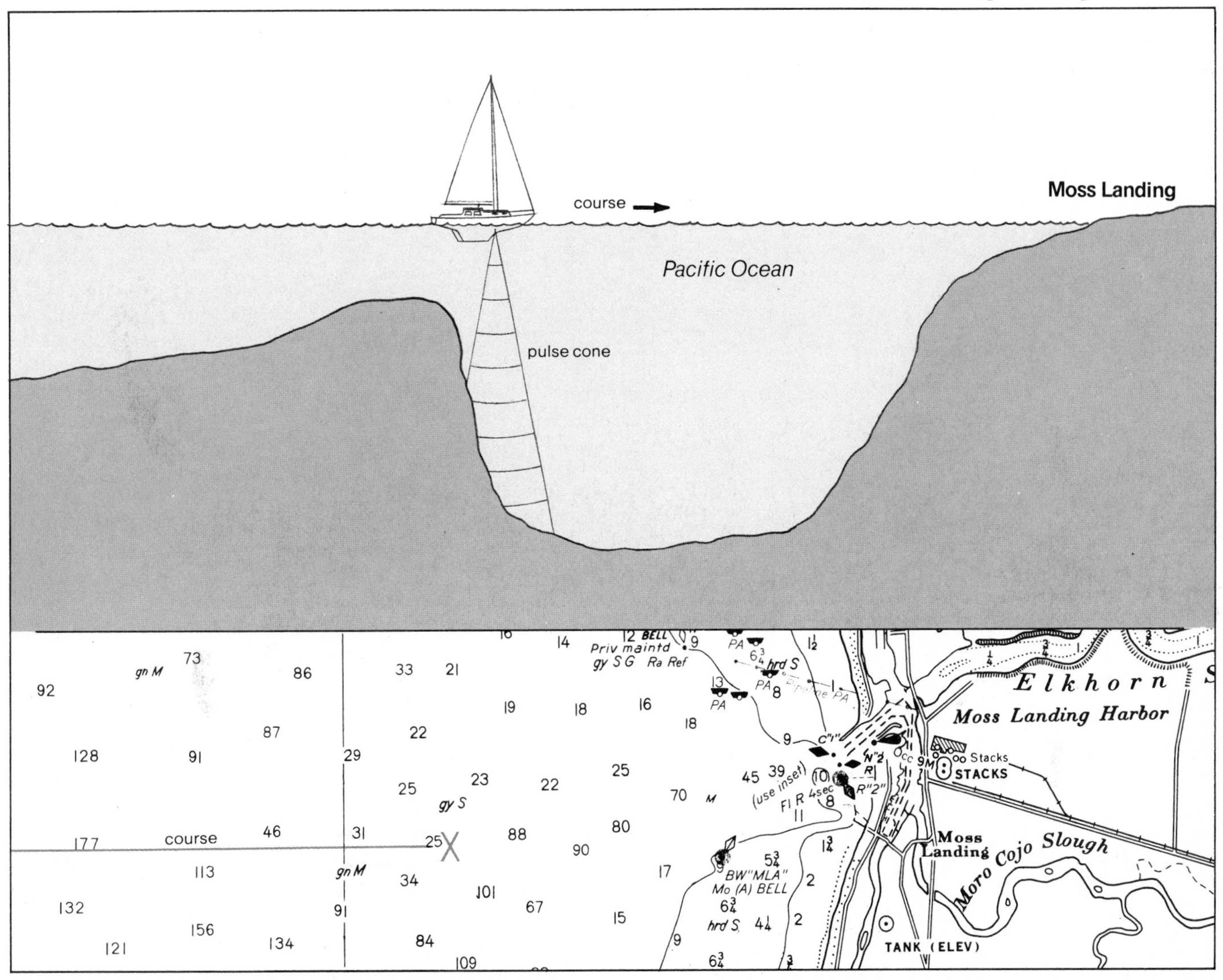

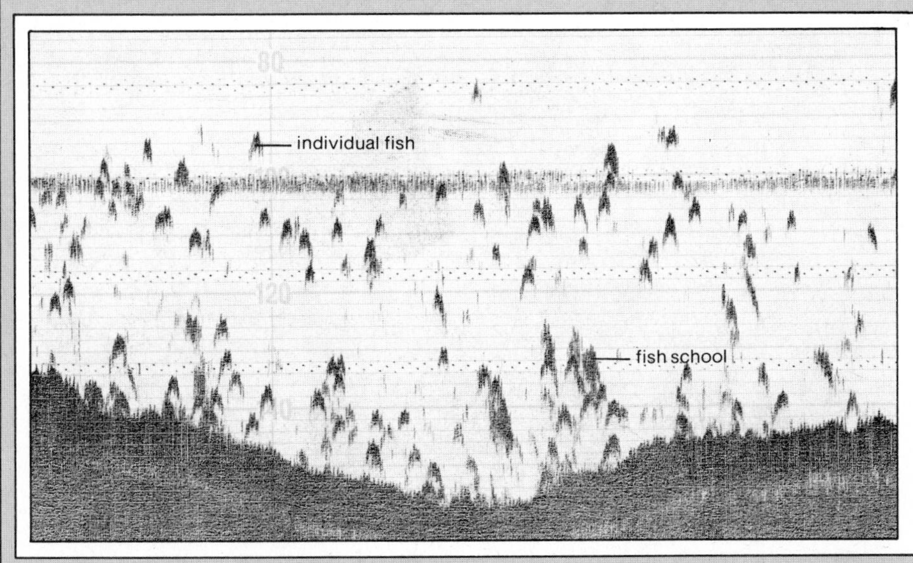

Fish by the Fathom

Though common depth finders give readings on bottom contours, some sensitive and sophisticated models can locate fish by painting pulse echoes on a moving tape. A small section of such a tape appears at left. The dark area along the lower edge represents the bottom, which a grid on the chart shows to vary from about 130 to 155 feet. The inverted-V shapes above the bottom are fish—both individuals and schools; some fishermen, with practice, claim that they can identify species. The sum total of such electronic wizardry has brought not only better fishing, but also cries of alarm from some conservationists who argue that the angler now has an unfair advantage over his quarry.

This typical RDF receiver has three bands: MARINE for ship-to-shore distress calls, and time and weather broadcasts; B.CAST for commercial stations; and BEACON for regular RDF radio beacons. The directional antenna rests inside a rotating bar. When the antenna points toward a transmitter, the needle on the null meter moves to "0." Controls on the unit's face (from left) turn on the set, switch it to direction finding, adjust its sensitivity and tune it.

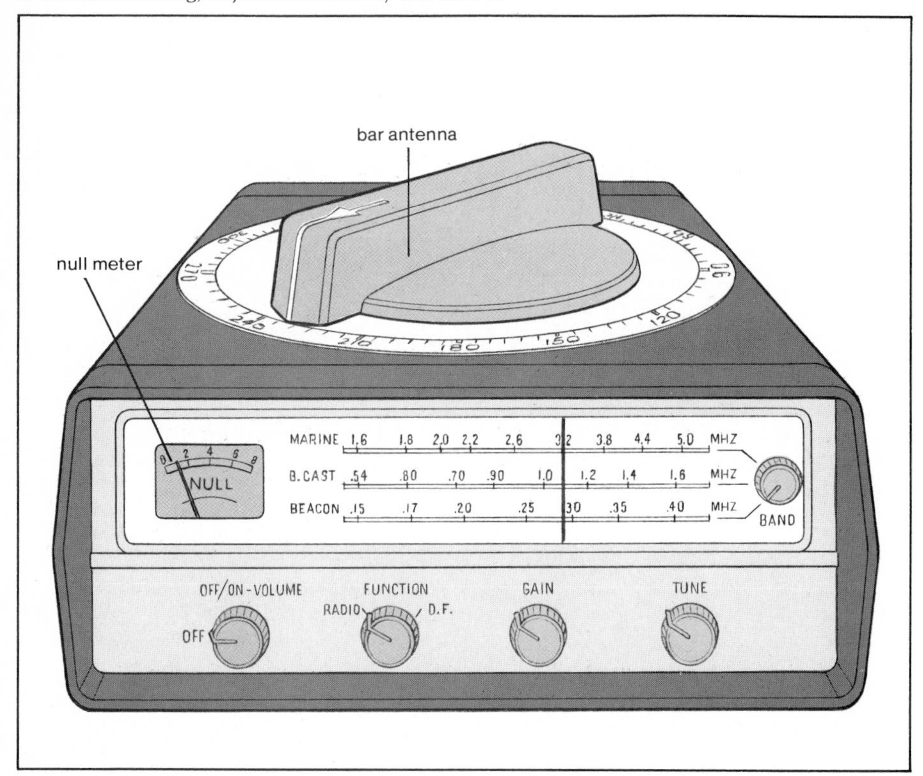

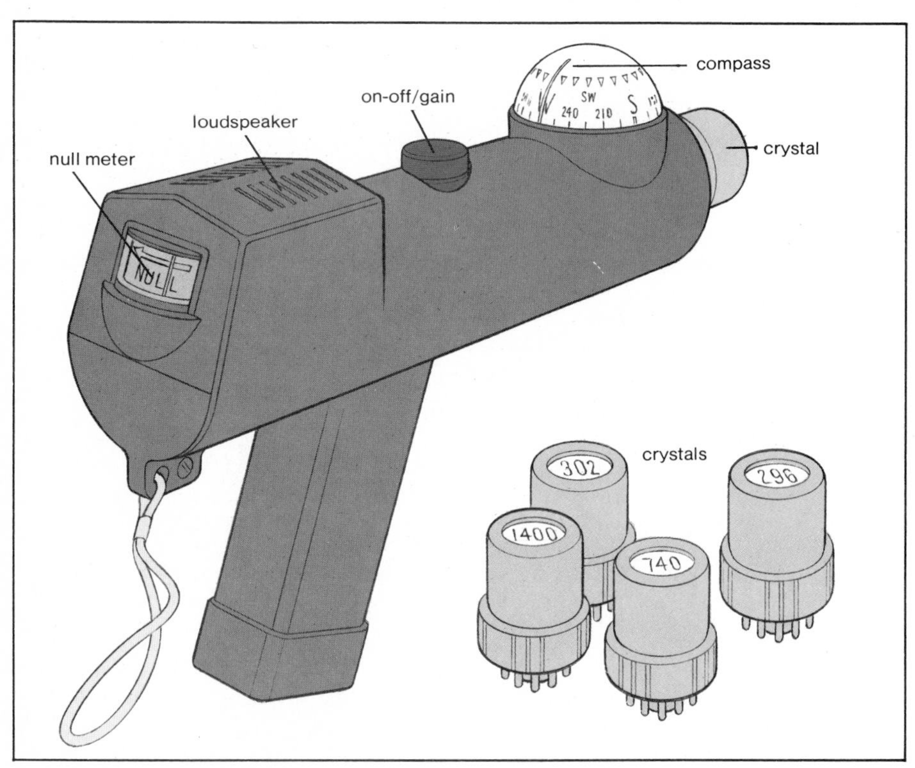

The directional antenna in this hand-held RDF set is built into its barrel; the end of the barrel accommodates plug-in radio crystals that are pretuned to fixed frequencies (note that channel numbers are marked on the spare crystals beneath the barrel). When the barrel is pointed at a transmitter, the unit registers a null on the meter at its rear. On top of the receiver are a loudspeaker for identifying the signals from beacons, an on-off switch and a compass for bearings.

Bearings by Radio Beam

After depth finders, the most widely used electronic aids to navigation are radio direction-finding (RDF) receivers. Capable of providing accurate position fixes well beyond sight of land, RDF equipment extends the yachtsman's safe horizons, while adding an extra measure of security for sailing at night and in bad weather.

As its name indicates, an RDF unit is fundamentally a radio. Sets like the one at left have faces and knobs that resemble those of everyday table radios. And the more flexible, modern hand-held units *(bottom left),* though their design hardly calls to mind that of a conventional radio, operate on the same principle as an old-fashioned crystal set.

The heart of an RDF receiver is a bar-shaped directional antenna, made of ferrite, that is connected to a so-called null meter on the face of the set. Ferrite is an iron compound exceptionally good at picking up radio waves. It converts the radio signals into a small flow of electricity that deflects the meter according to the current's strength. The antenna produces the smallest amount of current when it is pointed directly toward a transmitter: the null position. Once a null is found, the relative bearing of its source can be converted into a compass bearing *(opposite and overleaf)* that is accurate to within three or four degrees—adequate for most piloting situations.

Though any commmercial AM radio station within the clear range of an RDF unit can be used for navigating, the most reliable source of signals is the network of special-frequency marine radio beacons maintained all around the nation's waters by the Coast Guard. The exact locations of their transmitting towers are marked on charts, and the towers are placed near the water's edge so their signals are not bent by passing over land, as is often the case with those of commercial stations. Over 200 of these radio signposts guide mariners in coastal waters and lakes. To aid in its identification, each beacon has an assigned frequency and a special signal, patterned on the Morse code, that it sends repeatedly at close intervals 24 hours a day. These, along with detailed listings of lighthouse locations, are available in booklets called light lists *(page 72)*, published by the Coast Guard.

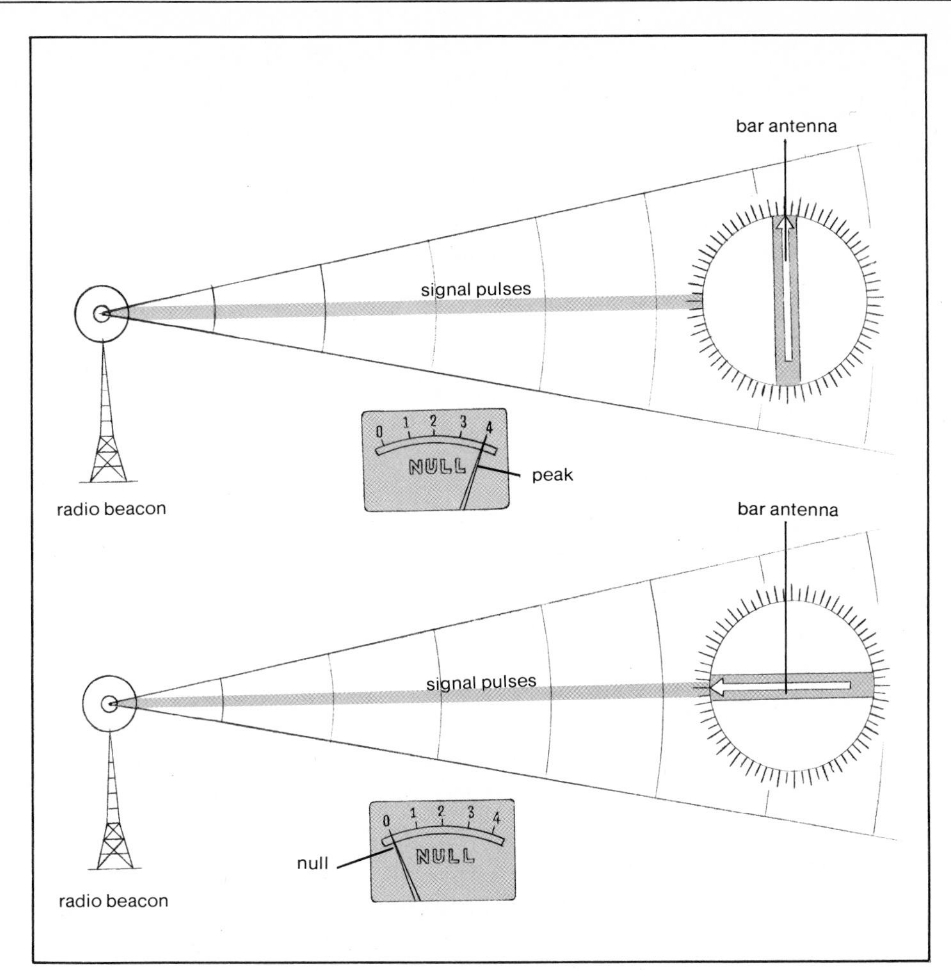

In the upper drawing, the bar antenna of an RDF unit is turned broadside to a radio beacon, and thus picks up strong signal pulses. This produces electric current within the RDF unit that deflects the null-meter pointer to the right, or peak, position. With the bar turned head-on to the beacon (lower drawing), the antenna picks up very little of the beacon's signal, and the meter pointer remains stationary at its null position.

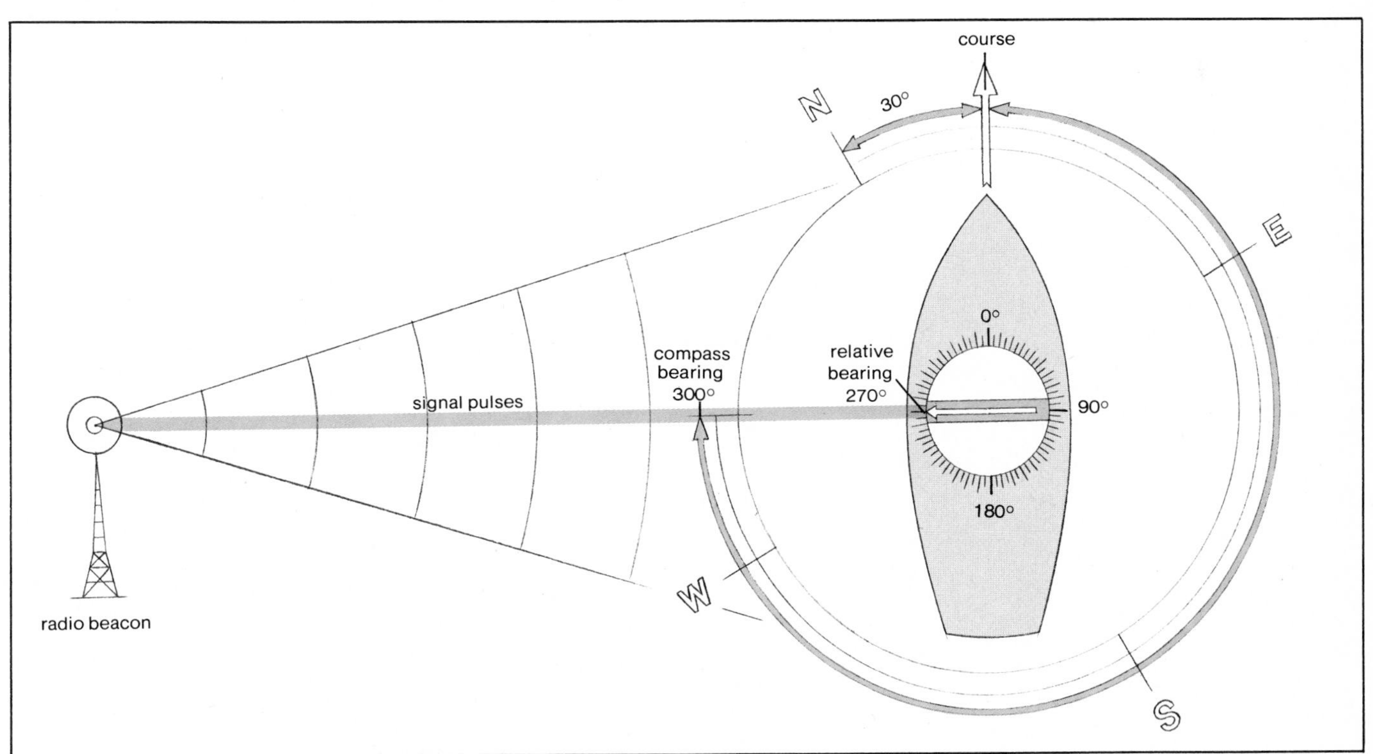

To locate a beacon, the relative bearing of all nulls must be translated into compass bearings. On hand-held RDF receivers, a built-in compass provides an instantaneous magnetic bearing. Otherwise the conversion is made by adding the vessel's compass course to the bearing given by the RDF. In this example, the RDF aboard a boat sailing a compass course of 30° shows a relative bearing to a radio beacon of 270°; thus the compass bearing to the beacon is 300°.

This stylized excerpt from the light list for Lake Michigan shows a typical network of electronic lighthouses positioned to aid navigators in taking RDF fixes. The beacons are marked here with solid blue dots and keyed to identifying boxes. Heading each box is the station's transmitting frequency. Each beacon sends for 60 seconds, rotating in the order indicated by the Roman numerals. Next are the stations' locations, the specific dot-dash code each sends and its range in miles. Short-range beacons, carrying 10 miles or less, are designated by blue circles. They send a continuous signal of half-second dashes.

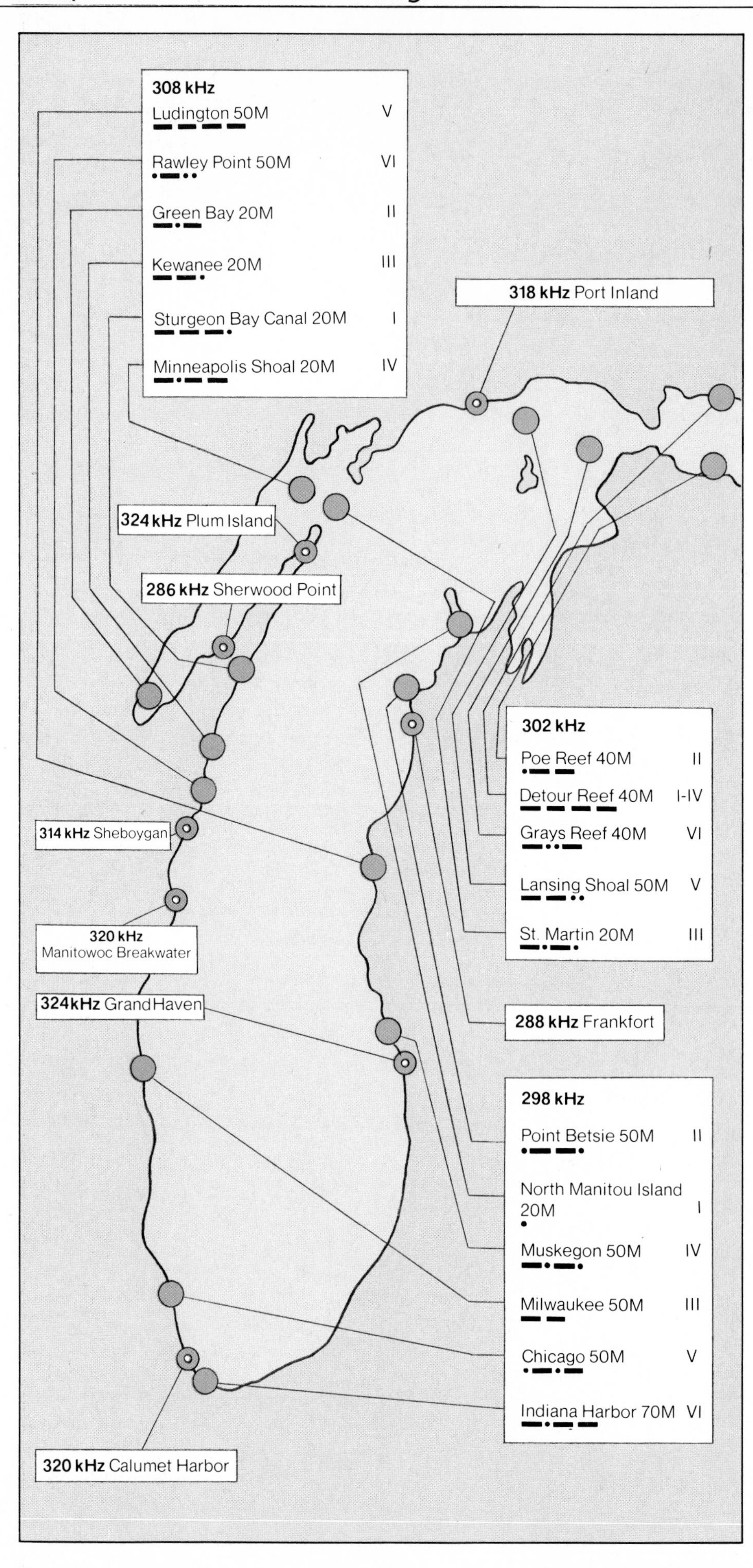

In a typical RDF exercise, a navigator crossing Lake Michigan from Milwaukee to Benton Harbor checks his course with RDF fixes, then homes in on a local radio station. At 1015, the skipper takes a fix on the Milwaukee and Muskegon radio beacons (he is out of range of Grand Haven's marker beacon) and sets a course for Benton Harbor. Two hours later, beyond the range of all the beacons along the southern part of Lake Michigan except the ones at Milwaukee and Indiana Harbor, he takes another fix. Finding himself off course, he swings to a new heading that brings him within range of Benton Harbor's commercial broadcast station—and a straight run home.

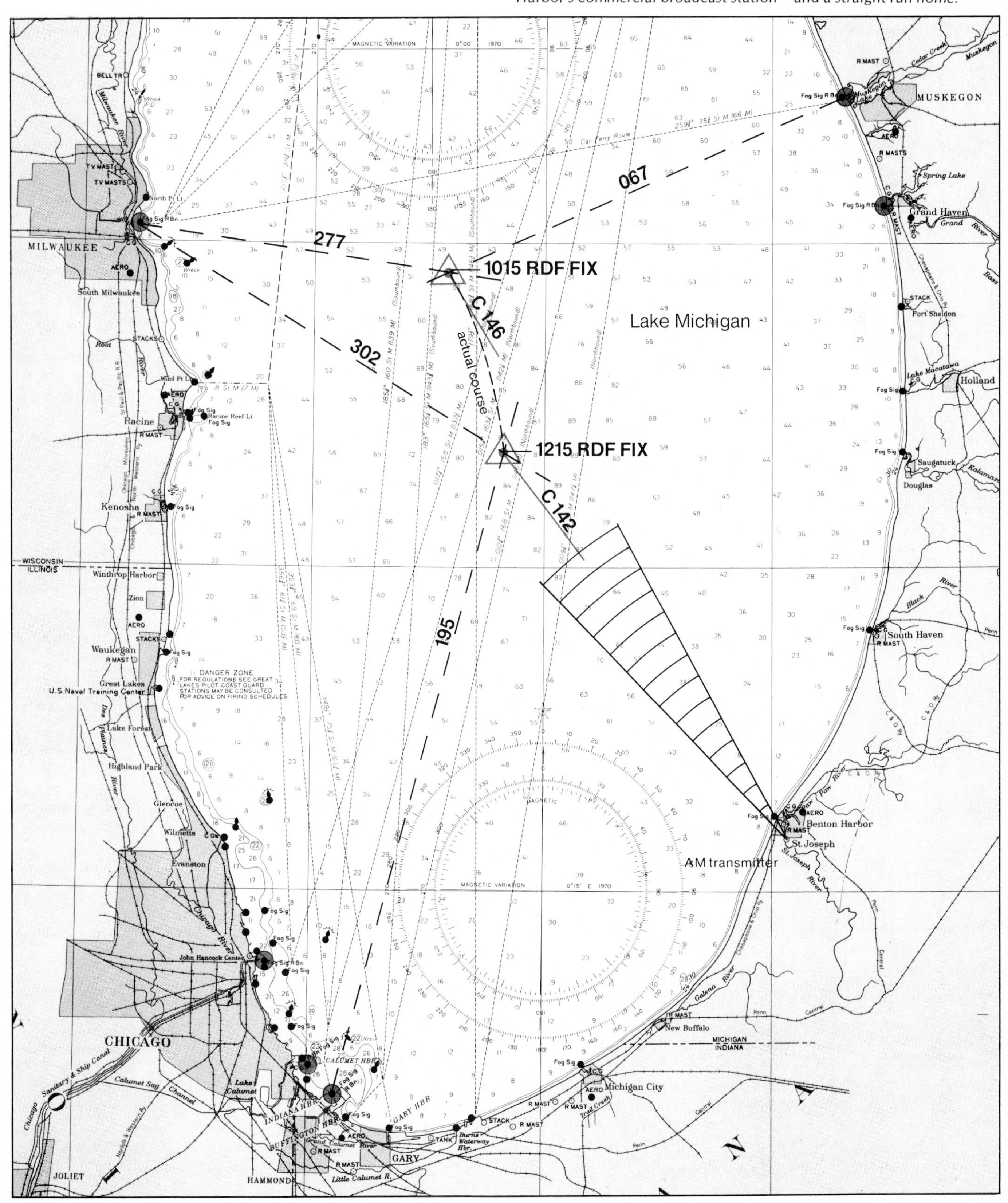

A shipboard omni unit has three simple controls: an on-off volume switch; frequency dials for tuning in on specific stations; and a knob that rotates a calibrated bearing card, marked off by degrees. When a boat homes in on the bearing that coincides with the indicator line, the hanging pointer bisects the circle. If the boat strays, the pointer swings left or right. The word FROM in the direction window means that the bearing reads from the omni station to the boat.

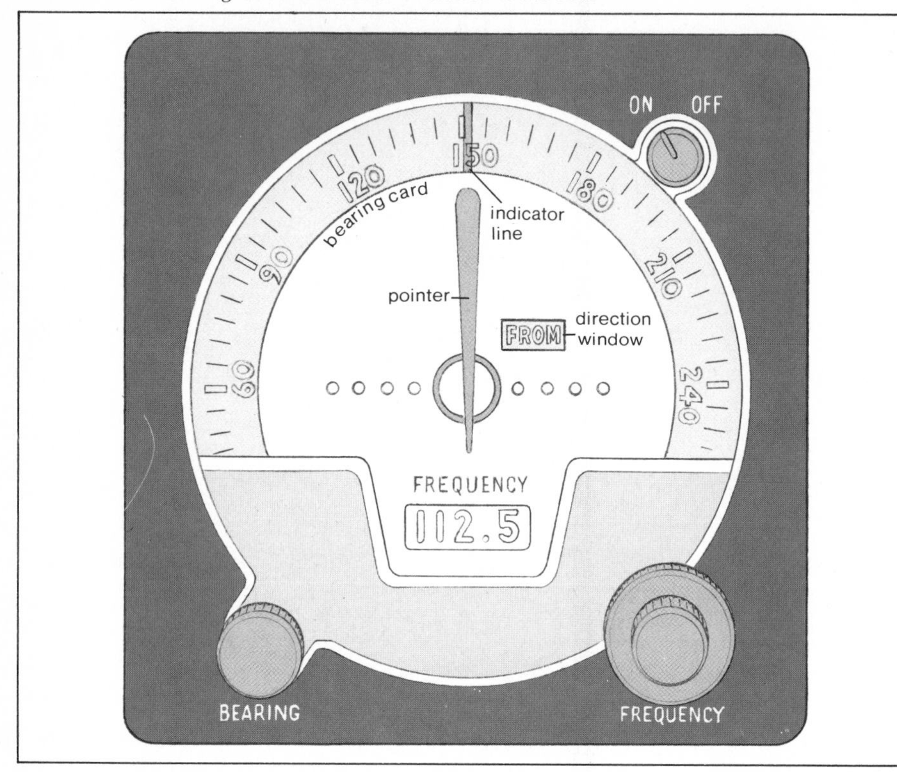

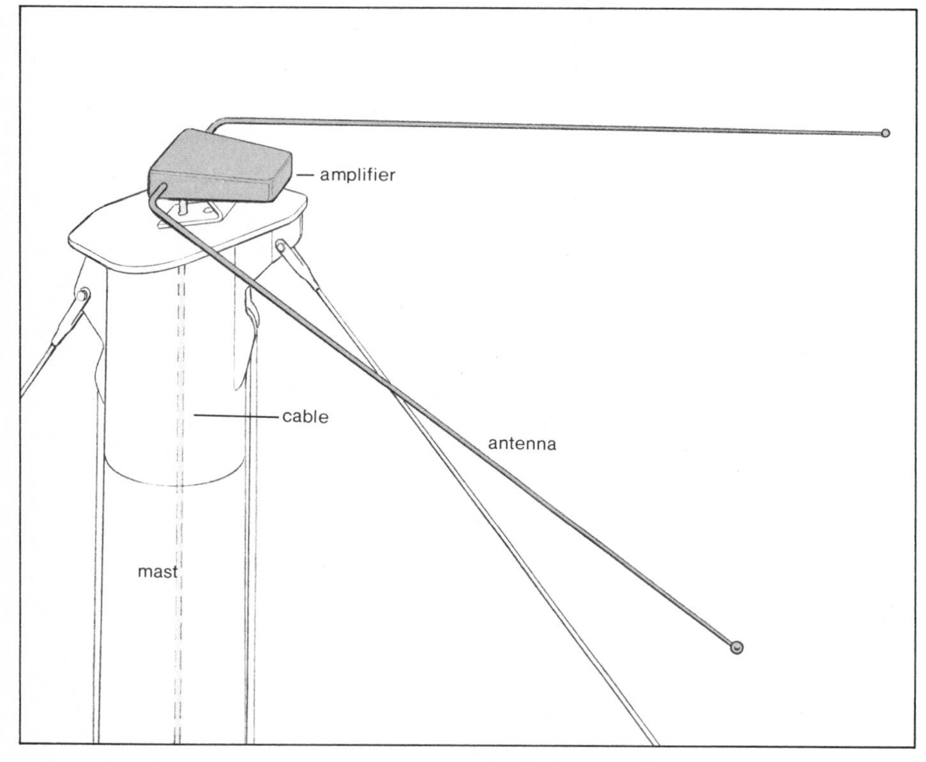

V-shaped omni antennas are permanently mounted as high as possible —on a powerboat's cabintop or, as here, on a sailboat's masthead. The antenna's arms are attached to a low-powered amplifier that boosts the strength of incoming impulses. The impulses then travel by a cable down the mast to the receiver. Because omni signals do not carry beyond the horizon, the antenna's height determines the set's range—about 60 miles for an antenna atop a 40-foot mast.

A Twist on RDF

A giant step up from conventional radio direction-finding equipment, both in accuracy and expense, is the highly sophisticated system called omni, which allows a yachtsman to tune in on specialized radio beacons that were originally designed for use by aircraft.

An omni receiver, which costs about four times as much as most RDF sets, will fix a vessel's line of position to within two compass degrees—as against almost twice that margin of error for RDF. Furthermore, omni systems are easier to use, and their signals are all but immune to atmospheric static that may disrupt RDF. Omni's major drawback is its short range; unlike ordinary radio beams, which can be bounced off the atmosphere, omni beams go in a direct line, and thus become ineffective beyond the horizon.

The key element in an omni system is the complex, very high frequency (VHF) beam sent out by each transmitting station. The beam is actually a composite of two VHF radio waves. When transmitted together, these two waves combine into a signal whose nature varies depending upon the direction in which it travels. Thus the portion of the signals that are sent out to the north differs from the signals aimed east or west.

An omni receiver detects these differences and displays them as bearings between the station and the boat. The bearings, known as radials, give the compass direction either from the station to the boat, in which case the omni receiver designates them as "from" radials *(top left)*, or, conversely, from the boat to the beacon, in which case they are designated "to" radials.

To get a bearing from an omni beacon, the yachtsman first tunes his receiver to the station's frequency; in the example at left, the frequency is 112.5 megahertz. Next he spins his bearing dial until the set's pointer hangs vertically. His bearing—shown here as 150°— appears under an indicator line at the top of the set. Then, if he wants to home in on this bearing, he simply steers his course so that the omni's pointer remains vertical.

Omni information—including the location of transmitters—is not given on standard nautical charts. But the boatman can easily add the necessary data to his charts *(right)*. Transmitter locations and beacon frequencies are available from the U.S. Department of Commerce, which publishes detailed aviation maps called sectional aeronautical charts. These charts can also be obtained at local airports.

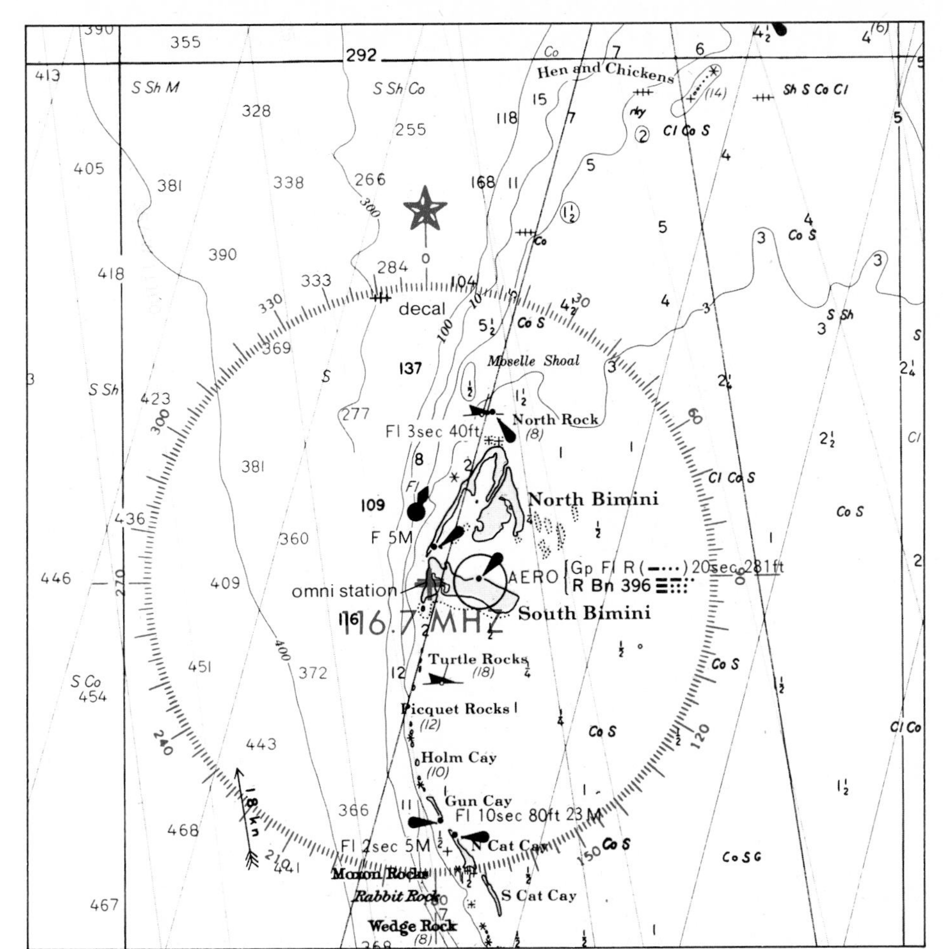

A chart segment of the Bahamas, prepared for use in omni navigation, has been marked with a cross at the precise location of the South Bimini omni station, and the station's broadcast frequency noted beside it. (The "aero" transmitter just east of the omni station is Bimini's regular airport beacon.) A transparent compass-rose decal—available at most chart stores—has been pasted down with its center on the station and its zero line on magnetic north. To find his line of position, a navigator draws a line from the station through the bearing on the decal that matches the FROM reading on his omni set.

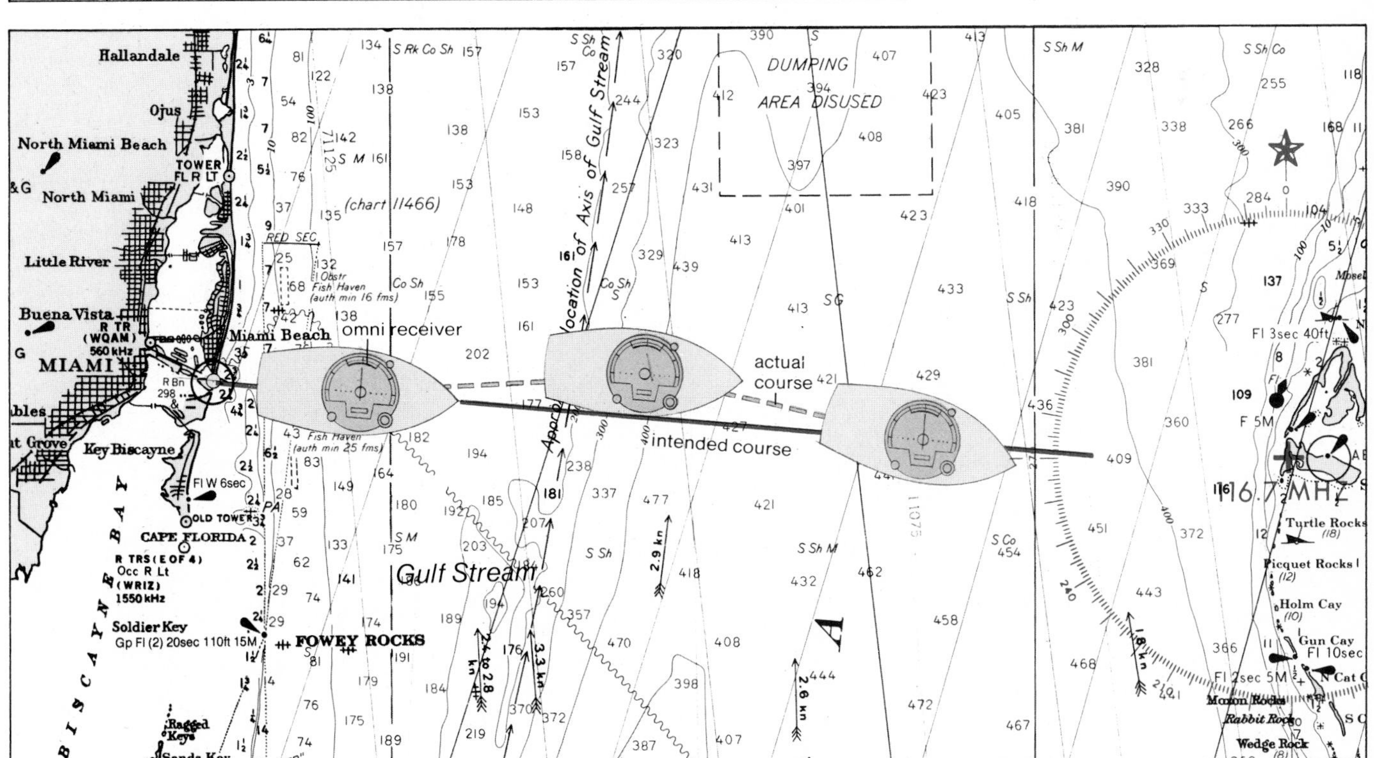

Cruising to Bimini from Miami across the north-flowing Gulf Stream (pages 164-165), a boat homes in on the Bimini omni beacon. Out of Miami, the boat heads on course along the 272 omni radial, and the receiver's pointer is centered. En route, the current carries the craft to port, causing the pointer to drift to the right. Noting the error, the skipper alters his course to starboard to line up on the radial again, thus bringing the pointer back—and keeping his boat on course.

On this simplified drawing of a radar receiver, the knobs to the right of the scope control the picture. The brilliance knob regulates the intensity of the image, while the tuning knob brings it into focus. The range knob selects the radius of the picture on the scope; the boat's own position is marked by its cross hairs. The on-off switch may be set to impose concentric range rings on the screen, and the anti-clutter and gain knobs partially block out unwanted signals.

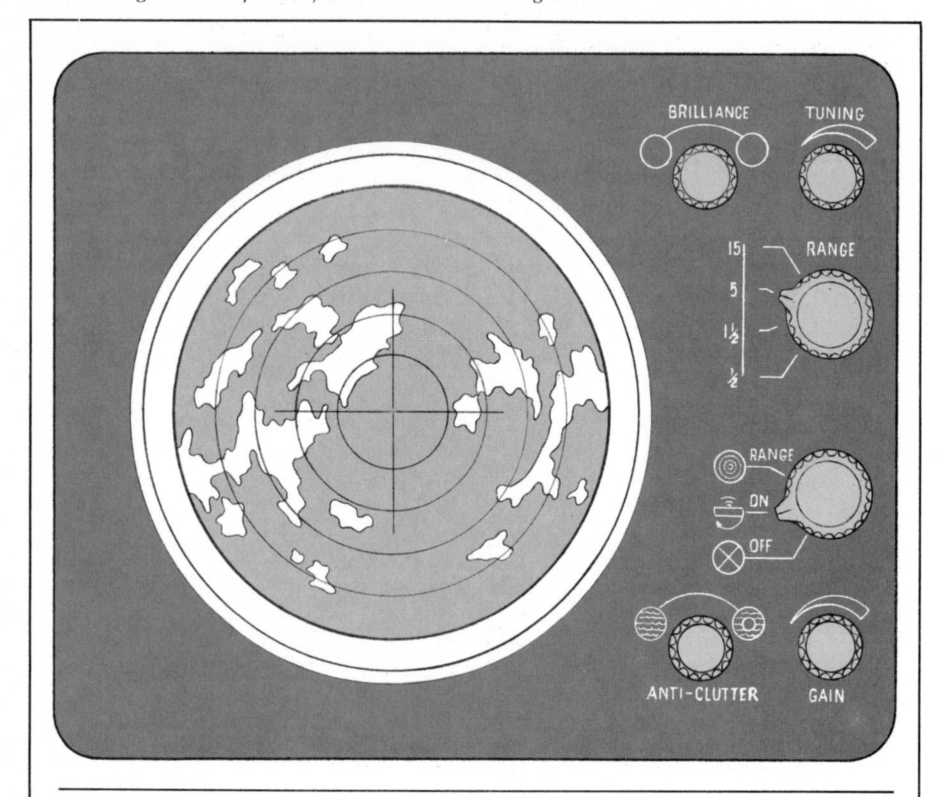

A radar's sophisticated two-way antenna consists of two major components. The slender horizontal scanner at the top, which houses the antenna's sending and receiving unit (blue), spins around at the rate of 20 times every minute, sweeping the water as far as the horizon with its SHF radio beam. The bulkier fixed unit underneath contains the driving motor and cables for carrying impulses to and from the sending and receiving unit and the scope below.

The Super Scanner

While most electronic navigating equipment delivers its message in the numerical language of directional bearings or water depths, one particular device gives the skipper a direct visual image. This is radar, whose viewing screen *(left)* reveals not only the presence, but also the distance, direction and even the shape of objects around a boat. Though some skill is needed to understand a radar picture, any navigator who learns how to read it can pilot his boat through tricky channels and heavy maritime traffic in the darkest night or the murkiest fog.

To create a radar picture, a transmitter aboard ship sends out a superhigh-frequency (SHF) radio signal from a revolving two-way antenna *(bottom left)*. As the antenna turns, scanning the water's surface, its SHF beam is reflected by nearby objects. These reflections then bounce back to the boat and the antenna picks them up. A receiver translates them into electronic images called blips that are flashed onto the radarscope, a cathode ray tube much like the tube in TV sets.

In reading a radarscope, a skipper must make some quick and expert visual interpolations, since—as on pages 138 and 139—the picture on the screen differs markedly from the world as seen by the naked eye. This is because some features—particularly objects made of metal—reflect radar beams better than others. Special buoys with metal radar reflectors, for example, show up as enormous phosphorescent splotches *(page 146)*, far out of proportion to their actual size. Other features, such as low-lying rocks, or small wood or fiberglass boats, may not appear at all. In addition, severe rain, snow or hail can mask sections of a screen with random streaks, known as clutter. And the center of the screen often blazes with a mystifying jumble of blips, called "sea return," which are simply a reflection from waves near the ship.

Experienced operators, however, interpret radar's visual quirks with relative ease. They can distinguish between the fleeting blip of a moving boat and the steady flare from a buoy. They learn to relate shapes on the scope to landmarks delineated on their charts. They keep in mind the limited range of radar waves, which are effective only to the horizon *(opposite, above)*. And since radar sets used aboard most pleasure craft produce their sharpest, most complete pictures for objects within a radius of five or six miles, most skippers use them primarily for close-in piloting in tight quarters.

The beam emanating from the radar antenna of the powerboat below sweeps out (blue) until it intercepts a sailboat on the horizon. Then part of the beam rebounds (blue-gray) back to the powerboat. The sailboat does not stop all the radar pulses. Some of them pass through nonreflecting surfaces such as the sail—and others miss the boat entirely. But since the waves travel in straight lines, they never reach the headlands at far right, which lie below the horizon.

Collision Insurance

Because radar beams reflect poorly—or not at all—from wood or fiberglass boats, many small-craft skippers invest in compact but highly efficient radar reflectors like the one at right. Commonly about 15 inches in diameter, the reflectors are made of thin, interlocking metal discs from which radar waves bounce strongly no matter at what angle they strike. Usually kept folded and stowed away, they can be quickly assembled and hoisted aloft—the higher the better—for cruising at night or in bad weather. Though simple and inexpensive, these ingenious reflectors can provide an increasingly important form of anticollision insurance, as more and more vessels rely on radar to guide them through crowded waters in bad weather.

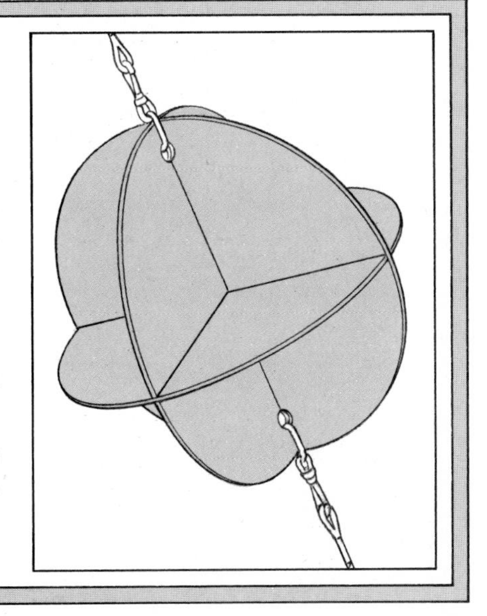

The circular pattern of glowing blips in the radarscope of a boat in Los Angeles Harbor reflects the locations—and in some cases the actual shapes—of objects around the vessel. The boat's position is marked by a bright dot at the scope's exact center. The thin white line slanting from this dot to the upper left is from the beam of the revolving antenna. The heavier, angled lines above and below the boat indicate piers and breakwaters, and the nebula of blips beyond the upper piers is from buildings on shore—as can be seen by comparing the radar picture with the chart at right. Some blips, however, have no counterparts on the chart. The spattering of light immediately surrounding the boat, for example, is reflection from nearby waves, while the small, ragged patch of brightness just below the vessel is the echo coming from a passing power cruiser.

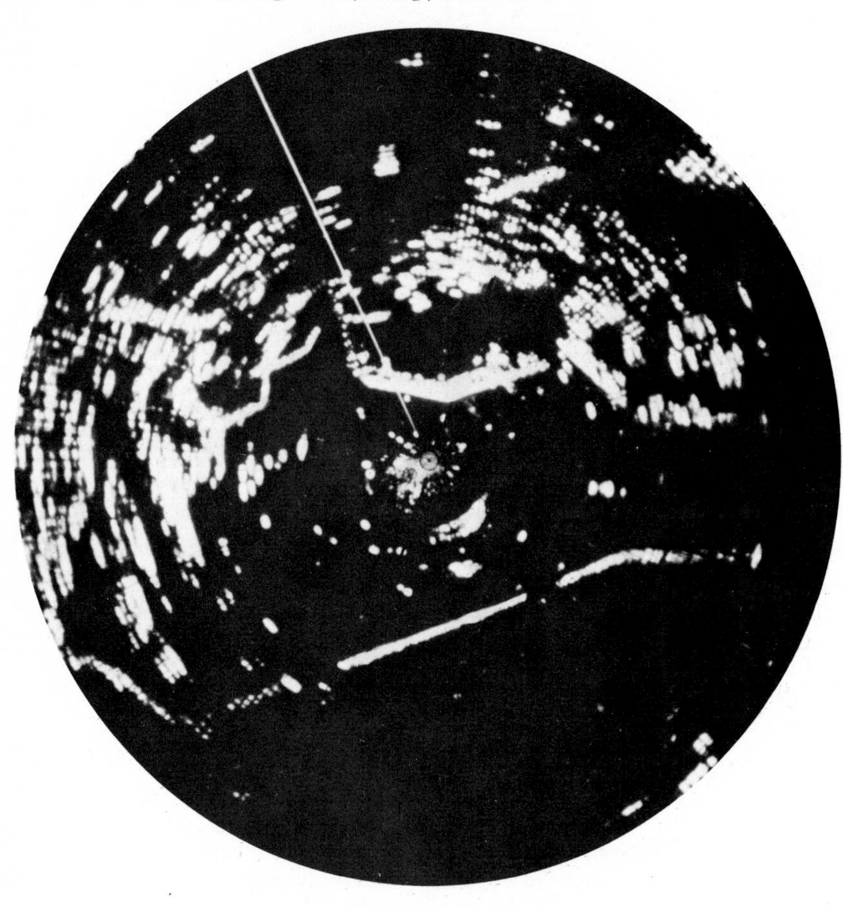

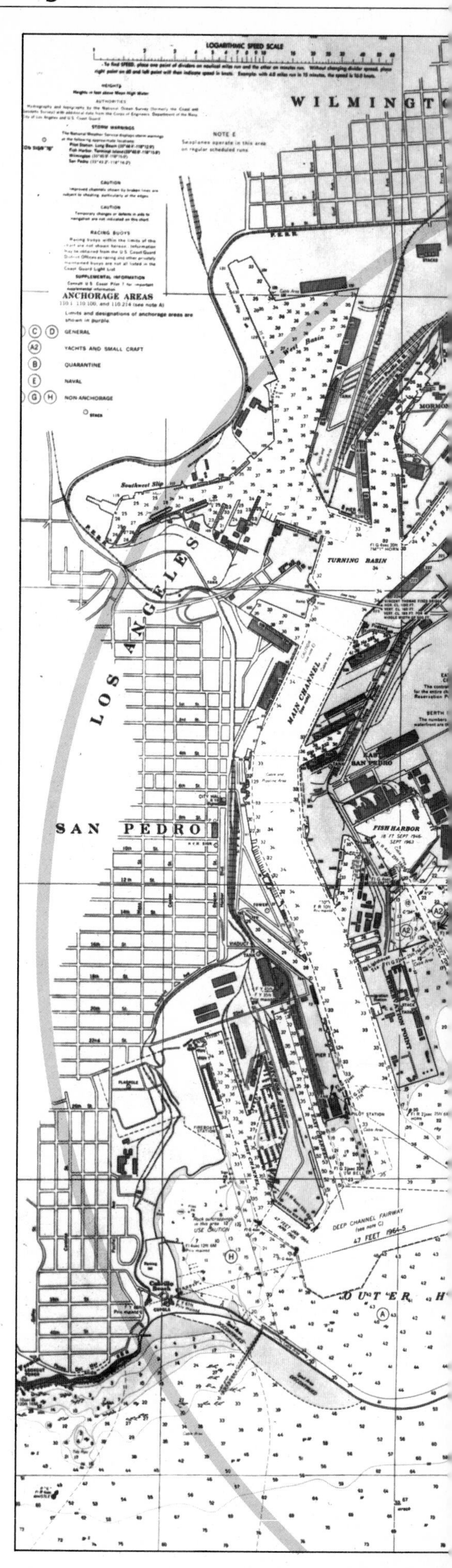

On a chart of Los Angeles Harbor, a blue circle encloses the area covered by the picture seen on the radar screen (above), and a blue X marks the position of the boat. The circle's radius is about three miles; the area of detailed radar coverage is roughly 28 square miles.

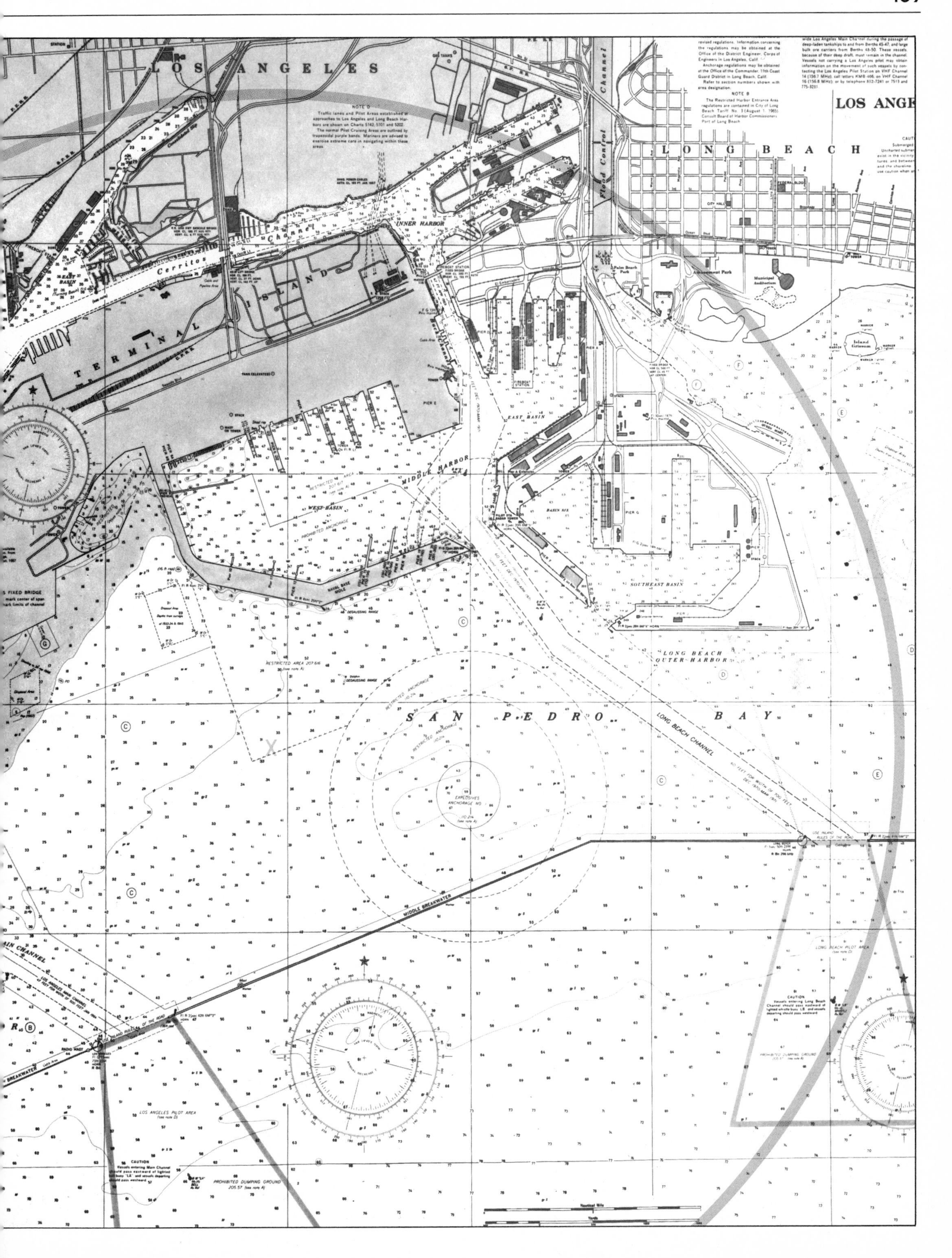
LOS ANGELES
revised regulations. Information concerning the regulations may be obtained at the Office of the District Engineer, Corps of Engineers in Los Angeles, Calif.
Anchorage regulations may be obtained at the Office of the Commander, 11th Coast Guard District in Long Beach, Calif.
Refer to section numbers shown with area designation.
NOTE B
The Restricted Harbor Entrance Area regulations are contained in City of Long Beach Tariff No. 3 (August 1, 1965). Consult Board of Harbor Commissioners Port of Long Beach
wide Los Angeles Main Channel during the passage of deep-laden tankships to and from Berths 45-47, and large bulk ore carriers from Berths 48-50. These vessels, because of their deep draft, must remain in the channel. Vessels not carrying a Los Angeles pilot may obtain information on the movement of such vessels by contacting the Los Angeles Pilot Station on VHF Channel 14 (156.7 MHz), call letters KMB-466, on VHF Channel 16 (156.8 MHz); or by telephone 832-7241 or 7513 and 775-3231.
LOS ANGE
NOTE D
Traffic lanes and Pilot Areas established at approaches to Los Angeles and Long Beach Harbors are shown on Charts 5142, 5101 and 5202.
The normal Pilot Cruising Areas are outlined by trapezoidal purple bands. Mariners are advised to exercise extreme care in navigating within these areas.
Flood Control Channel
LONG BEACH
FEDERAL BLDG
CITY HALL
Palm Beach Park
Municipal Auditorium
Island Grissom
INNER HARBOR
Cerritos Channel
TERMINAL ISLAND
EAST BASIN
MIDDLE HARBOR
WEST BASIN
PROHIBITED ANCHORAGE
PIER A
PIER E
PIER F
PIER G
BASIN SIX
SOUTHEAST BASIN
LONG BEACH OUTER HARBOR
SAN PEDRO BAY
LONG BEACH CHANNEL
RESTRICTED ANCHORAGE
EXPLOSIVES ANCHORAGE
MIDDLE BREAKWATER
MAIN CHANNEL
LONG BEACH PILOT AREA
CAUTION
Vessels entering Long Beach Channel should pass eastward of lighted whistle buoy LB and vessels departing should pass westward
PROHIBITED DUMPING GROUND
LOS ANGELES PILOT AREA
CAUTION
Vessels entering Main Channel should pass eastward of lighted bell buoy "LA" and vessels departing should pass westward.
PROHIBITED DUMPING GROUND 205.57 (see note A)
Nautical Mile
Yards

By Master and Slave

Of all the magic boxes available to the yachtsman, none surpasses loran for navigational precision over great distances. Loran's wide reach is implicit in its name, which stands for long-range navigation. By means of synchronized, intersecting radio waves from a network of land-based transmitters, loran can pinpoint a boat's position with quarter-mile accuracy, even when the vessel is as far as 1,000 miles from land. Closer to shore, loran's precision is correspondingly greater. Loran receivers are compact, easy to install, consume little power and are simple to operate. But loran costs more than almost any other type of electronic gear a yachtsman can buy.

The principle of loran is essentially simple. A radio station transmits signals to two distant slave stations, which then retransmit the signals. The receiver picks up both the master transmission and the slave transmissions, and measures the elapsed time between the first signal and each of the others. These two time figures are displayed as a pair of numbers on the boat's receiver, and the boatman matches them to a loran grid, superimposed on a chart, to find his position. First, the unit picks up the master signal, which starts a pair of precision timers in the receiver. When a slave signal arrives, it stops one timer, and the elapsed time in microseconds (millionths of a second) appears on the control panel. The next slave signal stops the other timer and a second time interval flashes onto the panel.

These numbers represent specific intersecting grid lines on a loran chart. Each line is labeled with a code—SS7-Z and SS7-Y in the example on the opposite page—that identifies the particular master-slave signals. Following the code is a number that corresponds to the readings in microseconds that would appear on the loran receiver of any boat located along the line. The navigator notes the readings and finds the two intersecting grid lines—one on the SS7-Z axis, the other on the SS7-Y axis—that most nearly match the readings *(opposite)*. The point where the lines meet gives the navigator an approximate fix on his position, which he then refines by the method shown at the bottom of the opposite page.

On a loran receiver's control panel, all the controls are set for automatic operation. The knobs at bottom are tuned to one of the loran networks, in this case SS7. When the receiver locks into the network's master and slaves, the row of lights in the middle, labeled SIG, flash on. With the power switch pointing to TRACK, the set monitors the boat's progress, indicating its position in microsecond readings. Other lights and switches are for manual operation.

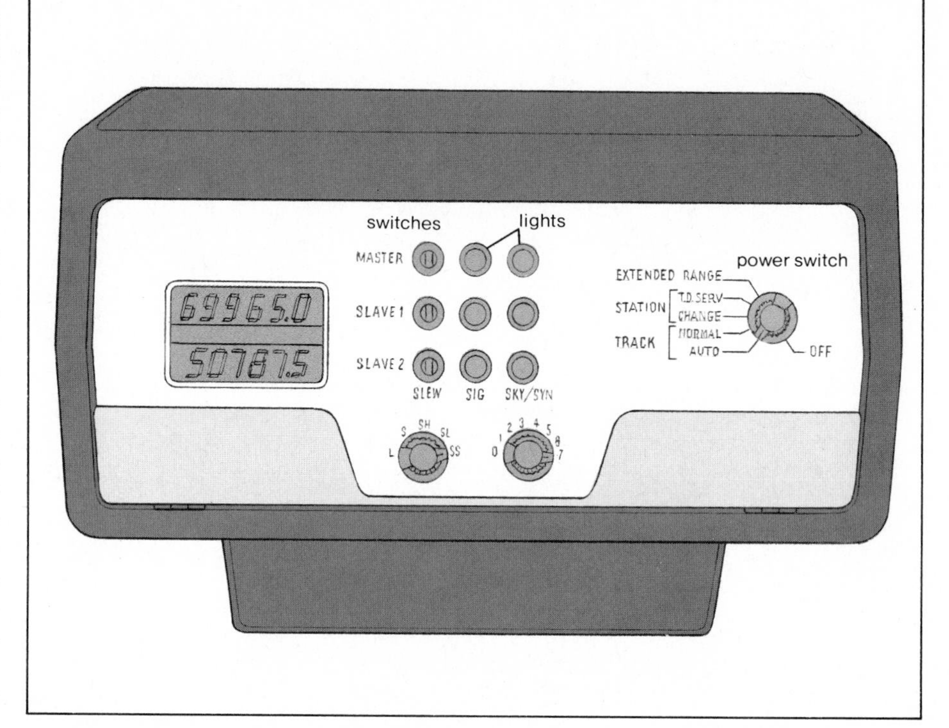

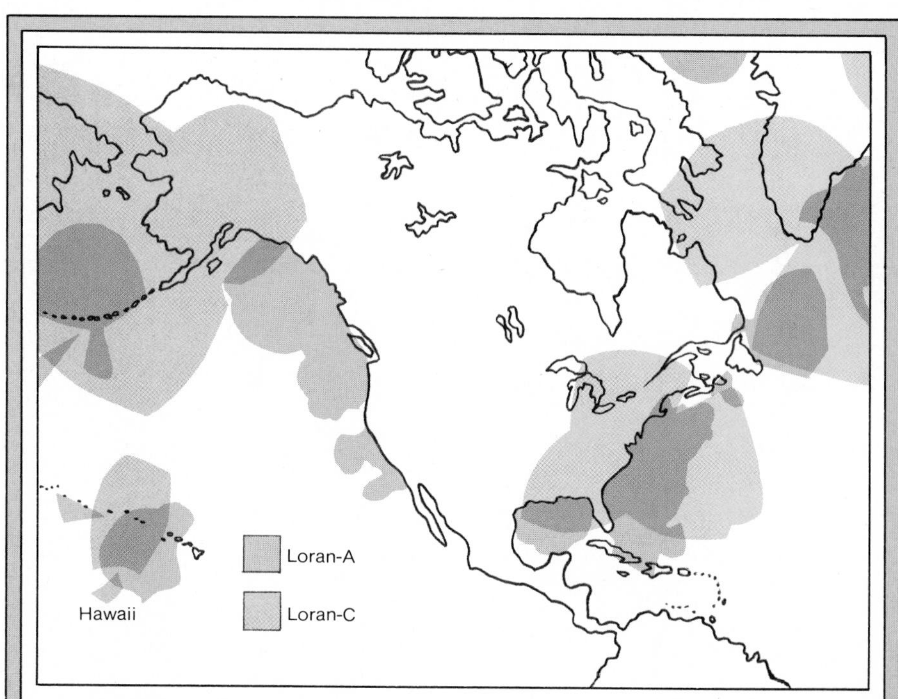

Loran's Double Standard

Two varieties of loran blanket the coastal waters of North America and Hawaii; their signals are strongest in the tinted areas. The gray patches contain networks for loran-A, the original system. But loran-A is being phased out in favor of loran-C, a more accurate version that already serves the areas shown in blue. Inside their respective zones, loran-A can fix a boat's position to within two miles, while loran-C is accurate down to 1,500 feet. With some sacrifice in precision, both systems can be used outside the shaded areas.

The first step in plotting a loran position is to match the numbers on the receiver with the loran grid of a chart. Here, a skipper following a course from Atlantic City to Montauk Point notes that the upper number on his receiver (opposite) lies between lines SS7-Z-69960.0 and SS7-Z-69980.0. Similarly, the lower number falls between lines SS7-Y-50750.0 and SS7-Y-50800.0. These four lines intersect to form a grid square, here tinted blue, that serves as a rough fix.

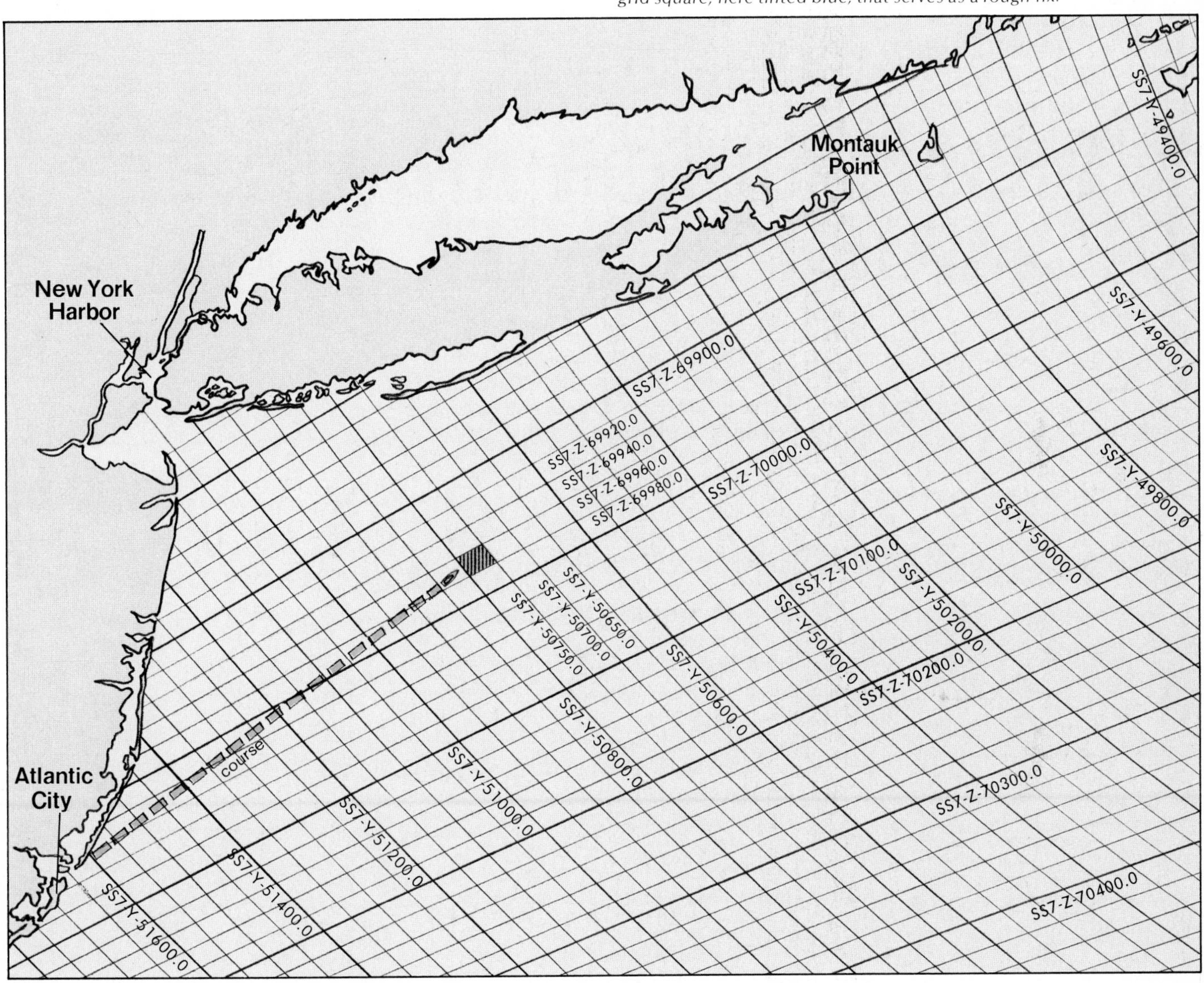

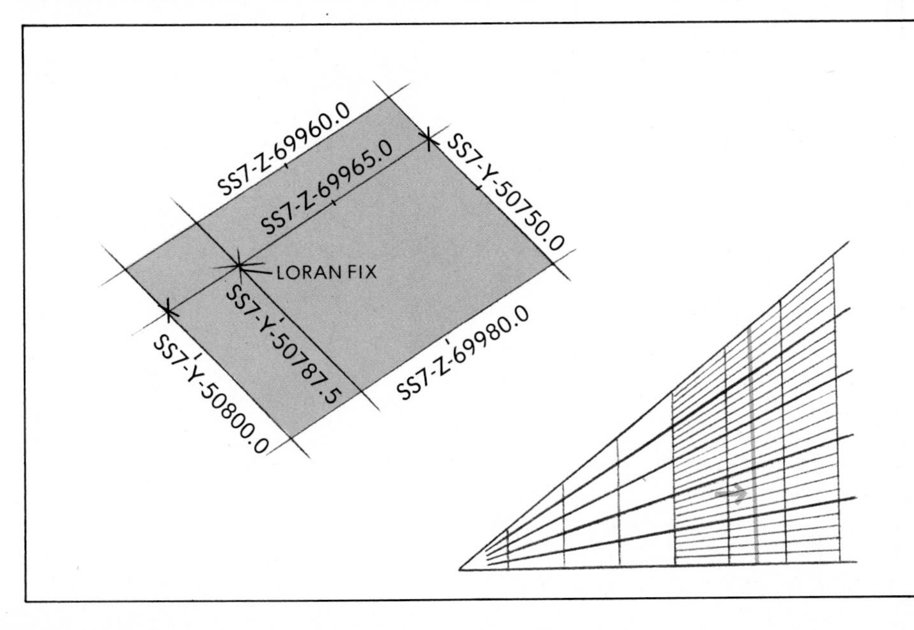

To refine his fix, the skipper measures how far along the grid square each number lies; e.g., 69965.0 on the SS7-Z axis is about one fourth of the way between the 69960.0 and 69980.0 lines. In order to find this distance the skipper refers to a wedge-shaped scale on his loran chart. He marks off the distance between the grid lines 69960.0 and 69980.0 on the chart; then, with dividers, he finds the same distance on the scale (blue line), measuring between the scale's converging boundary lines. He next takes one fourth of this distance (blue arrow) and transfers it to the grid square (black X's) for one line of position. He repeats the procedure for the second line and gets his fix.

RICH HAUL FOR AN AUTOMATED TRAWLER

The 85-foot fishing trawler *Alliance,* heading out of Point Judith, Rhode Island, on a fishing trip, is carrying the ultimate in electronic gear. Festooned atop her cabin and her superstructure is an array of antennas attesting to the presence on board of some $11,000 worth of futuristic marine technology.

Alliance's two co-owners and her three-man crew fish regularly near the edge of the continental shelf, some 50 to 75 miles away from shore. And without the electronic gear boxes, all hands could soon drift into bankruptcy.

Alliance is a lineal descendant of the sailing craft that fished New England waters for 300 years. To find their course —and the fish—those old-time sloops and schooners had only a compass, a lead line and a lookout. Often they became lost in a fog or storm, had their nets torn by unseen rocks, even sank when steamers running blind in bad weather rammed them. Amid these many perils, the catch depended primarily on chance—but, nevertheless, in those days of plentiful fish and relatively few fishing boats, the chances were generally good.

Today the picture has changed. Escalating costs, heavy competition and dwindling schools of fish force modern trawlers to search ever harder for their catch.

Despite this, *Alliance's* sophisticated electronic aids regularly guide her home with her hold bulging with 40,000 pounds of iced fish. Her radar warns of hazards, and picks out buoys and coastline contours; loran pinpoints the ship's location, guiding her to areas where fish are known to be or away from areas where wrecks endanger nets. Supersensitive depth recorders give the navigator eyes underwater, so that no school of fish hidden beneath the boat escapes his gaze. So vital have these electronic aids become that the skipper of *Alliance* says flatly, "I wouldn't go fishing without this equipment."

The fishing boat Alliance leaves her home port of Point Judith, Rhode Island, on the start of a three-day cruise to the fishing grounds near the edge of the continental shelf. Positioned on her cabin roof is a radar antenna; her superstructure carries the antennas for a wind-velocity gauge, loran, a radio and a two-way marine radiotelephone.

The skipper of Alliance steers his craft across Block Island Sound en-route to the fishing grounds. Arrayed next to him at the ready are the boat's electronic crew members. These include, from left: a wide-screen depth finder to provide a display of bottom contours; two loran sets for instant position fixes; above the lorans, an extra-sensitive depth finder that can locate fish; a radarscope with its viewing hood; and to the left of the skipper's head, two radio receivers.

On a chart of the Atlantic Ocean off southern New England, the captain plans a triangular course to put Alliance at the edge of the continental shelf. The course's outgoing leg runs about 75 miles southeast, past Block Island. The base line cuts across a productive area for butterfish, which bring good prices.

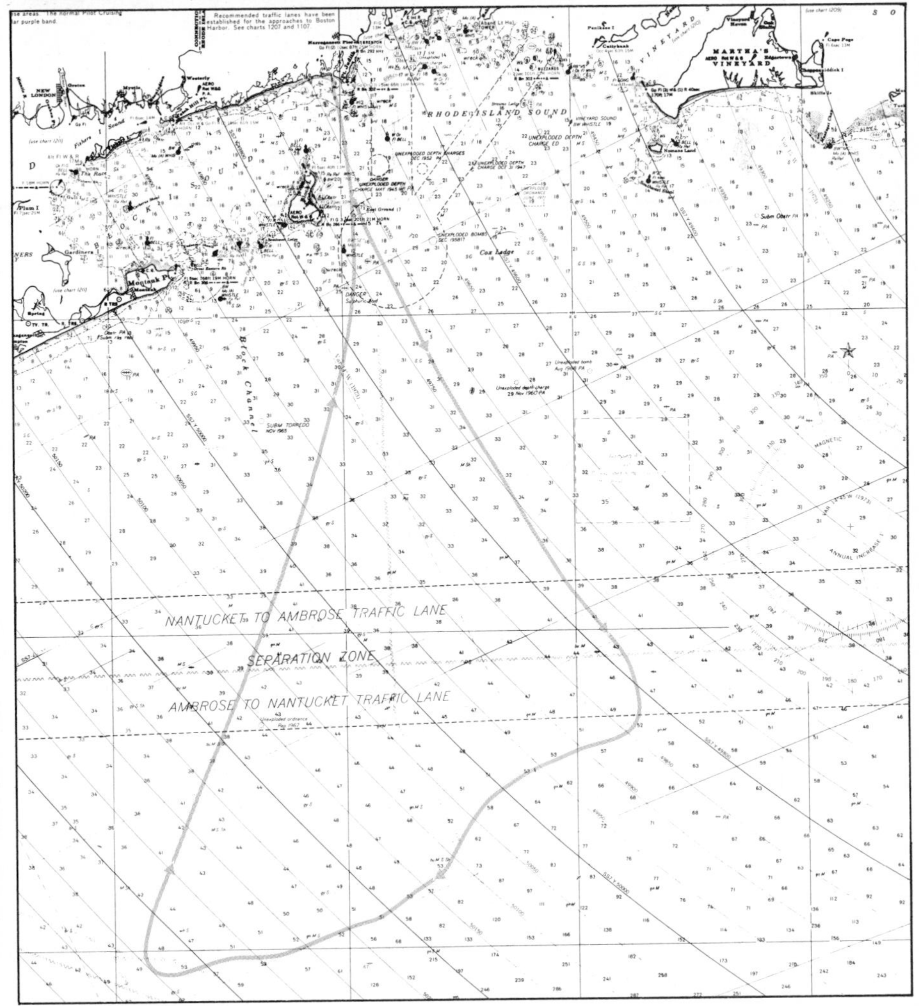

As he comes abreast of Block Island in poor visibility, the skipper of Alliance peers at his radarscope to pick up the familiar shape of the island, thus reaffirming his position and making sure no vessels are in his path. In the fleeting blips that flash on the scope, experience has taught him to recognize the shoreline, buoys, any small craft and even rain showers that may surround him. At bottom is a photographic reproduction of his view in the scope.

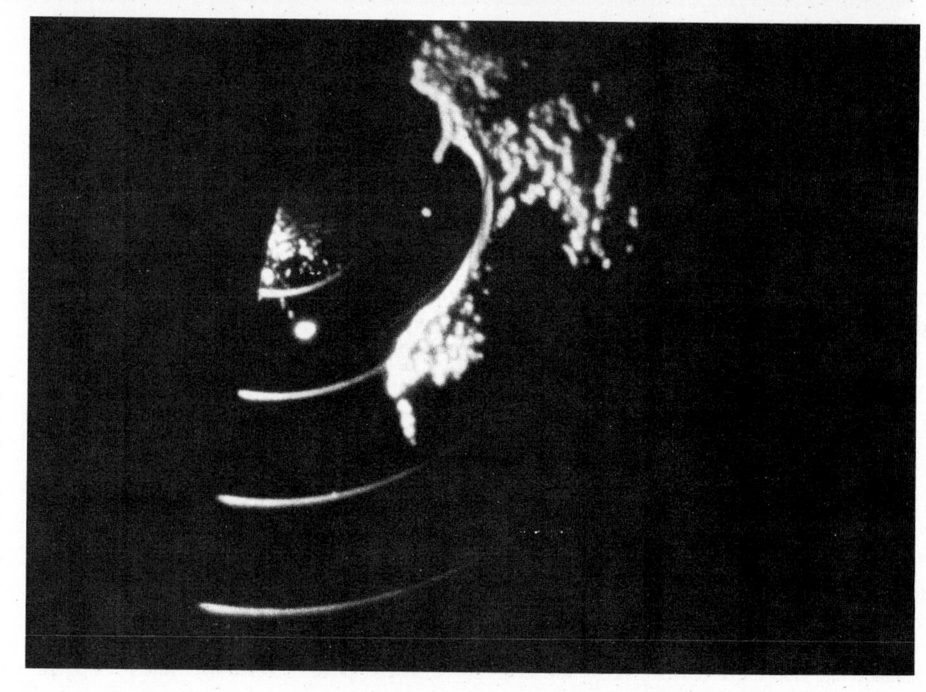

Alliance's radar shows the eastern coastline of Block Island, with the island's southern tip at the top of the screen. Alliance is at the center point of the four concentric arcs, which indicate distances of one, two, three and four nautical miles from the vessel. The mass of blips around the boat are harmless reflections from waves, which the skipper knows he can safely ignore. The small dot inside the crescent of the coast is caused by a bell buoy. The big, bright dot outside the first ring is from a radar-reflecting buoy.

Consulting his chart as he nears the fishing ground, the skipper rechecks the exact locations of bottom obstructions—marked by Xs—that would foul his nets. Next to the Xs he has noted the loran coordinate numbers (pages 140-141) that identify their locations. He has also recorded the numbers in the logbook at left. The flashing numbers on the loran set (bottom) indicate his own position; by checking the chart, he knows whether he can safely drop his nets.

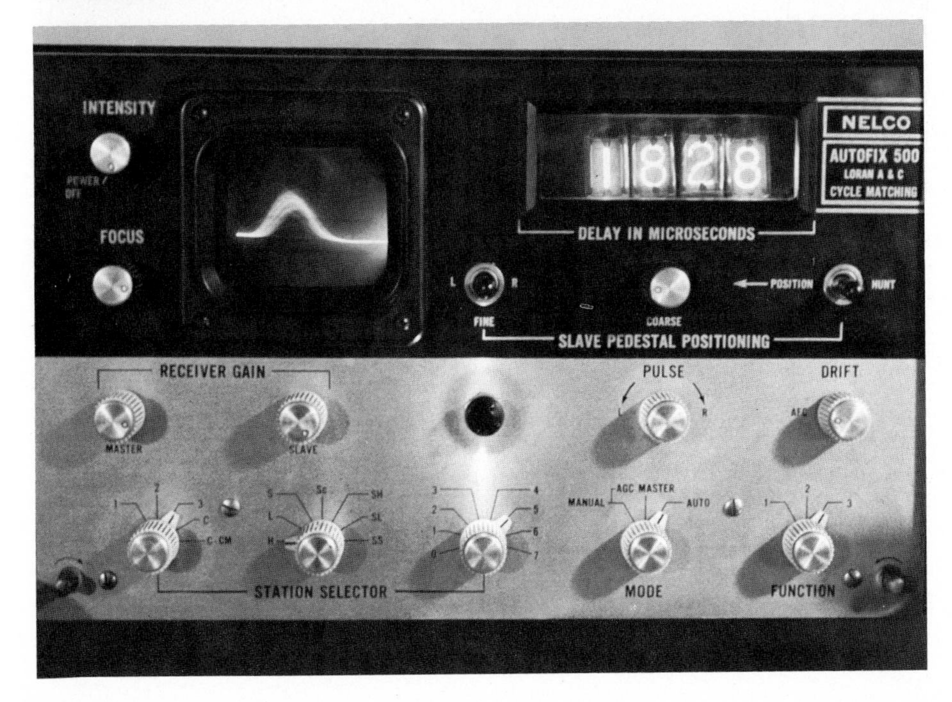

The readout panel of a loran receiver shows a four-digit number (upper right) that identifies the loran coordinate the boat is crossing. By finding the spot on the chart where this number has been printed, the captain pinpoints the location of his vessel. The wavy line on the scope (upper left) indicates that the equipment is correctly tuned to the shore-based loran broadcasting station; an incorrect tuning-dial setting would produce a line that oscillated wildly

Alliance's main depth recorder displays by print-out a profile of the smooth, sloping plain of the continental shelf. At this point the vessel is nearing the shelf's edge—which is prime fishing ground—and the skipper switches on his extra-sensitive depth indicator for any signs of fish (bottom).

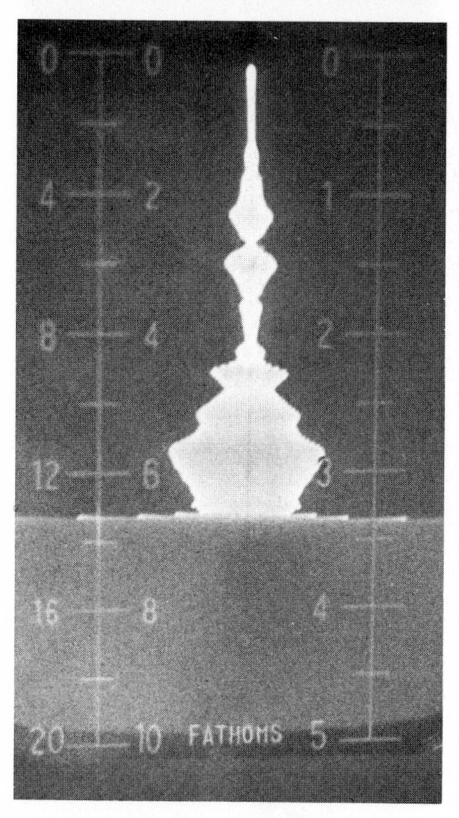

This dramatically varied light pattern on Alliance's electronic depth scope is produced by sound waves echoing off fish. The echoes, relatively weak compared with those from the bottom, are amplified by the sensitive scope. The wide base of the pattern indicates a tight grouping of fish near the bottom.

Knee-deep in the butterfish spotted on Alliance's scope, a crewman secures the vessel's net around a winch drum that hauls the net up. The enormous catch will be quickly stowed into the hold and covered with crushed ice; and Alliance will head home after another successful voyage—thanks to the lift from her electronic gear.

6

When the ocean retreats from Southend-on-Sea, England, a mile-wide mud flat uncovers in the Thames estuary *(opposite),* as though the land had heaved up out of the sea. Some six hours later the waters return with a rush. The owner of the stranded sailboat at left knows from long observation how the local tides and currents behave, and he has prepared for them. His craft has twin keels that hold it upright when low tide dries out the estuary. The skipper also knows exactly when the tide will come in again to float him clear.

Few tidal flows are as severe or dramatic as the ones in the Thames estuary. Yet all along the world's seacoasts the tide rises and falls at least once a day,

COPING WITH CURRENT AND TIDE

and in most cases twice. This enormous movement of water generates tidal currents that swirl in and out of bays, coves, straits and estuaries, flooding when the water rises, ebbing when it recedes. Even in inland areas where the tide does not reach, water levels may fluctuate with periods of rainfall or drought, and currents of varying strength flow down rivers to the sea. Almost anywhere he sails, in fact, a boatman travels across a surface that is itself in continuous motion, a kind of watery magic carpet that carries him up and down and back and forth according to its own physical laws. To navigate across this moving surface with any degree of precision, every boatman must —like the Thames skipper—have a clear idea of the tides and currents at any given moment. For example, since the soundings on nautical charts show water depths only at the time of mean low water, a navigator using a depth finder to determine his position must calculate the tide level at the moment he takes his reading, and add it to the charted depth.

In calculating both currents and tides, the navigator's task is further complicated by the idiosyncratic time schedule of tidal movements. The exact moments of high and low water, and also the periods of flood and ebb current, vary with every location and change every day. However, these variations can be predicted with some degree of accuracy. Every year the National Ocean Survey (NOS) publishes four volumes of tide tables *(pages 152-153)* that give tide predictions for most of the navigable world. The volume entitled *East Coast of North and South America,* for example, estimates tide levels for some 2,000 places from Greenland to Tierra del Fuego. To keep each volume within manageable size, full daily predictions are listed for only a few principal points, called reference stations. All the remaining locations, or local stations, are keyed to one of the reference stations. And the tables include brief annotations that allow the navigator to compute the differences between the tides at any local station and its reference station.

Although currents in any given area generally relate to the times and extent of tidal rise and fall, the correspondence is rarely exact. The NOS, therefore, publishes a separate set of tidal current tables *(pages 154-155)* that predict current times, speeds and directions. These, too, are organized around reference stations and local stations, and allow the navigator to calculate currents for any day of the year. Also, for 13 of the nation's busiest coastal areas, the NOS issues tidal current charts *(pages 156-157)* that graphically show current patterns, hour by hour, throughout the cycle of currents.

But while the tide and current tables give fairly accurate estimates of the water's movement, their predictions are hardly ever exact. Strong winds, heavy rain, even low barometric pressure can radically alter local tide levels. And one of the world's mightiest currents, the 45-mile-wide Gulf Stream sweeping northward up the Florida coast, is caused solely by the trade winds flowing steadily across the Atlantic Ocean. Piloting through it *(pages 162-167)* is one of the supreme tests of a navigator's skill.

High and dry for the moment, a small sloop sits firmly on its twin keels, awaiting the rush of the next high water across the tidal flat in the Thames estuary at Southend-on-Sea, England.

Timetables for Tides

When coming into an area like Jekyll Sound *(right)*, which has a six-foot mid-channel shoal, a skipper needs to know how much water he will have under his hull when he gets there. To figure this, he must consult three different listings *(opposite)* in the area's tide tables and make a few quick calculations. The work sheet at right, below, simplifies this process.

In the example shown, the skipper plans to arrive at Jekyll Point on June 1, 1975, at 4:30 p.m. To figure out the tide levels, he looks up Jekyll Point in the tide tables index, and learns that the nearest reference station is Savannah River Entrance, listed in the section of the tide tables labeled Table 1 *(opposite, top)*.

From Table 1, the skipper finds the Savannah River tide levels for the afternoon of June 1 (shaded gray in this example). On his work sheet, he copies the exact times of high and low water, and the height of each (color-keyed to the table in the same gray tint). These levels will differ slightly, but significantly, from the times and heights at Jekyll Point.

To calculate the correct figures for Jekyll Point, the skipper now turns to Table 2; the figures in the first two columns labeled "differences" tell him (blue-gray tint) that the tides there occur 28 minutes later than at the reference station. He notes these figures on his work sheet, and adds them to the Savannah River data to get the Jekyll Point times. He uses the next two figures in the table to correct the height of both high and low tide.

Next, the skipper works out the figures he needs to make use of the third table, which allows him to calculate the water level at 4:30 p.m., the time at which he will pass the shoal near Jekyll Point. He gets his first figure by subtracting the high-water time (1347) from the low-water time (2007), giving him the duration of the tide fall (6 hours 20 minutes). Then he computes the time difference between high tide (1347) and his moment of arrival (1630) and notes the result (2 hours 43 minutes). Finally he subtracts the low-tide level (1.1 feet) from the high-tide level (5.7 feet) to get the tidal range (4.6 feet).

Now he finds those three figures in Table 3, as shown. This table gives the skipper a number (shaded blue) that enables him to make the key calculation; he subtracts 1.8 from the high-water height of 5.7 feet and gets the tide level at 4:30 p.m. — 3.9 feet. Adding this figure to the charted depth of six feet over the shoal, he finds that he has plenty of water — 9.9 feet — in which to pass with safety.

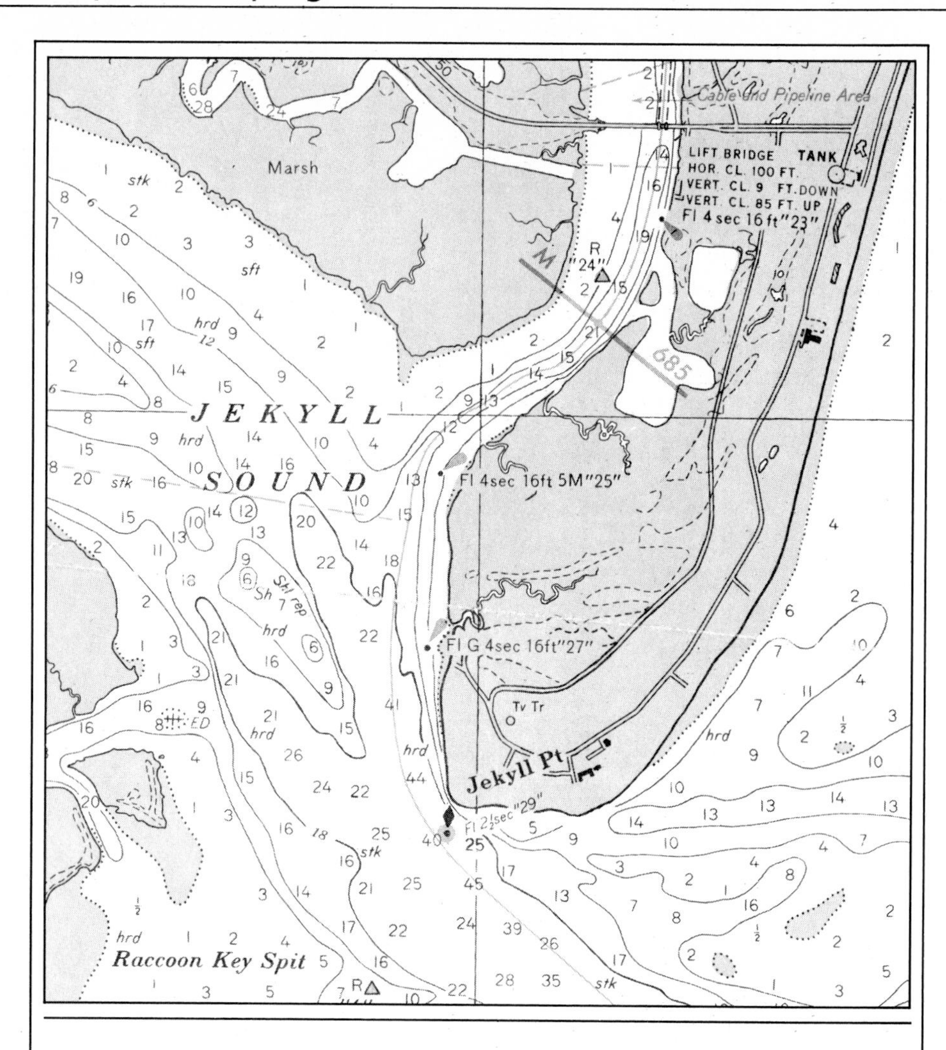

TIDE-TABLE WORK SHEET

Tidal Data for Desired Location — date: June 1, 1975

Reference station: Savannah River Entrance, Georgia
High water: (time) 1319 hrs. **(height)** 6.0 ft.
Low water: (time) 1939 hrs. **(height)** 1.1 ft.

Local station: Jekyll Point
High-water time difference: +28 mins. **High-water height difference:** – 0.3 ft.
Low-water time difference: +28 mins. **Low-water height difference:** 0.0
High water: (time) 1347 hrs. **(height)** 5.7 ft.
Low water: (time) 2007 hrs. **(height)** 1.1 ft.

Height of Tide at a Desired Time — date: June 1, 1975

Time: 1630 hrs. **Locality:** Jekyll Point
Duration of rise or fall: 6 hrs. 20 mins. (2007 hrs. – 1347 hrs.)
Time from nearest high or low water: 2 hrs. 43 mins. (1630 hrs. – 1347 hrs.)
Range of tide: 4.6 ft. (5.7 ft. – 1.1 ft.)
Height of nearest high or low water: 5.7 ft.
Correction to height: – 1.8 ft.
Height of tide at desired time: 3.9 ft. (5.7 ft – 1.8 ft.)

Height of tide at 1630 hrs.: 3.9 ft.
Charted water depth: 6.0 ft.
Depth of water at 1630 hrs.: 9.9 ft.

SAVANNAH RIVER ENTRANCE, GA., 1975 — 101

TIMES AND HEIGHTS OF HIGH AND LOW WATERS

APRIL Day	Time H.M.	Ht. Ft.	APRIL Day	Time H.M.	Ht. Ft.	MAY Day	Time H.M.	Ht. Ft.	MAY Day	Time H.M.	Ht. Ft.	JUNE Day	Time H.M.	Ht. Ft.	JUNE Day	Time H.M.	Ht. Ft.
1 TU	0551 1148 1802	-0.2 6.3 0.1	16 W	0503 1050 1717 2319	0.3 6.2 0.2 7.3	1 TH	0615 1213 1826	0.3 6.0 0.7	16 F	0539 1138 1759	0.0 6.4 0.2	1 SU	0049 0719 1319 1939	6.2 0.5 6.0 1.1	16 M	0044 0716 1331 1954	7.1 -0.4 7.0 0.1
2 W	0025 0647 1242 1857	6.9 0.3 6.0 0.5	17 TH	0551 1145 1810	0.4 6.1 0.3	2 F	0044 0709 1305 1923	6.5 0.6 5.9 1.0	17 SA	0002 0634 1239 1903	7.3 0.1 6.5 0.3	2 M	0137 0811 1408 2037	6.0 0.5 6.1 1.1	17 TU	0143 0816 1435 2100	6.8 -0.4 7.2 0.1
3 TH	0121 0746 1339 2002	6.4 0.7 5.7 0.8	18 F	0017 0651 1247 1916	7.1 0.5 6.1 0.4	3 SA	0137 0805 1400 2025	6.2 0.7 5.9 1.1	18 SU	0100 0737 1343 2012	7.1 0.0 6.7 0.2	3 TU	0227 0901 1500 2132	5.8 0.5 6.3 1.0	18 W	0246 0916 1541 2201	6.6 -0.5 7.4 -0.1
4 F	0224 0848 1442 2104	6.2 0.8 5.7 0.9	19 SA	0118 0756 1355 2028	7.0 0.4 6.3 0.3	4 SU	0232 0858 1457 2122	6.0 0.7 6.0 1.0	19 M	0203 0839 1452 2117	7.0 -0.2 7.0 0.0	4 W	0319 0951 1552 2223	5.8 0.3 6.6 0.8	19 TH	0351 1013 1644 2300	6.5 -0.6 7.7 -0.2
5 SA	0326 0940 1543	6.0 0.7 5.8	20 SU	0222 0902 1504	7.0 0.1 6.7	5 M	0327 0947 1551	5.9 0.5 6.2	20 TU	0308 0938 1558	6.9 -0.5 7.4	5 TH	0415 1036 1644	5.8 0.1 6.9	20 F	0454 1107 [illegible]	6.5 -0.7

Table 1 *in the tide tables for the East Coast predicts times and heights of high and low water at 48 key points, or reference stations, such as Savannah River Entrance, Georgia (left), for every day of the year. Time listings are in standard time for the area, indicated on a 24-hour clock. On Sunday afternoon, June 1, for example, high water is at 1319, or 1:19 p.m., and low water at 1939, or 7:39 p.m. Heights for these two tides are 6.0 feet and 1.1 feet above the area's charted depths. These figures, transposed to a work sheet (opposite), provide a start for determining water levels at other spots in the area.*

No.	PLACE	POSITION Lat.	POSITION Long.	DIFFERENCES Time High water	DIFFERENCES Time Low water	DIFFERENCES Height High water	DIFFERENCES Height Low water	RANGES Mean	RANGES Spring	Mean Tide Level
		° ′	° ′	h. m.	h. m.	feet	feet	feet	feet	feet
	GEORGIA — Continued St. Catherines and Sapelo-Sounds — Continued *Time meridian, 75°W.*	N.	W.	on SAVANNAH RIVER ENT., p. 100						
2756	Dallas Bluff, Julienton River-------	31 35	81 19	+0 50	+1 01	+0.7	0.0	7.6	8.9	3.8
2757	Blackbeard Island-------------------	31 32	81 12	+0 20	+0 19	0.0	0.0	6.9	8.1	3.4
2758	Dog Hammock, Sapelo River-----------	31 32	81 16	+0 31	+0 23	+0.2	0.0	7.1	8.3	3.6
2759	Pine Harbor, Sapelo River-----------	31 33	81 22	+1 05	+1 01	+0.3	0.0	7.2	8.4	3.6
2760	Eagle Creek, Mud River-- -----------	31 31	81 17	+0 23	+0 16	+0.3	0.0	7.2	8.4	3.6
276[illegible]	[illegible]	[illegible]	[illegible]	[illegible]	[illegible]	[illegible]	[illegible]	[illegible]	[illegible]	[illegible]
	St. Andrew Sound									
2797	Jekyll Point------------------------	31 01	81 26	+0 28	+0 28	-0.3	0.0	6.6	7.7	3.3
2799	Jointer Island, Jointer Creek-------	31 06	81 30	+1 02	+0 49	+0.3	0.0	7.2	8.4	3.6
	Little Satilla River									
2801	2½ miles above mouth--------- -	31 04	81 30	+0 47	+0 49 +1 20	-0.1	0.0	6.8	8.0	3.4

Table 2 *of the tide tables shows how the tides at various local stations differ in time and height from tides at the reference stations in Table 1. At Jekyll Point, high water is 28 minutes later than at Savannah River Entrance, as indicated by the "+ 28" in the high-water time-difference column. To find the moment of high water at Jekyll Point on the afternoon of June 1, this figure must be added to the time of the afternoon high water at Savannah River Entrance. In addition, high water is 0.3 feet lower than at the reference station, so this figure must be subtracted from the Savannah River Entrance tide level.*

Time from the nearest high water or low water

Duration of rise or fall h. m.	h. m.	h. m.	h. m.	h. m.	h. m.	h. m.	h. m.	h. m.	h. m.	h. m.	h. m.	h. m.	h. m.	h. m.	h. m.
4 00	0 08	0 16	0 24	0 32	0 40	0 48	0 56	1 04	1 12	1 20	1 28	1 36	1 44	1 52	2 00
4 20	0 09	0 17	0 26	0 35	0 43	0 52	1 01	1 09	1 18	1 27	1 35	1 44	1 53	2 01	2 10
4 40	0 09	0 19	0 28	0 37	0 47	0 56	1 05	1 15	1 24	1 33	1 43	1 52	2 01	2 11	2 20
5 00	0 10	0 20	0 30	0 40	0 50	1 00	1 10	1 20	1 30	1 40	1 50	2 00	2 10	2 20	2 30
5 20	0 11	0 21	0 32	0 43	0 53	1 04	1 15	1 25	1 36	1 47	1 57	2 08	2 19	2 29	2 40
5 40	0 11	0 23	0 34	0 45	0 57	1 08	1 19	1 31	1 42	1 53	2 05	2 16	2 27	2 39	2 50
6 00	0 12	0 24	0 36	0 48	1 00	1 12	1 24	1 36	1 48	2 00	2 12	2 24	2 36	2 48	3 00
6 20	0 13	0 25	0 38	0 51	1 03	1 16	1 29	1 41	1 54	2 07	2 19	2 32	2 45	2 57	3 10
6 40	0 13	0 27	0 40	0 53	1 07	1 20	1 33	1 47	2 00	2 13	2 27	2 40	2 53	3 07	3 20
7 00	0 14	0 28	0 42	0 56	1 10	1 24	1 38	1 52	2 06	2 20	2 34	2 48	3 02	3 16	3 30
7 20	0 15	0 29	0 44	0 59	1 13	1 28	1 43	1 57	2 12	2 27	2 41	2 56	3 11	3 25	3 40
7 40	0 15	0 31	0 46	1 01	1 17	1 32	1 47	2 03	2 18	2 33	2 49	3 04	3 19	3 35	3 50
8 00	0 16	0 32	0 48	1 04	1 20	1 36	1 52	2 08	2 24	2 40	2 56	3 12	3 28	3 44	4 00
8 20	0 17	0 33	0 50	1 07	1 23	1 40	1 57	2 13	2 30	2 47	3 03	3 20	3 37	3 53	4 10
8 40	0 17	0 35	0 52	1 09	1 27	1 44	2 01	2 19	2 36	2 53	3 11	3 28	3 45	4 03	4 20
9 00	0 18	0 36	0 54	1 12	1 30	1 48	2 06	2 24	2 42	3 00	3 18	3 36	3 54	4 12	4 30
9 20	0 19	0 37	0 56	1 15	1 33	1 52	2 11	2 29	2 48	3 07	3 25	3 44	4 03	4 21	4 40
9 40	0 19	0 39	0 58	1 17	1 37	1 56	2 15	2 35	2 54	3 13	3 33	3 52	4 11	4 31	4 50
10 00	0 20	0 40	1 00	1 20	1 40	2 00	2 20	2 40	3 00	3 20	3 40	4 00	4 20	4 40	5 00
10 20	0 21	0 41	1 02	1 23	1 43	2 04	2 25	2 45	3 06	3 27	3 47	4 08	4 29	4 49	5 10
10 40	0 21	0 43	1 04	1 25	1 47	2 08	2 29	2 51	3 12	3 33	3 55	4 16	4 37	4 59	5 20

Correction to height

Range of tide Ft.	Ft.	Ft.	Ft.	Ft.	Ft.	Ft.	Ft.	Ft.	Ft.	Ft.	Ft.	Ft.	Ft.	Ft.	Ft.
0.5	0.0	0.0	0.0	0.0	0.0	0.0	0.1	0.1	0.1	0.1	0.1	0.2	0.2	0.2	0.2
1.0	0.0	0.0	0.0	0.0	0.1	0.1	0.1	0.2	0.2	0.2	0.3	0.3	0.4	0.4	0.5
1.5	0.0	0.0	0.0	0.1	0.1	0.1	0.2	0.2	0.3	0.4	0.4	0.5	0.6	0.7	0.8
2.0	0.0	0.0	0.0	0.1	0.1	0.2	0.3	0.3	0.4	0.5	0.6	0.7	0.8	0.9	1.0
2.5	0.0	0.0	0.1	0.1	0.2	0.2	0.3	0.4	0.5	0.6	0.7	0.9	1.0	1.1	1.2
3.0	0.0	0.0	0.1	0.1	0.2	0.3	0.4	0.5	0.6	0.8	0.9	1.0	1.2	1.3	1.5
3.5	0.0	0.0	0.1	0.2	0.2	0.3	0.4	0.6	0.7	0.9	1.0	1.2	1.4	1.6	1.8
4.0	0.0	0.0	0.1	0.2	0.3	0.4	0.5	0.7	0.8	1.0	1.2	1.4	1.6	1.8	2.0
4.5	0.0	0.0	0.1	0.2	0.3	0.4	0.6	0.7	0.9	1.1	1.3	1.6	1.8	2.0	2.2
5.0	0.0	0.1	0.1	0.2	0.3	0.5	0.6	0.8	1.0	1.2	1.5	1.7	2.0	2.2	2.5
5.5	0.0	0.1	0.1	0.2	0.4	0.5	0.7	0.9	1.1	1.4	1.6	1.9	2.2	2.5	2.8
6.0	0.0	0.1	0.1	0.3	0.4	0.6	0.8	1.0	1.2	1.5	1.8	2.1	2.4	2.7	3.0
6.5	0.0	0.1	0.2	0.3	0.4	0.6	0.8	1.1	1.3	1.6	1.9	2.2	2.6	2.9	3.2
7.0	0.0	0.1	0.2	0.3	0.5	0.7	0.9	1.2	1.4	1.8	2.1	2.4	2.8	3.1	3.5
7.5	0.0	[illegible]	0.2	0.3	0.5	0.7	1.0	[illegible]	1.5	[illegible]	[illegible]	[illegible]	3.0	[illegible]	3.8

Table 3 *provides the navigator with the "correction to height" that allows him to determine the tide level at a particular spot at any time. On the work sheet opposite, he has calculated the duration of rise or fall, time from nearest high or low water, and range of tide as 6 hours 20 minutes, 2 hours 43 minutes, and 4.6 feet, respectively. He finds the 6:20 figure in the left-hand column, tracks it across to 2:43 in the table (the closest figure is actually 2:45), then follows that column down until it intersects the line from 4.5 (the nearest range figure to 4.6). The lines meet at the desired correction number—1.8. Since the tide is falling, he subtracts 1.8 from high water to arrive at the Jekyll Point tide level—3.9 feet.*

Forecasting Currents

Just as tide tables and work sheets help sailors figure out the heights of tides, so the tidal current tables help them forecast the speed and time of currents.

Suppose a skipper wants to cut into Blynman Canal in Gloucester, Massachusetts *(right)*, on June 18, 1975. If the current is flowing out of the canal with any force when he gets there, he may have trouble entering. So to establish the time, strength and direction of the various currents at the canal he refers to the tidal current tables and makes some quick calculations on the work sheet below.

He begins by consulting the nearest reference station, in this case Boston Harbor. Looking up Boston Harbor in Table 1 *(opposite, top)* under the column for June, he finds the periods of slack water, and also the times and velocities of the maximum ebb and flood currents. He expects to arrive at Blynman Canal around midday on June 18, but he is not sure precisely when. So he copies down all the figures for the various daytime currents (shaded gray, to key them to the work sheet).

Next, referring to Table 2, the skipper looks up the differences between the Blynman Canal currents (shaded blue-gray) and those at Boston Harbor. Following the steps described on the opposite page, he calculates the times of the two slack-water periods at Blynman, and the time and velocity of the maximum ebb and flood currents. He also notes down the directions of the ebb and flood—listed in degrees relative to true north.

As soon as the skipper nears the canal and can predict his exact arrival time—in this case 1400 hours, or 2 p.m.—he can turn to Table 3 and figure out what the current will be doing at that moment. He must first calculate two key figures from the data he has already entered on his work sheet. He determines the interval between his arrival time (1400) and the nearest slack water (1147); it is 2 hours 13 minutes. Now he wants to find the interval between the nearest slack water (1147) and the nearest maximum current (1507); it is 3 hours 20 minutes. Plotting these two intervals on Table 3, he finds the correction factor: 0.9 (blue shading). From his work sheet, the skipper notes that the maximum current will be flooding at 3.42 knots. He multiplies this figure by the correction factor to obtain the velocity when he reaches the canal: 3.07 knots. From Table 2 he has found that the current will be flowing at 310° true—the westerly bearing of the canal—giving him a welcome three-knot push through the channel.

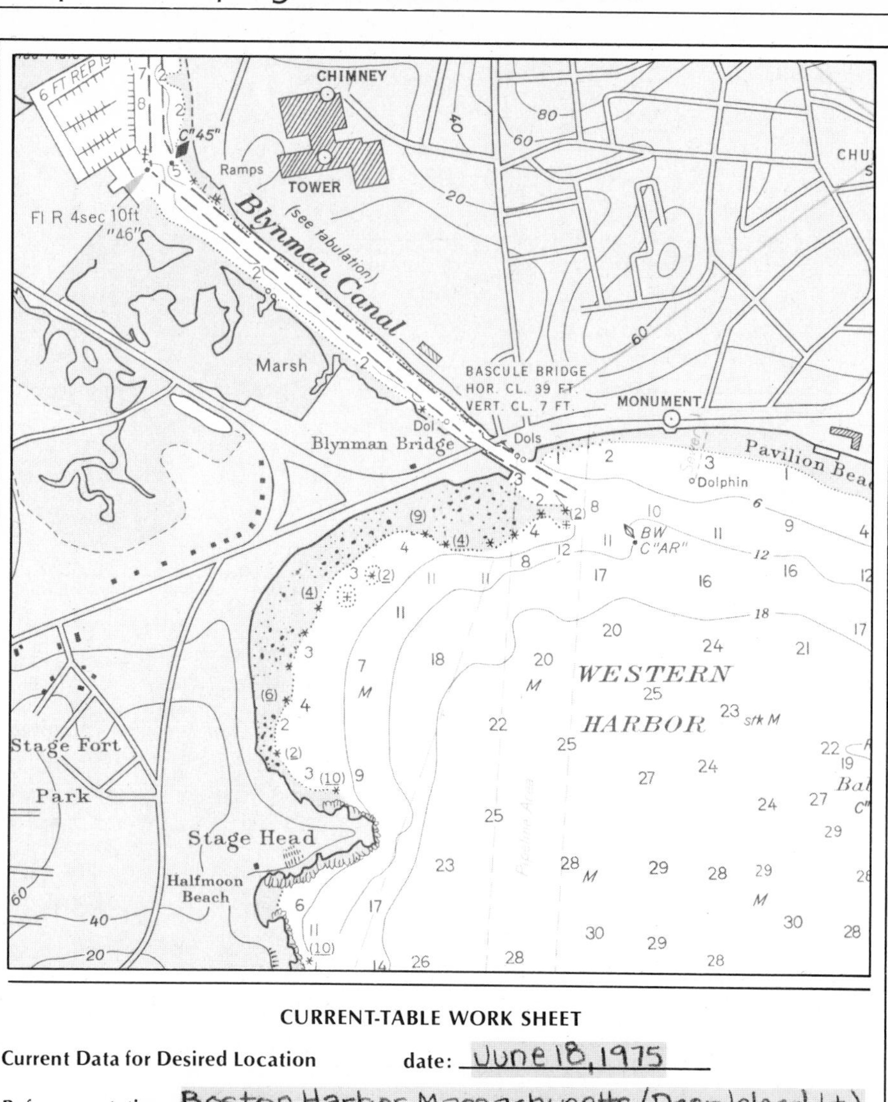

CURRENT-TABLE WORK SHEET

Current Data for Desired Location **date:** June 18, 1975

Reference station: Boston Harbor, Massachusetts (Deer Island Lt.)

Time:	Velocity:
0613 hrs.	Slack
1003 hrs.	1.3 Ebb
1227 hrs.	Slack
1552 hrs.	1.9 Flood

Local station: Blynman Canal Entrance (Gloucester Harbor)

Time difference: **Slack water:** -0.40

Maximum current: -0.45

Velocity ratio: **Maximum flood:** 1.8

Maximum ebb: 2.5

Direction (degrees true): Flood 310° **Ebb** 130°

Time:	Velocity:
0533 hrs.	Slack
0918 hrs.	3.25 Ebb
1147 hrs.	Slack
1507 hrs.	3.42 Flood

Velocity of Current at a Desired Time **date:** June 18, 1975

Time: 1400 hrs. **Locality:** Blynman Canal Ent.

Interval between slack and desired time: 2 hrs. 13 mins. (1400 hrs. - 1147 hrs.)

Interval between slack and maximum current: 3 hrs. 20 mins. (1507 hrs. - 1147 hrs.)

Maximum current: (ebb) 3.42

Correction factor: 0.9

Velocity at desired time: 3.07 (3.42 X 0.9) **Direction (degrees true):** 310°

BOSTON HARBOR (DEER ISLAND LIGHT), MASS., 1975

F-FLOOD, DIR. 260° TRUE E-EBB, DIR. 085° TRUE

MAY								JUNE							
DAY	SLACK WATER TIME H.M.	MAXIMUM CURRENT TIME H.M.	VEL. KNOTS	DAY	SLACK WATER TIME H.M.	MAXIMUM CURRENT TIME H.M.	VEL. KNOTS	DAY	SLACK WATER TIME H.M.	MAXIMUM CURRENT TIME H.M.	VEL. KNOTS	DAY	SLACK WATER TIME H.M.	MAXIMUM CURRENT TIME H.M.	VEL. KNOTS
1		0021	1.7F	16	0236	0517	1.3E	1		0137	1.4F	16		0120	1.8F
TH	0308	0703	1.4E	F	0903	1218	1.7F	SU	0416	0822	1.1E	M	0410	0751	1.4E
	0936	1255	1.6F		1511	1739	1.1E		1040	1405	1.4F		1031	1354	1.9F
	1546	1934	1.1E		2118				1654	2052	1.0E		1644	2030	1.4E
	2152								2308				2303		
2		0115	1.5F	17		0036	1.6F	2		0229	1.3F	17		0224	1.8F
F	0400	0802	1.2E	SA	0330	0618	1.3E	M	0508	0916	1.0E	TU	0510	0859	1.3E
	1029	1348	1.5F		0956	1315	1.7F		1130	1457	1.4F		1128	1452	1.9F
	1641	2036	1.0E		1606	1918	1.1E		1745	2147	1.0E		1743	2135	1.4E
	2249				2217										
3		0212	1.4F	18		0139	1.6F	3	0003	0324	1.3F	18	0007	0326	1.8F
SA	0456	0901	1.1E	SU	0428	0803	1.2E	TU	0603	1007	1.0E	W	0613	1003	1.3E
	1123	1444	1.4F		1053	1415	1.7F		1221	1549	1.4F		1227	1552	1.9F
	1739	2131	1.0E		1704	2049	1.2E		1836	2238	1.0E		1844	2237	1.5E
	2347				2321										
4		0307	1.3F	19		0243	1.7F	4	0057	0417	1.3F	19	0111	0427	1.8F
SU	0554	0954	1.1E	M	0530	0920	1.3E	W	0657	1058	1.0E	TH	0718	1104	1.4E
	1217	1539	1.4F		1152	1516	1.8F		1310	1639	1.4F		1327	1651	1.9F
	1835	2226	1.1E		1805	2156	1.3E		1926	2328	1.1E		1945	2338	1.7E
5	0045	0405	1.3F	20	0025	0347	1.7F	5	0150	0508	1.4F	20	0213	0527	1.8F
M	0652	1050	1.1E	TU	0633	1024	1.3E	TH	0751	1147	1.0E	F	0821	1202	1.4E
	1310	1630	1.4F		1251	1616	1.9F		1359	1728	1.5F		1425	1747	2.0F
	1928	2319	1.1E		1905	2257	1.5E		2013				2044		
6	0140	0456	1.4F	21	0128	0448	1.8F	6		0015	1.2E	21		0031	1.7E
TU	0747	1139	1.1E	W	0736	1125	1.4E	F	0240	0557	1.4F	SA	0312	0622	1.9F
	1359	1719	1.5F		1349	1712	2.0F		0842	1236	1.0E		0922	1257	1.5E
	2016				2004	[illegible]	1.7E		[illegible]	[illegible]	1.6E		1520	[illegible]	[illegible]

Table 1 *of the tidal current tables lists the four daily periods of slack water at Boston, and the times and velocities of the peak flood (F) and ebb (E) currents. The boatman refers to the entries in the table that correspond to his approximate arrival time at his local station—in this case the daytime hours of June 18 (gray shading). Thus he notes that the morning slack water is at 0613 hours, and that at 1003 hours there will be an ebb current of 1.3 knots. He then transfers these figures to the work sheet on the opposite page, along with the figures for the afternoon slack water and flood current.*

No.	PLACE	POSITION Lat.	POSITION Long.	TIME DIFFERENCES Slack water	TIME DIFFERENCES Maximum current	VELOCITY RATIOS Maximum flood	VELOCITY RATIOS Maximum ebb	MAXIMUM CURRENTS Flood Direction (true)	MAXIMUM CURRENTS Flood Average velocity	MAXIMUM CURRENTS Ebb Direction (true)	MAXIMUM CURRENTS Ebb Average velocity
		° ′	° ′	*h. m.*	*h. m.*			*deg.*	*knots*	*deg.*	*knots*
	MASSACHUSETTS COAST—Continued	N.	W.	on BOSTON HARBOR, p.16							
	Time meridian, 75°W.										
390	Merrimack River entrance	42 49	70 49	+0 40	(*)	1.3	1.1	285	2.2	105	1.4
395	Newburyport, Merrimack River	42 49	70 52	+1 10	+0 40	0.9	1.1	290	1.5	100	1.4
400	Plum Island Sound entrance	42 42	70 47	+0 15	-0 10	0.9	1.2	315	1.6	185	1.5
405	Annisquam Harbor Light	42 40	70 41	+0 20	-0 05	0.8	0.8	200	1.0	015	1.3
410	Gloucester Harbor entrance	42 35	70 40	*Current too weak and variable to be predicted.*							
415	Blynman Canal ent., Gloucester Hbr	42 37	70 40	-0 40	-0 45	1.8	2.5	310	3.0	130	3.3
420	Marblehead Channel	42 30	70 49	+0 40	+0 40	0.3	0.2	285	0.4	105	0.4
425	Nahant, off East Point	42 25	70 54	-0 20	-0 20	0.5	0.5	235	0.8	085	0.7
430	Lynn Harbor entrance	42 25	70 57	-0 05	-0 05	0.3	0.3	325	0.5	170	0.5
435	Winthrop Beach, 1.2 miles east of	42 23	70 57	-0 05	-0 30	0.2	0.2	195	0.4	095	0.2
	BOSTON HARBOR APPROACHES										
440	Stellwagen Bank	42 24	70 24	*Current too weak and variable to be predicted.*							
445	Boston Lightship, 3 miles SSE. of	42 20	70 45	*Current too weak and variable to be predicted.*							
450	North Channel, off Great Faun	42 21	70 56	-0 05	-0 25	0.7	1.1	200	1.2	025	1.4
455	Hypocrite Channel	42 21	70 54	-0 30	-0 30	0.7	0.7	255	1.2	070	1.0
460	Nantasket Roads entrance	42 19	70 53	0 00	-0 20	1.0	1.0	260	1.4	085	1.5
465	[illegible]ck Rock C[illegible]	42 1[illegible]	70 55	[illegible]	[illegible]	0.7	0.9	220	1.2	[illegible]	[illegible]

Table 2 *shows the differences between the Boston Harbor currents and those at Blynman Canal (blue-gray shading). In the first time-difference column, the boatman finds that slack water at Blynman is 40 minutes earlier; thus the Blynman slack occurs at 0533 and 1147. The next column indicates that maximum currents are earlier by 45 minutes; so the Blynman ebb is 0918, the flood 1507. From the two velocity-ratio columns he finds that the Blynman ebb will be stronger by a multiple of 2.5 knots, the flood by a multiple of 1.8 knots. Thus the maximum ebb current at Blynman is 3.25 knots, the flood 3.42.*

TABLE A

Interval between slack and desired time (h. m.)	Interval between slack and maximum current: 1 20	1 40	2 00	2 20	2 40	3 00	3 20	3 40	4 00	4 20	4 40	5 00	5 20	5 40
	f.	*f.*	*f.*	*f.*	*f.*	*f.*	*f.*	*f.*	*f.*	*f.*	*f.*	*f.*	*f.*	*f.*
0 20	0.4	0.3	0.3	0.2	0.2	0.2	0.2	0.1	0.1	0.1	0.1	0.1	0.1	0.1
0 40	0.7	0.6	0.5	0.4	0.4	0.3	0.3	0.3	0.3	0.2	0.2	0.2	0.2	0.2
1 00	0.9	0.8	0.7	0.6	0.6	0.5	0.5	0.4	0.4	0.4	0.3	0.3	0.3	0.3
1 20	1.0	1.0	0.9	0.8	0.7	0.6	0.6	0.5	0.5	0.5	0.4	0.4	0.4	0.4
1 40	---	1.0	1.0	0.9	0.8	0.8	0.7	0.7	0.6	0.6	0.5	0.5	0.5	0.4
2 00	---	---	1.0	1.0	0.9	0.9	0.8	0.8	0.7	0.7	0.6.	0.6	0.6	0.5
2 20	---	---	---	1.0	1.0	0.9	0.9	0.8	0.8	0.7	0.7	0.7	0.6	0.6
2 40	---	---	---	---	1.0	1.0	1.0	0.9	0.9	0.8	0.8	0.7	0.7	0.7
3 00	---	---	---	---	---	1.0	1.0	1.0	0.9	0.9	0.8	0.8	0.8	0.7
3 20	---	---	---	---	---	---	1.0	1.0	1.0	0.9	0.9	0.9	0.8	0.8
3 40	---	---	---	---	---	---	---	1.0	1.0	1.0	0.9	0.9	0.9	0.9
4 00	---	---	---	---	---	---	---	---	1.0	1.0	1.0	1.0	0.9	0.9
4 20	---	---	---	---	---	---	---	---	---	1.0	1.0	1.0	1.0	0.9
4 40	---	---	---	---	---	---	---	---	---	---	1.0	1.0	1.0	1.0
5 00	---	---	---	---	---	---	---	---	---	---	---	1.0	1.0	1.0
5 20	---	---	---	---	---	---	---	---	---	---	---	---	1.0	1.0
5 40	---	---	---	---	---	---	---	---	---	---	---	---	---	1.0

Table 3, *part A (or in certain special cases part B), of the tidal current tables furnishes a correction factor that allows the navigator to find the current velocities at any time not accounted for by Tables 1 and 2. First he determines the interval between slack and desired time (2 hours 13 minutes), then finds the closest approximation in the left column (2:20). Now he figures the interval between slack and maximum current (3 hours 20 minutes). Reading across from 2:20 and down from 3:20, he finds the correction factor —0.9. That enables him to get the current velocity at the time he wants—3.07 knots.*

Patterns of Flow

For certain heavily traveled boating areas the National Ocean Survey has prepared annotated charts providing instant readings on the speed and direction of tidal currents. These tidal current charts are issued in booklets containing sets of 12, one for each hour of the current cycle. The four charts on these pages are from the set for Block Island Sound, near Connecticut. The data on such charts are based on the current at the area's reference station—in this case a tide-ripped narrows called The Race. To determine what the current is doing at a specific hour of a particular day, the navigator must check the tidal current tables *(pages 154-155)* for that day's listings at the reference station.

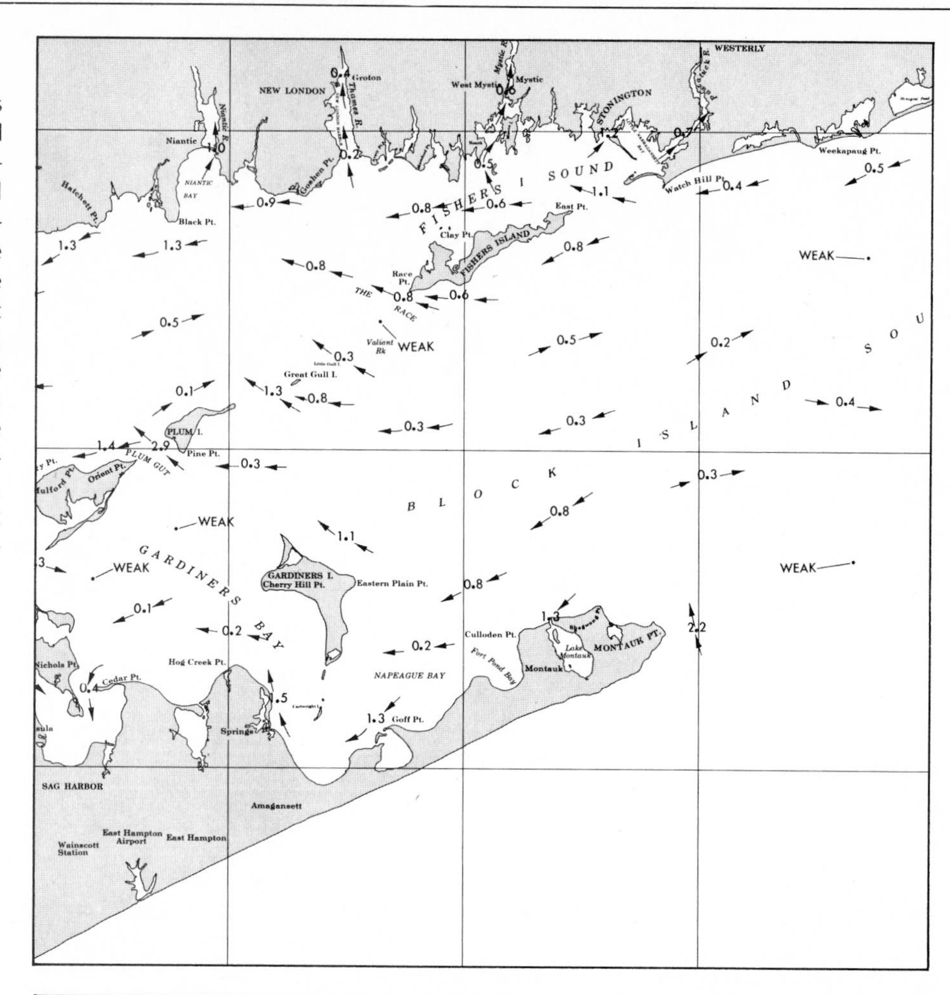

Slack water; flood begins. *When currents are slowest at The Race (top center, running southwest of Fishers Island), there are weak and conflicting currents all across the surrounding waters, as indicated by the labeled arrows. But a 2.9-knot current has already begun to stream northwest into Long Island Sound through a narrow channel that is called Plum Gut (left, middle).*

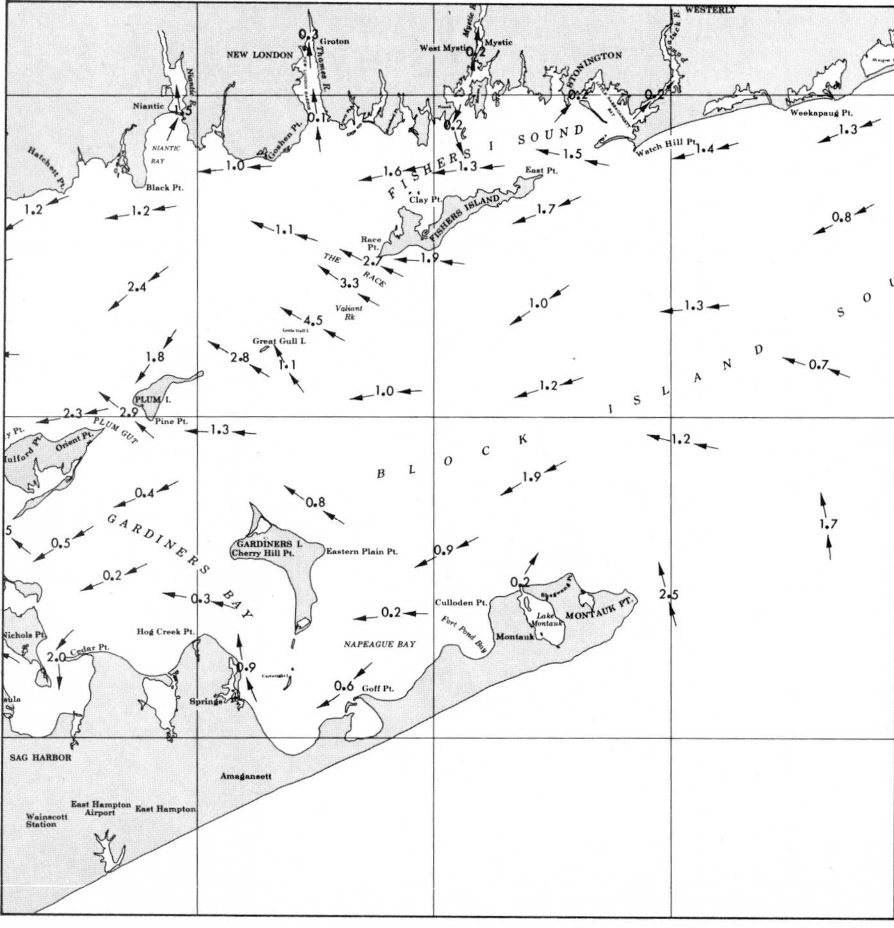

Maximum flood. *Three hours after slack water at The Race, currents flood into Long Island Sound at speeds up to 4.5 knots. As in all current charts, designated velocities are for the twice-monthly periods of spring tides, when currents run strongest. To adjust the figures for periods of weaker currents, the boatman can refer to the front of the current-chart booklet, where there is a correction table and instructions for using it.*

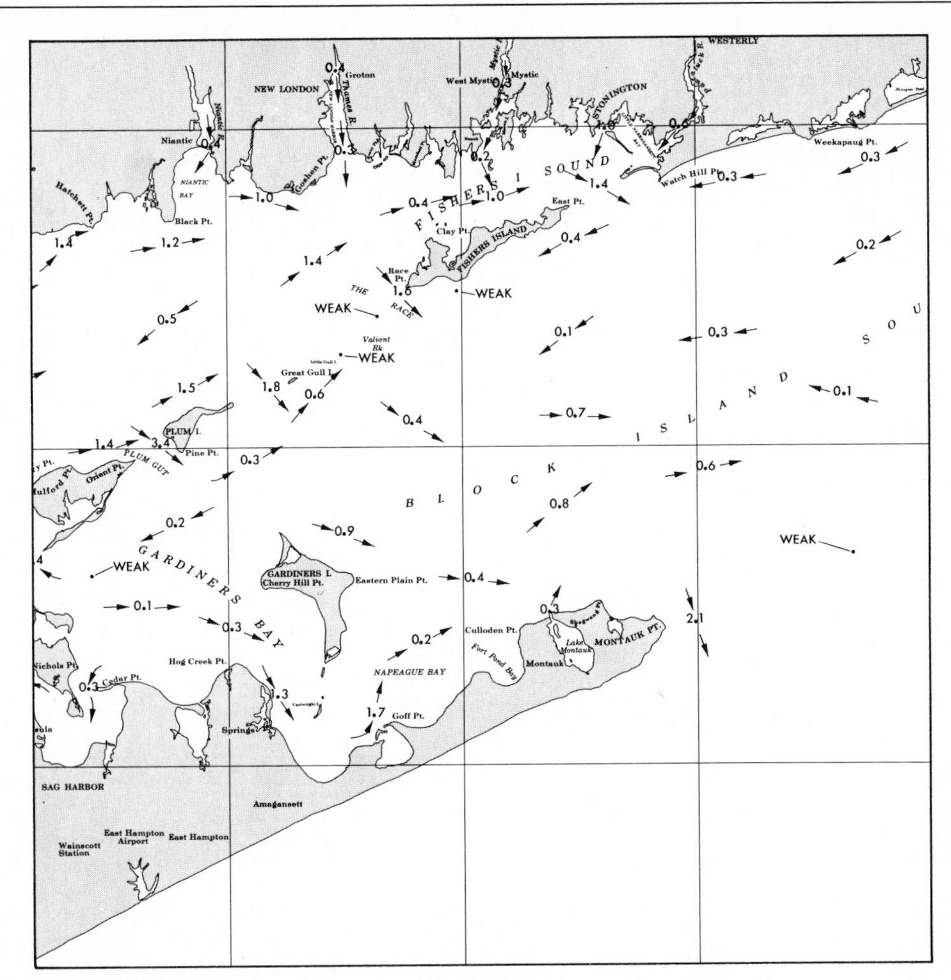

Slack water; ebb begins. *Just as the current turns at The Race, flows are weak and contrary throughout most of the nearby area. But along the north and south shores of Long Island Sound (top left corner), eastward-running currents have begun to quicken, and in the narrow sluice of Plum Gut, the ebb current has already reached 3.4 knots.*

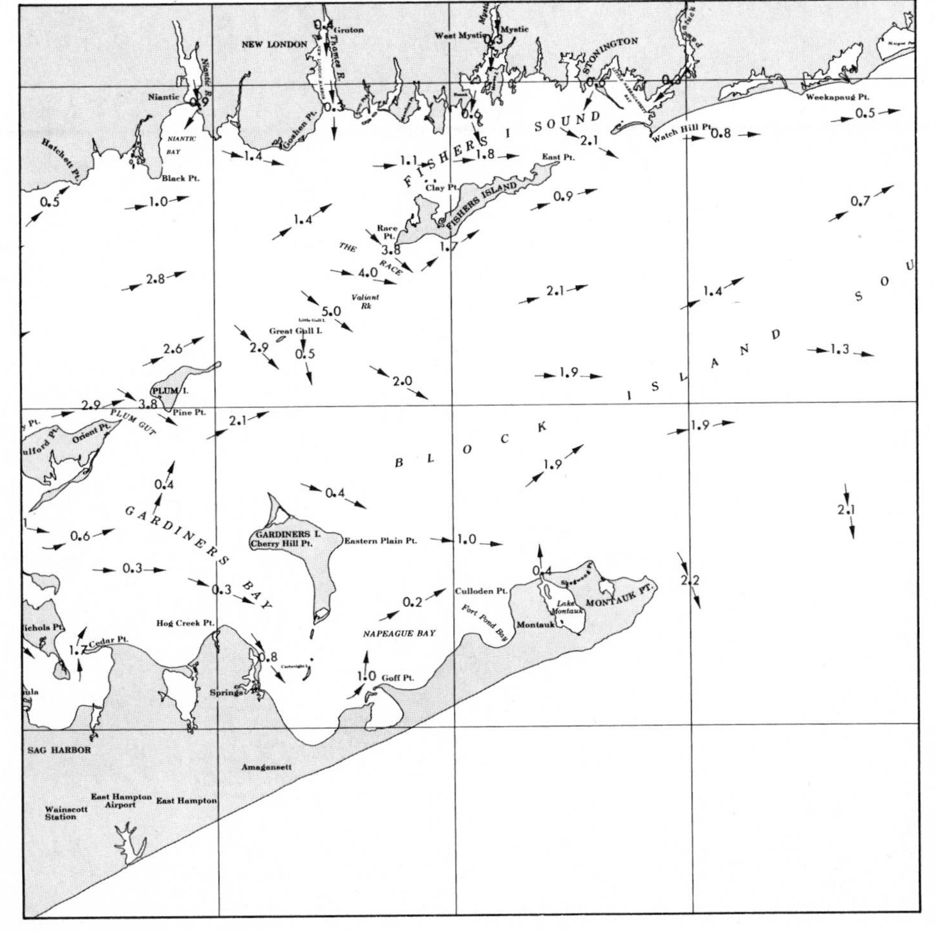

Maximum ebb. *Three hours after slack water at The Race, the ebb current surges southeasterly at speeds up to five knots, and the water now empties through Plum Gut at 3.8 knots. But at one channel, between Plum and Great Gull islands, the flow is only 2.9 knots, making this the easiest passage for a boat heading west into Long Island Sound.*

Working the Angles

Once the strength and direction of the current in a given place on a given day and hour have been calculated, as in the work sheet on page 154, they become vital statistics in plotting a course.

When a boat is running directly with or against the current, figuring the effect is a matter of simple arithmetic: running with a four-knot current adds four knots to the craft's progress over the bottom; bucking the current cuts progress by four knots. In either case, the skipper simply points his bow in the direction of his next mark and sails ahead.

More commonly, however, navigators must contend with a current that runs at an angle to the boat's intended path. The crosscurrent sweeps the boat sideways —and the longer the vessel stays in the current, the farther off course it will be carried, as shown in the diagram at right. So the skipper must adjust his heading in advance to compensate.

Some skippers are experienced enough at traveling through currents to make the proper adjustment by means of an educated guess, especially where distances are short. Over long distances, however—or when visibility is poor or navigational hazards threaten—more accurate methods are essential. One common approach is to work out a current triangle like that at the top of the opposite page.

The triangle is a graphic representation of the strength and direction of the current, and its effect on a moving boat. One line indicates the boat's intended path, or track, and the distance it travels in a given period of time. Since this distance depends on how fast the boat is moving, the length of the line also serves to represent the boat's speed (that is, a line covering 10 miles of chart and two hours of travel time indicates a speed of five knots). A second line, laid down from the destination end of the first line, shows the direction of the current and—by its length —the current's speed. The triangle's third leg provides the answer: the new heading the boat must take and the speed at which it must travel.

In practice, the current triangle may be plotted directly on a chart *(opposite, below)*. Note that the current's direction is shown in degrees relative to true north —the way it is reported in the tidal current tables; the navigator should therefore refer to the compass rose's outer circle when plotting the current on his chart. Other directions—for his course and track—are plotted in degrees magnetic, using the rose's inner circle.

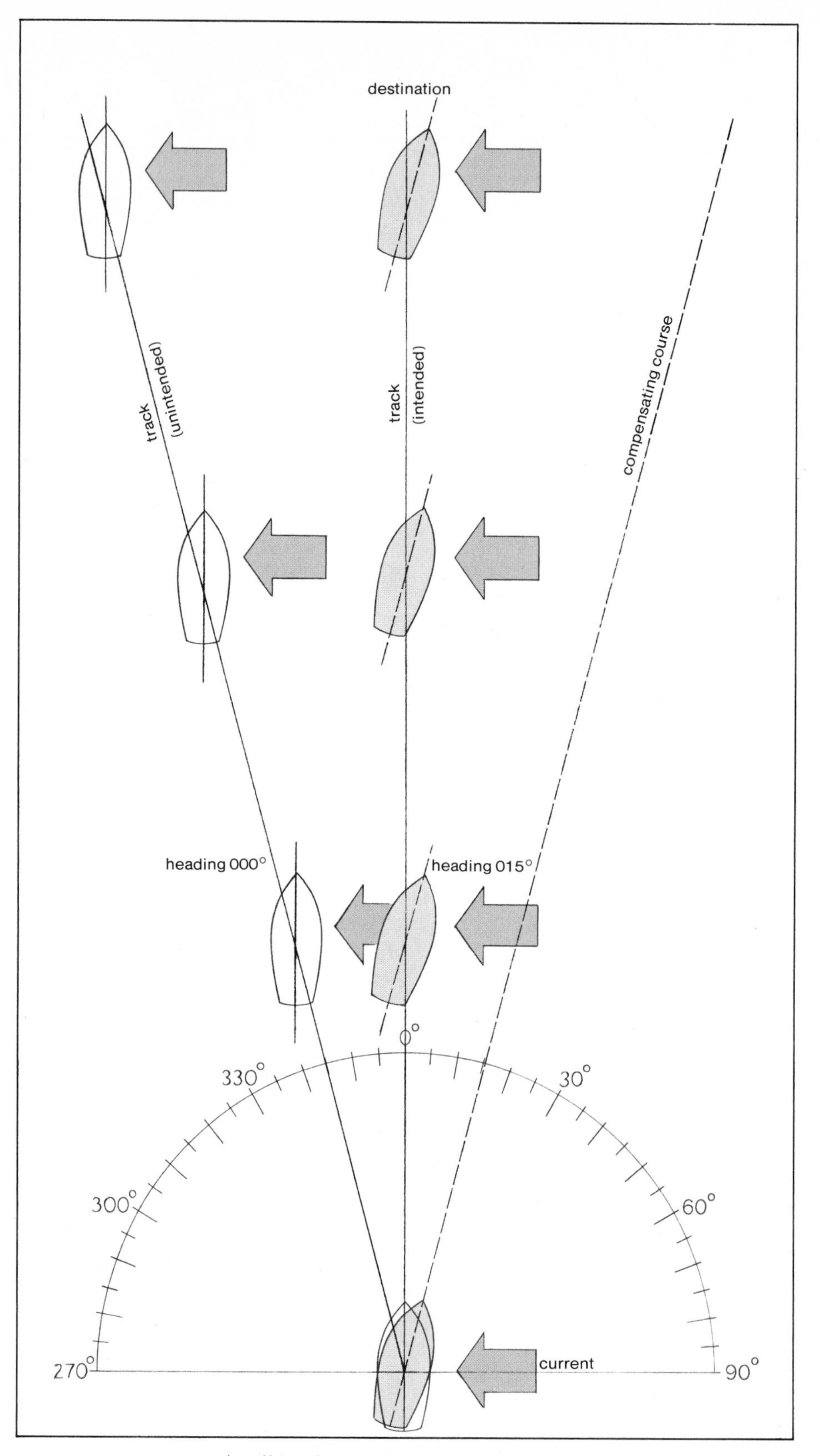

The effect of current on a boat's progress—and the way to correct for it—is shown by the diverging tracks of the two vessels in this diagram. Both are bound for a destination that bears 000°; and both move through a crosscurrent. The white boat heads straight for its objective, making no allowance for this flow; consequently, the current carries it progressively to port of its intended track. The gray boat, however, has anticipated the current, and heads into it slightly, at about 15°. Though the vessel's bow will always be pointed a bit to starboard of its goal, its actual track will lead right there.

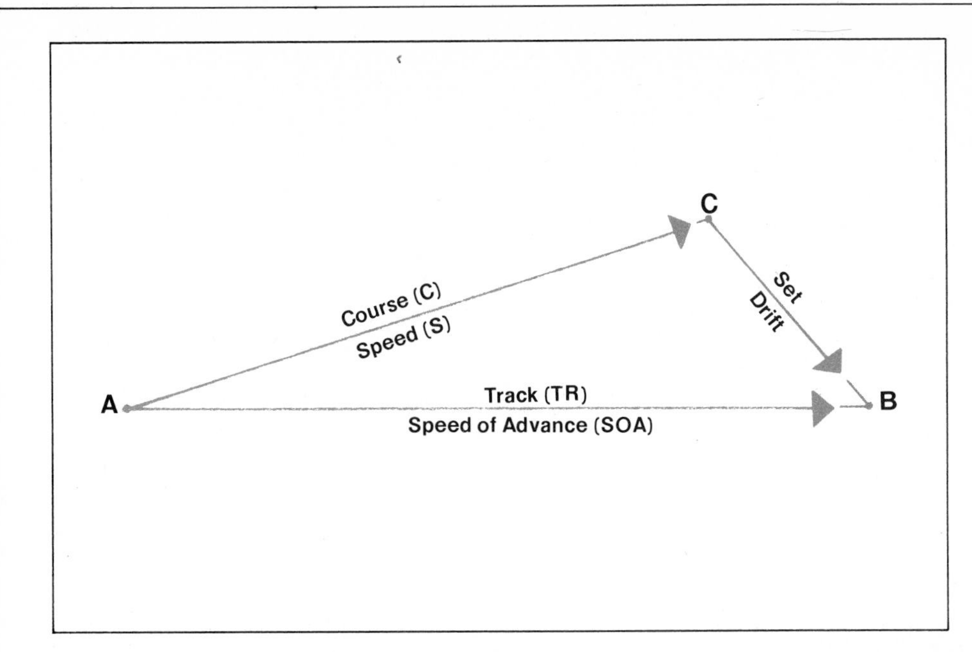

On this current triangle—with its own special shorthand—point A is the boat's starting position, B its destination. Line AB represents the boat's intended track (TR) and speed of advance (SOA); BC shows the current's speed, or drift, and its direction, or set; AC gives the boat's corrected course and speed.

Using a current triangle, the navigator has figured his corrected course from nun "2" to gong "3." He drew his intended track (TR) and measured the distance (three miles). He entered his cruising speed (six knots) as his SOA, and his estimated travel time (30 minutes). He then drew his current line in degrees true (T) and measured off the distance the two-knot current will travel in a half hour (one mile). Lastly, he drew a line from nun "2" to the outer end of the current line to get his heading. The current will push him forward, as well as sideways, so he can cut his speed through the water to five knots.

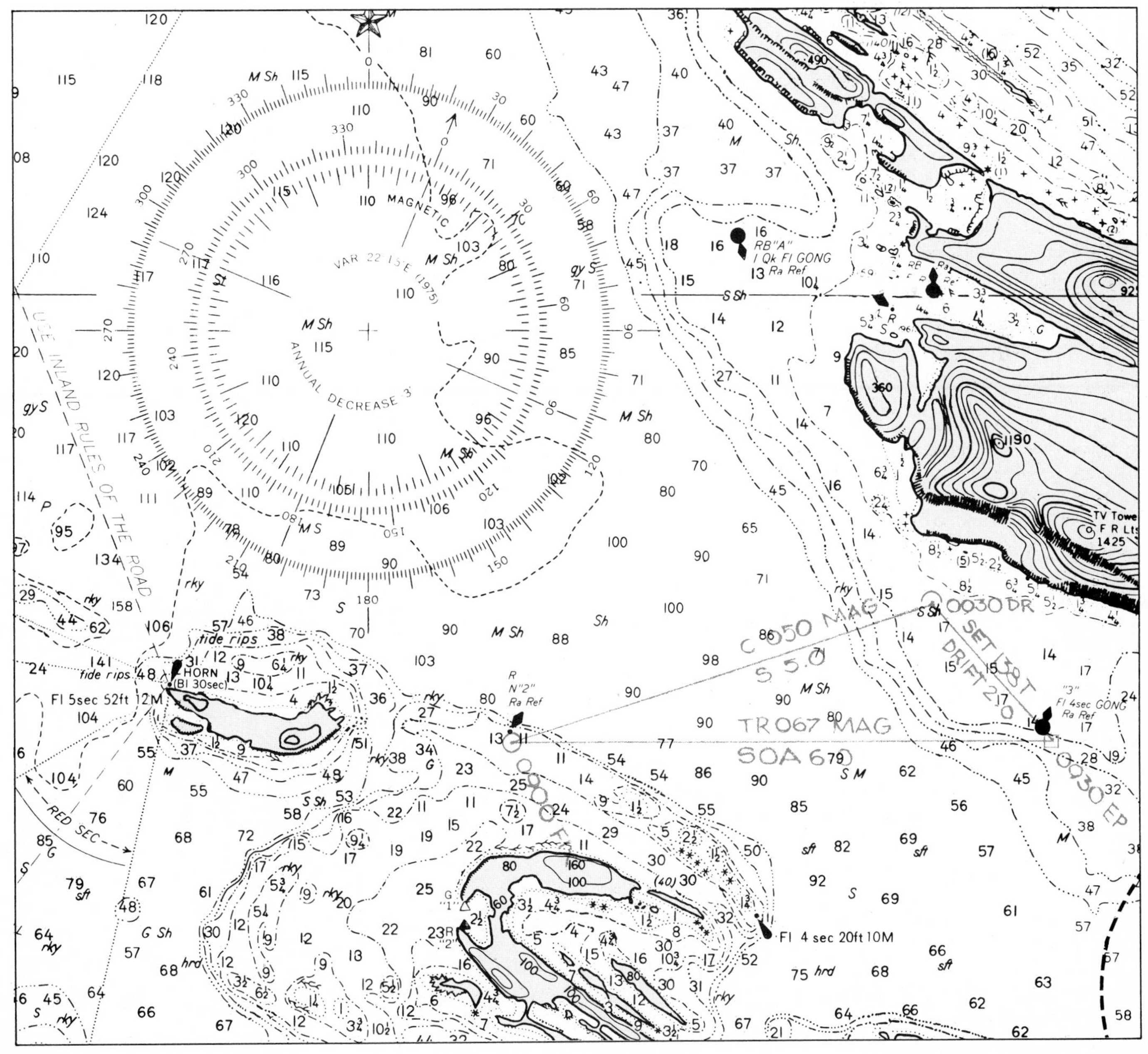

How to Read a River

Unlike currents in tidal channels, which may reverse themselves as often as four times a day, a fresh-water river flows in only one main direction. Yet from bank to bank the internal dynamics of a river at any point can be extremely complex. As the illustrations on these pages show, the flow of every stream, whether it is the lordly Mississippi *(right)* or an unnamed creek in the New Jersey Pine Barrens, varies from spot to spot, depending on the bends and twists the river takes, and on the conformation of its bottom.

The current is strongest along a river's main channel, where the water is deepest. In the shallows near shore, the current tends to grow weaker; as the river bottom rises, it creates an increasing degree of drag on the water, slowing it down. Depending on a river bed's particular contours, the forward flow may stop altogether near the bank, or it may even be sent into a reverse spin, eddying upstream before being pulled back into the faster downriver current.

If the river is fairly straight, the main current is usually in the middle. But wherever the river curves, the main current is thrown as though by centrifugal force to the outside bank *(opposite, below)*. There, the current's impact erodes the bank and deepens the bottom just under it; as a result, the current speeds up. Along the inside of the curve, however, the current slackens, leaving deposits of silt that build up into shoals. Because of this constant erosion and sedimentation, the river's bottom conformation continually changes; the boatman cruising along the stream should pay special attention both to navigation aids and to his depth finder.

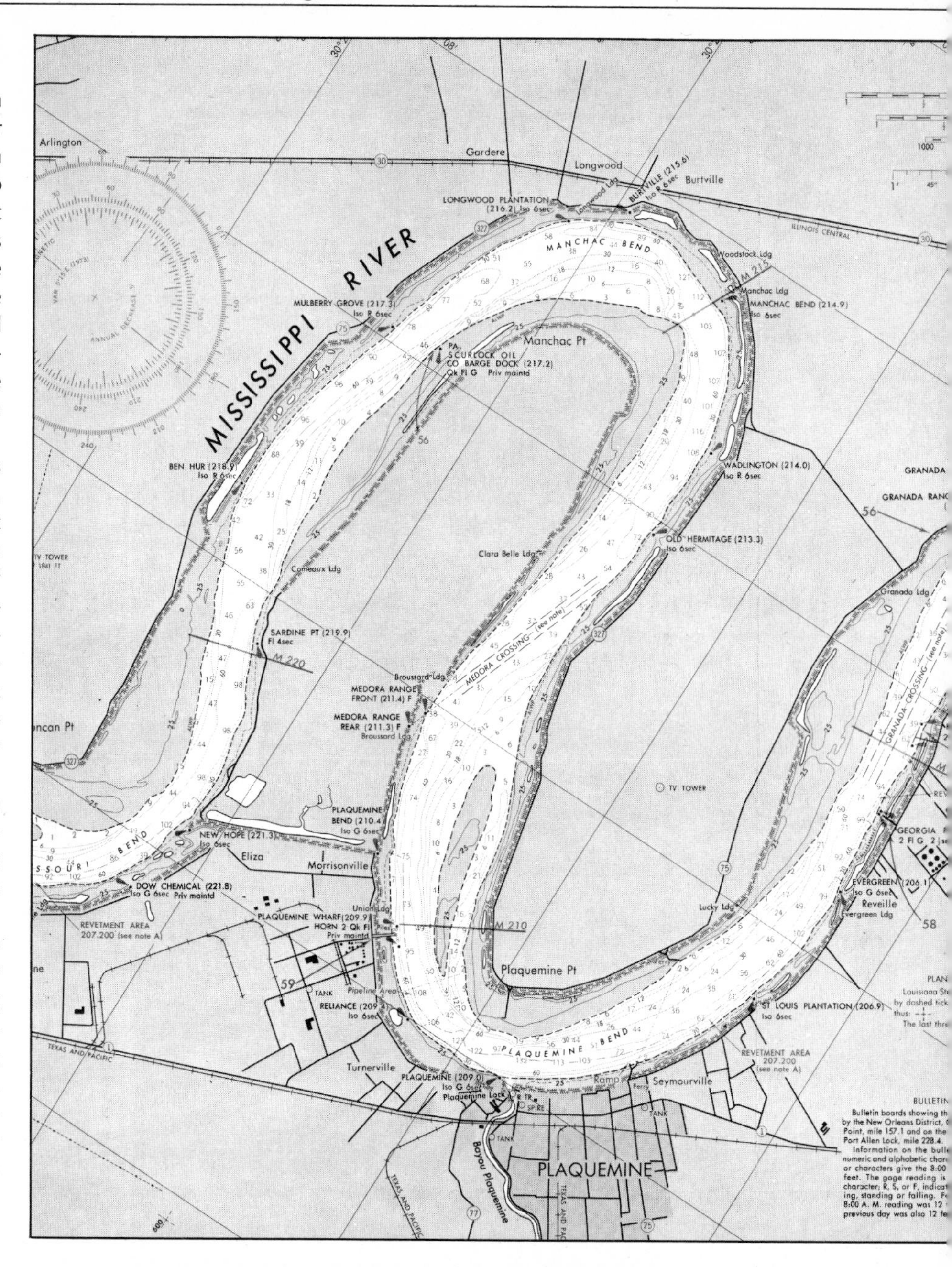

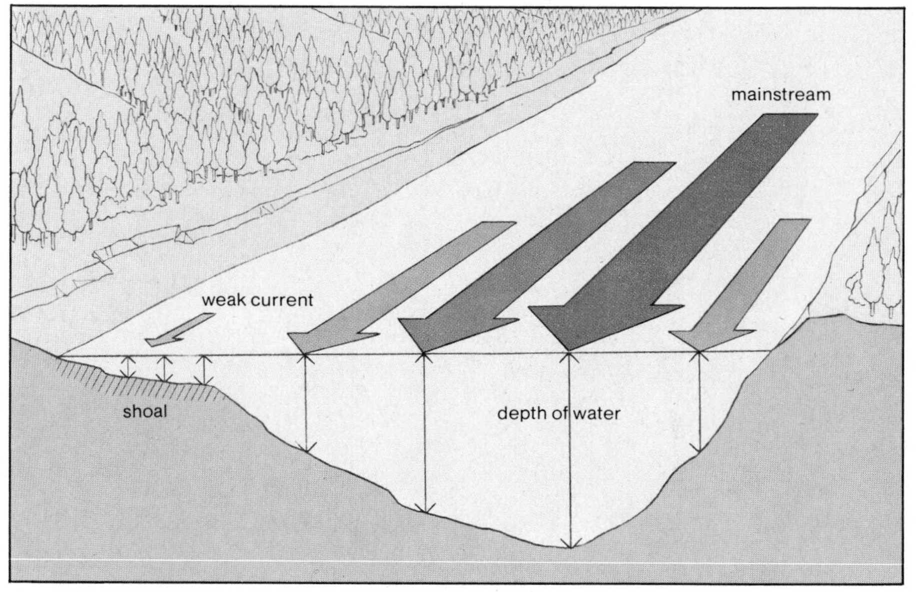

As a river flows along its bed, contours of the bottom and the banks constantly modify the speed of the current, as represented by the arrows in the diagram at right. The mainstream (wide, dark-tinted arrow) moves deepest and fastest; the skipper traveling downriver may add several knots to his forward speed by riding it. Conversely, a boatman who is headed upriver can stay in shallower water where there are weaker currents (paler arrows) to go against.

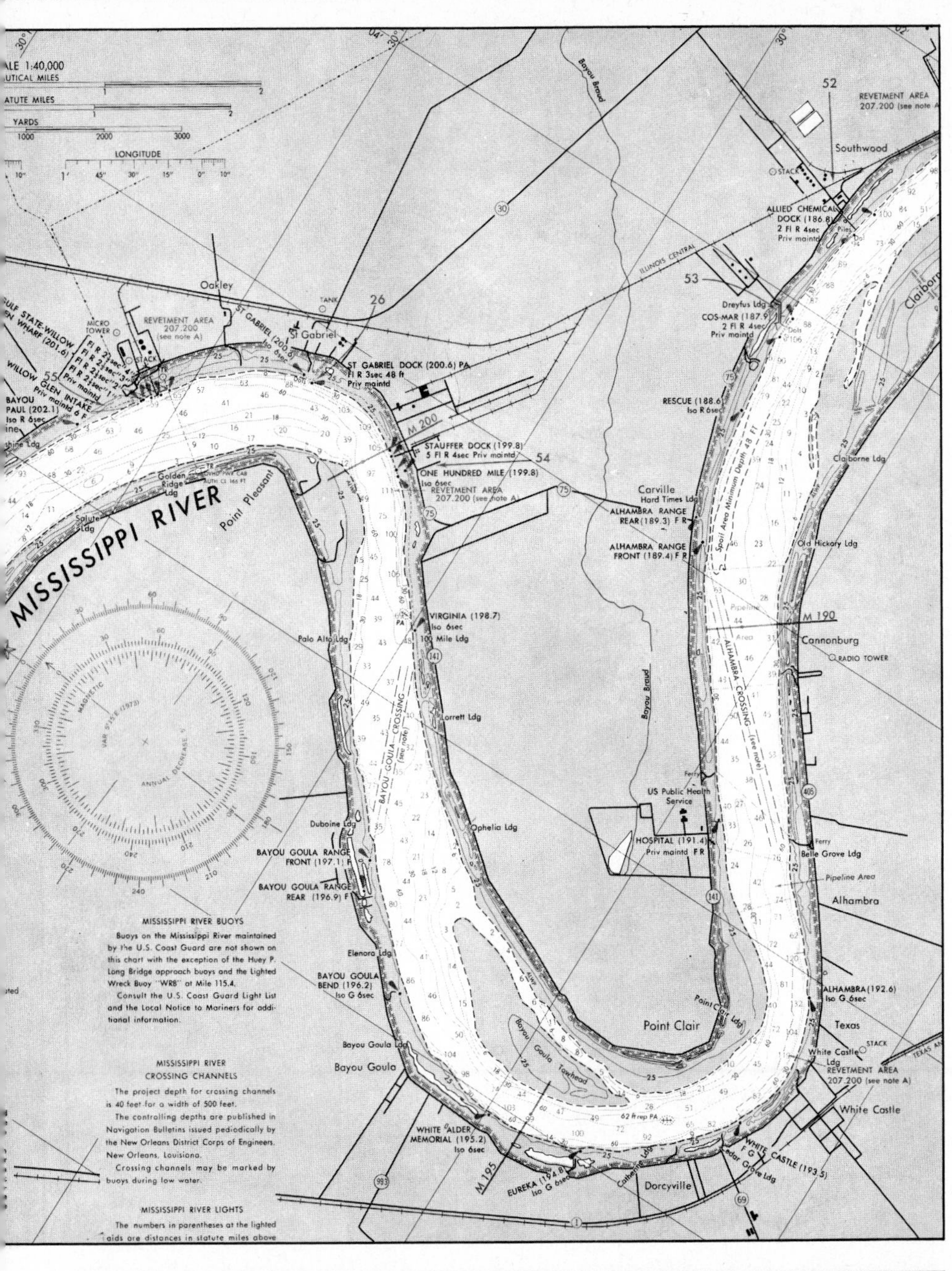

A charted stretch of the Mississippi River just south of Baton Rouge, Louisiana, demonstrates the typical placement of deep and shoal water as a river rounds each bend. Although this graphic information, when translated into current patterns (below), can save a boatman hours of travel time, he should remember that river depths are unstable at curves, where the antagonistic forces of shoal building and erosion are at constant war. In hugging the insides, therefore, he should factor in a judicious safety margin in using charted river depths.

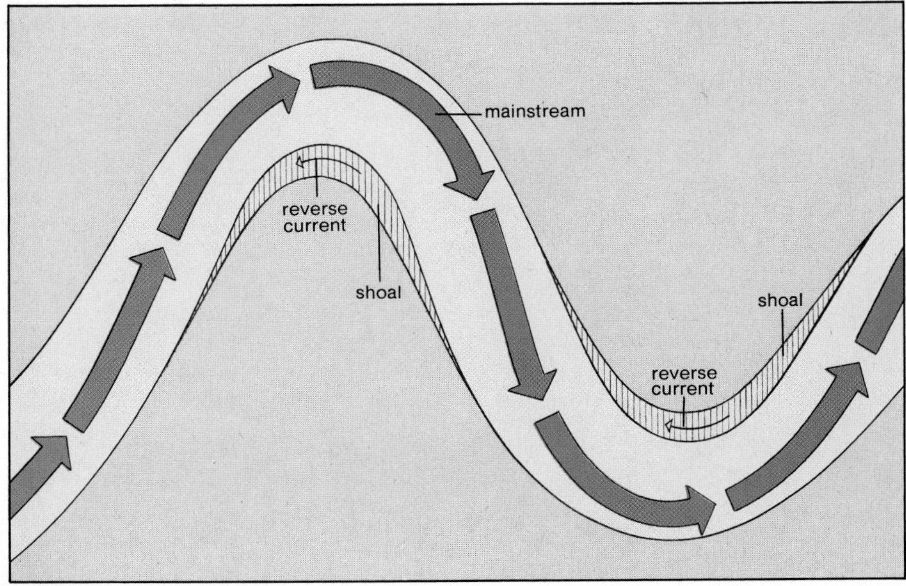

When flowing through a series of curves a river's mainstream, represented here by heavy blue arrows, caroms from the outer wall of one bend to the outer wall of the next. Currents on the inside of each bend move considerably slower and may occasionally swing around completely to create a backwater over shoals, as shown. By keeping to the inside while traveling upstream, the boatman not only can avoid the main current —which can move at five and a half knots along the Mississippi during the spring runoff —but may even get a lift from the eddies.

Catching a bone in her teeth, the 79-foot ketch Kialoa churns through Gulf Stream waters off Florida. Built by California racing enthusiast Jim Kilroy, the vessel is equipped with the finest in navigation gear, including omni, loran and a sea thermometer that registered Kialoa's entry into the warm flow of the Stream itself.

Racing the Gulf Stream

No condition of tide or current challenges a navigator's skill more thoroughly than does the broad river of wind-driven tropical water known as the Gulf Stream, which sweeps up the eastern coast of North America and out into the Atlantic. The speed of this current—and even its exact location—changes in often mystifying and unpredictable ways. But for the navigator of a sleek ocean racer like the one at left, a knowledge of just where the main flow of the Gulf Stream may be and how fast it is moving on any given day can mean the difference between winning a trophy or finishing somewhere in the ruck.

The vessel challenging the Stream on these pages is the ketch *Kialoa,* shown during her run in the 1975 Ocean Triangle Race between Florida and the Great Bahama Bank. The navigator, Scott Perry *(right, standing),* had to contend with light, fluky winds at the start, and an unexpected westward shift in the Gulf Stream's axis. To prepare for the current's erratic behavior, Perry armed himself with a sheaf of information on the flow in past years that helped him estimate its probable strength and position. To determine just when *Kialoa* entered the Stream, he referred to a simple but effective device —a sea thermometer that jumped a telltale 4° in the current's warm waters. In addition, Perry closely monitored *Kialoa*'s progress through the Stream's path with a steady sequence of omni and loran fixes. Perry's careful navigating paid off, as *Kialoa* sailed the 132-mile course in just 15 and a half hours, bringing her home well ahead of the fleet.

Minutes before the 9 a.m. starting gun, helmsman Kilroy and navigator Scott Perry, holding a stopwatch, prepare for a dual struggle with the Gulf Stream and competing boats. In any race whose course crosses the Stream, the boat that best calculates—or guesses—the current's speed and location may receive a boost that means victory.

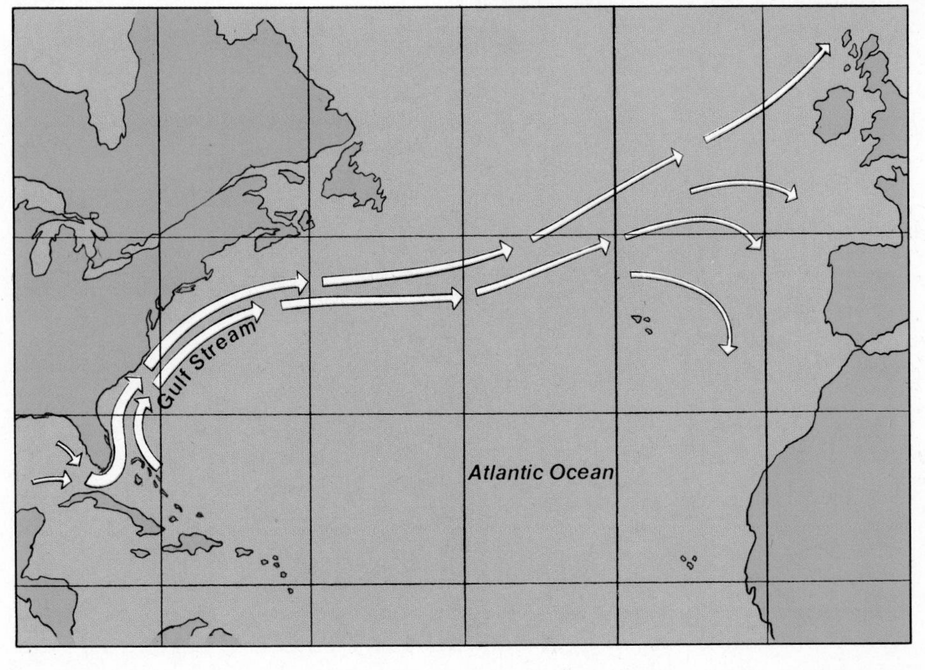

The Gulf Stream begins where wind-driven feeder currents from the Gulf of Mexico and surrounding tropical waters funnel through the narrow straits between Florida and Cuba. From there the Stream surges northward up the Atlantic coast, saltier and significantly warmer than the sea around it. Diminishing to a sluggish drift as it veers eastward across the Atlantic, the Stream splits into subsidiary currents and then finally dissipates against the coasts of Europe and West Africa.

Tucked belowdecks in the navigator's nook, Perry keeps a running record of Kialoa's progress in a logbook. Depth soundings, wind direction and speed, boat speed, and sea temperatures can be instantly assessed by reading the various dials and gauges in the console behind the chart table. On the table, next to a blue-jacketed NOS Coast Pilot volume for the Florida area, is a pocket computer that allows Perry to test in advance the effect of different headings on Kialoa's forward progress toward the next mark.

Gulf Stream
Fort Lauderdale
Great Isaac
Miami

The course of the Ocean Triangle Race runs east-northeast from the Miami sea buoy, around Great Isaac Light, west to the Fort Lauderdale sea buoy and south again to the starting point. The Gulf Stream, tinted in progressively darker shades of blue to indicate the strength of its flow, is a major factor throughout the race, but especially on the first two long legs. About 45 miles wide at this point, the current runs north at an average three to four knots along its strongest axis, slightly to the west of center, and diminishes by about a knot along the edges.

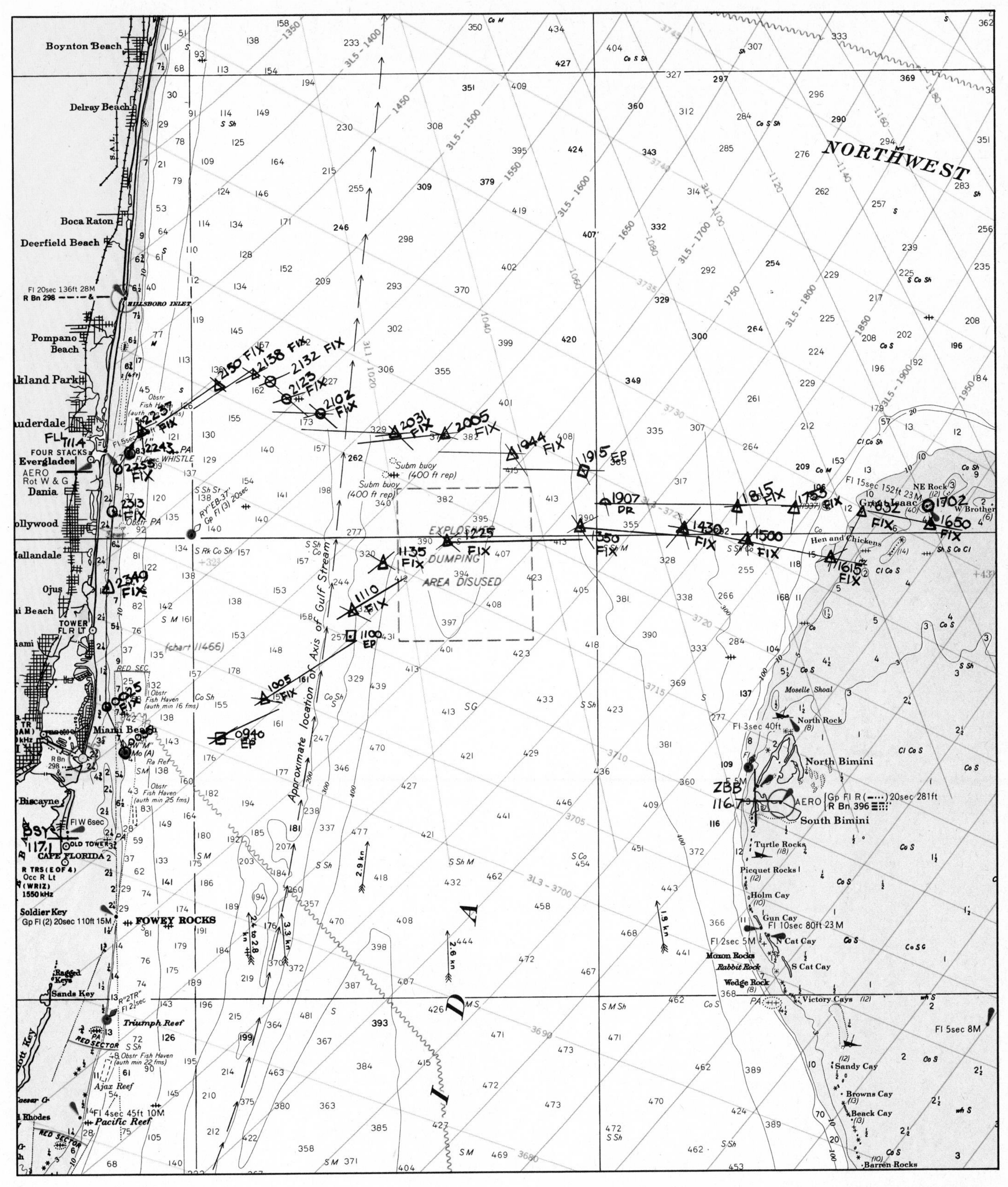

On this chart of Kialoa's progress, the sequence of Perry's fixes shows that even the best-laid plots often need revising to account for wind and current shifts. Sailing in light air for the first half of the outbound leg, and carried steadily north by the Gulf Stream, Kialoa edged well above the direct course line. Then, at 1150, she picked up a strong northeasterly wind that carried her to the first mark. On the second leg, to offset the current, Perry called for a heading slightly south of the straight-line, or rhumb-line, course. But an unexpected one-knot increase in the current's strength and a five-mile westward shift of its axis sent Kialoa north again as she neared the second mark.

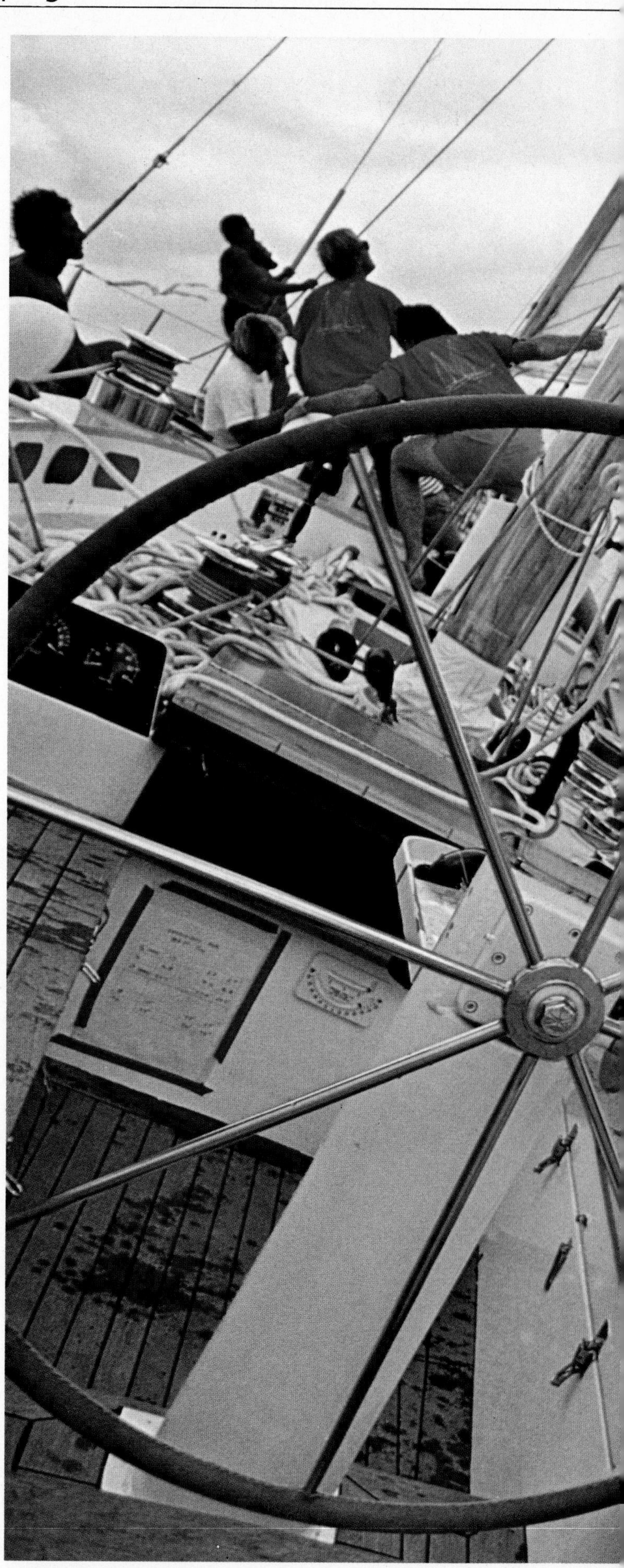

Driving hard into a 22-knot wind, helmsman Kilroy urges Kialoa on through choppy Gulf Stream seas. The crew has taken a reef in the mizzen, and now checks the trim of the main. The strong breeze held steady until the end of the race, giving the 42-ton Kialoa a powerful push toward the finish line.

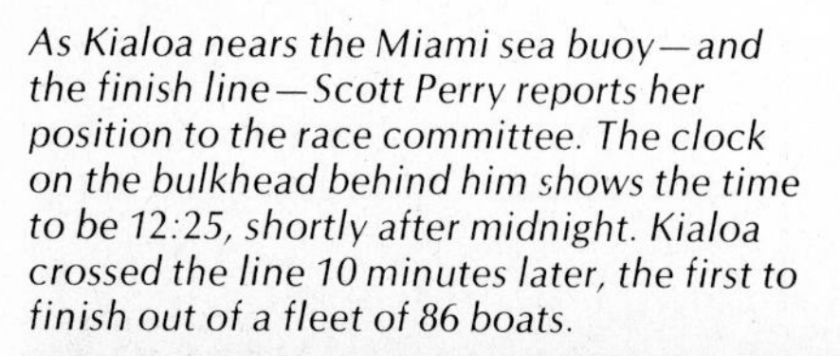

As Kialoa nears the Miami sea buoy—and the finish line—Scott Perry reports her position to the race committee. The clock on the bulkhead behind him shows the time to be 12:25, shortly after midnight. Kialoa crossed the line 10 minutes later, the first to finish out of a fleet of 86 boats.

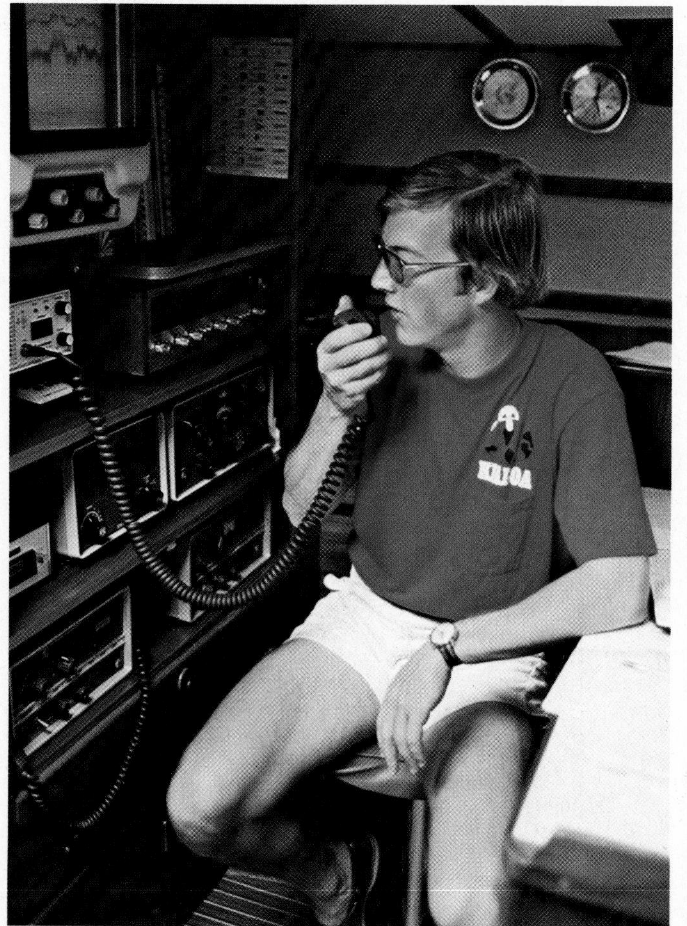

Pilot's Guide to Navigation Aids

The position and pertinent features of any aid to navigation, from the smallest buoy to the tallest light station, are marked on charts in a concise language of symbols, abbreviations and terse notations. Each symbol has its own distinctive shape, and is exaggerated in scale for easy recognition. Often the symbols are colored in significant ways, e.g., reddish-purple for a red nun. A complete listing of symbols is included in the light lists and Chart No.1; samples of the most common are given below.

Lights

A magenta teardrop or disc indicates a lighted aid. Abbreviated labels, and sometimes additional symbols, define the light's particular nature.

Position of Light

Indicated by a black dot beneath the teardrop, or at the center of the disc.

Riprap around Light

Boulders called riprap, piled around a light's base to protect the structure from waves.

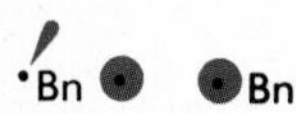

Light Beacon

A beacon equipped with an identifying light.

Aeronautical Light

A light intended to guide airplane pilots, but that can also be used by mariners.

Lightship

A permanently anchored ship that serves as a lighted aid to navigation.

Sector Light

A colored light shining over a precise area, usually of danger, shown by dotted lines.

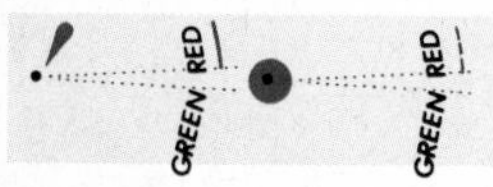

Directional Light

A light that marks a safe channel (dotted lines) by bracketing it with two color sectors.

Buoys and Day Beacons

Buoys are symbolized by an elongated diamond shape, which may be color coded and labeled. Triangles indicate day beacons.

• ◦ **Position of Buoy**

Indicated by a black dot—or sometimes by a circle—just below the diamond.

Light Buoy

Indicated by a magenta teardrop or disc accompanying the buoy's position mark.

Nun

A buoy with a conical top.

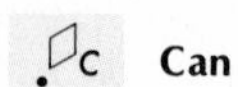

Can

A buoy that is cylindrical in shape.

R "2" R "2" **Starboard-Hand Buoy**

A red even-numbered buoy, left to starboard by a boat returning to harbor; the diamond may be tinted or uncolored.

"1" **Port-Hand Buoy**

A black odd-numbered buoy, left to port by a returning boat; the diamond is tinted black.

Mid-Channel Buoy

A buoy with black and white vertical stripes, used to mark the center of a channel.

Junction Buoy

A buoy with horizontal bands of red and black, marking the junction of two channels; may also mark wrecks or other obstructions.

Y **Quarantine Buoy**

A yellow buoy designating an anchorage where boats from foreign ports await clearance.

Fish-Net Buoy

A buoy with black and white horizontal bands that warns of commercial fish nets.

Anchorage Buoy

A solid-white buoy, indicating that portion of a congested area where boats may anchor.

Priv maintd **Private Aid to Navigation**

A privately owned and maintained buoy.

△Bn **Day Beacon**

A fixed, unlighted aid to navigation.

⊙MARKER **Range Marker**

Sometimes accompanied by a dotted line that shows the direction of the range.

Special-Purpose Buoy

An orange-and-white buoy—used mainly by the government—to mark restricted areas.

Radio Installations

A small circle with an interior dot pinpoints radio towers or beacons. A larger magenta circle marks radio beacons intended specifically for navigation.

Radio Beacon

A beacon for taking bearings by RDF.

R TR (WBAL) 1090 kHz **Commercial Broadcasting Station**

Radio tower; the station's call letters and broadcast frequency are indicated.

AERO R Bn 302 **Aeronautical Radio Beacon**

A beacon for airline pilots, also usable by boatmen equipped with RDF; always accompanied by the beacon's broadcast frequency and its Morse-code signal.

Fog Signals

These warning sounds can be identified by the characteristics of their noisemaking device—which is always noted on the chart.

DIA **Diaphone**
A signal activated by compressed air that begins with a high-pitched blast and ends with a deeper tone.

SIREN **Siren**
Similar to the whine of a police siren.

HORN **Horn**
Electrically powered signal with a slightly higher pitch than that of an automobile horn.

WHIS **Whistle**
A low-pitched, mournful hoot that is activated by wave motion.

BELL **Bell**
A single tone, irregularly repeated, similar in sound to a church bell.

GONG **Gong**
A multitoned signal produced by four separate gongs striking at random.

Supplementary Notations

Besides the standard abbreviations that are given above, some aids are accompanied on the chart with other abbreviated information. For example, 10 M means that a light's range is 10 nautical miles. And Alt. Fl. W 30sec, R 30sec describes a light's signature as alternating 30-second flashes of white and red.

Alt	**Alternating**	B	**Black**
M	**Nautical mile**	Bu	**Blue**
m; min	**Minutes of time**	G	**Green**
Ra Ref	**Radar reflector**	Or	**Orange**
Rot	**Rotating**	R	**Red**
sec	**Seconds of time**	W	**White**
SEC	**Sector**	Y	**Yellow**

Glossary

Abeam A direction at right angles to the centerline of the boat.

Back The wind is said to back when it changes in a counterclockwise direction, as from northeast to northwest. The opposite is to veer.

Beacon A freestanding or fixed aid to navigation, smaller than a light station.

Beam The width of the boat at its widest part. A boat is "on her beam ends" when heeled over 90°.

Bear To lie in a specified direction from a designated reference point; also, to move or tend to move in a certain direction.

Bearing The direction in which an object is seen, or the direction of one object from another, expressed in compass points or degrees. A true bearing is one expressed in degrees relative to true north; a magnetic bearing is one expressed in degrees relative to magnetic north.

Binnacle Housing of the compass.

Bone in her teeth A colloquial phrase implying that a boat is moving through the water at considerable speed. The "bone" is the bow wave thus produced.

Bow The forward part of the boat. (The word prow, cherished by poets, describes a ship's ornamented stem and is otherwise avoided by seamen.)

Box the compass To name the 32 points of the compass in sequence from north through east, south, west, back to north.

Buoy A floating aid to navigation used to mark the navigable limits of channels, indicate hazards, define anchorages, post local regulations, etc.

Can An unlighted cylindrical buoy.

Cardinal mark A navigation aid—used in the Uniform State Waterway Marking System—that is color-coded to indicate the compass direction around which it should be passed. A red-topped cardinal mark may be passed to the south or west, a black-topped one to north or east.

Chart recorder A highly sensitive depth finder in which the readings are noted by stylus traces on moving tape, often used by fishermen to locate schools of fish.

Clutter Unwanted reflections on a radar screen, commonly from rain, snow or sleet.

Cocked hat A small polygon formed by three or more bearing lines intersecting on a chart. The position of the ship from which the bearings have been taken is assumed to be within that polygon.

Compass card A circular card marked either in degrees or compass points to indicate the direction a boat is heading in—or that an object bears from the boat.

Compass point One of 32 divisions of the compass card equal to an arc of 11¼ degrees. The cardinal points are north, east, south and west; the intercardinal points are northeast, southeast, southwest and northwest.

Compass rose Two concentric circles, each divided into 360 degrees or 32 points, printed on nautical charts and used for laying off courses or bearings. The outer circle is graduated in degrees true, the inner circle in degrees magnetic.

Contour line A line on a chart connecting points of equal depth or elevation.

Controlling depth The minimum depth of a specified channel.

Countercurrent A current flowing in a direction opposite to that of the principal current.

Course The direction in which a ship is steering in making her way from point to point during a voyage. A magnetic course is the direction of the ship's heading relative to magnetic north; a compass course is the direction of the ship's heading based on the ship's compass (including errors of deviation and variation).

Course line The graphic representation on a chart of a ship's course, normally used in constructing a dead-reckoning plot.

Danger bearing A line drawn on a chart from a visible, charted object to a navigational hazard. The navigator uses the magnetic bearing of this line to warn him when his course is leading him too close to the danger.

Day beacon An unlit beacon.

Daymark The colored and numbered or lettered sign placed on many beacons to identify them. Most daymarks are coated with reflective material to make them visible in a searchlight beam at night.

Dead reckoning The process of projecting a ship's position based on the course steered and the distance run since the vessel's last known position; commonly abbreviated as DR.

Depth finder An instrument for measuring the depth of the water by means of a timed sonic pulse; also known as depth sounder or echo sounder.

Deviation The error in a magnetic compass caused by magnetic influences on board a boat. Deviation is described as being easterly or westerly according to whether the ship's compass is deflected east or west of magnetic north.

Diaphone A compressed-air sound-signal apparatus used in light stations to produce warning signals during fog.

Directional antenna A bar antenna used by radio direction finders to locate the bearing of a radio station.

Dividers An instrument with two pointed legs, hinged where the upper ends join; used to measure distances on a scale and transfer them to a chart, or vice versa.

Doubling the angle on the bow A method of obtaining a running fix by measuring the angles in a triangle formed by the boat's course line and two successive bearings taken on the same object.

Draft The depth a vessel extends below the waterline.

Drift The speed, in knots, of a current.

Drum lens A nonrotating Fresnel-type lens often used on lighted buoys.

Ebb The tidal movement of water away from the land and toward the sea, as in ebb current; the falling of the water level from high tide to low tide, as in ebb tide.

Estimated position (EP) In piloting, an approximate position obtained from incomplete data; less accurate than a fix.

Fathom A nautical measure equal to six feet; used for measuring water depths, and also for indicating the lengths of lead lines, cordage and anchor chains.

Fathom line A line on a chart connecting equal water depths and thereby marking the contours of underwater geographical features.

Fetch The distance along open water or land over which the wind blows; to achieve a desired destination under sail, particularly with an adverse wind or tide.

Fix A boat's position as marked on a chart, established by taking bearings on two or more known landmarks (visual fix) or two or more radio sources (electronic fix).

Flashing Description of a light—fixed on a navigation aid—that flashes on and off. The period of light is always briefer than the period of darkness.

Flood The movement of water toward the land and away from the sea; the rising of the water level from low tide to high tide.

Fore and aft A boat's longitudinal axis.

Fresnel lens A glass lens composed of an aggregation of prisms that concentrate and direct light in horizontal beams.

Gain control A device installed on marine radio receivers to improve the clarity of radio signals; also used for the same purpose on radar sets.

Genoa A large headsail set on the headstay and overlapping the mainsail.

Hand bearing compass A hand-held compass incorporating a sighting apparatus and used primarily for taking bearings.

Head The forward part of a boat, including the bow and adjacent areas; the uppermost corner of a triangular sail; a seagoing lavatory.

Heading The direction in which a boat's head is pointed.

Height of tide The amount of water above or below mean low water at any given time in the tide cycle.

Helm The device, usually a tiller or wheel, connected to the rudder, by which a boat is steered.

Intracoastal Waterway The system of inland waterway channels running along the Atlantic and Gulf coasts of the United States from Manasquan Inlet, New Jersey, to the Mexican border in Texas; commonly abbreviated as ICW.

Isophase Description of a light—fixed on a navigation aid—that flashes on and off at equal intervals.

Jibe To turn a boat's stern through the wind so that the sails swing from one side of the boat to the other, putting the boat on another tack.

Ketch A boat with a two-masted rig in which the larger, or mainmast, is forward, and the smaller mizzenmast is stepped aft—but forward of the rudder and usually of the helm.

KiloHertz (kHz) A unit, equal to one thousand cycles per second, used to describe radio frequency.

Knot A nautical mile equal in distance to one minute of latitude, or 1.15 statute miles; a common contraction for speed expressed in nautical miles per hour.

Landfall A sighting of or coming to land, also the land so approached or reached; the land first sighted at the end of a sea voyage.

Lead When pronounced "leed," the direction of a line; when pronounced "led," the metal weight at the end of a line used for taking soundings.

Lead line A line marked off in fathoms and weighted at one end with a lead, used for measuring water depths; also called a sounding line.

Leeway The lateral movement of a ship caused by the force of the wind.

Leg A section of a vessel's track or plotted course along a single heading; in a race, one of the marked portions of the course; also, the path a sailboat takes between tacks when beating to windward.

Life lines Safety lines and guardrails rigged around a boat's deck to prevent the crew from being washed overboard.

Line of position A straight line somewhere along which a ship is presumed to be. The line may be determined either by ranges, or by visual or electronic bearings.

Log A device for measuring the rate of a ship's motion through the water; also, a ship's journal or written record of the vessel's day-by-day performance, listing speeds, distances traveled, weather conditions, landfalls and other information.

Loran A radio positioning system that allows navigators to make position fixes by the reception of synchronized low-frequency radio transmissions. The word loran is an acronym for *lo*ng-*ra*nge *n*avigation.

Lubber line A mark on the inside of the compass bowl that indicates the fore-and-aft—or athwartships—line of a boat.

Magnetic north The spot on the earth toward which magnetic compass needles tend to point.

Mainsail The sail set on the after side of the mainmast, usually the biggest working sail; often called simply the main.

Mark The generic term for navigation aids such as buoys and beacons.

Mean high water The average level of high tide for any area.

Mean low water The average level of low tide for any area.

MegaHertz (mHz) A unit, equal to one million cycles per second, used to describe radio frequency.

Mizzen The sail set on the aftermast of a yawl or ketch.

Neap tide A tide of less than average range, occurring at the first and third quarters of the moon.

Null The compass point at which a radio direction finder's directional antenna receives the weakest signal from a given RDF station, thereby indicating the station's bearing.

Nun A partially conical, unlighted buoy.

Occulting Description of a light—fixed on a navigation aid—that is eclipsed at regular intervals. The duration of light is always greater than the duration of darkness.

Omni A navigation system that provides bearings by means of a VHF radio signal; also known as visual omni range (VOR). The system was originally designed for aviators, but is also used by mariners.

Parallel rules Two rulers connected by metal straps that allow the rules to separate but remain parallel; used in chart work to apply the readings on a compass rose to various plotted course and bearing lines, or vice versa.

Piloting The act of guiding a vessel, and fixing her position, by means of visible landmarks and aids to navigation, charts and various instruments.

Port The left side of a boat, when looking forward.

Quarter Either side of a boat's stern.

Radar A means of locating objects by reflected superhigh-frequency radio pulses. The word radar is an acronym for *ra*dio *d*etection *a*nd *r*anging.

Radial A term used by operators of omni sets to designate bearings either to or from an omni transmitter.

Radio beacon Marine radio transmitters operated by the Coast Guard and positioned along U.S. coastal waters and the Great Lakes to aid boatmen in piloting by means of radio direction-finding equipment; designated R Bn on nautical charts.

Radio direction finder (RDF) A specialized marine radio capable of establishing the bearing of the station whose signal it is receiving.

Range The alignment of two prominent objects or landmarks that gives a navigator a line of position; two fixed navigation aids whose alignment helps to guide a vessel through a channel; the distance at which a lighted navigation aid may be seen.

Range lights Two navigation lights, one higher than the other and located some distance apart, set upon ranges.

Reef To reduce sail area without removing the sail entirely, done by partially lowering the sail and securing loose fabric along the foot of the sail or the boom.

Relative bearing A bearing stated as a direction relative to the ship's fore-and-aft line, expressed in compass points or degrees from her bow, beam or quarter, as in "two points off the starboard bow."

Rhumb line The path a boat follows when sailing toward a specific point on the compass; on a Mercator chart, a straight line.

Run To sail before the wind; also, the narrowing part of the hull, aft, underwater.

Running fix A position determined by the intersection of two lines of position obtained from bearings taken at different times, often on the same object.

Sea buoys The first buoys a mariner encounters when approaching a channel or harbor entrance from the sea.

Sea return A term used to describe radar reflections from waves around the boat. Most radar sets have sensitivity knobs to reduce sea return.

Sector A colored segment in the sweep of a navigation light. A red sector, for example, warns of dangerous waters.

Set The direction in which a current is moving, expressed in compass degrees; also, the direction in which a boat is pushed by current or wind.

Shadow pin A vertical pin mounted at the center of a compass card, used in taking bearings.

Slack water The period of little or no current about halfway between maximum flood and maximum ebb currents.

Sounding Water depth at a given spot, measured in feet or fathoms; a chart notation of water depth, at mean low water; the act of measuring water depth with a lead line or a depth finder.

Speed of advance (SOA) The average speed in knots needed to cover a given distance over the bottom in a given amount of time.

Spring tide A tide of greater than average range, occurring around the times of new and full moons.

Starboard The right side of a boat, looking forward.

Superhigh frequency (SHF) A designated band of the radio spectrum, from 3,000 to 30,000 mHz.

Swinging ship The process of determining the deviation of a ship's compass by putting the vessel through a sequence of headings.

Tidal current The horizontal movement of water caused by the ebbing and flooding of the tide.

Tidal range The amount of change in an area's water level from low tide to high tide; e.g., an area covered by two feet of water at low tide and six feet of water at high tide has a tidal range of four feet.

Tide The alternate rising and falling of the surface level in bodies of water, caused primarily by the gravitational forces of the sun and the moon on the earth. Tide is always the vertical movement of water (as opposed to the horizontal movement of tidal currents), although, colloquially, tide is used to refer to both currents and changes in water level.

Track (TR) The path a boat actually travels over the bottom.

Transducer The sending-receiving device of a depth finder that transmits sonic pulses to the bottom, and then picks up the echoes.

Trim To adjust the set of a sail relative to the wind.

True north The geographic North Pole; the chart direction to the North Pole, where, on a globe, the lines of longitude converge.

Variation The difference, expressed in degrees of an angle, between the direction of true north and magnetic north at any point on the surface of the earth. Variation is designated as east or west depending on whether the magnetic needle is deflected east or west of true north.

Veer The wind is said to veer when it shifts in a clockwise direction, as from north to northeast. When the wind shifts counterclockwise, it is said to back.

Very high frequency (VHF) A designated band of the radio spectrum, ranging from 30 to 300 mHz.

Bibliography

Navigation

Bowditch, Nathaniel:
American Practical Navigator. U.S. Navy Hydrographic Office, 1962.
American Practical Navigator. U.S. Government, 1966.

Dunlap, G. D., *Navigation and Finding Fish with Electronics.* International Marine Publishing Company, 1972.

Dunlap, G. D., and H. H. Shufeldt, *Dutton's Navigation and Piloting.* Naval Institute Press, 1972.

Hobbs, Richard R., *Marine Navigation 1: Piloting,* Fundamentals of Naval Science Series. Naval Institute Press, 1974.

Kals, W. S., *Practical Navigation.* Doubleday & Company, Inc., 1972.

Mixter, George W., *Primer of Navigation.* D. Van Nostrand Co., Inc., 1960.

Shufeldt, H. H., and G. D. Dunlap, *Piloting and Dead Reckoning.* Naval Institute Press, 1970.

Simonsen, Capt. Svend T., *Simonsen's Navigation.* Prentice-Hall, Inc., 1973.

Taylor, E. G. R., *The Haven-finding Art.* Hollis & Carter, 1958.

Townsend, Sallie, and Virginia Ericson, *The American Navigator's Handbook.* Thomas Y. Crowell Co., 1974.

Charts

Bagrow, Leo, *History of Cartography.* Translated by D. L. Paisley, revised and enlarged by R. A. Skelton. Harvard University Press, 1964.

Brindze, Ruth, *Charting the Oceans.* The Vanguard Press, Inc., 1972.

Brown, Lloyd A., *The Story of Maps.* Little, Brown and Company, 1949.

Greenhood, David, *Down to Earth: Mapping for Everybody.* Holiday House, 1944.

Howse, Derek, and Michael Sanderson, *The Sea Chart.* Fletcher & Son Ltd. (England), 1973.

General

Andrews, Howard L., and Alexander L. Russell, *Basic Boating: Piloting and Seamanship.* Prentice-Hall, 1964.

Brindze, Ruth, ed., *The Experts' Book of Boating.* Prentice-Hall, Inc., 1959.

Chapman, Charles F., *Piloting, Seamanship, & Small Boat Handling.* Motor Boating and Sailing, 1972.

French, John, *Electrical and Electronic Equipment for Yachts.* Dodd, Mead & Co., 1974.

Freuchen, Peter, *Peter Freuchen's Book of the Seven Seas.* Julian Messner, Inc., 1957.

Gaskell, T. F., *The Gulf Stream.* The John Day Company, 1973.

Marchaj, C. A., *Sailing Theory and Practice.* Dodd, Mead & Company, 1964.

History

Beaver, Patrick, *A History of Lighthouses.* The Citadel Press, 1973.

Cotter, Charles H., *A History of Nautical Astronomy.* American Elsevier Publishing Company Inc., 1968.

Hale, John R., *Age of Exploration.* TIME-LIFE BOOKS, 1966.

May, Commander W. E., *A History of Marine Navigation.* W. W. Norton & Company, Inc., 1973.

Morison, Samuel Eliot:
Admiral of the Ocean Sea: A Life of Christopher Columbus. Little, Brown and Company, 1942.
The European Discovery of America: The Southern Voyages. Oxford University Press, 1974.

Morison, Samuel Eliot, trans. and ed., *Journals and Other Documents on the Life and Voyages of Christopher Columbus.* The Heritage Press, 1963.

Government Publications

Chart No. 1: United States of America, Nautical Chart Symbols and Abbreviations. Prepared jointly by Defense Mapping Agency Hydrographic Center and National Ocean Survey (Department of Commerce, National Oceanic and Atmospheric Administration). Published by Defense Mapping Agency Hydrographic Center. Washington: 1974.

Significant Aspects of the Tides. U.S. Department of Commerce, National Ocean Survey, Educational Pamphlet #5, January 1971.

Tidal Currents. U.S. Department of Commerce, National Ocean Survey, Educational Pamphlet #4, February 1972.

Where to Buy Charts

Most marine supply stores carry a full complement of the government charts, tables, light lists and piloting guides needed to navigate local waters. If the boatman finds that the store is out of stock, however, or if he requires charts or other publications for distant areas, he can obtain the necessary materials by writing directly to the appropriate issuing office, as listed below.

1. National Ocean Survey, Distribution Division, C44, 6501 Lafayette Avenue, Riverdale, Maryland 20840. Telephone: (301) 436-6990. Publishes charts for all U.S. coastal areas, the Great Lakes, sections of major rivers; *Coast Pilots,* tide tables, tidal current tables, tidal current charts, *Chart No. 1;* catalogues of NOS charts. Distributes *Notice to Mariners.*

2. Defense Mapping Agency Depot, 5801 Tabor Avenue, Philadelphia, Pennsylvania 19120. Telephone: (215) 697-4262. Issues charts of foreign waters, a chart catalogue and *Notice to Mariners.* Distributes *Chart No. 1.*

3. U.S. Army Corps of Engineers. The district office in each state issues charts and chart lists for inland lakes and waterways.

4. Lake Survey Center, 630 Federal Building, Detroit, Michigan 48226. Publishes charts of the Great Lakes and connecting rivers, Lake Champlain and New York State Canals, and a chart catalogue.

5. Superintendent of Documents, Government Printing Office, Washington, D.C. 20402. Distributes light lists.

6. Hydrographic Chart Distribution, Canadian Hydrographic Service, Surveys and Mapping Building, 615 Booth Street, Ottawa, Ontario, Canada. Distributes Canadian charts and marine publications.

Acknowledgments

For help given in the preparation of this book the editors wish to thank the following: Aqua Meter Instrument Corp., Roseland, New Jersey; Stanley Baldwin, Fairhaven, Massachusetts; The Bertram Yacht Company, Miami, Florida; Commander Ransom K. Boyce, First Coast Guard District, Boston, Massachusetts; Chris-Craft Industries, New York, New York; Goldberg Marine Distributors, Incorporated, New York, New York; Theodore Haendel, U.S. Merchant Marine Academy, Kings Point, New York; Hammond Map Store, New York, New York; Fred Hernandez, Bertram Yacht Co., Miami, Florida; Richard Humphrey, Staten Island, New York; P. S. Iskowitz, Aids to Navigation School, Governors Island, New York; Kenyon Marine, Guilford, Connecticut; H. Lewkowitz, New York, New York; Lion Yachts, Stamford, Connecticut; James McCauley, Nelson Bourret, Paul Bennet, Point Judith Fishing Cooperative, Point Judith, Rhode Island; Robert Merriam, Merriam Electronics, Point Judith, Rhode Island; National Oceanic and Atmospheric Administration, National Ocean Survey, Department of Commerce, Washington, D.C.; New York Nautical Instrument & Service Corp., New York, New York; Robert D. Ogg, Danforth, Portland, Maine; Henry E. Olsen, City Island, New York; Scott Perry, Lexington, Kentucky; E. S. Ritchie &. Sons, Inc., Pembroke, Massachusetts; J. J. Scholz, Sun Electric Corporation, Crystal Lake, Illinois; E. M. Volek, Aids to Navigation School, Governors Island, New York; James Woodward, Ninth Coast Guard District, Federal Office Building, Cleveland, Ohio.

Picture Credits *Credits from left to right are separated by semicolons, from top to bottom by dashes.*

Cover—Richard Meek for SPORTS ILLUSTRATED. 6,7—Paul A. Darling. 9—Jim Molloy for *The Providence Journal.* 12—Photo by Dennis L. Crow, background chart by National Oceanic and Atmospheric Administration (NOAA), National Ocean Survey (NOS). 14,15,16—NOAA, NOS. 17—NOAA, NOS; chart symbols drawn by Nicholas Fasciano. 18,19—NOAA, NOS. 20—Chart symbols drawn by Fred Wolff. 21—Drawings by Nicholas Fasciano. 22,23—Photos by John Zimmerman—chart by NOAA, NOS. 24—Maps drawn by Nicholas Fasciano. 25—NOAA, NOS. 26—From *Mapmaking: The Art That Became a Science* by Lloyd A. Brown by permission of Little, Brown & Co., redrawn by Nicholas Fasciano. 27—Defense Mapping Agency Hydrographic Center. 28 through 31—NOAA, NOS. 32,33—NOAA, NOS—Defense Mapping Agency Hydrographic Center; U.S. Army Corps of Engineers, Little Rock and Tulsa Districts. 34 through 37—Enrico Ferorelli. 38,39—National Maritime Museum, Greenwich, England. 40,41—Photo Bibliotêque Nationale, courtesy of the Département des Cartes et Plans, Bibliotêque Nationale, Paris. 42 through 45—Derek Bayes, courtesy of the National Maritime Museum, Greenwich, England. 46—B. Evans from Sea Library. 48,49—Drawings by William G. Teodecki. 50,51—Drawings by Dale Gustafson. 52,53—Drawing by Nicholas Fasciano. 54,55—Drawings by Dale Gustafson. 56,57—Drawings by Nicholas Fasciano. 58,59—Drawings by Dale Gustafson. 60,61—Drawings by Nicholas Fasciano. 62—Drawings by Dale Gustafson. 63—Drawing by Nicholas Fasciano. 64—Bruce Roberts from Rapho/Photo Researchers. 65—Drawings by William G. Teodecki. 66—Roy Porello. 67—Thomas E. Mahnken Jr.—drawings by William G. Teodecki. 68—U.S. Coast Guard. 69—Drawing by William G. Teodecki—U.S. Coast Guard. 70—John Chang McCurdy. 71—Drawings by William G. Teodecki. 72—NOAA, NOS—signal chart drawn by Walter Johnson. 73—U.S. Coast Guard. 75—Peabody Museum of Salem. 76,77—U.S. Coast Guard, courtesy Brown Brothers; U.S. Coast Guard, courtesy Mariner's Museum. 78,79—Nathaniel Stebbins from The Society for the Preservation of New England Antiquities; Wide World. 80—Peabody Museum of Salem. 81—No credit. 82—Ken Kay. 84—Drawing by Roger Metcalf—drawing by Dale Gustafson. 85—Drawing by Roger Metcalf—drawings by Dale Gustafson (3). 86—Drawings by Roger Metcalf. 87,88—Drawings by Dale Gustafson. 89,90—Drawings by Roger Metcalf. 91—Tables and graph drawn by Rosi Cassano. 92—Photo by Ken Kay, chart by NOAA, NOS. 93—Drawing by Roger Metcalf—chart and graph drawn by Rosi Cassano. 94—Photo by Ken Kay, chart by NOAA, NOS—drawing by Fred Wolff. 95,96,97—Photos by Ken Kay, chart by NOAA, NOS. 98,99—Drawings by Rosi Cassano. 100,101—NOAA, NOS. 102 through 123—Photos by Stephen Green-Armytage, charts by NOAA, NOS. Map on 105 drawn by Nicholas Fasciano. 124—Enrico Ferorelli. 126—Drawings by Fred Wolff. 127, 128—Drawings by Roger Metcalf. 129—Drawing by Roger Metcalf—NOAA, NOS—Ross Laboratories. 130—Drawings by Fred Wolff. 131,132—Drawings by Roger Metcalf. 133—NOAA, NOS. 134—Drawings by Fred Wolff. 135—NOAA, NOS, bottom inset drawing by Roger Metcalf. 136—Drawings by Fred Wolff. 137—Drawing by Roger Metcalf—drawing by Fred Wolff. 138,139—John Zimmerman; NOAA, NOS. 140—Drawing by Fred Wolff—map by Roger Metcalf. 141—Drawings by Roger Metcalf. 142 through 149—Marvin Newman, charts on 145 and 147 by NOAA, NOS. 150—Sue Cummings. 152—NOAA, NOS—work sheet drawn by Rosi Cassano. 153—NOAA, NOS. 154—NOAA, NOS—work sheet drawn by Rosi Cassano. 155,156,157—NOAA, NOS. 158—Drawing by Fred Wolff. 159—Composite from NOAA, NOS charts, current triangle drawn by Rosi Cassano. 160,161—NOAA, NOS—drawings by Fred Wolff. 162—Eric Schweikardt. 163,164—Eric Schweikardt—drawings by Fred Wolff. 165—NOAA, NOS, inset course drawn by Rosi Cassano. 166,167—Eric Schweikardt. 168—Drawings by Fred Wolff.

Index

Page numbers in italics indicate illustrations.

Printed in U.S.A.